George Alfred Raikes

Historical Records of the First Regiment of Militia

Or Third West York Light Infantry

George Alfred Raikes

Historical Records of the First Regiment of Militia
Or Third West York Light Infantry

ISBN/EAN: 9783337250546

Printed in Europe, USA, Canada, Australia, Japan

Cover: Foto ©ninafisch / pixelio.de

More available books at **www.hansebooks.com**

QUEEN'S COLOUR.

REGIMENTAL COLOUR.

HISTORICAL RECORDS

OF THE

FIRST REGIMENT OF MILITIA;

OR,

Third West York Light Infantry.

BY

CAPTAIN G. A. RAIKES,

3rd West York Light Infantry Militia;
Lieutenant-Instructor of Musketry Hon. Artillery Company;
Author of "Militia Reform," &c.

With Illustrations.

LONDON:
RICHARD BENTLEY & SON, NEW BURLINGTON STREET,
Publishers in Ordinary to Her Majesty.

1876.

LONDON:
BARRETT, SONS AND CO., PRINTERS,
SEETHING LANE.

HENRY MORSE STEPHENS

[*Entered at Stationers' Hall.*]

TO

MY BROTHER OFFICERS

OF THE

FIRST REGIMENT OF MILITIA,

OR,

Third West York Light Infantry,

THIS VOLUME IS INSCRIBED.

CONTENTS.

CHAPTER I.

THE YORKSHIRE MILITIA PREVIOUS TO 1757.

                                                                                         PAGE

The County.—Wapentakes and Subdivisions.—Population and Quota.—Militia Established previous to the Regular Army.—Anglo-Saxon Militia or Fyrd.—The Feudal System.—The Militia during the Thirteenth and Fourteenth Centuries.—Lords-Lieutenant.—Yorkshire Militia in the Reign of James I.—Origin of word "Militia."—Reorganisation of Militia by Charles II., 1660.—Pay of Horse and Foot during Training.—Trophy Money.—Yorkshire Regiments and Officers in 1697.—Condition of the Militia, 1715.—Colonel Thornton's Company in 1745.—The Yorkshire Blues.—The Independents 1

CHAPTER II.

FROM 1756 TO 1796.

EMBODIED FROM 6TH SEPTEMBER, 1759, TO 25TH SEPTEMBER, 1762.

The New Militia of 1757.—The Yorkshire Militia.—Riots at York.—Formation of the three West York, the two North York, and East York Regiments.—List of First Officers appointed to the Regiment.—Brigadier-Generals of Militia.—Sergeants approved by the King.—Letter from Marquis of Rockingham.—List of Arms and Accoutrements supplied to the Regiment.—Royal Warrant for the supply of Powder, &c. to the Militia.—Embodiment of the West York Militia.—Warrant for Necessaries.—The Clothing.—Militia Pay and Subsistence.—Regiment ordered to Sunderland.—Return to York.—Inspected by His Royal Highness the Duke of York.—Proceed to Newcastle-on-Tyne.—Thence to Nottingham.—Warrant to Disembody the three West York Regiments.—Votes of Thanks of House of Commons.—The West York Militia reorganised in two Regiments.—List of the Officers.—The Militia from 1765 to 1796 15

CHAPTER III.

FROM 1796 TO 1802.

EMBODIED FROM 5TH MARCH, 1798, TO 22ND APRIL, 1802.

PAGE

The Supplementary Militia.—Formation of New Regiments.—Royal Warrant to embody the Supplementary Militia.—Establishment of the five West York Regiments.—Clothing and Accoutrements. Second half of the Supplementary Militia Embodied in May.—Regiment ordered to Hull.—Letter from General Sir R. Abercromby.—Regiment called out to suppress Riots at Hull.—Vote of Thanks. Volunteers into Army.—Mode of Wearing the Hair.—Meeting of Lords-Lieutenant and Colonels of Militia.—Supplementary Militia reduced July, 1799.—Further Reduction in October.—Russian Prisoners at Hull.—Letter of the Lord-Lieutenant relative to Disbanding the 3rd and 4th and Retaining the 5th Regiment.—His Letter to Colonel Sir George Cooke.—General Order respecting the Dress of the Infantry.—Regiment proceeds from Hull to Sunderland.—Thence to Berwick and Tweedmouth.—Stationed in Scotland.—Regiment Augmented August, 1801.—Returns to Doncaster, February, 1802.—Disembodied 22nd April.—Vote of Thanks from Parliament 51

CHAPTER IV.

FROM 1803 TO 1814.

EMBODIED FROM 11TH MARCH, 1803, TO 24TH JUNE, 1814.

Establishment increased to 809.—Regiment embodied.—Ordered to York.—Supplementary Men called out in July.—Regiment proceeds to Colchester.—Encamps on Elmstead Heath.—Orders in case of Invasion.—Two Companies Equipped as Rifles.—Officers' Dress in 1804.—Alarm Beacons in Yorkshire.—Encampment at Coxheath.—Quartered at Feversham and Ospringe.—Quota again reduced in 1805.—Quota increased in 1807.—Standing Orders issued by Col. Bryan Cooke in 1809.—The White Rose of York conferred as a Badge, 1811—Regiment embarked for Ireland, December, 1811.—The Battalion of Detachments of Militia.—Quarters in Ireland.—Warrant to hold Courts-Martial.—Volunteers into the Army, 1805-1814.—Regiment returns to England, May, 1814.—March from Plymouth to Doncaster.—Letter from the Lord-Lieutenant.—Disembodied 24th June.—Thanks from Secretary of State and Commander-in-Chief.—Vote of Thanks from Parliament.—Pay of Disembodied Staff.—Establishment of the Regiment ... 85

CHAPTER V.

FROM 1814 TO 1852.

DISEMBODIED PERIOD.

Bugles to be worn by Light Infantry and Rifles.—Part of the Militia Embodied, June, 1815, to February, 1816.—Uniform of Regimental Staff.—Training Suspended 1814-19.—The Training at Doncaster, 1820, and Pontefract, 1821.—Training at Doncaster, 1825.—Sergeants armed with Fusils instead of Pikes, 1830.—Green Tufts to be worn by Light Infantry.—Sir Robert Peel's Protest on the Gold Lace Question.—The Last Training at Pontefract, 1831.—Regiment Recommended to be made Light Infantry.—Order of Precedence of Militia Regiments previous to 1833.—Numbers as finally decided.—Staff Reduced, 1835.—Ordered to be completed, 1845.—Regiment to wear Silver instead of Gold Lace.—The Contingent Fund.—Captain and Adjutant Rawson 133

CHAPTER VI.

FROM 1852 TO 1856.

EMBODIED FROM 26TH MAY, 1854, TO 30TH JUNE, 1856.

Militia raised by Voluntary Enlistment, 1852.—Four New Regiments formed in Yorkshire.—Disembodied and Retired Allowances to Officers.—Regiment made Light Infantry.—Establishment Increased.—The Training, 1853 and 1854.—Regiment Embodied and sent to Berwick.—Embarks for Dublin.—Volunteers required for Regular Army.—The Depôt.—Regiment Volunteers for Foreign Service.—Coatees changed for Tunics.—Order of Precedence of Militia Regiments Revised.—Presentation of New Colours.—Regiment Embarks at Belfast for England.—Royal Warrant to Disembody the West York Militia.—Thanks of the Queen and Parliament 152

CHAPTER VII.

FROM 1857 TO 1875.

EMBODIED FROM 1ST OCTOBER, 1857, TO 2ND MAY, 1860.

Royal Warrant to Embody the Regiment.—Regiment sent to Aldershot.—Thence to Carlisle, Ashton-under-Lyne, and Tynemouth. —Volunteers supplied to the Army.—Establishment when Embodied.—Militia made liable to serve in all parts of United Kingdom.—Regiment Disembodied.—Recruiting from the Militia.— Scheme for dividing the Riding between the Six Regiments.—

Training Suspended, 1861.—Establishment reduced to 700 Privates, 1864-7.—Alteration in Uniform.—Formation of the Militia Reserve.—Property Qualification Abolished.—Honorary Rank.—Reserve and Auxiliary Forces.—Commissions in the Line offered to Subalterns.—Establishment of Brigade Depôts.—Rank of Ensign abolished for that of Sub-Lieutenant.—Clothing of Men changed from Red Tunics to Scarlet Kerseys.—White Rose to be worn on Uniform.—The Annual Training 1862-1875 181

APPENDICES.

APPENDIX A.—Succession of Officers of the Regiment 203
" B.—Alphabetical List of Officers 219
" C.—Officers appointed to, or received from, the Regular Army and Militia, and the Regiments to which they were appointed or received 252
" D.—Lords-Lieutenant of the West Riding 259
" E.—Property Qualification of Militia Officers 260
" F.—Chronological Summary of the Change of Quarters of the Regiment 262
" G.—Alphabetical List of Places where the Regiment has been Quartered 271
" H.—Enrolled Strength of the Regiment, of each rank, in every year, from 1758-1875 287
" I.—Date, Place, &c. of Annual Trainings when the Regiment was Disembodied 290
" J.—List of Half-yearly and Annual Inspections, &c. ... 292
" K.—Miscellaneous Returns 294
" L.—Summary of Statutes relating to Volunteering into the Army 305
" M.—Ditto, fixing the Quota of Militia 308
" N.—Alphabetical List of Parishes in each Wapentake, showing the number of Men liable to be raised by Ballot for the Regiment, from 1802 to 1852 ... 311
" O.—Ditto, showing the number of Supplementary Men to be raised between the years 1803 and 1813 ... 316
Records of First West York Supplementary Regiment (called also the Third West York Militia), from 1797 to 1799 325

ILLUSTRATIONS.

	PAGE
THE REGIMENTAL COLOURS ... ... (*Frontispiece*)	
UNIFORM OF THE MILITIA, 1759	40
A PRIVATE OF THE GRENADIER COMPANY, 1804-1814	86
PORTRAIT OF COLONEL BRYAN COOKE, M.P.	104
HEAD-QUARTERS, DONCASTER	164
COLONEL FERRARS LOFTUS	169
BADGES WORN, 1811-1852	172
BADGES NOW WORN BY THE REGIMENT	200

A PORTRAIT OF COLONEL GEORGE CHOLMLEY IS PRESENTED WITH
    THIS VOLUME ... ... Page 142

PREFACE.

"AN HISTORICAL ACCOUNT IS TO BE KEPT IN EVERY CORPS, OF ITS SERVICES, &c.; STATING THE PERIOD AND CIRCUMSTANCES OF THE ORIGINAL FORMATION OF THE REGIMENT; THE MEANS BY WHICH IT HAS, FROM TIME TO TIME, BEEN RECRUITED; THE STATIONS AT WHICH IT HAS BEEN EMPLOYED, AND THE PERIOD OF ITS ARRIVAL AT AND DEPARTURE FROM SUCH STATIONS. . . . . THE BADGES AND DEVICES WHICH THE REGIMENT HAS BEEN PERMITTED TO BEAR, AND THE CAUSES ON ACCOUNT OF WHICH SUCH BADGES AND DEVICES, OR ANY OTHER MARKS OF DISTINCTION, WERE GRANTED, ARE TO BE STATED; ALSO THE DATES OF SUCH PERMISSION BEING GRANTED. ANY PARTICULAR ALTERATION IN THE CLOTHING, ARMS, ACCOUTREMENTS, COLOURS, HORSE FURNITURE, &C., ARE TO BE RECORDED, AND A REFERENCE MADE TO THE DATES OF THE ORDERS UNDER WHICH SUCH ALTERATIONS WERE MADE. THE VARIOUS ALTERATIONS WHICH MAY BE MADE IN THE ESTABLISHMENT OF THE REGIMENT, EITHER BY AUGMENTATION OR REDUCTION, ARE ALSO TO BE STATED IN THIS BOOK."—*Queen's Regulations and Orders for the Army*, Section 23, para. 44.

THERE are, probably, but few Regiments in Her Majesty's Service in which the book above referred to, and known generally as the "Digest of Services," is kept with the care and attention which it deserves. In the Militia, regiments have always had permanent head-quarters in some county town, and it might therefore be reasonably expected that all regimental books and papers would be complete. Unfortunately, such is far from being the case. In most regiments the books belonging to the earlier periods are almost all wanting, and few can boast of a complete set previous to the year 1852; valuable Order Books, and volumes of Returns having been destroyed or disposed of as waste paper, on the plea of insufficient space or accommodation.

The first step towards publishing the Records of Regiments was taken in 1836, when a General Order was issued from the Horse Guards stating that, with a view to doing the fullest justice to Regiments and Officers, the King had been pleased to direct that an Account of the Services of every Regiment in the British Army should be published, under the superintendence and direction of the Adjutant-General. The Records of nearly all the Cavalry—upwards of twenty—and about forty regiments of Infantry, were therefore prepared by Richard Cannon, Esq., of the Adjutant-General's Office, and published between the years 1837 and 1851, since which time they have been discontinued. It being impossible for any one individual to accomplish such a task as compiling the history of some seventy Regiments in the space of a few years, especially without having access to the books in the possession of regiments, these volumes are merely interesting sketches of some sixty or a hundred pages, no attempt having been made to give anything in detail.

Of late years the Records of several regiments have been published in a more or less complete form, notably the History of the Grenadier Guards, by Lieut.-General Sir F. W. Hamilton, K.C.B.; the History of the Royal Artillery, by Major Duncan, R.A.; that of the 43rd Monmouthshire Light Infantry, by Sir R. G. A. Levinge, Bart.; and the 52nd Oxfordshire Light Infantry, by Captain Moorsom.

In the Militia the Records of only five regiments have as yet been published (in addition to those of the Eight Lancashire Regiments, which are comprised in one volume), viz., the 25th, or South Devon; 59th, or Royal Sherwood Foresters; 69th or Royal North Gloucester; 80th, or Royal Tyrone Fusiliers; and 118th, or 3rd Royal Surrey. Having chiefly been used as Depôt Battalions to supply the Army with officers and men when required during war, and, therefore, having few exciting scenes or gallant deeds to recount, many think there is nothing worthy of record. To those, however, who take a pride or interest in the Service, or in their Regiments, such records of the past, although only of usefulness and not of glory, cannot fail to have

much interest, and they have also a beneficial effect in maintaining that *esprit de corps*, without which a regiment loses half its value. Moreover, but little is known of the history of the "Old Constitutional Force," as no book yet published gives anything approaching to a complete or correct account of this branch of the Service, which has always been acknowledged to be the First, and often the only Reserve on which the country has been able to depend with confidence in time of need. Such a work is much wanted, and the subject is worthy of a good historian. Napier, in his History of the Peninsula War (vol. i. p. 11), in speaking of the Regular Troops, says:—"Of these 50 and 60,000 were employed in the colonies and in India; *the remainder were disposable, because from* 80 *to* 100,000 *Militia, differing from the regular troops in nothing but the name, were sufficient for the home duties.*" Lord Castlereagh (Secretary of State for Foreign Affairs), in a speech delivered in the House of Commons on the 11th of November, 1813, in which he states that the Militia during the eight preceding years had furnished 100,000 men to the Army, said (Hansard's Parliamentary Debates, vol. xxvii, pp. 86, 87):—
"We could not have kept possession of Portugal, or have sent forces to co-operate in the deliverance of the Peninsula at large, and to take up that menacing position on the frontiers of France which our Army now occupies. We should have been shut up within the bounds of our insular policy, and we could not have set that glorious example to other nations, or borne our share in the general exertions which have been made for the deliverance of Europe. Parliament ought always, therefore, to bear in recollection that it is to the Militia we owe the character we at present enjoy in Military Europe, and that without the Militia we could not have shown that face which we have done in the Peninsula."

This volume lays no claim to being a history in the ordinary sense of the term, but merely a record, as complete as it is possible to make it, of the Services of the Regiment. To enter into the general history of the Militia, or even of the other Yorkshire Regiments, or to introduce references to passing events, would only tend to make it unconnected, and swell the volume out of all reasonable proportion to the subject. For the same reason all criticism on the policy of the various measures has been purposely avoided; but, at the same time, all the principal changes made in the Force have been carefully noted.

In July, 1873, these pages were commenced, and a considerable portion of the first part appeared in *Colburn's United Service Magazine* for March, April, May, June, August, and October, 1874. Since then, almost half as much again has been added, some omitted, and the whole re-written. The references in the foot-notes have been made complete and corrected, and the Appendices are here given for the first time.

In performing this work, it has been my endeavour to carry out what I believe to have been the original intention of the Order quoted at the commencement of this Preface, by rendering it complete in every possible detail likely at any time to be of service. I have also done my best to make it accurate and reliable, and at the same time to arrange all the details so as to be clear and precise, with the view of, in a great measure, taking the place of the large accumulation of Correspondence and Returns which go to form the greater portion of a regiment's records, and out of which it is difficult to ascertain any required particulars without great labour and loss of time. It would have been comparatively easy to compile a history of more interest to the general reader, in less than half the time, by omitting many of the details and references here given; the Appendices alone having required for their preparation more than double the time occupied by the remainder of the book.

The earliest Regimental Order Book commences on the 18th of June, 1810, and the Returns in 1808; but both are very incomplete between the years 1815 and 1853; these, with a few Sub-division Books relating to the enrolment of men in the different Wapentakes, are all that remain of a previous date to the year 1852, since which time the records may be said to be complete, with the exception of some important Returns which are wanting as late as the year 1859.

The Regimental Records hitherto published have never contained any complete Returns even of the establishment of the regiments, or of the names and services of the officers. The latter have, in the present case, entailed great labour, as the roll in the possession of the Regiment is far from being complete. Every name has consequently been taken from the *London Gazette*, and Army Lists, amounting to several hundred volumes; and in many instances, where the spelling of the names, or dates of commissions have varied, reference has been made to the Regimental Pay Lists for the period. Several officers—about half-a-dozen—appear to have resigned, and been reappointed; or other individuals of the same name were appointed; but, on comparing the signatures in the Pay Lists, they appear so much alike in every case, that in all probability they are the same persons, although no record exists to show positively which supposition is correct.

Every line previous to the year 1810 has been collected, little by little, from various sources; and in every case, where the information is not derived from the MS. books in possession of the Regiment, the authority is given, partly as a guarantee of accuracy, and because it may possibly prove of assistance to other workers in the same field of research; and also as an acknowledgment of the assistance and information derived from the works of others. The best authorities have always been first consulted, and in most cases the information is taken from the original MS. books or letters themselves.

For the earlier part of my work—indeed, by far the greatest portion—I am indebted for the materials to the Public Record Office, where I have been laid under especial obligations to Alfred Kingston, Esq., for the kindness and assistance I have at all times received from him. The remainder has been principally collected from the Libraries of the British Museum and this Institution; at which latter place I have to thank T. D. Sullivan, Esq. (late 56th Regiment), the Librarian and Assistant-Secretary. In addition to the above places, I have obtained more or less information from the Prince Consort's Library, Aldershot; the Tower, Woolwich, Chelsea, and the Libraries of the House of Commons, and the Corporation of the City of London, at the Guildhall. It has been found almost impossible to obtain any information in detail relating to the uniform and equipment at various periods; and the Print Room of the British Museum, the Fine Art Library at South Kensington, and the Army Clothing Depôt, have been searched without success.

I have also to express my thanks to the authorities of the Home Office, War Office, and Horse Guards, for having permitted me to have access to everything I asked for. Some of the Returns could not have been completed had I not been allowed to refer to the originals at the War Office.

In May, 1870, a short account of the Regiment and the Militia of the West Riding was published, in a series of four articles, in the *Doncaster Gazette*, by William Sheardown, Esq., of that town, from which I have quoted in several places, duly noted. For several occurrences between 1800 and 1810, I am indebted to Major Manwaring, who supplied me with a number of extracts from the Regimental Order Books, copied by him some years ago; the originals having since disappeared. It was my wish to give portraits of all the past Commanding Officers of the Regiment; but I regret that I have only succeeded in obtaining two, one of which was kindly lent to me by Philip Bryan Davies Cooke, Esq., of Owston (the grandson of Colonel Cooke). I have also to thank Major Chantrell and Lieutenant Vincent for supplying me with some of the old badges worn by the Regiment, of which illustrations are given. With the exception of the Head-quarters and the Colours, the illustrations have been done by the Heliotype process. Sir Albert William Woods, Garter King of Arms and Inspector of Colours, kindly furnished me with drawings, in their proper colours, of the Colours of the Regiment, a reduced copy of which is given as a frontispiece.

In conclusion, I can only hope that these pages may prove useful to those interested in the subject, and that this volume—which is principally intended for reference and use by the Regiment—will encourage all ranks to strive to maintain in every sense the high position of THE FIRST REGIMENT OF MILITIA.

G. A. R.

ROYAL UNITED SERVICE INSTITUTION,
    WHITEHALL YARD,
        8th December, 1875.

HISTORICAL RECORDS

OF

THE FIRST REGIMENT OF MILITIA;

OR,

THIRD WEST YORK LIGHT INFANTRY.

CHAPTER I.

THE YORKSHIRE MILITIA PREVIOUS TO 1757.

CONTENTS.—The County.—Wapentakes and Subdivisions.—Population and Quota.—Militia established previous to the Regular Army.—Anglo-Saxon Militia or Fyrd.—The Feudal System.—The Militia during the Thirteenth and Fourteenth Centuries.—Lords-Lieutenant.—Yorkshire Militia in the Reign of James I.—Origin of word "Militia."—Reorganisation of Militia by Charles II., 1660.—Pay of Horse and Foot during Training.—Trophy Money.—Yorkshire Regiments and Officers in 1697.—Condition of the Militia, 1715.—Colonel Thornton's Company in 1745.—The Yorkshire Blues.—The Independents.

YORKSHIRE, as is well known, is the largest county in the United Kingdom, being nearly as large as Wales, and in population comes next after Lancashire and Middlesex. Its extreme length from north to south is about 90 miles, and the greatest breadth from east to west about 115 miles, containing an

B

FIRST REGIMENT OF MILITIA; OR,

area of 5,983 square miles, and a population of 2,436,355.*
Yorkshire has from an early period been divided into three
Ridings, each of which has a Lord-Lieutenant, a Commission of
the Peace, and a separate Court of Quarter Sessions, but there is
only one Sheriff of the whole county.

The County is divided into twenty-six Wapentakes,† six of
which are in the East Riding, which include the Municipal
Boroughs of Beverley, Kingston-upon-Hull, and Hedon, which
was incorporated in 1860.

There are eleven Wapentakes in the North Riding, which
include the two Liberties of Langbaurgh, and Whitby Strand,
and the Municipal Boroughs of Middlesborough, Richmond, and
Scarborough.

In the West Riding there are nine Wapentakes, the City and
Liberty of Ripon, the Municipal Boroughs of Bradford, Don-
caster, Halifax, Leeds, Pontefract, Sheffield, Wakefield, and also
the Boroughs of Dewsbury, incorporated in 1862, Batley and
Huddersfield, both incorporated in 1868, Barnsley in 1869, and
Rotherham in 1871.

The Ainsty ‡ of the City and Shire of York (which is about
thirty-two miles in circumference, and contains sixteen parishes)
was formerly a Wapentake of the West Riding, but by the 27
Henry VI. it was annexed to the city, and remained so until the
year 1836, when it was united with the North Riding for county
elections, for registration purposes with the East Riding, and
the West Riding for all other purposes. §

---

* Lewis's Topographical Dictionary of England, **Vol. IV.**

† *Wapentake*, from the Saxon Wœpen-tac or Hundred.

‡ Some have supposed the word **"*Ainsty*"** to be derived from "*Ancientcy*,"
denoting its antiquity. **Camden conjectures** that its etymology may be
more plausibly referred **to the German** word "*Antossen*," implying a
boundary **or limit. Drake derives it from the** old Northern word "*Anent*,"
which **signifies** opposite or **contiguous, and says it** was called the *Ainsty*
long before **it was** annexed **to the City.—Allen's History** of York, Vol. I.,
page 466.

§ **The** Census, 1871, **Vol. I., page 435.**

The County contains several small "Shires,"* viz., the Shire of the City of York, the Shire of the Town of Hull in the East Riding, and in the West Riding the Shire of Craven in the north-west, and Hallamshire around Sheffield. The Wapentakes are also divided into Parishes, which are mostly very large, and sub-divided into Townships, † the Wapentake of Straforth and Tickhill contains also the Soke ‡ of Doncaster.

The Soke of Doncaster contains Balby-with-Hexthorpe, Doncaster, Loversall, Rossington, Long Sandall, and Wheatley.

The West Riding is forty-eight miles long from north to south, ninety-five miles broad from east to west, and about three hundred and twenty miles in circumference, containing 2,450 square miles. It is divided into twenty-five Petty Sessional Divisions; the City of York (a county in itself), the Boroughs of Doncaster, Leeds, and Pontefract, and the Liberty of Ripon (including the city) have Commissions of the Peace, and separate Courts of Quarter Sessions; and the Boroughs of Batley, Bradford, Dewsbury, Halifax, Huddersfield, Sheffield, and Wakefield have Commissions of the Peace.

The Riding contains thirteen Lieutenancy Sub-divisions, which, with some exceptions, are generally identical with the Wapentakes.

For Parliamentary purposes the West Riding is divided into three Divisions: The Eastern Division, which includes the City

---

* Alfred the Great is said to have divided the country into "Shires," which he subdivided into three parts, called *trythings*. Each *trything* was divided into "*Hundreds*," or "*Wapentakes*," and these again into "*tythings*," or dwellings of ten householders.—Encyclopædia Britannica, 8th Edition, Vol. II., page 481.

† *Township*. The district or territory of a town.

‡ *Soke*. A territorial district in some parts of England, in which a particular privilege is enjoyed or a particular power exercised, such as exemption from customary burdens, and the power of a Lord to hold a Court of his tenants and administer Justice. In some counties there is an intermediate division between the Shire and Hundreds, as the *Lathes* in Kent, and *Rapes* in Sussex, in which latter county there are six of these divisions, which are sub-divided into Hundreds. (Blackstone's Commentaries on the Laws of England).—Latham's "Johnson's Dictionary."

of Ripon and Boroughs of Knaresborough, Leeds, and Pontefract. The Northern Division, which includes the Boroughs of Bradford and Halifax. The Southern Division includes the Boroughs of Dewsbury, Huddersfield, Sheffield, and Wakefield.

The Liberty and the Borough of Ripon are not included in the West Riding for the purpose of the county rate, but are rated separately.

The West Riding has twenty-one Police Divisions. The Cities of Ripon and York and all the Municipal Boroughs, with the exception of Barnsley, Batley, Hedon, and Rotherham, have their own police.

It contains 724 Civil Parishes, Townships, or Places, and parts of six other Townships, viz., Lower Dunsforth, Upper Dunsforth, Humberton, and Milby, which extend into the North Riding, part of the Township of Crowle, which extends into Lincolnshire, and part of the Township of Awkley, which extends into Nottingham.

The nine Wapentakes and thirteen Sub-Lieutenancy Districts are as follows:—*

WAPENTAKE.	Area in Acres.	Population.		
		Males.	Females.	Total.
1. AGBRIGG, including Boroughs of Batley, Dewsbury, Huddersfield, and Wakefield, contains 2 Sub-Lieutenancy Districts, viz.:—				
Upper Division of Agbrigg	72,458	86,810	87,562	174,372
Lower „ „	88,991	76,611	80,978	157,589
2. BARKSTON ASH	91,362	13,768	14,119	27,887
3. CLARO, including City of Ripon	268,317	27,793	28,840	56,633
4. MORLEY, including Boroughs of Bradford and Halifax ...	142,896	229,880	247,476	477,356
5. OSGOLDCROSS, including Boro' of Pontefract	113,851	24,331	24,119	48,450
6. SKYRACK, including Borough of Leeds	116,297	161,149	168,905	330,054
Carried forward ...	894,172	620,342	651,999	1,272,341

* The Census, 1871, Vol. I., pp. 435, 436, and Table 6, p. 443.

Wapentake.	Area in Acres.	Population.		
		Males.	Females.	Total.
Brought forward	894,172	620,342	651,999	1,272,341
7. STAINCLIFFE and EWCROSS, including Boro' of Barnsley, contains 2 Sub-Lieutenancy Districts, viz. :—				
Staincliffe East	168,090	29,473	30,594	60,067
,, West and Ewcross	287,982	13,603	12,515	26,118
8. STAINCROSS	84,962	35,095	32,891	67,986
9. STRAFORTH and TICKHILL, including Boroughs of Doncaster, Sheffield, and Rotherham, contains 3 Sub-Lieutenancy Districts, viz.:				
Lower Division of Straforth and Tickhill	120,150	23,044	23,843	46,887
Upper ditto ditto	161,033	177,034	170,938	347,972
York City and Ainsty	53,970	25,584	27,656	53,240
Total	1,770,359	924,175	950,436	1,874,611

Previous to the year 1852 each regiment was raised exclusively in certain Wapentakes. The quota of 809 appointed to be raised for the Regiment in each Wapentake, Town, and Village in 1802, and the supplementary men raised in 1803, 1809, and 1813, by which the numbers were increased by one-half, or to 1,214, is given in Appendices N and O. The former continued to be the regular establishment of the Regiment until 1852, when men were raised by voluntary enlistment only, and the establishment was increased to 1,036.

The Militia existed a long time previous to the establishment of either a mercenary or a standing army, and frequently constituted the sole military organisation of its times. Sir W. Blackstone and many others agree in attributing to Alfred the Great the foundation of a military system (about the year 878), out of which a national Militia was subsequently formed, and, after many changes, was gradually organised on its present footing in the reign of George II., in the year 1757.

The Anglo-Saxon Militia, or Fyrd, consisted of all the male

population capable of bearing arms, who were compelled, under pain of various penalties, to be efficiently armed according to their means, either to repel invasion or to preserve the peace.*

The Feudal System was introduced by William the Conqueror, about the year 1086. The land was then divided into Knight's Fees, or Fiefs, to the number, it is said, of 60,000, the owners of which were obliged to attend the king annually, with their vassals, for a period of forty days, or, if unable or unwilling to do so, had the option of paying "scutage"—a tax arbitrarily fixed by the king, until the Magna Charta, in 1215, required that it should be assessed by Parliament.

During the thirteenth and fourteenth centuries every man had to serve at his own expense, and provide arms according to his means. He was not liable to leave his county, except in case of invasion or insurrection, and could not, under any pretext, be ordered abroad. The soldiers employed by the sovereign on foreign expeditions were paid by the Crown; noblemen and gentlemen agreeing to serve, with a certain number of men, at a fixed rate of pay for each man.

From the reign of Henry VIII. (about 1545) the Lords-Lieutenant were inseparably associated with the Militia, the right of issuing commissions to the officers being vested in them, subject only to the approval of the sovereign, together with the command of the whole force of Militia in their respective counties,† which they retained until February, 1872, when an Order in Council was issued, re-vesting in the Crown the jurisdiction of the Lords-Lieutenant of Counties in respect of the Militia. A general muster,‡ taken throughout the whole of England and Wales at the beginning of the reign of James I., in 1603, gives the number of able men and armed men, from which it appears that there were 16,345 pyoners, 935 demilances, and 6,777 high

---

* For an account of the Militia, Posse Comitatus, Assize of Arms, &c., see Scott's History of the British Army, Vol. I., pp. 244-261.

† Encyclopædia Metropolitana, Vol. XXII., and Encyclopædia Britannica (8vo. edition), Vol. XV.

‡ Military MSS. in the possession of the Royal United Service Institution.

horses. "Besydes what the Noblemen, Earls, baronnes, lords, Abps, Bishops and prelatts of England can make, which is supposed to be about 20,000 Armed Men and about 4000 Horses." Of the above numbers, Yorkshire furnished the following proportions:—

	Able Men.	Armed Men.	Pyoners.	Demilances.	High Horses.
The County	16,000	11,000	700	120	340
York Cittie	6,000	2,000	500	6	20

From the reign of Charles II., in 1660, our standing army dates its origin, and the Militia was again reorganised.

It is uncertain at what period the word "Militia" was first applied to the men raised for defence by each county. Many think it was about this time, as, during a debate in the House of Commons, in February, 1641, as to whether the command of the Militia was vested in the Crown or in Parliament, Mr. Whitlocke says:—" I do heartily wish that this great word, this new word, this hard word, the Militia, might never have come within these walls." * Bacon, however, in his essay, " Of Kingdoms and Estates," published many years earlier, makes use of this word, saying : " Therefore, let any Prince, or State, thinke soberly of his forces, except his *Militia* of natives be of good and valient soldiers." †

The earliest statutes under which the present Militia Force now serves were partially repealed by the Statute Law Revision Act of 1863. These Acts ‡ placed the Militia of each county under the command of the Lord-Lieutenant, who had the appointment of deputies and all officers, the Crown having the power of displacing them at any time. This force, which consisted of both *horse* and foot, was provided by, or at the expense of, the owners of property—not of land exclusively. No person was charged with providing and equipping a horseman, whose income was less than £500 per annum, or whose estates in goods or money were less than £6,000, and so, proportionate, for a greater estate. No person was required to provide a foot-soldier

---

* Parliamentary History, Vol. II., p. 1,078.
† Montague's Bacon's Essays, Vol. I., p. 100.
‡ 13 Charles II., c. 6 ; 14 Charles II., c. 3 ; and 15 Charles II., c. 24.

and arms unless he had an annual income of £50, or an estate of £600. No person was liable to provide or contribute for both horse and foot, and those who were charged with finding men were not obliged to serve in person. When called out for training and exercise, the horseman received 2s. (shortly afterwards raised to 2s. 6d.), and a foot-soldier 1s. per diem. In the event of rebellion or invasion, the persons who provided the men had to supply each with a month's pay in advance, which was reimbursed out of the public Treasury; but they were not liable to provide a second month's pay until the first had been made good. The ammunition, drums, colours, and other necessaries, were provided out of county rates, known as "trophy money;" the assessment for Yorkshire amounting to £3,043 8s. 10d. Not more than one-fourth the assessment—£70,000 a-month*—could be levied in any one year, except in case of danger, when the whole amount might be raised for three consecutive years. In default of not doing their duty or attending training, they were liable to a fine of 5s., or twenty days' imprisonment.

The men were not compelled to march out of the kingdom "*otherwise than by the laws of England ought to be done.*" The regiments were only required to assemble once a-year, and in companies not oftener than four times a-year, and not for a longer period than four days at a time. Power was afterwards given to the Lords and Deputy-Lieutenants to assemble men for training for any period they thought most convenient, but not exceeding fourteen days in any year.

In the year 1697, during the reign of William and Mary, the Duke of Leeds was Lord-Lieutenant of all three Ridings, and the Militia of the whole county consisted of eight Infantry regiments and the same number of troops of Cavalry.†

The North Riding had 3 Regiments of Infantry and 3 Troops of Horse, viz., Richmondshire Regiment, 7 companies of 326 men, commanded by Col. Sir Christopher Wandesford; Cleveland Regiment, 6 companies, 303 men, commanded by Col. Sir Thos. Pennyman; Bulmer Regiment, 5 companies, 276 men, commanded by Col. Sir B. Bourcher. The Bulmer Troop, 56 men;

---

* Grose's Military Antiquities, Vol. I., p. 27; and 12 Charles II., c. 21.
† Egerton MSS., British Museum, 1626, Press 541 G.

Cleveland Troop, 57 men, and Richmondshire Troop, 62 men. Total, 18 Companies with 905 men, and 3 troops with 175 men, or 1,080 in all. "This is a true list of the Militia within our riding, according as they were last mustered. We know of none not charged to the Militia, except the Peers, who are not chargeable by us."

The East Riding had one regiment of Foot of 8 companies, commanded by the Marquis of Carmarthen as Colonel, 679 strong, and 2 Troops of Horse, of 64 men each, or 128, making a total of 807 men. "They were mustered in May, 1696, and appeared in very good order, and now that they are empowered to receive their contributions, we cannot doubt of their entire obedience whenever His Maty's service shall require It.

"The Lord Howard and the Countess of Winchelsey have each of them £500 per annum, in the East Riding, but have not for many years sent their horses."

A LIST OF THE MILITIA OF THE WEST RIDING IN YORKSHIRE.

THE DUKE OF LEEDS LORD-LIEUT.

OFFICERS' NAMES.	NO. OF MEN.
The Lord Fairfax...	Coll.
John Carvill, Gent.	Capt.-Lieut.
——— ———	Ens.
Sir W. Lowther, Knt...	Lt.-Coll.
James Greenwood, Gent.	Lieut.
——— ———	Ens.
Henry Fairfax, Esq.	Major.
Mr. Brooks ...	Lieut.
——— ———	Ens.
Wm. Fairfax, Esq.	1st Capt., dead.
——— ———	Lieut.
——— ———	Ens.
John Moore, Esq.	2nd Capt.
Henry Wickham, Gent.	Lieut.
——— ———	Ens.
John Batt, Esq. ...	3rd Capt.
— Beaumont, Gent.	Lieut.
——— ———	Ens.
6 Companies	544

FIRST REGIMENT OF MILITIA; OR,

OFFICERS' NAMES.	NO. OF MEN.
Sir Henry Goodrick, Barr.	Coll.
John Dodson, Esq.	Capt.-Lieut.
Wm. Clarke, Gent.	Ens.
Cyrill Arthington, Esq.	Lt.-Coll.
John Beeckwith, Gent.	Lieut., dead.
——— ———	Ens.
Richard Redman, Esq.	Major, dead.
Mr. — Craven	Lieut.
Mr. — Buck	Ens.
Wm. Jennings, Esq.	1st Capt.
Chr. Lyster, Gent.	Lieut.
——— ———	Ens.
Cuthbt. Waide, Esq.	2nd Capt., dead.
——— ———	Lieut.
——— ———	Ens.
Wm. Serjeantson, Gent.	3rd Capt.
(Sent in his commission.)	
——— ———	Lieut.
——— ———	Ens.

" So that in this Regiment 3 companies are unofficered.

6 Companies	528
Sir Mich. Wentworth, Knt. ...	Coll., dead.
Thos. Edmonds, Esq.	Capt.-Lieut.
Mr. Mitch. Burley	Ens.
Wm. Wombwell, Esq.	Lt.-Coll.
Mr. Barnard Allott	Lieut.
Mr. — Wheatley	Ens.
John Gill, Esq.	Major.
Mr. Watts	Lieut., dead.
Mr. Firth	Ens.
John Bradshaw	1st Capt.
Mr. — Shirtliffe, Gent.	Lieut.
Mr. — Thorp	Ens., dead.
Rich. Washington, Esq.	2nd Capt.
Godfrey Washington, Esq., Gent,	Lieut.
——— ———	Ens., dead.

THIRD WEST YORK LIGHT INFANTRY.

OFFICERS' NAMES.		NO. OF MEN.
Wm. Wentworth, Esq.	3rd Capt.	
Tho. Waterhouse, Gent.	Lieut.	
Mr. Fretwell	Ens.	
6 Companies		520
Lord Marquis of Carmarthen ...	Coll.	
John Peckett, Gent.	Capt.-Lieut.	
Joseph Kinger, Gent.	Ens.	
Wm. Roundell, Esq.	Lt.-Coll., dead.	
Roger Wynn, Gent.	Lieut.	
Thos. Scott, Gent.	Ens.	
Robert Waller, Esq.	Major.	
Ambrose Girdler, Gent.	Lieut.	
Mr. — Lawn (gone away)	Ens.	
Richard West, Esq.	1st Capt.	
Tho. Maie (?), Gent.	Lieut.	
Oswold Buckle, Gent.	Ens.	
Thos. Thomlinson, Gent.	2nd Capt.	
Richard Lambert	Lieut., dead.	
— Richardson	Ens.	
Wm. Thompson, Gent.	3rd Capt., dead.	
Edw. Baldock, Gent.	Lieut.	
John Blith, Gent.	Ens.	
Wm. Hesletine, Gent.	4th Capt.	
Benjamin Mason, Gent.	Lieut.	
John Wise, Gent.	Ens.	
7 Companies		520

"This is the City of Yorke Regiment, four companys whereof are raised in the City, and three in the Ayncitty, and encrease and decrease according to the number of the Inhabitants.

OFFICERS' NAMES.		NO. OF MEN.
Thos., Lord Fairfax	Capt.	
Rich. Nettleton, Esq.	Lieut.	67
———— ————	Cornett	
———— ————	Quarter-Mastr.	
Henry Hitch, Esq.	Capt.	
Tho. Kirke, Esq.	Lieut.	74
John Dyneley, Esq.	Cornett.	
Wm. Lastells, Gent.	Quarter-Mastr.	

OFFICERS' NAMES.			NO. OF MEN.
Tho. Fawkes, Esq.	… …	Capt.	⎫
Wm. Hardcastle, Gent.	… …	Lieut., dead	⎬ 72
John Norton, Gent.	… …	Cornett	⎪
Wm. Helm, Gent.	… …	Quarter-Mastr.	⎭

	3 Troops … …	213

ABSTRACT.

Lord Fairfax Regt.,	… …	6 comps. …	544
Sir H. Goodrick's Regt.	… …	6 comps. …	528
Sir. M. Wentworth's Regt.	… …	6 comps. …	520
Lord Carmarthen's Regt.	… …	7 comps. …	520
		25 „ …	2,112
	Horse, 3 Troops	…	213
			2,325

Duke of Norfolk.	Earle of Thanett.
Duke of Devonshire.	Earle of Bridgwater.
Lrd. Arch Bp. of Yorke.	Earle of Holdernesse.
Earle of Strafford.	Lord Viscount Wharton.
Earle of Scarsdale.	Lord Viscount Lonsdale.
Earle of Huntingdon.	

"These Lords, not having been of late charged by their Peers, do not send in their Horse.

| Duke of Somerset … | 1 | Marq. of Hallifax … | 4 |
| E. of Burlington … | 2 | E. of Radnor … | 3 |

"These usually send in their number of Horse.

"Upon the last charge and since, the number of Horse has been advanced, by reason whereof the number of Foot has been something diminished, and upon that alteration there are severall small Estates within the severall Weapentakes of the Westriding which did contribute to Foot, and are at present uncharged, the Deputy Lts. of the parts aforesaid, reserving them to supply such persons as upon complaint shall be adjudged to be overcharged." *

The old Militia, although a popular, was a badly organised and unreliable force. In the Rebellion of 1715 the Militia of one

---

* Egerton MSS., British Museum, 1626, Press 541 G.

county took nine months to assemble; but the force did good service in doing the duty of the Regular troops in garrison. A writer at this period gives an account of the Posse Comitatus and Militia of Cumberland and Westmoreland, amounting to some three or four thousand men, under the Earl of Carlisle, Lord Lonsdale, and a number of half-pay Officers, taking to their heels on the appearance of the Rebels, who were on their way from Penrith to Appleby, in November, 1715, and whom they were sent to stop. Much could certainly not be expected from troops who mustered in country churchyards, and went through such movements as could be performed by a handful of men.*

About the year 1745, Colonel (then Captain) Thornton, of Thornville, near York, raised and maintained a company of seventy-five men at his own expense, with which he marched to Scotland, and was present at the battle of Falkirk, on the 17th of January, 1746. The sergeants and drummers received 1s. 2d., the corporals 1s. 1d., and the privates 1s., per diem.† On the formation of the Militia in 1758, he was appointed to the command of this Regiment, and afterwards commanded the 2nd West York Militia for many years.

During the rebellion of 1745, the City as well as the County of York gave the most unequivocal proofs of loyalty. The Archbishop projected an Association, consisting of more than 800 of the principal nobility, gentry, and clergy of the county, which was formed at the Castle of York, on the 23rd of September, 1745. A subscription was immediately commenced, and the sum of £31,420 was raised for the support of the Government and the defence of the county. John Raper, the Lord Mayor, convened a meeting of the inhabitants for the same purpose, when the subscription in the City amounted to £2,420, and to £220 in the Ainsty. With these sums four companies of Infantry, of seventy men each, exclusive of sergeants, cor-

---

* A Scheme for Establishing a Constitutional Militia, 1747, p. 9 ; and An Essay on the Expediency of a National Militia, 1757, pp. 17 and 19.
† Eboracum, or History of the City of York, Vol. I., p. 225.

porals, and drummers, were raised, and designated the "Yorkshire Blues." They remained embodied about four months, the officers serving without pay, and the sergeants receiving fourteen shillings, the drummers ten shillings, and the privates seven shillings per week. Another military body, called the "Independents," was formed, for the defence of the City, by the gentlemen and other principal inhabitants. Their uniform and accoutrements were purchased at their own expense, and the corps remained under arms ten months.* This was probably the first Volunteer Corps ever established in the kingdom.

---

* Eboracum, or History of the City of York, Vol. I., pp. 222-5 ; Allen's History of York, Vol. I., p. 116 ; Sheahan and Whellan's History of York, Vol. I., pp. 268-9.

CHAPTER II.

FROM 1756 TO 1796.

EMBODIED FROM 5TH SEPTEMBER, 1759, TO 25TH SEPTEMBER, 1762.

CONTENTS.—The New Militia of 1757.—The Yorkshire Militia.—Riots at York.—Formation of the three West York, the two North York, and East York Regiments.—List of First Officers appointed to the Regiment.—Brigadier-Generals of Militia.—Sergeants approved by the King.—Letter from Marquis of Rockingham.—List of Arms and Accoutrements supplied to the Regiment.—Royal Warrant for the supply of Powder, &c. to the Militia.—Embodiment of the West York Militia.—Warrant for Necessaries.—The Clothing.—Militia Pay and Subsistence.—Regiment ordered to Sunderland.—Return to York.—Inspected by His Royal Highness the Duke of York.—Proceed to Newcastle-on-Tyne.—Thence to Nottingham.—Warrant to Disembody the three West York Regiments.—Vote of Thanks of House of Commons.—The West York Militia reorganised in two Regiments.—List of the Officers.—The Militia from 1765 to 1796.

1756.—In the year 1756, defensive measures having become urgent, Parliament * again had recourse to the Militia, which was then first organised in its present form (the ballot clauses being for the first time introduced) as a *permanent* provision for the defence of the realm, and the expense of the force ceased to be a charge on property, each county having to provide a fixed quota of men. †

---

* Lords' Journals, Vol. XXIX., p. 4, King's Message recommending the framing of a National Militia.

† Appendix H. (8), p. 243 of the Report of the Commission on Recruiting, 1866.

It was under this Act * that the oldest existing English and Welsh regiments, were first raised, most of them being formed during the two following years. The Irish Militia was not organised until the year 1793;† and the Scotch until 1797.‡

1757.—The preamble of the Act for England of 1757 states that, "*Whereas a well-ordered* and *well-disciplined Militia is essentially* necessary to the *Safety,* Peace, *and* Prosperity *of this Kingdom; and* whereas the *Laws now* in being for the *Regulation of the Militia,* are defective and ineffectual," &c. That from and after the 1st of May of that year the King would appoint Lords-Lieutenants, who were empowered to assemble and arm the Militia, and appoint deputies who must be approved by His Majesty, and grant Commissions to the proper number of Officers, submitting their names to the King within one month after appointment. The Lords-Lieutenant had the chief command of the Militia in their respective counties, and all those already appointed, including Deputy-Lieutenants were to stand good. The Deputy-Lieutenants and Officers of Militia were required to have a "Property Qualification," one-half of which had to be within the county for which they served. The Property Qualification was several times revised, and finally abolished in the year 1869.§

When the Militia was called out in case of invasion or imminent danger, officers might be promoted for extraordinary merit without reference to the above qualification, provided that no officer was promoted above the rank of Captain unless he had the qualification for that rank. At the end of every four years such a number of officers were to be discharged as should be equal to the number who were qualified and willing to serve. The Adjutant and Sergeants were appointed from the army.

---

* 30 George II., c. 25, which received the Royal Assent on the 28th June, 1757 (see Appendix M).

† 33 George III., c. 22.

‡ 37 George III., c. 103; and 42 George III., c. 91.

§ The amount required to qualify for each rank at different periods is given in Appendix D.

The quota was fixed at 32,000,* of which Yorkshire supplied 2,360, viz.: for the West Riding, with the City and County of the City of York, 1,240; for the North Riding, 720; and for the East Riding, with the town and county of Kingston-upon-Hull, 400. Three officers were allowed to every eighty men, who had to serve three years, after which they were not liable to serve again unless it came to their turn by rotation.

The Deputy-Lieutenants, and not the Commanding Officer, had the power to grant discharges, which were given annually on the Tuesday before Michaelmas to those who were entitled to them. Within one month after the return of the Rolls the Lords and Deputy-Lieutenants were to meet and form the Militia into *Regiments*, appointing the necessary officers; but if the companies were less than *seven* they were formed into *Battalions*, under the command of the Lord Lieutenant and one field officer. Until three-fifths of the men were enrolled, and a similar proportion of the officers had accepted commissions, neither pay, arms, or clothing were issued, nor the Adjutant or Sergeants appointed.

The men were punished by the Justices of the Peace for absence or disobedience; viz., for the first offence a fine of two shillings, or "be set in the stocks for an hour;" second offence a fine of four shillings or four days in the House of Correction; and for a third and every subsequent offence a fine of six shillings, or one month in the House of Correction. Any man drunk on duty was fined ten shillings.

They were not liable to serve out of the United Kingdom. It was in this Act that it was first laid down that the officers were to rank with officers of the Regular Army, as equal in degree, but as junior of their respective ranks; and that officers of the Regular Army should not sit in any court-martial on the trial of a Militiaman, or Militia officer on the trial of a Regular soldier.†

---

* The House of Commons fixed the quota at upwards of 60,000, but it was reduced by the Lords to one-half that number.—Parliamentary History, Vol. XV., pp. 739 and 782.

† Gentleman's Magazine, Vol. XXXII., pp. 225-230.

The Training of the Militia then extended throughout the year. On the first Monday in each month from March to October inclusive, they exercised in half companies, and assembled in companies on the third Monday in each of these months. The men were not obliged to go more than six miles from home, and with this view the places of assembly were fixed to suit the convenience of the men as much as possible. The companies assembled in regiments or battalions on Tuesday, Wednesday, Thursday, and Friday, in Whitsun week, and in the event of this being inconvenient at any time on account of fairs or markets, the Deputies-Lieutenant and Justices of the Peace were empowered to change the days to any other within that week, excepting Sundays. Instead of drilling during harvest, the time might be made up by drilling on Tuesday and Wednesday in Easter week. The drills were to be for six hours a-day, but not more than two hours under arms at a time.

At the annual regimental Training in Whitsun week the officers and men were billeted in the public-houses, the landlords having to provide "diet and small beer for officers under the rank of Captain at a shilling, and privates fourpence per diem."

The power of the officers to award punishment was extremely limited, almost all cases having to be decided by the magistrates. For being drunk, a man was fined ten shillings, or had to sit in the stocks for an hour. Disobedience to an officer was punished, during the time of training, by fines; for the first offence, half-a-crown, or committed to the House of Correction for four days; for the second offence, a fine of five shillings, or seven days in the House of Correction; and for a third and every subsequent offence, a fine of forty shillings, or one month in the House of Correction.

The captain of each company might either keep the arms, clothes, and accoutrements in his possession, or order them to be kept by whom he chose. The churchwardens had to provide chests for that purpose, in which the arms, &c., were carefully locked-up; and if the person intrusted with their care should at any time deliver them out, unless for exercise or by proper authority, he incurred a penalty of six months' imprisonment.

At the end of his three years' service, a Militiaman was entitled to his clothing.

Captains were allowed to increase their companies if called out for active service, subject to the permission of the Lord-Lieutenant, and provided that the men were disciplined, properly equipped, and signed an agreement to serve during such period of active service, and submit to the Militia Laws.*

THE YORKSHIRE MILITIA.—The new regulations for levying the Militia, which obliged the poor to contribute equally with the rich, produced a spirit of insubordination in the North and East Ridings of York,† and, on the 13th of September, 1757, a large body of the countrypeople from more than thirty parishes (principally from the Wapentake of Buckross, in the East Riding) went to Birdfall, the seat of Henry Willoughby, Esq., the High Sheriff, and demanded a repeal of the Militia Act.‡ On the 15th of September, a number of farmers and countrypeople (principally from the Wapentake of Bulmer, in the North Riding) assembled at York, with intent to prevent the constables from presenting the lists of men subject to the ballot. Armed with guns, clubs, scythes, and other unlawful weapons, they proceeded to the Cockpit House, without Bootham Bar, where the Deputy-Lieutenants and Chief Constables were to have assembled; and, not meeting with the first-named officers, as they expected, they forced the lists from such constables as were in attendance; and, after drinking all the liquors, they demolished the house. At length the rioters were prevailed upon to disperse by the Lord Mayor and High Sheriff; and at the ensuing assizes several of them were tried and acquitted. One man, named George Thurloe, received sentence of death; but his punishment was afterwards commuted to transportation for life. Another, of the name of Cole, was condemned and

---

* The **Complete Militia Man,** a Compendium of Military Knowledge, 1760, pp. 99, 100, 105-111; and Grose's Military Antiquities, Vol. I., pp. 19, 26.

† These riots were not confined to Yorkshire; there were also Militia riots in several other counties.

‡ Eboracum, or the History and Antiquities of the City of York, 1788; published anonymously by T. Wilson and R. Spence, Vol. I., pp. 227-8.

executed for being the leader of a riot, on the same occasion, in the East Riding.*

The Right Hon. G. H. Lane, then Lord Mayor of York, in a letter dated 1st October, 1757, to the Secretary of State (enclosing the sworn depositions of the witnesses on which several of the rioters had been committed for trial), says :—"The Rioters who did the mischief came from neighbouring villages, and, to the number of over a hundred, plundered the House of Mr. Wm. Bowes, in Bootham. We have had frequent disturbances about the high price of corn, and now the Militia—by no way disagreeable if properly handled; and the truth is, the necessitous (who are by much the majority) are endeavouring to promote a levelling principle (which is constantly made use of in the meetings) which would prove fatal to the peace and happiness of our Constitution; and they think, by the Militia Act, the poor are to defend the rich."†

1758.—The *London Gazette* for 1758 contains numerous notices from the Lords-Lieutenant of Counties in England and Wales of meetings about to be held to select properly qualified persons to officer the Militia. The one issued for the West Riding is as follows:—

" WENTWORTH, *July* 1*st*, 1758.

" The Deputy-Lieutenants, and Gentlemen qualified to serve in the Militia of the West Riding of the County of York, and of the City of York, and County of the same, or Ainsty of York, are desired to meet at the Red Lion, in Pontefract, on Monday, the 24th Day of July Instant, in order that all Gentlemen, qualified according to the Act passed last Session, and willing to accept of Commissions, may deliver, or cause to be delivered, to His Majesty's Lieutenants of the several Places aforesaid, their Names, specifying the Rank in which they would serve.

" ROCKINGHAM."

Similar notices were issued, at the same time, for meetings to be held for the East Riding, at the " Tiger," Beverley, on Tues-

---

* Sheahan's and Whellan's History of York, Vol. I., pp. 269-70, 1855 ; and Hargrove's History of York, 1818, Vol. I., pp. 234-35.

† Home Office, Domestic Series, George II., No. 138; Allen's History of York, Vol. I., pp. 190-91.

day, the 25th of July; and for the North Riding at the "Post-house," Richmond, on Saturday, the 5th of August.

Some difficulty was at first experienced in completing the number of officers required, especially in the East Riding, where it was necessary to hold several meetings for that purpose. Colonel Thornton's Regiment (now the 3rd West York), which was raised in the Wapentakes of Claro, Staincliffe, and Ewcross was the first completed, the list of officers having been approved by the King on the 27th of January, 1759; the warrant for arms and accoutrements being dated the 31st of May.

Sir George Savile's Regiment (now the 2nd West York), which was raised in the Wapentakes of Agbrigg and Morley, was the next completed, the names of the officers being approved by the King on the 13th February; the warrant for arms and accoutrements was of the same date as Colonel Thornton's Regiment.

Lord Downe's Regiment (now the 1st West York) was the last completed, and was raised in the Wapentakes of Osgoldcross, Straforth and Tickhill, Staincross, Barkston Ash, and part of Skyrack. The names of the officers were approved by the King on the 29th of June, the warrant for arms and accoutrements bearing date the 27th of July.* All three Regiments were embodied for the first time on the 5th of September, 1759.

Lord Downe's Regiment, however, was always known as the First Battalion, Sir George Savile's Regiment retaining its place as the Second Battalion; so that Colonel Thornton's, although actually the First, became the Third Battalion, probably in consequence of the regiments taking precedence according to the rank of their commanding officer.

In the North Riding the names of the officers were submitted for the King's approval by the Lord-Lieutenant, in a letter dated the 2nd of January, 1759; and three-fifths of the officers and men were certified by him to be completed on the 19th of May. The warrant for the supply of the necessary arms and accoutrements, &c., was dated the 21st of May, 1759, for the Richmondshire Battalion, under the com-

---

* War Office Militia Letter Book, Sept. 1758—Sept. 1760.

mand of Colonel Sir Ralph Milbanke, Bart., and the 20th of June for the Cleveland and Bulmer Battalion, commanded by Colonel Duncombe. The two regiments were first embodied on the 2nd of July, 1759.

In the East Riding the names of the officers were submitted by the Lord-Lieutenant in a letter dated the 9th of June, 1759, and the three-fifths were certified by him to be complete on the 3rd of December, the warrant for arms, &c., bearing the same date. The regiment was first embodied on the 1st of January, 1760.

A War-Office letter, dated the 1st of September, 1759, orders that Militia Regiments are not to have any fixed rank or precedence of one before another; but the first which arrives in any camp, garrison, or quarters, shall have seniority there, and the others in the order they arrive. On the 26th of June, the following year, regiments were directed to draw lots for precedence, whilst serving together, without prejudice to their pretensions; but this arrangement was not to interfere with the rank previously arranged between regiments of the same county.*

1759.—The following is the letter from the Secretary of State, intimating the King's approval of the names of the first officers appointed to the regiment:—†

"WHITEHALL, *January* 27*th*, 1759.

"My Lord,

"Having laid before the King the List your Lordship transmitted to me, some time since, of Persons who have offer'd to serve as officers in the Militia raised within the City of York and County of the same City, and within the several Wapentakes or Hundreds of Claro, Staincliffe, and Ewcross, part of the West Riding of the County of York; I have the satisfaction to acquaint

---

* Military Orders and Instructions for the Wiltshire Battalion of Militia from 1758 to 1770, pp. 55-6, and 130. This is an 8vo volume of over 500 pages, published at Chelsea in 1772, and contains all the Regimental Orders during that period, besides much interesting matter. There is a copy in the British Museum, King's Library, 58, d. 4.

† War Office Militia Letter Book, Vol. I., Sept., 1758—Sept., 1760; and Vol. II., pp. 39-40.

your Lordship that His Majesty does not disapprove of any of the Persons mentioned in the said List.

"I am, with great truth and regard, &c.

"HOLDERNESSE."

"THE NAMES of the officers for His Majesty's approbation, in One Battalion of the Militia, consisting of Three Hundred and Eleven private men, proposed to be divided into Eight companies, raised within the City of York, and County of the same City, and within the several Wapentakes or Hundreds of Claro, Staincliffe, and Ewcross, part of the West Riding of the County of York.

COLONEL.—William Thornton, Esq.
LIEUTENANT-COLONEL.—Daniel Lascelles, Esq.
MAJOR.—William Tufnell Joliffe, Esq.

CAPTAINS.
- Sir Cecil Wray, Bart.
- Josias Morley, Esq.
- William Weddal, ,,
- William Meeke, ,,
- Henry Duncombe, ,,
- Mann Horsfield, ,,

LIEUTENANTS.
- William Foster, Esq.
- James Morley, ,,
- William Nowel, ,,
- George Hassell, ,,
- George Iveson, ,,
- Edward Norton, ,,
- Samuel Wand, ,,
- George Thompson ,,

ENSIGNS.
- Richard Clapham, Gent.
- Richard Taylor, ,,
- David Swails, ,,
- Miles Staveley, ,,
- William Sands, ,,
- Richard Dewes, ,,
- Isaac Webster, ,,
- John Wilks, ,,
- John Horner, ,,
- John Allinson, ,,
- Christopher Wharton, ,,
- Samuel Wiggins, ,,

"The above-named Gentlemen are humbly presented to His Majesty for his Royal Approbation, to be Commission Officers of the Militia ; They being Persons properly qualified, and willing to accept such Commissions.

"ROCKINGHAM."

The following is a copy of the commission appointing the first adjutant to the regiment :—

"GEORGE THE SECOND, by the Grace of God, King of Great Britain, France, and Ireland, Defender of the Faith, &c. To Our Trusty and well-beloved Richard Dawson, Jun., Gent., GREETING : We do, by these Presents, constitute and appoint you to be Adjutant to the Militia Battalion of Foot, for Our City of York, and County of Our same City, the several Wapentakes of Claro, Staincliffe, and Ewcross, Part of the West Riding of Our said County of York, commanded by Our Trusty and Welbeloved William Thornton, Esq. You are, therefore, carefully and diligently to discharge the Duty of Adjutant, by doing and performing All, and all manner of Things thereunto belonging. And you are to observe and follow such Orders and Directions, from Time to Time, as you shall receive from Our Lieutenant, of the West Riding of Our said County of York, or, any other Your superior Officer, according to the Acts of Parliament, in this Case made, and provided. GIVEN at our Court at St. James's, the Thirteenth Day of February, 1759, in the Thirty-Second Year of Our Reign.

"By His Majesty's Command,
"HOLDERNESSE."

At this period the rank of Brigadier-General was held by Militia officers in certain counties. By a warrant, dated the 22nd of February, 1760, Henry, Earl of Darlington, was appointed "Brigadier-General of Our Militia Forces for the County of Durham." Sir James Lowther was also made Brigadier-General of the Militia of Cumberland and Westmoreland, and the Earl of Shaftesbury Brigadier-General of the Militia of Dorset.*

It was then usual to submit the names of the Sergeants as well as the officers for the approval of the Crown. The following

---

* War Office Militia Letter Books, Vol. II., pp. 21-2 and 25 is the list submitted by the Lord-Lieutenant of **the West Riding.**

"The names **of the** Sergeants for His Majesty's Approbation and appointment **in the Militia Battalions** raised within, and for, the West Riding **of the County of York, City of York, and County of the same City, or** Ainsty of **York:—**

NAMES.	REGIMENTS SERVED IN.	HOW LONG.	
		Years.	Months.
Joseph Lane	Lord Geo. Beauclerk's	32	6
Geo. McCulloth	,,	26	3
Abraham Crosland	,,	19	4
John Fraizer	,,	18	6
William Hurst	...	30	0
Richard Hayl	Gen. Howard's	14	0
Joseph Swift	...	...	...
Robert Cooper	...	...	...
George Naylor	Col. Cotterel's	...	...
John Baxly	Col. Pool's	25	0
Richard Horner	Sir Robt. Rich's	3	6
Andrew Shields	Lord Albemarle	30	5
Wm. Henderson	Kerr's, Now Cope's	30	8
Wm. Wright	...	...	...
Nicholas Thornber	Yorkshire Blues	...	...
Benjamin Warren	Col. Hodgson's	...	...
Wm. Deighton	...	...	...
John Cundale	Sir John Mordaunt's	...	...
Christopher Solisby	...	...	...
Abraham Jellson	Under the King of Prussia	...	...
William Crnsk	...	...	...

"*Wentworth, August* 16*th*, 1759."

"WHITEHALL, *August* 24*th*, 1759.

"His Majesty does very well approve of the several Persons mentioned in the foregoing **List to be appointed Sergeants in** the Militia Forces raised within, **and for the West Riding of** the County of York, City of **York and County** of the same City, or Ainsty of York. "HOLDERNESSE."

On the 30th of May, 1759, the House of Commons resolved to present an Humble Address **to the King, that he will be** pleased to direct the Lords-Lieutenants to use their **utmost** diligence and **attention to carry out** the Militia Acts.*

---

* Commons' Journals, Vol. XXVIII., p. 600.

In compliance with this Resolution, a Circular was sent to the Lords-Lieutenants of Counties, dated Whitehall, June 5th, 1759:—

"My Lord,

"I am commanded by the King; in consequence of an Humble Address from the House of Commons, to signify to your Lordship His Majesty's Pleasure that you do use your utmost Diligence and Attention to carry into execution the several Acts of Parliament made for the better ordering of the Militia Forces of that part of Great Britain, called England.*

"I am, &c.,
"W. PITT."

Another circular of the same date was also sent directing the Lords-Lieutenant to report what progress had been made in their respective counties in carrying out the Militia Acts:—†

"WHITEHALL, June 5th, 1759.

"The King having, by a Most Gracious Message, acquainted His Parliament‡ with His having received repeated Intelligence of the actual Preparations making in the French Ports to invade This Kingdom, and of the imminent Danger of such Invasion being attempted, to the end that His Majesty may (if He shall think proper), cause the Militia, or such Part thereof as shall be necessary, to be drawn out and embodied, and to march as occasion shall require; I am commanded to signify the King's Pleasure to your Lordship that you do forthwith transmit to one of His Principal Secretaries of State, for His Majesty's Information, an account of what Progress has been made in the West Riding of the County of York, in the Execution of the Acts of Parliament past in the 30th and 31st years of His Majesty's Reign, for the better ordering of the Militia Forces in the several Counties of That Part of Great Britain called England; and also an exact Return of the actual state and condition of the Militia

---

* Militia (Home Office), No. I., 1759. As early as July out of the quota of 32,000 men, 17,436 were officered and nearly completed, and 6,280 were embodied and on duty.—Annual Register, Vol. II., p. 273; and Gentleman's Magazine, Vol. XXIX., p. 384.

† Militia (Home Office), No. I., 1759.

‡ On 30th May, Lords' Journals, Vol. XXIX., p. 524; and Commons' Journals, Vol. XXVIII., p. 600.

in the County above mentioned under your Direction, in order that the King may be fully informed, how soon the whole, or any part of the Militia of the said County may be in readiness to be **drawn out and embodied,** if His Majesty shall think proper, and **to march as Occasion shall** require.

"I am, &c.,
"W. Pitt."

In reply to this Circular, the Lord-Lieutenant returned the following answer:—*

"Sir,

"The Militia of the West Riding of Yorkshire—City of York, &c.—are divided into Three Battalions, for the greater Convenience of the Officers for assembling and Disciplining the men.

"The Battalion commanded by Colonel Thornton is completed in number of Officers.

"The Battalion commanded by Sir George Savile wants some few Lieuts. and Ensigns, but has above the three-fifths.

"The Battalion proposed to be commanded by Lord Downe is also near completed in the full number of Officers.

"The two first Battalions have been for some time entitled to their Arms, Pay, &c., and accordingly some weeks ago I laid the proper estimate before the Treasury, and believe that the Arms and Clothing, &c., will be delivered to those two Battalions within three weeks.

"The other Battalion will be put in order very soon. The necessary number of Officers were *not* completed till a Meeting at which I attended last Thursday at Pontefract.

"The Private Men were returned Balloted upon the first Militia Act in 1757, and many of them have learnt part of their exercise.

"If any part of the West Riding of Yorkshire, as being very inland, was thought a proper place for French Prisoners to be sent to, I believe that in three weeks' time, the Militia of the West Riding could undertake to guard them, and if the number sent was sufficient to occasion three or more companies of Militia to be assembled, by letting the Companies serve in

---

* Militia (Home Office), 1759, No. 1.

rotation at fortnightly Guards, it would greatly tend to expedite the Disciplining the Militia in those Parts, and would be very agreeable to the Gentlemen to be able to flatter themselves with the thought of being in any Degree serviceable at this juncture.

"I am, Sir,
"With great truth and Regard,
"Your Most Obedient and Humble Servant,
"ROCKINGHAM.
"WENTWORTH, *June* 25*th*, 1759."

The following correspondence took place between the Secretary of State and the Board of Ordnance, relating to the application for arms for the Yorkshire Militia :—

"WHITEHALL, *May* 31*st*, 1759.*

"Gentlemen,
"The Marquis of Rockingham, His Majesty's Lieutenant for the West Riding of the County of York, having, agreeable to the Acts of Parliament, for the better ordering the Militia Forces in that part of Great Britain called England, certified and returned, to the King, that Three-Fifths of the Two Battalions of Militia for the West Riding of the County of York, have been chosen and enrolled, and that Three-Fifths of the Commissioned Officers for the same, have been appointed and taken out their Commissions, and entered their Qualifications, and His Lordship having in consequence thereof, desired that the necessary Arms, Accoutrements, &c., may be delivered for the use of the said Two Battalions of Militia; I am to signify to you His Majesty's Pleasure, that you do accordingly direct the Arms, Accoutrements, &c., agreeable to the List enclosed, to be provided and delivered free of any Expense of Carriage at such Place in the West Riding of the County of York, as the Marquis of Rockingham, His Majesty's Lieutenant thereof, shall judge most convenient, and to such Person or Persons as shall be duly Authorized by His Lordship to receive the same.

"I am, Gentlemen, &c.,
"*Board of Ordnance.*"   "HOLDERNESSE."

---

* War Office Militia Letter Book, Vol. I.; and King's Warrants (Tower), Vol. IV., p. 76; and see also Commons' Journals, Vol. XXVIII., p. 642.

THIRD WEST YORK LIGHT INFANTRY.

A Return of Arms, Accoutrements, and Ammunition necessary for Two Battalions of the Militia for the West Riding of the County of York, consisting of 32 Sergeants, 32 Drummers, and 720 Rank and File, to be formed into 16 Companies:—

	Sir George Savile's.	Col. Thornton's.
"Silk Colours—the **one an** Union, the other a * ——— Sheet, with the Arms of ——— ...	2	2
Oilskin **cases** for ditto, lined with Baize	2	2
RANK AND FILE.		
Short Musquets, with Bayonets, **Scabbards, Wood Rammers** and tanned Leather Slings	400	320
Cartouch Boxes with Belts **and** Frogs	400	320
Small Hangers, with Brass **Hilts,** Scabbards, and tanned Leather Waist-Belts	400	320
Brushes and Wires	400	320
Iron Wiping Rods	16	16
SERJEANTS.		
Halberts...	16	16
Large Hangers with **Brass Hilts, Scabbards,** and tanned Leather Waist-Belts	16	16
DRUMMERS.		
Drums compleat, with the Arms of ———	16	16
Drum Carriages and Ticken, Drum Cases—each	16	16
Small Hangers, **with** Brass Hilts, Scabbards, **and** Waist-Belts, **the same as the Drum Carriages**	16	16
AMMUNITION.		
Powder for { Service (Barrels)	4½	3½
Powder for { Exercise "	5	4
Musquet { Ball (Cwt.)	9	7½
Musquet { Flints	1,600	1,280
Musquet { Formers	16	16
Fine Paper—Rhms. Quires	5·5	4·4
Leather Powder Bags	8	8
Spare Musquet Rammers	80	64

"*Office of Ordnance*, 16th *May*, 1759.
"ROCKINGHAM."

---

* The Regimental Colour of **Lord Downe's Regiment was Green, with the** Arms of the Lord Lieutenant.

The subjoined extracts, relating to the preceding correspondence, are taken from the Proceedings of the Board of Ordnance:—*

"*7th June*, 1759.
"By the Board.

"The Right Honorable Earl of Holdernesse, His Majesty's Principal Secretary of State, by Letters of the 31st Ultimo, signified the King's pleasure that the Arms, &c., mentioned in the List enclosed be forthwith Issued for use of the Militia of the West Riding of the County of York, and delivered free of any Expense of Carriage, at such place as the Marquis of Rockingham shall judge proper, and to such Person or Persons as shall be Authorized by His Lordship to receive the same.

"The same was Ordered accordingly."

12*th June*.—"The Marquis of Rockingham having by Letter of the 7th inst. desired that the Arms, &c., for the West York Militia, may be sent to Doncaster by the Road Waggons, if the Board have no objections thereto,

"Ordered, that his Lordship be acquainted that the sending them by water will be greatly cheaper, and that they will be down time enough, but if his Lordship hath any objection thereto, they will be sent as he desires."†

The following Warrant was issued authorizing the supply of the necessary ammunition for the Militia:—‡

"GEORGE R.

"Whereas it has been humbly represented unto Us that Ammunition is immediately wanted for Our Militia Forces, OUR WILL and PLEASURE is that out of the Stores, remaining within the Office of Our Ordnance, you cause Powder, Ball, and Flints to be delivered to all the Regiments of Militia, that already are, or which hereafter may be called out for Our Service, in the same Proportion as Ammunition is delivered to Our Regular Forces, computing Eighteen Barrels of Serviceable and Thirty Six Barrels of Triumph Powder, to every Nine Hundred Men;

---

* Ordnance Minutes (Tower) (Surveyor-General), Vol. XX., p. 607.
† Idem, Vol. XX., p. 620.
‡ King's Warrants (Woolwich), Vol. IV., pp. 92-3; and Commons' Journals, Vol. XXVIII., p. 642.

it is likewise OUR WILL and PLEASURE that one Waggon with a proper Number of Horses and Drivers do attend each Battalion of Our Militia Forces that Encamps, in order to carry their spare Ammunition. And OUR FURTHER WILL and PLEASURE is that you cause the following allowance of Ammunition, to be from Time to Time, delivered for Exercise of such of Our Militia Forces as are not called out for service, viz.,—

Powder 1 lb. per man, which, at ¼ oz. per cartridge, will make 64 rounds.

Ball
Flints   } In Proportion,
Fine Paper

the same to be issued Half Yearly (upon the Commanding Officer certifying the last Allowance to be nearly expended), free of any Expence, at such Place in each County as the Lord-Lieutenant shall judge most convenient, and to such Person as shall be duly authorised to receive and indent for the same. And you are hereby required to insert the Whole Charge hereof in your Estimates to be, from Time to Time, presented to Parliament. And for so doing this shall be as well to you, as to all others Our Officers and Ministers herein concerned, a sufficient Warrant.

"Given at Our Court at Kensington the Ninth Day of July, 1759, in the Thirty-Third Year of Our Reign.

"By His Majesty's Command,

"*To Our Right Trusty and Wellbeloved*   "W. PITT.
Cousin and Councillor JOHN VIS-
COUNT LIGONIER, *Master-General of*
Our Ordnance."

It appears to have been necessary, when the Militia was disembodied, to issue a similar Warrant, authorising a supply of ammunition for practice during the period of the Annual Training to be given to regiments, as the following letter will show:—*

"WHITEHALL, 18*th May*, 1763.

"The King thinks it reasonable that all the Militia should have an allowance of ammunition for their Annual Exercise, of

---

* Ordnance Entry Book, Vol. I., p. 195; and King's Warrants (Woolwich), Vol. VI., p. 21.

the same species, and in the same proportion, as is allowed to His Majesty's Regular Forces for the like purposes."

In July the Regiment was increased to ten companies and 400 men, by the addition of two Companies, containing four sergeants and eighty rank and file, a Warrant being issued, dated 27th of that month, for supplying them with the necessary arms and accoutrements.*

Two months after his previous letter of the 25th of June, the Lord-Lieutenant wrote to inform the authorities that the West York Militia was complete, and anxious that their services should be accepted :—†

"Sir,—

"The Militia for the West Riding of Yorkshire has been for some Time completed in Officers and Men, and being very desirous that in case of need they may be able to be of some Service in Defence of His Majesty's Royal Person and Government, I must now in their Behalf, and at their Request, apply to you, Sir, for the favour of their being called out and sent upon any service where they may possibly be of any use.

"The Difficulty of learning the Men their Discipline without being assembled and embodied for some time, and the impossibility of being of Service without Discipline is so apparent that unless the Men are called out I believe no utility can be expected from them.

"The Militia for the West Riding is divided into Three distinct Regiments, of about 400 men each. As Lord-Lieutenant, I have the Honour to Command them while in this County; and if these Regiments are ordered upon any service out of their County, I most humbly apply to His Majesty, to enable me in any manner He thinks proper, to have the Command of them wherever they go.

"If the Militia here was assembled and Embodied for six weeks, I don't doubt but in that time they would have learnt the Platoon Exercise so well, that they would be capable of acting on the Material Business of their service. Many of the

---

* King's Warrant Book (Tower), Vol. IV., p. 105 ; and War Office Militia Letter Book, Vol. I., Sept. 1758—Sept. 1760.

† Militia (Home Office), 1759, No. 1.

Companies can do great part of the exercise, but the difficulty we have laboured under in procuring Sergeants has made great difference in the forwardness of the Companies—for want of being equally successful in having the benefit of good Sergeants.

"I am, &c.,

"WENTWORTH, *August 29th*, 1759." "ROCKINGHAM.

The Establishment of the Regiment was then ten companies, one colonel, one lieut.-colonel, one major, seven captains (the three field officers each had a company), ten lieutenants, ten ensigns, one adjutant, one quartermaster, one surgeon, twenty sergeants, twenty corporals, twenty drummers, and 400 privates. The 2nd West York and East York had the same establishment. The 1st West York had only eight companies, with sixteen sergeants, sixteen corporals, and sixteen drummers, but 408 privates, and the same number of field and staff officers as the other regiments. The two North York Battalions consisted of nine companies each, and 342 privates.*

Orders had been sent as early as June and July to several regiments to make preparation for being embodied; and within a few days after the Lord-Lieutenant had written to express his desire that the West Riding Militia should be embodied, the following order was received:—†

"It is His Majesty's Pleasure that you cause the Militia of the West Riding of the County of York with the City and County of the City of York under your Command, to assemble immediately at such place or places as you shall think proper, and march from thence by such Routes and in such Divisions as you shall think most convenient, to York, where they are to be quartered, and follow such Orders as they shall receive from Major-General Whitmore. Wherein, &c.

"Given at the War Office, this 6th day of Sept., 1759.

"By His Majesty's Command,

"BARRINGTON.

"*To the* MARQUIS OF ROCKINGHAM,
*His Majesty's Lieutenant for the West
Riding of the County of York.*"

---

* Militia Miscellaneous (Treasury) Establishment Books, 1759, p. 16.
† Militia Marching Book, Vol. LXXXIV., p. 26.

To this Order the Lord-Lieutenant sent the following reply :—*
"Sir,

"I received with **Great Pleasure** the Favour of your Letter, with the agreeable **Orders for** the Militia of the Riding to be drawn out and embodied.

"I have appointed the Field Officers of each Regiment to meet me on Monday, and no time shall be lost in executing His Majesty's Orders.

I beg leave, thro' you, Sir, to present my Most Respectful Duty and Thanks to His Majesty for the **Great** Honour he has done me in Complying with the Humble Request I made to him of Enabling me to attend the Militia of this Riding wherever the Service and Defence of this Country may call them.

"I am, Sir, &c.,

"ROCKINGHAM.

"WENTWORTH, *September 8th*, 1759."

The regiments were not kept long inactive after having been assembled, as but little more than a month had elapsed from the date of the Warrant for their being embodied, when the following orders were received :—†

"It is His Majesty's Pleasure that you **cause** two of the three Battalions of the Militia for the **West Riding of** the County of York, to March immediately by the shortest and most convenient Route from York to Hull, Beverley, Wigtown, Burton, and Bewton, where they are to be quartered, and remain until further Orders. Wherein, &c.

"Given at the War Office, this 20th day of October, 1759.

"By His Majesty's Command,

"BARRINGTON.

"*To* MAJOR-GENERAL WHITMORE, *or Officer Commanding the Militia for the West Riding of the County of York, at York.*"

The following Warrant for paying a Contractor for the first supply of necessaries for the Militia is of some interest, and shows the cost of various articles at this period.‡

---

* Domestic Series, George II., No. 143.
† Militia Marching Book, Vol. LXXXIV., p. 37.
‡ King's Warrant Book (Treasury), Vol. XLIII., p. 185.

"GEORGE R.

"Our Will and Pleasure is that out of such Monies as are in or shall come to your hands for the Contingent uses of Our Land Forces, or out of such Monies as are in or shall come to your hands for this use, you pay unto John Trotter the sum of £2,394 11s. 7d., in full satisfaction for providing divers Camp Necessaries, &c., for the use of the Militia, according to the account of Particulars hereunto annexed, and for so doing this, with the acquittance of the said John Trotter, or of his Assigns, shall be your Warrant and Discharge.

"Given at Our Court at Kensington this — day of September, 1759, in the 33rd year of Our Reign.

"By His Majesty's Command,
"BARRINGTON.

"We have been made acquainted with the aforegoing Warrant.
"Whitehall Treasury Chambers, 9th October, 1759.
"R. NUGENT.
"J. GRENVILLE.
"NORTH.

"THE RIGHT HON. LORD VISCOUNT BARRINGTON."

DR. TO JOHN TROTTER.

"For Sundry Necessaries provided for different Regiments of Militia :—

	£	s.	d.
To 8,990 Knapsacks, at 2s. 6d.	1,123	15	0
„ 5,528 Pair of Gayters, at 2s. 6d.	691	0	0
„ 749 Tin Kettles, at 1s. 8d.	62	8	4
„ 749 Kettle Bags, at 6d.	18	14	6
„ 3,596 Tin Canteens, at 10d.	149	16	8
„ 3,596 Haversacks, at 1s.	179	16	0
„ Packing up the several Articles delivered with Matts, Cord, &c., Cartage to the Inns, Cartage to Rumford and Hampstead, and Cartage of Gayters to and from Salisbury for the Warwick Militia	14	0	6
	2,239	11	0
„ Poundage on this Bill, Fees of Warrant, Countersigning and Entry	155	0	7
	£2,394	11	7

The price of Articles appears to have varied slightly; the following was generally the price charged to regiments for some of the principal articles issued by the Ordnance:—

		£	s.	d.
Ticking Bell Tents	each	2	12	0
Camp Colours	,,	0	15	0
Drum Cases	,,	0	10	0
Copper Kettle, with bags	,,	0	14	0
Water Flask 1s. 6d., covered with leather 1s. 8d. extra	,,	0	3	2
Large Tin Canteens	...	0	1	0
Hand Hatchets	...	0	2	0
Knapsack	...	0	2	6
Powder Bags	...	0	7	0
Haversack	...	0	1	0
Pouches and Shoulder Belts	...	0	9	9
Waist Belts	...	0	4	6
Slings	...	0	2	0
For Pioneers.				
Axe Cases and Belts	...	0	9	3
Saws ditto	...	0	14	7
Caps	...	0	12	0
Aprons	...	0	2	0

CLOTHING.—The supply of Clothing for the Militia, when first embodied, was not sufficient to meet the requirements of the Service. At one of the usual Board Meetings of the Lords of the Treasury, on the 9th of October, 1759, "A Letter from Lord Barrington was read, stating that complaint had been made to him from most of the Colonels of the Militia of the Inconvenience which the men laboured under since they have been embodied for want of sufficient clothing; praying their Lordships' directions whether the same sum should be allowed each Militia man according to an Estimate delivered in, to be paid out of the contingencies, or whether every Regiment should receive a sum equal to the amount of the off-reckonings of a Regiment of Foot of the like numbers during the time of their being embodied. The

Lords are of opinion that the allowance should be made, and that the money should be paid to the Colonels of every Regiment to be by them laid out in the Clothing.

"Issue to the Paymaster of the Forces to be applied to the above service £10,000." *

In consequence of this decision, warrants were made out for the payment of the sums required by the several regiments, the amount of which varied in proportion to their strength. The following warrant was issued for the Third West York Regiment :—†

"GEORGE R.

"Whereas it hath been most humbly represented unto Us that the embodied Militia in General must sooner or later be exposed to great inconveniences on account of the deficiencies of the Clothing provided for them by Our Parliament, and We, having been most humbly besought to grant them such a sum of Money as in addition to Our Parliamentary Allowance will enable the respective Colonels of Our said Militia to supply their men with the several Articles of Clothing which are usually furnished to Our other Regiments of Foot, which We, thinking reasonable, are graciously pleased to consent to. Our Will and Pleasure therefore is, that out of such Monies as are in or shall come to your hands for the Contingent uses of Our Land Forces, or out of such other Monies as are in or shall come to your hands for this use, you pay without deduction unto our Trusty and Well-beloved Colonel Thornton the sum of £473 6s. 8d., being the amount of the additional allowance which We have thought fit to grant for the Battalion of the West Riding Yorkshire Militia under his Command at the rate of £2 4s. 7d. for every Sergeant, £1 0s. 5d. for every Corporal, Drummer, and Private Man, and for so doing this with the acquittance of the said Colonel Thornton or of his assigns shall be your Warrant and Discharge.

---

* Treasury Minute Book, Vol. XXXIII., pp. 228-229.
† King's Warrant Book (Treasury), Vol. XLIII., p. 199 ; and Commons' Journals, Vol. XXVIII., p. 671.

"Given at Our Court at Kensington this 23rd day of October 1759, in the 33rd year of Our Reign.

"By His Majesty's Command,

"BARRINGTON.

"*To Paymaster (of the) Forces.*

"We have been made acquainted with the aforegoing.

"Whitehall Treasury Chambers, 23rd October, 1759.

"H. B. LEGGE.
"R. NUGENT.
"J. GRENVILLE."

The Lord-Lieutenant applied for the necessary arms and accoutrements for forty men to complete the three regiments of the West Riding, the warrant for which was issued on the 4th of December.*

1760.—On the 12th February, 1760, Lord Barrington read a Memorial regarding the furnishing of clothing to the embodied Militia to the Lords of the Treasury, who were of opinion "that an Estimate of the charge of Clothing all the embodied Militia should be laid before Parliament, the service being new, and that a sum should be proposed to be voted on account for that service." † In compliance with this recommendation the following estimate was prepared for the year 1760 :—‡

	£	s.	d.
851 Sergeants, at £3 10s. 0d.	2,978	10	0
846 Corporals, at £1 15s. 0d.	1,480	10	0
683 Drummers, at £2 0s. 0d.	1,366	0	0
16,598 Privates, at £1 10s. 0d.	24,897	0	0
	£30,722	0	0

The estimate which was prepared for the year 1761, amounted to £56,568 15s. 2d. for the clothing of 22,804 non-commissioned officers and men, § viz. :—

---

* War Office Militia Letter Book, Vol. I. ; King's Warrants (Tower), Vol. IV., p. 188 ; and Commons' Journals, Vol. XXVIII., pp. 950-1.

† Treasury Minute Book, Vol. XXXIII., p. 284.

‡ Commons' Journals, Vol. XXVIII., p. 851.

§ Idem, p. 947.

				£	s.	d.
1,015 Sergeants	...	...	... each	5	14	7
1,007 Corporals	...	...	... „	2	15	5
806 Drummers	...	...	... „	3	0	5
19,976 Privates	...	...	... „	2	5	7

The sum for clothing the Regiment at the above rates, according to a Warrant, dated the 21st of May, 1761, was £1,096 10s. 0d. For the year 1762, £60,706 4s. 1d. was the estimated cost for the same purpose, the numbers being increased to 24,471 men.*

Warrants were also issued for clothing the several regiments of Militia in 1760, that for the Third West York Regiment amounting to £715.†

"GEORGE R.

"It having been represented that the several Corps of Embodied Militia are in great Want of Clothing. Our Will and Pleasure therefore is that out of such Monies as are in or shall come to your hands for Clothing the Embodied Militia for this current year, you pay without deduction unto our Trusty and Well-beloved Colonel William Thornton for Our Battalion of Militia for the West Riding of the County of York the sum of £715, for Clothing of Our said Battalion under his Command, at the rate of £3 10s. for every Sergeant, £1 15s. for every Corporal, £2 for every Drummer, and £1 10s. for every Private Man. And for so doing this, with the acquittance of the said Colonel William Thornton, or of his assigns, shall be your Warrant and Discharge. Given at Our Court at Kensington, this 23rd day of June, 1760, in the 33rd year of our Reign.

"By His Majesty's Command,
"BARRINGTON."

"We have been made acquainted with the aforegoing Warrant. Whitehall Treasury Chambers, 25th June, 1760.

"H. B. LEGGE.
"NORTH.
"JAMES OSWALD."

---

* Commons' Journals, Vol. XXIX., p. 33.
† King's Warrant Book (Treasury), Vol. XLIV., p. 14.

The uniform then consisted of a long red coat, the skirts of which were lined with the colour of the facings of the regiment, and were made to hook back; the waistcoat (which was made long) and the breeches were red, with white, or sometimes black gaiters; the hair was powdered and tied up.

"Orders for Holding Courts Martial," dated 15th March, 1760, were sent to the Regiment, and were also addressed to the Colonels of all Regiments, both Regulars and Militia, countersigned by the Earl of Holderness. *

MILITIA PAY.—The Militia contributed towards the support of Chelsea Hospital, the same as the Regular Army, according to the following rates.†

"GEORGE R.

"Whereas there has been usually deducted out of the Pay of Our Forces Twelve Pence out of every Twenty Shillings. Our will and Pleasure therefore is, And We do hereby direct and authorize you to make the same deduction of Twelve Pence out of every Twenty Shillings, which you shall Issue pursuant to this Establishment of our Embodied Militia Forces (the non-commissioned officers and private men of the several Regiments or Battalions excepted), which said deductions are to be applied to the Use of our Royal Hospital near Chelsea, or such other uses as shall hereafter be directed by Warrant. And you are to keep a distinct account thereof in writing to be from Time to Time laid before Us, Our High Treasurer, or Commissioner of Our Treasury for the Time being.

"Given at Our Court at St. James's, the 17th day of Dec., 1760, in the First Year of Our Reign.

"By His Majesty's Command,
"H. B. LEGGE. NORTH. JAMES OSWALD."

"*To Our Right Trusty, and Wellbeloved Counsellor,*
HENRY FOX, *Paymaster-General of Our Guards, Garrisons, and Land Forces in Great Britain and Forces Abroad, and to the Paymaster-General of Our said Forces for the Time being.*"

---

* Military Entry Book, Vol. XXV., p. 560.
† Militia Miscellaneous; Treasury Establishment Books, 1759-62.

UNIFORM OF THE MILITIA 1759.

Another Warrant, in similar terms, was issued at the same time authorizing the deduction of one day's pay annually for the same purpose.

The daily Rates of Pay and Subsistence were as follows:—

Pay.

	Per Diem.
	s. d.
Colonel as Colonel 12/0 (in lieu of servant 2/0)	14 0
Lieut.-Colonel as Lieut.-Colonel	7 0
Major as Major	5 0
Captain 8/4 (in lieu of servant 1/0)	9 4
Lieutenant 4/2 (in lieu of servant 0/8)	4 10
Ensign 3/0 (in lieu of servant 0/8)	3 8
Adjutant	4 0
Quartermaster 4/0 (in lieu of servant 0/8)	4 8
Surgeon	4 0
Sergeants	1 0
Corporals	0 8
Drummers	0 8
Privates	0 6
Agents' allowance per Company	0 6

Subsistence.

	Per Diem.
	s. d.
Colonel and Captain, in lieu of his servant	18 0
Lieut.-Colonel and Captain...	13 0
Major and Captain	11 6
Captain	7 6
Lieutenant	3 6
Ensign	3 0
Adjutant	3 0
Quartermaster, in lieu of his servant	3 6
Surgeon	3 0
Sergeant	1 0
Corporal	0 8
Drummer	0 8
Fifer...	0 8
Private	0 6

The Regiment was first employed out of the County in June, 1760, when they were sent to Sunderland to relieve the North York Militia.*

"It is His Majesty's Pleasure that you cause the Battalion of Militia of the West Riding of Yorkshire under your Command at York, to March from thence by such Routes and in such divisions as you shall think most convenient, to Sunderland (acquainting this Office the day on which they begin their March, and when they will arrive at Sunderland), where they are to be quartered and remain until further Orders. Wherein, &c. Given at the War Office, the 25th day of June, 1760.

"By His Majesty's Command,

"BARRINGTON."

"To COLONEL THORNTON, or Officer Commanding
the Battalion of Militia of the West Riding of
York, at York."

Their stay at Sunderland, however, was very brief, as an order was received from the War Office, dated the 30th of August, 1760, directing them to march, as soon as they were relieved by the Durham Militia, by such routes and in such divisions as the Colonel thought fit, to Settle, Ingleton, and the towns adjacent; Skipton, Leeds, Otley, Ripon, Knaresborough, Green Hammerton, and the towns adjacent; and York. †

At this period the Militia were constantly employed in escorting prisoners of war from place to place, or in mounting guard over some of the prisons where they were detained in large numbers.

The following order was the first received for the Regiment to perform this duty :—‡

"The Lords Commissioners of the Admiralty having represented that two prisoners, who deserted from their Parole at Leeds, have been retaken and confined there, and their Lordships having desired that a proper Guard may be ordered to escort them from thence to York, it is His Majesty's Pleasure that (when applied to for that purpose) you cause a sufficient

---

* Militia Marching Book, Vol. LXXXIV., p. 153.
† Idem, p. 188.
‡ Idem, p. 225.

detachment to be made from the companies of the West Riding of Yorkshire Militia under your Command at Leeds, and be assisting in safely escorting the said two prisoners of war to York (halting as often for the benefit of the said prisoners as shall be thought proper); and, after performance of this service, the said detachment is to return to their present quarters.

"Wherein, &c. Given at the War Office, this 21st day of October, 1760.

"*To the Officers commanding the Companies of Colonel Thornton's Militia at Leeds.*"

A similar order, dated the 6th of December, 1760, was received by the detachment at Ripon, to furnish an escort for deserters from Richmond to York Castle.*

By an order, dated the 13th of December, the Colonel was directed to move the detachment quartered at Leeds to any other part of the county he thought proper, provided it did not interfere with the quarters of any of His Majesty's other Forces; and to acquaint the War Office with their station, where they were to remain until further orders.†

1761.—On the 2nd of June, 1761, orders were issued for the whole Regiment to assemble and march to York, and remain there.‡ On the 4th of August they were ordered to march to adjacent places two days before the Races, remain there until they were over, and then return. By a subsequent order, dated the 20th of August, they were ordered to Leeds for as long as the Colonel should think necessary.§ In September, having returned into quarters at York, orders were received, dated the 15th of September, to send detachments to Wakefield and Leeds, to escort French prisoners of war to York.||

On the occasion of the visit of H.R.H. the Duke of York to York, on the 19th of August, the Regiment lined Stonegate, through which he passed on his way to the Mansion House, where the Freedom of the City was presented to him. A grand

---

* Militia Marching Book, Vol. LXXXV., p. 6.
† Idem, p. 12.
‡ Idem, Vol. LXXXVI., p. 63.
§ Idem, pp. 126, 134.
|| Idem, p. 139.

banquet was given in the evening, to which the officers were invited. On the following morning, about seven o'clock, the Regiment was inspected by the Duke, at Knavesmire, on the race-course. His Royal Highness expressed great satisfaction at their appearance and evolutions, saying, "He never saw any veterans that exceeded them." After the inspection, he breakfasted with the Colonel and officers and a number of ladies and gentlemen, and then started for London.*

1762.—The Regiment remained at York until June, 1762, when they were relieved by Colonel Sir George Savile's Battalion; and orders, dated 12th June, were received for the Regiment to march to Newcastle-on-Tyne,† where they remained until the receipt of an order, dated 20th August, by which they were ordered to Nottingham.‡ Orders were next received, dated 19th November, ordering the Regiment to march from Nottingham to such towns and villages in the West Riding as the Colonel thought most convenient. § The Regiment probably went to York, as the next order was addressed to the Colonel in that city. A similar letter was sent at the same time to the commanding officer of all other Militia regiments, and, amongst others, to Colonel Savile, of the 2nd West York (also at York), and to Colonel Lister, of the 1st West York, at Doncaster; Colonel Sir Digby Legard, Bart., of the East Riding, at Beverley; Colonel Duncombe, of the Cleveland and Bulmer Battalion of North York, at Northallerton; and Colonel Sir Ralph Milbanke, Bart., of the Richmondshire Battalion of North York, at Newcastle. The letter was as follows:—||

"As the time is now drawing near when it may probably be thought expedient to disembody the Corps of Militia under your command, I am to signify His Majesty's Pleasure that, if

---

* Hargrove's History of York, 1818, Vol. I., p. 236; Eboracum, or the History and Antiquities of the City of York (anonymous), published by T. Wilson and R. Spence, 1778, Vol. I., p. 229; and Allen's History of the County of York, 1829, Vol. I., pp. 190, 191.

† Militia Marching Book, Vol. LXXXVII., p. 20.

‡ Idem, p. 71.

§ Idem, p. 127.

|| Idem, pp. 144, 145, 149, 150.

the Battalion under your command should not, in its present distribution, happen to be so conveniently quartered as it might be for the return of the non-commissioned officers and private men to the Respective Division of the County of York from which they were balloted, you are hereby empowered to march any Companies, Parties, or Detachments, belonging to the Battalion under your Command, from their present Quarters to any other place or places within the said County, for the greater convenience of the said Companies, Parties, or Detachments, at the time of their being disembodied; in doing which, you will follow your own discretion, and be governed by the good of the service and the convenience of the men and all Civil Magistrates. Given at the War Office, this 4th day of December, 1762.
" By His Majesty's Command,
" C. TOWNSHEND.
" *To* COLONEL THORNTON, *York.*"

This was shortly followed by a Letter to the Lord-Lieutenant, containing a Warrant, of the same date, ordering the Militia regiments of the West Riding to be disembodied :—*

" WHITEHALL, *December* 15*th*, 1762.
" My Lord,
" I have the Honour to transmit to your Lordship herewith His Majesty's Royal Sign-Manual, Ordering you to disembody the Militia for the West Riding of the County of York, which the King wishes may be done with all possible Dispatch. I must beg the favour of your Lordship to acknowledge the receipt of this Letter, and
" I am, &c.,
" EGREMONT."

With the exception of ten regiments, all the Militia was disembodied by the 25th of December; the last being the 3rd Devon, which was disembodied on the 11th of January, 1763.†

Several regiments, on being disembodied, received an allowance called " His Majesty's Bounty " ‡ (amounting to £6,265 4s.),

---

* War Office Militia Letter Book, Vol. III., pp. 102, 103, 113.
† Commons' Journals, Vol. XXIX., p. 867.
‡ Idem.

which was distributed amongst the non-commissioned officers and privates of thirty-nine regiments. The **3rd West York** does not appear in the list of regiments, and it is not stated for what reason the allowance was granted.

The House of Commons passed the following Vote of Thanks to the Militia for their services:—*

"JOVIS, 9 *die Decembris*, 1762.

"Resolved Nemine Contradicente,

"That the Thanks of this House be given to the Officers of the several Corps of Militia which are embodied, for the seasonable and meritorious Service they have done their Country; and that Mr. Speaker do signify the same by Letter to the Colonel or other Commanding Officer of each respective Corps."

On the 28th of January, 1763, the Speaker informed the House that he had received replies from most of the Commanding Officers of the Militia Regiments, who desired him to make their grateful acknowledgments for the great Honour done the Militia by the Notice which the House had been pleased to make of their endeavours to serve their King and Country.

The amount of pay received by the Regiment during the four years they were embodied, was in—†

					£	s.	d.
1759	...	111 days	...	...	2,573	7	0
1760	...	366 „	...	...	8,485	2	0
1761	...	365 „	...	...	8,279	8	4
1762	...	365 „	...	...	8,279	8	4

The strength and cost of the Yorkshire Militia at this period in each Riding, and the amount each received in each year was—

1759.‡

	BATTALIONS.	MEN.	AMOUNT.
West York	... 3	... 1,429 ...	£7,536 18 0
North York	... 2	... 856 ...	7,412 10 8
East York	... 1	not embodied.	
Total	... 6	2,285	14,949 8 8

* Commons' Journals, Vol. XXIX., pp. 393, 417.
† Treasury Establishment Books (**Militia** Miscellaneous), 1759-62; and Commons' Journals, Vol. XXVIII., p. 670.
‡ Treasury Establishment Book, 1759.

1760.*

	BATTALIONS.	MEN.	AMOUNT.
West York	3	1,429	£24,857 10 0
North York	2	856	15,414 14 0
East York	1	473	8,322 16 4
Total	6	2,758	48,595 0 4

1761.†

	BATTALIONS.	MEN.	AMOUNT.
West York	3	1,428	£24,601 0 0
North York	2	854	15,114 0 10
East York	1	461	7,105 6 8
Total	6	2,743	46,820 7 6

1762.‡

	BATTALIONS.	MEN.	AMOUNT.
West York	3	1,435	£23,530 6 8
North York	2	854	15,323 18 4
East York	1	455	7,008 0 0
Total	6	2,742	45,862 5 0

Colonel Sir George Savile, Bart., M.P., the Commandant of the 2nd West York Regiment, published a pamphlet in this year, in which he protested strongly against the ballot, and the use of the word "Militia." He states that nine out of ten men were substitutes, and that they were much preferred by the Officers. He also advocated an increase of pay so as to attract recruits.§

1763.—In this year all the three West York Regiments were reorganized into two regiments of 620 men each, the quota for the Riding remaining unaltered at 1240 men. The same course was pursued in some other counties where the number of regiments was out of proportion to the quota of men furnished.

---

* Commons' Journals, Vol. XXVIII., p. 859.
† Idem, p. 1,062.
‡ Idem, Vol. XXIX., p. 33.
§ An Argument concerning the Militia, 1762.

On the 22nd of October, 1763, the Earl of Huntingdon, then Lord Lieutenant of the West Riding, submitted the names of the gentlemen willing to serve in the "Northern Regiment of the West Riding," most of whom it will be observed had held Commissions in the Third Regiment, under Colonel Thornton, who was appointed to the command of the new Regiment.

The names were submitted of the gentlemen willing to accept Commissions in the "Southern Regiment of the West Riding," on the 4th of November.* The two Regiments thus formed were Officered as follows :—

FIRST, OR SOUTHERN REGIMENT OF THE WEST RIDING.	SECOND, OR NORTHERN REGIMENT OF THE WEST RIDING.
COLONEL.	COLONEL.
Sir George Savile, Bart.	Wm. Thornton †
LIEUT.-COLONEL.	LIEUT.-COLONEL.
Sir Geo. Dalston	John Lister
MAJOR.	MAJOR.
Richard Burton	Wm. Weddal †
CAPTAINS.	CAPTAINS.
Sir George Savile, Bart.	Wm. Thornton †
Sir Geo. Dalston	John Lister
Richard Burton	Wm. Weddal †
Wm. Radcliffe	Wm. Jackson
John Roebuck	Henry Stapleton
William Gream	Geo. Thompson †
Benjamin Farrand	Geo. Iveson †
George Cook	Geo. Hassel †
William Denton	John Wilks
Peter Willson Overend	Geo. Cooke
CAPT.-LIEUTENANT (QUARTERMASTER)	
Luck Annington	
LIEUTENANTS.	LIEUTENANTS.
Richard Zouch	Philip Stapleton
Abraham Woodhead	John Middleton

* War Office Militia Letter Books, Vol. III., pp. 154-5, 157-9.

† Late of Colonel Thornton's (3rd) Regiment. It will be observed that although the Northern, or Col. Thornton's Regiment, was first completed, the Southern, or Sir George Savile's Regiment, took rank as the First Regiment.

THIRD WEST YORK LIGHT INFANTRY. 49

LIEUTENANTS.
John Deykin
Edward Harrison
William Wilks
John Hawley
Ibbitson Stamer
Thomas Stevenson
George Swiney
John Burton

LIEUTENANTS.
Richard Kent
Samuel Storr
Francis Maud
Christopher Wharton *
Philip Sands *
Wm. Simpson
Charles Oates
Samuel Wand * ⎱ Lieuts. of
James Wiggins ⎰ Grenadiers
Isaac Toll
Charles Oates

ENSIGNS.
William Dawson
William Overend

ENSIGNS.
Richard Burton *
Edward Barker
William Dawson
James Wiggins
John Riston
William Robinson
Christopher Croft
Thomas Thornton
John Hutchinson
John Dupont
William Baynes
William Preston

SURGEON.
William Walker

1765–1777.—After being disembodied at the end of December, 1762, the Militia was only assembled annually for twenty-eight days' Training and Exercise, during the succeeding fifteen years, and nothing of interest occurred.

On the 3rd of March, 1778, the Militia was ordered to be embodied, in consequence of the American War, and served for exactly five years, being disembodied in March, 1783.

In the year 1786, an Act † was passed to amend and reduce into one Act the Laws relating to the Militia, which considerably increased the qualification of officers, but the quota of privates

---

* Late of Colonel Thornton's (or 3rd) Regiment.
† 26 Geo. III., c. 107.

E

for each county remained unaltered. By this Act the Clerks of Lieutenancy were directed to insert the names of the officers, with the dates of their commissions, in the *London Gazette*, in the same manner as those of the officers of the Regular Army. Lieut.-Colonels Commandant were to have the rank of Colonel after five years' service.

In December, 1792, a portion of the Militia was embodied, and in January and February, 1793, the remainder of the Force was called out and embodied in consequence of war with France, and remained so for upwards of nine years, being disembodied in April, 1802; but only for a few months, as they were again embodied in March the following year, and served until June, 1814. With the exception of the interval already mentioned, of about ten months, the Militia remained embodied for upwards of twenty years.

In 1794 an Act * was passed to increase the Militia, as the state of Public Affairs rendered it "highly necessary and expedient that the number of the Militia Forces should be augmented." The Lords-Lieutenant were, consequently, authorised to raise Volunteer Companies, or Volunteers to be attached to the existing Militia regiments, the officers of which Companies received temporary rank, but not higher than Lieutenant-colonel, and the men were entitled to the same bounty, pay, clothing, &c., as the Regular Militia. No volunteer companies, or men, were raised in the West Riding under this Act. During the following year no change of any importance took place, but in 1796 the Militia was largely augmented by the Supplementary regiments then raised.

---

* 34 Geo. III., c. 16 (see Appendix M).

CHAPTER III.

FROM 1796 TO 1802.

EMBODIED FROM 5TH MARCH, 1798, TO 22ND APRIL, 1802.

CONTENTS.—The Supplementary **Militia.**—**Formation** of New Regiments.— Royal Warrant to Embody the Supplementary Militia.—Establishment of the five West **York** Regiments.—Clothing and Accoutrements.— Second half of the **Supplementary** Militia Embodied in May.—Regiment ordered to Hull.—**Letter** from **General** Sir R. Abercromby.— Regiment called out to suppress Riots at Hull.—Vote of **Thanks.**— **Volunteers into** Army.—Mode of Wearing the Hair.—Meeting **of Lords-Lieutenant and** Colonels of Militia.—Supplementary **Militia reduced** July, 1799.—Further Reduction in October.—Russian Prisoners at Hull. —Letter of the Lord-Lieutenant relative to Disbanding the **3rd and 4th** and Retaining the 5th Regiment.—His **Letter** to Colonel **Sir George Cooke.**—General Order respecting the Dress of the Infantry.—Regiment proceeds from Hull to Sunderland.—Thence to Berwick and Tweedmouth.—Stationed in Scotland.—Regiment Augmented August, 1801.—Returns to Doncaster, February, 1802.—Disembodied 22nd April.—Vote of Thanks from Parliament.

1796.—THE SUPPLEMENTARY MILITIA.—In November, 1796, Parliament sanctioned the raising of a Supplementary Militia of 59,441 for England, and 4,437 for Wales, making, in addition to those raised as Volunteer Companies under the previous Act, a force of 94,618. *

1797.—On the 11th of January, the King, in a message to the House of Commons, informed them that in consequence of various advices of preparations made, and measures taken, in France, apparently in pursuance of the design openly and repeatedly professed, of attempting the invasion of the kingdom,

---

* 37 Geo. III., c. 3, 22 (see Appendix M); and Clode's Military Force of the Crown, Vol. I., p. 284.

His Majesty thought it right to communicate it to the House, to the end that His Majesty could call out and embody such of the Supplementary Militia as occasion should require. The House passed a unanimous vote of thanks to the King for his Message, and assured His Majesty that he might rely on the decided and continued support of the House.*

The large increase to the Regular Militia proposed to be added under the name of Supplementary Militia, seems to have been far from popular. A large number of Bills were circulated by the authorities throughout the country appealing to the loyalty and patriotism of the inhabitants to protect the country from the horrors of an invasion, and setting forth the advantages in pay and exemption from further service to those who would come forward. The following is a copy of the proclamation referred to :— †

"DEFENCE AGAINST INVASION.

" IN order to prevent any Mis-conception of the Measures taken for the Defence of the Kingdom against a French Invasion, All TRUE FRIENDS TO THEIR COUNTRY are desired to remark, that by the Act lately passed, a Force of SIXTY THOUSAND MEN will be ready in case of necessity on the shortest Notice, properly armed and clothed, and in readiness to join the MILITIA of their own Counties.

" Such a Force will leave no Doubt, if the Attempt should be made, of the Contest being brought to a speedy and successful Issue, and of the Country being delivered from all the Miseries and Horrors which would otherwise arise from the Landing of an Enemy.

"This Object will be effected with little Inconvenience to Individuals, compared with its importance to the Public.

"The Persons enrolled under this Act will, in the first Instance, only be called out and exercised *within their own counties, for the space of Twenty Days*, during which Time they will receive One

---

* Parliamentary History, Vol. XXXIII., pp. 1,303, 1,304.
† Militia (Home Office), No. 15, 1797.

Shilling per Day; and particular Provision is made for Supporting their Families during their absence.

"No *further Service* will afterwards be required from them unless in the event of an *Actual* Invasion, or the *immediate expectation of it*: in which case, no man who has any Regard for himself, his Family, or his Country, but would of his Own Accord, stand forward for the common Defence.

"The Service, however, of Persons enrolled under this Act will be doubly useful in Case of such Necessity, by their being armed and instructed beforehand, and conducted by proper Officers, selected from their own Neighbourhood.

"Their Service can at any Rate be wanted only for a short Time, and there is even the greatest Reason to hope that the knowledge of such Preparations may be sufficient to prevent the Enemy from being desperate enough to make an attempt which can only end in their Ruin.

"GOD SAVE THE KING, AND PROTECT OLD ENGLAND!"

When the Supplementary Militia was ordered to be raised, there was a great variety of opinion as to whether they should be divided amongst the existing regiments, or formed into separate corps by themselves, as it was feared by many that if the former plan were adopted, it would cause serious disturbances, and many of the Lords-Lieutenants protested strongly against the proposal, which, however, was carried into effect in all counties where the quota exceeded the number required to complete existing regiments. The Hon. Henry Lascelles, in a letter dated the 18th of January, 1797, says, that the Supplementary Militia must be kept distinct, and not attached to existing regiments, or it would cause a disturbance; and Lord Hawke, in writing to the Duke of Norfolk, from Yorkshire, on the 26th of the same month, says, "everything has hitherto been perfectly quiet and regular; the Magistrates still entertain apprehensions from the attaching a part of the Militia to the existing regiments." *

---

* Militia (Home Office), No. 15, 1797.

In the West Riding the quota of Supplementary Men was distributed on both systems, the 1st and 2nd West York each receiving an addition of between two and three hundred men, and the remainder being formed into three new regiments, known at first as the 1st, 2nd, and 3rd West York Supplementary Regiments; but as this caused some confusion they were afterwards numbered the 3rd, 4th, and 5th West York Regiments respectively.

This Regiment, therefore, which was at first the 3rd Supplementary Regiment, became the 5th West York Regiment, which number it retained until December, 1799, when the 3rd and 4th Supplementary Regiments were disbanded, and the Regiment once more became the 3rd West York.

The men liable to serve in the 5th West York Supplementary Regiment of Militia were balloted for in January, 1797, the quota for Doncaster being fifty, and they were sworn in before the Magistrates at the Town Hall on the 17th of February. The names of the officers were submitted for approval by the Duke of Norfolk, then Lord-Lieutenant, in a letter dated the 31st of March, 1797,* and they were gazetted in May, their Commissions being ante-dated to the 27th of February.

The first division assembled at Doncaster for twenty days' training, and a party of the 1st West York Regular Militia from Leeds, under the command of Captain Dixon, were sent to assist in drilling the men. The second division assembled on the 27th of the same month.

On the 14th of April, the second division of Supplementary Militia was inspected in Doncaster Field, by Colonel Sir George Cooke, Bart., who was accompanied by a number of officers. He expressed the greatest satisfaction at the precision with which the men went through a variety of evolutions, as well as the correctness of their firing. "The high state of discipline which the first division has acquired certainly does great credit to Captain Dixon, and the party sent down with him from the First West York Militia, for the purpose of training them."

The third division assembled at York on the 17th of April;

---

* Militia (Home Office), No. 15, 1797.

and the fourth division at Sheffield on the 12th of May, for a similar number of days' training. The fifth and last division assembled on the 5th of June.*

1798.—In January, 1798, an Act was passed to allow a number of Supplementary Militia, not exceeding 10,000 men, or one-fifth of the quota of any county, to enlist into the regular army, their places not being supplied by ballot.†

Another Act was passed in February, 1798, to enable the King to call out and embody one-half of the Supplementary Militia not later than the 10th of March, 1798, and the remainder whenever His Majesty thought proper.‡ The half to be embodied, being balloted for. The second half was assembled on the 14th of May.

The following Royal Warrant was immediately issued, authorising the men to be embodied in the West Riding of Yorkshire :— §

"GEORGE R.

"We, having resolved to embody a part of Our Supplementary Militia Forces raised under an Act passed in the Thirty-Seventh Year of Our Reign, Intituled 'An Act for providing an Augmentation to the Militia, to be trained and raised in the manner therein directed; and for enabling His Majesty to cause the same to be embodied, in case of necessity, for the defence of these Kingdoms;' the occasion therefore having been first communicated by Us to Our Parliament, in conformity to the said Act, Do hereby, in pursuance of an Act passed in the present Year of Our Reign, Intituled 'An Act to enable His Majesty to Order Out a certain proportion of the Supplementary Militia, and to provide for the necessary augmentation of

---

* Origin and Services of the Third West York Regiment of Militia, by W. Sheardown, Esq., Doncaster, 1870 ; published in May and June, 1870, in the *Doncaster Gazette*, and afterwards printed by the author for private circulation.

† 38 Geo. III., c. 17 (see Appendix L).

‡ 38 Geo. III., c. 18, 19 (see Appendix M); see also Militia (Home Office), No. 29.

§ War Office Militia Letter Book, pp. 92-96.

Men in the Several Companies of Militia, by incorporating the Supplementary Militia therewith,' order and direct you, with all convenient speed, to draw out and embody at Leeds, Wakefield, and Doncaster, within the West Riding of Our County of York, the portion of our said Supplementary Militia specified in the said last-mentioned Act, to be chosen by Ballot in the manner therein prescribed; and either to be incorporated with the Militia of the said West Riding of the County of York, or formed therewith into Companies, and into a Battalion or Regiment, Battalions or Regiments, or to be formed into Companies, a Battalion or Regiment, Battalions or Regiments, separate and distinct from the Militia of the said West Riding of the County of York, in such manner as the Provisions in the said several Acts and Our Instructions conformable thereto, and the exigencies of the case, shall require; and that you do cause the same to be held in every respect ready to March as occasion shall require, to such Posts within this Kingdom as We shall judge proper to Assign them, and to be put under the Command of such General Officer or Officers as We shall be pleased to appoint over them, and to obey such further Orders as shall be judged necessary for the safety and defence of this Kingdom. And for so doing this shall be your Warrant. Given at Our Court at Saint James's, the 20th day of February, 1798, In the Thirty-Eighth Year of Our Reign.

" By His Majesty's Command,
" PORTLAND.

" *To Our Lieutenant of the West Riding of Our County of York.*"

At a General Meeting of the Deputy-Lieutenants, held at Leeds on the 24th of February, 1798, an Order was made for all the Supplementary Militiamen for the several Wapentakes of the West Riding, to assemble at their respective divisions on the 5th of March following, for the purpose of being embodied.

The 1st Supplementary Regiment assembled at Leeds, the 2nd at Wakefield, and the 3rd at Doncaster, on the 5th of March; but they all received pay from the 20th of February, that being the date of the Warrant for embodiment, as authorised by the Act.*

---

* Militia Pay Lists, 1798.

Under an Order from the Horse **Guards, dated the 19th of
February**, each of the two Regular Regiments, **or 1st and 2nd
West York**, gave five sergeants, six corporals, and **eleven** men (to
be made non-commissioned officers), **who** were divided amongst
the three Supplementary Regiments, **being afterwards** replaced
by an equal number of Supplementary **men.***

On the 28th **of February**, the 2nd West **York**, at Ashford, was
ordered to send two detachments to train **the** Supplementary
Militia **about to be** embodied at Doncaster and Wakefield, an
equal number of the Supplementary men being sent back in
exchange. The **1st West York, at Horsham Barracks, was at
the same** time ordered **to send similar** detachments **to Leeds**
and Wakefield.† **On the 20th of March, the** 2nd West **York**
was ordered to send **another detachment** to Doncaster. ‡ **On the**
24th of March, the **strength of** the Regiment was 26 officers and
781 rank **and** file.

The establishment of the **five West York** Regiments was as
follows :—

Regiments.	Quota. From 1765 to 1796.	Supplementary Militia Raised 1797.	Total.
1st West York	620	553	1,173
2nd West York	620	550	1,170
3rd West York (1st Supplementary Regt.)	...	1,199	1,199
4th West York (2nd ,, ,,)	...	1,200	1,200
5th West York (3rd ,, ,,)	...	1,192	1,192
Total	1,240	4,694	5,934

None of the Regiments ever maintained the full establishment here given, as a large number of the first half of the quota which was embodied on the 5th of March volunteered into the army, one-fifth **of** the **full county** quota being permitted **to
do so.**

---

* Militia Miscellaneous (Home Office), 1798-1802, Vol. II., No. 20.
† Militia Marching Book, Vol. XCVI., p. 407.
‡ Idem, Vol. XCVII., p. 9.

Ten days after the Supplementary men had assembled, they were ordered to march to their respective regiments, and receive the following necessaries :—

SERGEANTS.			CORPORALS AND PRIVATES.		
Articles.	Value.		Articles.	Value.	
	s.	d.		s.	d.
1 Shirt	6	6	1 Shirt	5	6
1 pair of Stockings	3	0	1 pair of Stockings	1	6
1 pair of Shoes	6	0	1 pair of Shoes	6	0
1 pair of Long Gaiters	4	0	1 pair of Long Gaiters	4	0
Total	19	6	Total	17	0

The knapsacks were provided by the Government.* The clothing was provided for Militia regiments by the Colonel, who received a fixed sum for each man; but the rates allowed were not so high as in the Regular Army, and were the same as those allowed for the old Militia. The clothing consisted of coat, waistcoat, breeches, hat, feather and cockade, shirt and stock, shoes and stockings. The sum allowed per annum was, for each—†

	REGULAR ARMY.				MILITIA.		
	£	s.	d.		£	s.	d.
Sergeant	7	9	0¾	...	5	14	7
Corporal	4	19	4½	...	2	10	5
Drummer, Fifer	4	19	4½	...	3	0	5
Or Private	2	5	11⅔	...	2	10	5

In the Militia a suit of slop clothing for men serving broken periods was £1 15s. for all ranks. The estimated cost of a sergeant's coat, waistcoat, and breeches, was £2 16s. 10d.; drummer's, ditto, £2 19s. 10d.; and private's, £1 7s. 8d.; corporal's epaulets, 2s.

The accoutrements were furnished by the Ordnance if the Colonel thought fit to take them, and had to last twelve years—

---

* Militia (Home Office), No. 29; and G. O. Horse Guards, 24th April.
† Commons' Reports (Finance, 1797-1802), Vol. XII., p. 395, Appendix M, 4; and Vol. XIII., p. 670, Appendix G, 6.

consisting of a tanned leather waistbelt, ditto firelock sling and cartouch box; but they were of very bad quality, and very unsoldierlike; most Colonels, therefore, preferred to take the allowance, and pay the difference for buff accoutrements, the cost in each case being :—*

	War Office, for Buff Accoutrements.	Ordnance, for Tanned Leather Accoutrements.
	£ s. d.	£ s. d.
Sergeant...	1 4 0	0 9 0
Drummer	1 2 6	0 11 6
Corporal or Private ...	0 18 0	0 5 10

The articles consisted of swords and belts for sergeants and drummers, pouch and belts for rank and file, bayonets, belts, and firelock sling. At this period the West York Militia had green facings, with gold lace and epaulets; the North York, black facings, with gold lace and epaulets; and the East York, buff facings, silver lace, and epaulets. †

On the 23rd of April, Major-General Lord Mulgrave, having inspected the Regiment on the Race Common at Doncaster, issued the following :—

"General Order, April 23rd, 1798.—Major-General Lord Mulgrave cannot sufficiently express the satisfaction with which he has seen the steady and soldier-like appearance of the Regiment; their perfect performance of every part of their duty would do honour to a long established corps, and bears ample testimony of the zeal and exertions of the officers, and the attention and good conduct of the men."

A recruiting party of the Royal Artillery and 31st Foot was sent to Doncaster to recruit, but although the bounty was seven guineas, and the men were only enlisted to serve in Europe during the war, and until six months after a general peace, they only appear, according to the pay list, to have obtained twenty-four men.

Orders were sent from the War Office on the 28th of April for the 1st West York Regiment, at Horsham, to send ten men

---

* Commons' Reports, Vol. XIII., p. 673, Appendix H, 2.
† British Military Library, 1799, Vol. II., pp. 32-4.

to the 3rd Supplementary (5th) Regiment at Bawtry, and five men to the 4th Regiment at Halifax. The 2nd West York was directed to send ten men from Ashford to the 1st Supplementary (3rd) Regiment at Knaresboro', and five men to the 4th Regiment at Halifax.

By another Order from the War Office of the same date the Regiment was directed to march from Doncaster on the second day (Sunday excepted) prior to that which might be appointed for assembling the second half of the Supplementary Militia at that place, to the following quarters,—three companies to Bawtry, Blyth, and Tickhill, three companies to Rotherham, two to Worksop, and two to Hatfield and Thorne; but to leave such detachments at Doncaster as should be directed by the Adjutant-General.*

Orders were next received from the War Office, dated the 11th of May, directing that the detachment of the Supplementary Militia at Doncaster belonging to the 2nd West York Regiment, then stationed at Ashford, should march to join their Regiment on the 19th, in return for a similar number received from that Regiment.†

In May the Regiment was moved from Doncaster, in accordance with the Orders already quoted, and quartered at the following places in the neighbourhood, viz., one company at Blyth, two at Worksop, three at Rotherham, one at Bawtry, one at Tickhill, one at Hatfield, and one at Thorne.‡

The officer commanding the 5th Regiment at Bawtry received an Order, dated War Office, the 12th of May, directing the Regiment to march on Friday, the 25th instant, to Doncaster, to join the Supplementary Men assembled there, enlarging their quarters (if found necessary) with such adjacent place or places as the Colonel might judge most convenient. The 3rd Regiment was at the same time ordered to march from Knaresboro' to Leeds on the 21st inst., and the 4th Regiment from Barnsley to Wakefield on the 22nd inst., for the same purpose.§ Another

---

* Militia Marching Book, Vol. XCVII., pp. 57, 59, 61.
† Idem, pp. 90, 91.
‡ Militia Pay Lists, 5th West York, 1798.
§ Militia Marching Book, Vol. XCVII., p. 93.

Order, of the same date, was sent to "the Officer Commanding the Detachment of Supplementary Militia, of the West Riding of York at Wakefield," the second half of which was to assemble there on the 14th of May, directing him to send such part of the Supplementary Militia as were apportioned to the 5th Regiment to Doncaster, on the 22nd inst., to await the arrival of the Regiment, which they were to join there on the 25th inst.*

These men, to the number of 200, having joined, a second Major, Adjutant, and Sergeant-Major, were authorised, in consequence of the increased establishment, and were appointed by the Lord-Lieutenant to all the five West York Regiments.†

In consequence of intelligence having been received that the immense armaments, collected at Flushing, and supposed to be destined for England, had put to sea, orders were sent to the Lords-Lieutenant of the inland counties to collect and march their forces to a place of rendezvous on the coast.

On the 25th of May, the Regiment having reassembled at Doncaster (with the exception of the two companies at Hatfield and Thorne), the eight companies were sent on to Thorne, where the company stationed there joined them, and the nine companies then proceeded to Howden, where they were joined by the company from Hatfield, and the Regiment then proceeded to Hull. The pay lists contain an item of £2 13s. 11d. for taking the Regiment across Booth Ferry. The 3rd and 4th Supplementary Regiments were at the same time marched to Hull; the garrison being then under the command of Colonel Walter Fawkes.

A proposal to form distinct battalions for special service from the flank companies of different regiments met with great opposition from the Commanding Officers of Militia, and a long correspondence ensued on the legality of the proceedings between the Lords-Lieutenant of several counties and the Attorney-General. A Circular Letter, dated the 21st of March, 1798, was addressed to the Colonels of Militia in the Eastern District, ordering them to complete their flank companies

---

* Militia Marching Book, Vol. XCVII., p. 93; see also Monthly and Quarterly Returns.

† Militia (Home Office), No. 31, authorised by the 38 Geo. III., c. 55, dated 21st June.

to 100 rank and file, with a view of forming them into a battalion.

The Lords-Lieutenant, Colonels, and other Officers of Militia, *having seats in Parliament*, were in the habit of meeting at the Thatched House Tavern, under the presidency of Earl Fitzwilliam, for the purpose of discussing questions relating to the Militia Service. A Meeting was held to consider this question on the 15th of December, 1798, which resulted in a long correspondence on the subject between the President, Earl Fitzwilliam, on behalf of the Meeting, and the Attorney and Solicitor-Generals.*

The question was subsequently referred to the General Officers commanding districts, who were requested by the Duke of York, then Commander-in-Chief, in a letter dated 11th April, 1799, to favour him with their sentiments "upon this important subject, when you shall have given a full consideration to the various circumstances compromised in the Questions." The ultimate decision on the subject is not expressly stated; but the Militia Officers probably carried the point, as the battalion formed from the 31st Regiment and the 3rd West York and Nottingham Militia was soon broken up, and does not seem to have been afterwards re-formed. Amongst the replies sent by the General Officers commanding districts to the Commander-in-Chief, that of Lieutenant-General Sir Ralph Abercromby, K.B., dated Edinburgh, the 19th of April, 1799, enclosing the following memorandum on the subject, is the most interesting :—†

"The Formation of Grenadier Companies is of an ancient date. It arose from the Propriety of placing together the tallest and stoutest men of each Battalion, not only on account of their size, but from the Utility of having united in one company a chosen set of men, who could be detached without Inconvenience on any particular Service, or who might occasionally be formed during the Campaign, or during the War, into Battalions, under the command of distinguished Officers. Such has been the practice in the British Service, and the Reputation

---

* Militia Miscellaneous, 1798-1802, Vol. I., No. 19.
† Idem.

of the Grenadier Battalions stands hitherto unsullied and unrivalled.

"Light Infantry Companies are a later Institution. When the British Army became more numerous, and when it assumed a more respectable form, after our extensive conquests at the Peace of Paris, in 1763, and when the other Armies of Europe had formed numerous Corps of Light Infantry, it was found that Light Infantry was wanting. Great Britain possessed no species of men particularly fitted for that Service. The highly cultivated state of the country, the Manufacturing spirit of the Inhabitants, the severity of the Game Laws, and the disarming the Highlands of Scotland, had caused a total Disuse of Arms among the lower Ranks of men. For these Reasons it became necessary to select in each Battalion the Most Active young men, and to form them into Companies to act as Light Infantry. Companies thus composed of the fittest and aptest Men of each Battalion still wanted Experience. They required that their Minds should be trained to a Service for which their Bodies were so well adapted.

"It therefore became necessary to form them into Battalions, under active and Skilful Officers, who know not only how to inspire them with Courage, but to teach them Prudence, Vigilance, and Intelligence. Without such Instructions, Light Infantry Companies may please the eye on Parade, but they cannot be considered answering the End of their Institution.

"Until Great Britain shall have Corps of Light Infantry as a permanent part of their Military Establishment, the Light Companies of each Battalion should be formed into Battalions, not for the space only of a short Campaign, but during the War.

"The true use of these Battalions is not to be used on every occasion of Danger, Not to be the only Instrument a General Officer has in his Hands, But to perform the Real Duty of Light Troops. They must therefore, of course, be subject to be detached whenever they May be found most necessary.

"Battalions composed of less than 700 men cannot well afford to detach both their Flank Companies; and when at that Number, the Flank Companies must only bear a Relative proportion to the strength of the Battalion Companies. If the

Battalion Companies should fall short of their Establishment, the Flank Companies must do so too.

"Where a Battalion is a thousand strong, or upwards, it can well afford to keep the Flank Companies complete.—Some Inconvenience no doubt arises in detaching the Flank Companies, particularly to any Distance. But it certainly is not of great consequence. Their Clothing, Accoutrements, and Recruits, may, without Difficulty, be sent to them.

"R. A. ABERCROMBY, L.G.

"*Edinburgh,* 19*th April,* 1799."

In May, 1798, the Flank Companies of the Regiment, together with those of the 31st Foot, Nottingham Militia, North York Militia, and 3rd and 4th West York Supplementary Regiments, were formed into a separate brigade of two battalions for service in the Yorkshire District. The Grenadier Battalion was commanded by Lieut.-Colonel William Hepburn, of the 31st Foot, and the Light Infantry Battalion, by Lieut.-Colonel Carlton, of the Nottingham Militia. The staff was principally composed of officers from the 31st and Nottingham Regiments. Majors of brigade, Major H. Smith, and Major T. Smith. Adjutants, Lieutenants J. S. Hawkshaw, and R. B. Fearon, 31st Regiment. Quartermasters, Lieutenants T. G. Waggot, 31st Regiment, and T. C. Wooler, Nottingham Militia. Surgeons, Benjamin Worship, 31st Regiment, and Woldergofe. A detachment of the Royal Artillery, with the Grenadier and Light Infantry Battalions, were stationed between Tunstal and Roos.

The Regiment, when at Hull, was called out to suppress a riot on the 19th of July, for which service they received the thanks of the magistrates, who, at a meeting held the following day, the Mayor, John Sykes, Esq., in the chair, passed the following resolution:—

"That the Thanks of the Magistrates be given to Colonel Sir George Cooke, Bart., of the 5th West York Regiment of Militia, for his readiness in assembling his Corps last night in suppressing a riot of a very serious nature in the town, and that he be requested to represent to the Officers, and Corps in general, that the Magistrates entertain a due sense of the advantages derived from their steady conduct on the occasion."

At the end of July five companies went to Beverley, three to Burlington, and two into camp at Hilston.*

By a Warrant, dated the 3rd of August, 1798, Colours were ordered to be supplied to the three West York and North York Supplementary Militia, and twenty-two other regiments.

The troops stationed at Hull and the surrounding district at this time consisted of a detachment of the Royal Artillery, the 31st Foot, the 3rd, 4th, and 5th West York Supplementary Militia, the North York Supplementary Militia, and the Northumberland, Durham, and Nottingham Militia Regiments. These were encamped at Hornsea, Burstwick, Hilston, and Dimlington Camp, the brigade being under the command of Brigadier-General Smith, whose head-quarters were at Elston.

On the 18th of August the Colonels of the three West York Supplementary Regiments were made Brevet-Colonels in the Army, for as long as their respective regiments should remain embodied.† This brevet rank was given to Colonels of Militia of a certain standing in order to avoid their being commanded by young Colonels in the Regular Army, the multitude of new levies having then given that rank to very young soldiers.‡

An Order was issued, dated the 17th of August, stating that, as much confusion and inconvenience had arisen from the numbering of the Supplementary Regiments of Militia, His Majesty had been pleased to direct that the three Supplementary Regiments should be named the 3rd, 4th, and 5th West York Militia respectively. Two brass 6-pounders, and an ammunition waggon formed a portion of the equipment of the Regiment, which at the end of December was upwards of nine hundred strong.

In October the five companies stationed at Beverley, and the three at Burlington returned to Doncaster, and a detachment was sent to Yaxley, the two companies at Hilston returning to Hull.§ Previous to their leaving for their winter quarters, Major-General

---

* Pay Lists, 5th West York.
† *London Gazette*, 1798, p. 770.
‡ Grose's Military Antiquities, Vol. I., p. 48.
§ Militia Pay Lists, 5th West York.

Lord Mulgrave expressed his warmest approbation of the conduct of the several regiments. The Regiment, with the exception of the Flank Companies, was inspected at Doncaster, on the 31st of October, by Major-General C. Horneck, 499 privates being present on parade, and 35 gunners.

The following List of Necessaries, with which every man was to be provided, was published in Regimental Orders, on the 17th of December :—

3 Shirts,	1 Comb,	2 Buff Sticks,
2 pairs of Shoes,	1 Clubbing Iron,	1 Button Stick and
2 pairs of Stockings,	1 Black Ball,	Brush,
1 Stock,	1 Pouch Ball,	1 Forage Cap,
1 Picker and Crush,	4 Brushes,	A couple of Needles,
2 Flints,	1 Pouch Stick,	

1 Turnscrew and Worm, 1 Shaving Box and Razor, 1 Oil Bottle, and Thread, and 4 Crimping Irons to each Company.

1799.—In this year a number of Line regiments were ordered into certain districts to recruit from the Supplementary Militia, the 31st Foot being quartered at York, and the 35th at Beverley. The East Riding had to furnish 143 men, and the West Riding 782, or a total of 925. The 35th Foot was quartered in the North Riding, which had to find 226 men. The other regiments appointed to recruit from the Supplementary Militia were the 20th, 44th, 46th, 48th, 55th, 59th, 62nd, and 85th, a separate district being assigned to each. The counties of Kent, Bedford, Rutland, and in Wales were not allotted, but the quota required might be made up from them.*

Orders were issued from the Horse Guards, dated the 23rd of January, directing that only the Supplementary Men were to be enlisted. The bounty offered was seven guineas; to serve during the war, and until six months after peace had been concluded, and they were not liable to serve out of Europe. The recruit on enlisting received a guinea, on final approval two guineas, for necessaries to be provided at once, one guinea being retained

---

* Commander-in-Chief (Home Office), No. 11 ; and Militia Miscellaneous, 1798-1802, Vol. II, No. 20 ; and G. O. Horse Guards, 13th July, 1799.

to complete the necessaries at head-quarters, where the balance of three guineas was paid to him. The recruiting party were allowed a guinea for each man; one-sixth of the quota, or 10,663 men were required.

The following Orders regarding the Dress of the Officers and men were issued by the General Officer commanding the Yorkshire District, and the Officer commanding the Regiment:—

"MULGRAVE CASTLE, 2nd May, 1799.

"It having been notified to Major-General Lord Mulgrave that it is His Majesty's Pleasure that in future both Officers and Men of the Infantry, as well as Cavalry (excepting the Flank Companies), are to wear their hair cued, to be tied a little below the upper part of the collar of the coat, and to be ten inches in length, including one inch of hair to appear below the binding. It is His Lordship's most positive order that no officer or soldier in the Yorkshire District be permitted to cut his hair so as to prevent his wearing it cued, as above directed.

"H. FOSTER, *Aide-de-Camp.*"

"REGIMENTAL ORDERS, DONCASTER, 9th May, 1799.

"Colonel Sir George Cooke desires that in future the Officers at the Mess, and on the evening parade, will appear in white breeches, stockings, and shoes. If the Officers for their own accommodation wish at any time to substitute white pantaloons and half-boots in the place of breeches, stockings, and shoes, they are allowed to do so. . . . .

"The Non-commissioned Officers and Men have of late worn too much powder in their hair, they are again reminded that the hair should only appear grey, and that the comb should be drawn through the hair after it is powdered, there must be no powder on the face.

"The Commanding Officer orders that none of the Men shall have their hair cued till further Orders."

On the following day further Orders were issued on the subject:—

"Colonel Sir George Cooke orders that the Non-commissioned Officers and Privates shall be immediately provided with false cues, according to the pattern he has fixed upon; and he is highly gratified that an expedient has been hit upon which complies most punctiliously with His Majesty's express orders on this subject, and is at the same time effected at an expense to the men small in comparison of what they must have incurred if stuff Tails and Ribbons had been used. His Majesty's Order extending to all Officers as well as Non-Commissioned Officers and Privates, Colonel Sir George Cooke directs that the Officers will wear their hair in cue as near to the form of the cue ordered for the men as possible. The Sergeants of companies will see that the men, either from their own hair, or from their present clubs, supply the maker of the cues with as much hair as may be necessary to form the end of them."

The Morning Parade was then at half-past nine, the Officers' Mess at half-past three or four, and Afternoon Parade at six o'clock.

On the 7th of June the eight companies at Doncaster were ordered to march in three divisions to Hornsea and Roos to encamp. The two companies at Hull marched to Hilston camp, where they remained with the flank battalions until July, when they joined the Regiment at Hornsea, the Grenadier and Light Infantry battalions being broken up. The troops encamped in Holderness consisted of the Earl of Suffolk's Regiment of Militia at Burstwick, the 4th West York Militia at Skeffling, and the 5th West York at Hornsea.

At a meeting of Lords-Lieutenant, Colonels, and other Commanding Officers of Militia, and of Militia officers having seats in Parliament, held at the Thatched House Tavern, on Monday the 24th of June, 1799, Earl Fitzwilliam in the chair, it was "Resolved Unanimously. That the system of recruiting from the Militia, when embodied, is destruction of the Militia system, and degrading to all persons engaged in that service.

"Resolved Unanimously. That the raising recruits from the Militia, when disembodied, though in some degree infringing the Militia system, is such as, in the present situation of the country, this meeting will zealously support."*

An Act† received the Royal assent on the 12th of July,

---

* Militia Miscellaneous, 1798-1802, Vol. I., No. 19 ; Vol. II., No. 20.
† 39 Geo. III., c. 106 (see Appendix L).

to reduce the Supplementary Militia by volunteering into the regular Army.

The men were offered a bounty of ten guineas to enlist for five years, or during the war, and until six months after peace had been concluded; in the event of the quota of any County being complete according to the new establishment, one-fourth were allowed to enlist, no man being less than five feet four inches. If not complete the number was to be made up by men who subsequently joined. The Force might be further reduced by the Supplementary men who were raised in 1797, under the 37th Geo. III. c. 3 and 22,* being dismissed, but these were liable to serve again when required, unless they previously enlisted in the regular Army.

The quota for the West Riding of Yorkshire was thus reduced from 5,934 to 4,555, or about 911 for each of the five regiments.

By these measures many of the marching regiments, which were mere skeletons, were filled up, and the Government were enabled to send a large Force to Holland, which was subsequently reinforced by the same means.†

A Horse Guards Circular, dated the 12th of July, 1799, announced that a commission in the Line would be given to every subaltern with 60 men, or in the Royal Artillery with 120 men. From a Return dated Hornsea Camp, the 7th of August, we learn that 15 men volunteered into the 31st Foot, and 57 into the 35th Foot, or a total of 72.

Up to the 31st of August 102 men had volunteered, 77 of whom joined the 35th Regiment. Altogether 26,237 men were obtained under this Act.

From a Return made by the Deputy-Lieutenants, dated the 13th of September, 1799, it appears that 634 men from the West Riding volunteered into the regular Army, under the Act recently passed for the reduction of the Militia Forces.

Another Act‡ was passed in October, which authorised three-fifths of the quota of each county to volunteer. As the quota

---

* See Appendix M.
† Grose's Military Antiquities, Vol. I., p. 45.
‡ 39 & 40 Geo. III., c. 1 (see Appendix L).

for the West Riding was 4,555, the proportion amounted to 2,733. A subaltern's commission was offered for every 60 men, or commissions for one captain, one lieutenant, and one ensign for every 80 men volunteering as a company into one regiment. The captain and lieutenant were to have temporary rank, and the ensigns permanent rank in the Army; all the officers being entitled to half-pay when reduced, whether the rank was temporary or permanent.

In a General Order, dated Horse Guards, the 10th of October, 1799, His Royal Highness the Duke of York says "that, having witnessed the brilliant success which has already attended the efforts of His Majesty's Arms in Holland, and for which the country is so much indebted to the distinguished gallantry and zeal of the first volunteers from the Militia," he urges Militiamen to follow the example of their former comrades.

According to a Return dated the 13th of February, the Regiment had 1,011 privates, but in this month they had been reduced by volunteering into the Line to 549 men.

From a Return dated Adjutant-General's Office, 18th of October, it appears that of 45,821 men, being three-fifths of the quota for England and Wales, 26,173 volunteered, leaving the difference of 19,648 to be disembodied.* Of this number the West Riding supplied 785, of which 164 were from this Regiment; thus leaving 1,948 to be disembodied in the Riding, or 367 in the Regiment. The Lord Lieutenant, in a letter dated Wentworth, the 23rd of October, acknowledges the receipt of a War Office Circular of the 12th of October, directing him to disembody as many men of the West York Militia as exceeded the new quota of 1822.† On the 13th of November a letter was sent to the Lord Lieutenant, ordering that the 367 men of the Regiment in excess of the establishment were to be discharged, in accordance with a Warrant dated the 8th of December, which was enclosed.

In October the Regiment left Hornsea Camp for Hull, and was quartered in the Citadel Barracks, by order of Lieutenant-General Balfour. In Regimental Orders, dated Hull, the 20th of

---

* Commons' Journals, Vol. LXI., p. 639.
† Militia, No. 28, 1798-1802.

October, 1799, "The Sergeants are strickly forbid to pass the Streets with their pikes shouldered, except when passing an Officer, at which time they should leave the pavement. At all other times they must carry their pikes sloped on their shoulders, but carefully, to prevent their breaking windows or otherwise doing mischief. Any Sergeant who may, after this Order, be proved to break a lamp, or do other injury to the public, will not only be punished, but his pay will be stopped to repair the damage he may have occasioned."

The Sergeants' sashes were made of crimson worsted, intermixed with the colour of the facings of the Regiment. In those regiments which had crimson or scarlet facings, white was intermixed with the crimson groundwork, instead of the colour of the regimental facings.

A General Order, dated Hull, the 11th of November, directs " The usual firing party, with men sufficient to carry the body, to attend at the Marine Hospital this afternoon, precisely at half-past two o'clock, for the funeral of one Russian soldier, deceased.—H. MAXWELL, M. of B."

Another General Order, dated Hull, the 16th of December, directs that the funeral of Russians are to be in future conducted under the direction of the Russian officers in the citadel.

On the 26th of December, above forty sick Russians, with three officers, landed. The next day the following Order was issued: " The Sussex Yeomanry, Royal Artillery, East Norfolk, and 5th West York, Regiments of Militia, will be under Arms tomorrow morning at half-past eleven o'clock, in George Street, in order to be seen by the Russian Major-General Arbenoff.— H. MAXWELL, M. of B."

The following extracts from a letter from the Lord-Lieutenant to the Secretary at War explains the reason for disembodying the 3rd and 4th Regiments, and retaining the 5th as the Third Regular Regiment :—*

" MILTON, 22nd Nov., 1799.

" Having left Wentworth before your Packet containing His

---

* Militia, No. 28, 1798-1802.

Majesty's Warrant for disembodying certain proportions of the Militia of the West Riding Yorkshire, your circular of the 13th, and your Letter of Particular Instructions of the 15th inst., to which place it had been directed, it came to my hands only the day before yesterday.

"By the Circular, I collect that it is His Majesty's intention that the 1,822 Privates intended to be retained in actual service for the West Riding are to be formed into three Regiments, and, in conformity with this intention, that two out of the present five are to be reduced.

"That, in case of deficient numbers in the three retained, the deficiencies are to be made up from the two reduced.

"Permit Me to observe that, as the Quota of the Old Establishment had never been taken from one General Levy, but that each of the Two Regiments had always received its particular Quota from particular Wapentakes, so on the Establishment of the Supplementary a similar practice had been adopted, and each of the Three New Regiments had been likewise furnished by particular and distinct Wapentakes and Districts, as near as the rule could be made to apply.

"In a county full of Industry and Activity, such as the West Riding of Yorkshire is known to be, the return of a considerable number of industrious and useful hands will be considered as a very great benefit. Circumstanced, therefore, as the Regiments are, the total Reduction of any particular Regiments will throw the whole of the benefit upon the particular District which furnishes the Quota of that Regiment; whilst, on the contrary, to retain another Regiment entire will be to the total exclusion of some other districts from any share in that benefit.—A Measure producing so partial an effect will be viewed with jealousy, and, I am apprehensive, will occasion a considerable degree of uneasiness in those parts that continue deprived of the return of their industrious inhabitants. I am aware that the proposition made by the Lord-Lieutenant of Lancashire does not provide a remedy for this evil systematically, but I think it must prove one practically. Perhaps it may not produce arithmetical precision, but it will such a reasonable degree of equal distribution as to stifle complaint.

"For this reason, I anxiously hope that His Majesty will be graciously Pleased to direct me in executing his Warrant in the West Riding of Yorkshire, to pursue a plan that will spread the reduction pretty equally over all the Regiments, and thereby the benefits over all the Wapentakes.

"Such a plan may, without inconvenience, be carried into immediate execution with respect to the Three Regiments remaining in England, without waiting for the return from Ireland of the 1st and 2nd, because, as I explained above, the two last-mentioned, collectively taken, and the three first-mentioned, taken likewise, so each party separately affect the Riding generally. But, before anything can be done, it will be necessary to have most Accurate Returns of the Actual Strength of all the Regiments, for which I have written. . . . . With respect to the selection of Regiments, I collect from the Circular that it is His Majesty's intention that the 1st, the 2nd, and the 3rd Regiments should be retained in service, and that the 4th and 5th should be reduced. Under the existing circumstances of the different Regiments, it becomes my duty most humbly to recommend for His Majesty's consideration, to retain the 1st, 2nd, and 5th, and to permit me to reduce the 3rd and 4th.

"The merits of the Colonels and other officers of the two last-mentioned Regiments cannot have been surpassed during the time that those Regiments have been embodied. The urgency of the occasion on which they abandoned their private concerns and other avocations to come forward in defence of their Country and in support of His Majesty's Crown and Government, proved the warmth of their attachment to their Country, their stedfast Loyalty to His Majesty, and their just sense of the value of established Government. The steadiness of their respective Regiments under Arms has done credit to their diligence as Officers; whilst the exemplary discipline they maintained in those Corps manifested how fitly they were selected for command, and how justly they were entrusted with authority. In making, therefore, a proposal to reduce these two Corps, and to retain a junior Corps, I feel it necessary to express the sentiments of their merits impressed on my own mind, and at the same time to assure you that the same sentiment prevails universally throughout their own County. But, early after the close of the last Session of Parliament, I was given to understand, by the Commanding Officers of the 3rd and 4th, that nothing but the imminent and immediate danger of their Country should induce them to continue longer in this service. I have had the best grounds for knowing that the same determination prevailed through both the Corps of Officers—I mean, down to the Captains inclusive. I know nothing of the subalterns.

"It is, therefore, morally impossible that these two Corps should be kept up. I have, however, prevailed on the Officers of the 5th to remain together. It is on this account that I most strongly recommend the 5th Regiment to be retained, as the stock on which to engraft a Third Regiment of West Riding Militia.

"I have the honour, &c.,
"WENTWORTH FITZWILLIAM.
"*The* RIGHT HON. HENRY DUNDAS."

In reply, Mr. Dundas, in a letter dated Downing Street, the 27th of November, states that "The reasons adduced by your Lordship for retaining the 1st, 2nd, and 5th Battalions, and for reducing the 3rd and 4th, are perfectly sufficient to justify that arrangement, and His Majesty has been pleased to approve of your carrying it into effect."*

A War Office Circular, dated the 3rd of December, was addressed to "Sir George Cooke, Bart., Colonel of the 5th West York Militia," of which the following is an extract:—

"Sir,—The King having been Pleased to sign a Warrant directed to the Lord-Lieutenant of the West Riding of Yorkshire for disembodying a portion of the Militia of that Riding; in consequence of which you may soon expect to receive Orders

---

* War Office Militia Letter Book, Vol. II., pp. 28, 29.

from the Lord-Lieutenant for disembodying a portion of the Regiment under your command, &c.

"I have the honor, &c.,
"WM. WINDHAM."

The quota of the West Riding was acccordingly reduced to 1,822 men, by disbanding the 3rd and 4th Regiments, which commenced on the 19th and was completed on the 31st of December.

All the Officers on reduction received six months' pay, and the non-commissioned Officers and men fourteen days' pay, viz.:—

		s.	d.	£	s.	d.
Sergeants	...	at 1	6¾ =	1	1	10½
Corporals	...	at 1	2¼ =	0	16	7½
Drummers	...	at 1	1¾ =	0	16	0½
Privates	...	at 1	0 =	0	14	0

In addition to this, they received their clothing and knapsacks (War Office Circular, 22nd November, 1799), and "half-mounting," either in kind or value, viz.:— *

SERGEANTS.		s.	d.	CORPORALS, DRUMMERS AND PRIVATES.		s.	d.
1 Shirt ...	...	... 6	6	1 Shirt ...		... 5	6
1 pair of Stockings		... 3	0	1 pair of Stockings		... 1	6
1 pair of Shoes ...		... 6	0	1 pair of Shoes ...		... 6	0
Total		... 15	6	Total		... 13	0

The number discharged from the Regiment was more than counterbalanced by a draft of 399 privates from the 3rd and 4th Regiments. The 5th Regiment then became the 3rd Regiment of the Regular Militia, and the establishment which was proposed by the War Office Circular of the 3rd of December, as

---

* Militia, No. 28, 1798-1802.

above quoted, was adopted, viz., ten companies, one colonel, one lieut.-colonel, one major, seven captains, one captain-lieutenant, eleven lieutenants, eight ensigns, one adjutant, one quartermaster, one surgeon, one sergeant-major, one quartermaster-sergeant, thirty sergeants, thirty corporals, twenty-two drummers, and 607 privates. The establishment of the other two regiments was the same.

"The Paymaster and Surgeon's Mate not being borne on the establishment of Militia Corps, are not distinguished in the above state, but the usual pay and allowances will be granted them, as also the allowance of the Paymaster's Clerk"

Of the twenty-eight Regiments of Supplementary Militia twenty-three (or twenty-four including the 2nd Sussex, which, however, was not a distinct corps, but formed part of the 1st Sussex), were disbanded. The five Regiments retained were the 2nd and 3rd Lancashire, West Somerset, 2nd Surrey and 5th West York.*

The Regiment contributed a large sum to a fund for the relief of the widows and children of the killed and wounded British soldiers in Holland; to this fund the Corporation of Doncaster contributed fifty guineas.

The Lord-Lieutenant, Earl Fitzwilliam, in a letter to the Colonel, Sir George Cooke, Bart., dated Milton, the 14th of December, 1799, informing him that the Government had accepted the offer of the 5th Regiment to remain embodied, says:—"Allow me here to observe how greatly the obligation which you and the officers of your Regiment have already conferred upon your Country by your past services is enhanced by the promise of their continuance. The Country feels the obligation as it ought to do, and rejoices that so considerable a proportion of its favourite and best defence is to be continued under the command of those who have shown how wisely they were selected for command by the fit use they made of it. In the full confidence of obtaining the general approbation, I therefore request you, sir, and the officers, to continue in the command of the 5th

---

* Return, dated 21st July, 1801; Militia Miscellaneous, Vol. II., No. 20.

Regiment, but which will hereafter be called the Third, as soon as the 3rd and 4th shall be reduced, a measure which will take place immediately."

1800.—A General Order, dated Horse Guards, the 24th of February, for the Infantry of the Army states that

" It is His Majesty's pleasure that in future the use of Hats is to be entirely abolished throughout the whole of the Infantry, and instead thereof Caps are to be worn. . . . . . The Grenadiers to wear these Caps occasionally when they do not use their proper Grenadier Caps. . . . The tufts used by the Grenadiers to be white, those of the Light Infantry dark green.—All soldiers to wear the button of their respective Regiments in the centre of the cockade, except the Grenadiers, who will use the grenade. The Caps are to be made of a sufficient size to come completely on the soldiers' heads. They are to be worn straight and even, and brought forward well over the eyes. The Field, Staff, and Battalion Company officers to continue to wear hats. Officers of the Grenadier and Light Infantry Companies to wear Caps similar to those ordered for their Companies."

A Regimental Order of the 4th of May, directs that "Officers of the Grenadier Company are in future at all times to wear their hair plaited up behind; they will wear their Caps on Sundays and field days—Hats at other times."

A Warrant, dated the 25th of May, 1797, for increasing and regulating the pay of soldiers, allowed a stoppage for Messing of 4s. 6d. a-week in the Dragoons, and 4s. in the Infantry, with an allowance of small beer gratis. By War Office Circular, dated the 8th of March, 1800, an allowance of 1d. per diem was made to each Non-commissioned Officer and Private, instead of the allowance of small beer.

By a Warrant, dated the 17th of March, 1800, the amount of pay to be set apart for a soldier's Mess was raised to 5s. 1d. in the Dragoons, and 4s. 7d. in the Infantry.

The Regiment received orders in June to march from Hull, where they had been stationed since the previous October, in three divisions, by **the following routes to Durham,** Darlington, and Northallerton :—

		1st Division. 4 Companies.	2nd Division. 3 Companies.	3rd Division. 3 Companies.
Thurs.	5th June,	Beverley	—	—
Friday	6th „	Weighton and Pocklington	Beverley	—
Saturday	7th „	York	Weighton and Pocklington	Beverley
Sunday	8th „	Halt	Halt	Halt
Monday	9th „	Boroughbridge	York	Weighton and Pocklington
Tuesday	10th „	Northallerton	Boroughbridge	York
Wednes.	11th „	Darlington	Northallerton	Boroughbridge
Thurs.	12th „	Halt	Halt	Halt
Friday	13th „	Durham	Darlington	Northallerton

Orders were first received on the 2nd of June, ordering the Regiment to march by the above route to Sunderland, but a subsequent order, on the 10th of June, directed the several divisions to remain at the above places until further orders.*

When halted at York, on the 7th and 8th of June, the Regiment was inspected by General Staveley. In Regimental Orders of the 8th of June the Commanding Officer states that he is much pleased with the appearance of the division before Major-General Staveley, and he hopes they will do equal credit to themselves on the parade to-morrow, when General Staveley will pay them the compliment of coming to see them march off. The Commanding Officer cannot resist the pleasure of extracting the following paragraph from a York paper of Saturday last :—

"On Wednesday last, the 3rd West York, commanded by Colonel Sir George Cooke, received their route for Sunderland. It is a Regiment of as stout soldier-like men as any in the Kingdom; and their conduct, whilst quartered at Hull, has been highly creditable to both Officers and Men."

The detachments remained at Durham, Darlington, and Northallerton, from the 13th to the 22nd of June, and on the following day marched to Sunderland Barracks. Colonel Sir

---

* Militia Marching Book, Vol. XCVIII., pp. 152, 158.

George Cooke being the senior officer the command of the Garrison devolved upon him. On the 3rd of July the Light Company was sent to South Shields.

The Regiment was inspected by Major-General Murray, on the 18th of September, 477 privates being present under arms, who reported that "The Battalion presents a very remarkable fine body of young men, in a very high state of good order, steadiness, and discipline.—Marching particularly well.—The whole system regular and carefully attended to."

Marching Orders were received, dated the 29th of October, for the Regiment to march in three divisions from Sunderland Barracks to Berwick and Tweedmouth by the following route:—*

	1st Division. 4 Companies.	2nd Division. 3 Companies	3rd Division. 3 Companies.
Wednes. 5th Nov.,	Newcastle and Gateshead	—	—
Thurs. 6th „	Morpeth	Newcastle and Gateshead	—
Friday 7th „	Alnwick	Morpeth	Newcastle and Gateshead
Saturday 8th „	Bedford and adjacent places	Alnwick	Morpeth
Sunday 9th „	Halt	Halt	Halt
Monday 10th „	Berwick and Tweedmouth	Bedford and adjacent places	Alnwick
Tues. 11th „		Berwick and Tweedmouth	Bedford and adjacent places
Wednes. 12th „	—	—	Berwick and Tweedmouth

On the 28th of November the Regiment marched from Berwick to Stirling, where six companies were quartered, two being sent to Falkirk and two to Linlithgow, this was the first occasion the Regiment was quartered in Scotland. The Regiment was inspected by General Sir James St. Clair Erskine, Bart., with very satisfactory results.

A Horse Guards Circular, dated the 15th of December, directed the Colours to be sent to the Ordnance Office at the Tower of London, for the purpose of being altered to the new

---

* Militia Marching Book, Vol. XCVIII., pp. 195, 196.

pattern, which, by order of His Majesty was to be adopted on the approaching Union of Great Britain and Ireland.

1801.—In May the Falkirk and Linlithgow companies joined head-quarters at Stirling, and the Regiment was again inspected by General Sir James St. Clair Erskine, Bart., who spoke in high terms of the appearance of the men. On the 1st of June two companies returned to Falkirk and two to Linlithgow. On the 6th of August the six companies stationed at Stirling, and the four companies at Falkirk and Linlithgow marched to Edinburgh, where they were quartered in the Castle, with the exception of two companies which were sent on to Leith. The command of the Castle, in which there were a number of French prisoners, devolved upon **Colonel Sir** George Cooke, Bart.

On the 21st of July an **Order** was issued for **all Militia** Officers on leave to join their Regiments immediately.

The **Lord-Lieutenant**, in a letter dated Scarborough, the 7th of August, acknowledges the receipt of a **Warrant**, on the 5th inst., to re-embody the men who were disembodied in 1799, and states that he has given the necessary instructions to that effect. The Deputy-Lieutenants, at a meeting held at Leeds on the 25th of August, ordered **70 sergeants, 74 corporals, and 7** drummers of the West Riding to be re-embodied; of which number **24 sergeants, 25 corporals, and 4** drummers belonged to the Regiment.*
The number of re-embodied men who marched to join the Regiment, according to a Return dated Quartermaster-General's Office, 19th September, was **34 sergeants, 25 corporals, 5 drummers, and 217 men.** The number of privates re-embodied in England was **7,815.** † These men had been dis-embodied in 1799, being in excess of the reduced quota. ‡

The **Augmented Establishment** assigned under the Secretary of State's authority to the Regiment in consequence of the addition of the re-embodied men appears, from a Return dated Doncaster, 28th March, 1802, to have been **1 colonel, 1 lieut.-colonel, 2 majors, 7 captains, 11 lieutenants, 5 ensigns, 1 pay-**

---

* Militia, No. 28, 1798-1802 ; and Militia, **No. 38,** 1802-1809.
† Militia Miscellaneous, **1798-1802,** Vol. II., No. 20.
‡ See page 70.

master, 2 adjutants, 1 quartermaster, 1 surgeon, 1 assistant-surgeon, 2 sergeant-majors, 2 quartermaster-sergeants, 66 sergeants, 52 corporals, 27 drummers, and 809 privates. Of this number, 1 major, 1 adjutant, 1 sergeant-major, 1 quartermaster-sergeant, 26 sergeants, 12 corporals, and 5 drummers, were supernumeraries.

In September the Regiment was inspected by Lieutenant-General Vyse, who added his testimony to the high character they had earned.

On the 21st of August a number of re-embodied men assembled at Doncaster, and were at first ordered to Ripon, which was subsequently changed to Leeds by an Order dated the 14th of August.* On the 14th of September the detachment at Leeds was ordered to Berwick and Tweedmouth by the subjoined route:—†

- Friday   18th September, Harrogate and Knaresboro'
  Saturday   19th   „   Boroughbridge and Ripon
  Sunday   20th   „   Halt
  Monday   21st   „   Northallerton
  Tuesday   22nd   „   Darlington
  Wednesday   23rd   „   Durham
  Thursday   24th   „   Halt
  Friday   25th   „   Newcastle and Gateshead
  Saturday   26th   „   Morpeth
  Sunday   27th   „   Halt
  Monday   28th   „   Alnwick
  Tuesday   29th   „   Belford and adjacent places
  Wednesday   30th   „   Berwick

The detachment joined the Regiment at Edinburgh in October.

1802.—Orders were received, dated War Office the 19th of January, for the Regiment to proceed from Edinburgh to Berwick and Tweedmouth, and remain there until the 3rd of February, and then to proceed to Doncaster, and other places, according to route.

On the 23rd of January the eight companies at Edinburgh, and the two companies at Leith marched to Berwick, by order of

---

* Militia Marching Book, Vol. XCVIII., p. 323.
† Idem, p. 453.

Lieutenant-General Vyse, where they remained until the beginning of February, when they marched in four divisions by the following Route: five companies to Doncaster, three companies to Bawtry, and two companies to Pontefract and Ferrybridge.*

		1st Division. 3 Companies.	2nd Division. 2 Companies.	3rd Division. 3 Companies.	4th Division. 2 Companies.
W	3rd Feb.	Belford and adjacent	—	—	—
T	4th	„ Alnwick	Bedford and adjacent	—	—
F	5th	„ Morpeth	Alnwick	Bedford and adjacent	—
S	6th	„ Newcastle and Gateshead	Morpeth	Alnwick	Bedford and adjacent
S	7th	„ Halt	Halt	Halt	Halt
M	8th	„ Durham	Newcastle and Gateshead	Morpeth	Alnwick
T	9th	„ Darlington	Durham	Newcastle and Gateshead	Morpeth
W	10th	„ Northallerton	Darlington	Durham	Newcastle and Gateshead
T	11th	„ Halt	Halt	Halt	Halt
F	12th	„ Boroughbridge and Ripon	Northallerton	Darlington	Durham
S	13th	„ Weatherby and Tadcaster	Boroughbridge and Ripon	Northallerton	Darlington
S	14th	„ Halt	Halt	Halt	Halt
M	15th	„ Pontefract and Ferrybridge	Weatherby and Tadcaster	Boroughbridge and Ripon	Northallerton
T	16th	„ Doncaster	Pontefract and Ferrybridge	Weatherby and Tadcaster	Boroughbridge and Ripon
W	17th	„ Bawtry	Doncaster	Pontefract and Ferrybridge	Weatherby and Tadcaster
T	18th	„	—	—	Doncaster	Pontefract and Ferrybridge

The six-pounder field-pieces, with the ammunition, were left at Edinburgh Castle. Previous to their departure from Edinburgh the most distinguished mark of approbation of the conduct, both of the officers and men, was expressed by the public thanks of the inhabitants. In accordance with a Route dated the

---

* Militia Marching Book, Vol. XCIX., pp. 33, 34, 35.

12th of April the two companies at Pontefract and Ferrybridge returned to Doncaster, and two companies were sent to Rotherham.

The Secretary of State, in a letter to the Lord-Lieutenant, dated Downing Street, the 12th of April, enclosing a Warrant to disembody the Militia of the West Riding, says: "The first and most gratifying part of the duty I have to discharge, in obedience to the King's Commands, is to communicate to the Officers, Non-Commissioned Officers and Men, through your Lordship, the high sense with which His Majesty is impressed of their uniformly good Conduct since they have been embodied, and of their truly meritorious zeal and public spirit, under all the trying occurrences which have arisen to call forth their loyal exertions during the long and arduous contest in which we have been engaged."*

An Order was also received from the War Office, of the same date, directing the Colonel to march the Regiment to such places within the county as he thought fit, to carry out His Majesty's order for disembodying the Militia.† The Regiment was accordingly assembled at Doncaster and disembodied on the 22nd of April, after having been embodied for four years and two months.

Parliament again acknowledged the services rendered by the Militia to the Country, a Vote of Thanks being passed in both Houses; that by the House of Lords is here given:—

"*6th April*, 1802.

"Resolved Nemine Dissentiente, That the Thanks of this House be given to the Officers of the several Corps of Militia which have been embodied in Great Britain and Ireland during the course of the War, for the seasonable and meritorious Services they have rendered to their King and Country.

"Resolved Nemine Dissentiente, That this House doth highly approve of and acknowledge the services of the Non-Commissioned Officers and Men of the several Corps of Militia which have been embodied in Great Britain and Ireland during the

---

* War Office Militia Letter Book, Vol. II., p. 365.
† Militia Marching Book, Vol. XCIX., p. 84.

course of the War, and that the same be communicated to them by the Commanding Officers of the several Corps, who are desired to thank them for their Meritorious Conduct.

"Ordered, that the Lord Chancellor do signify the same Resolution by Letter to the Colonel or Commanding Officer of each respective Corps."*

On the same day the House of Commons passed a Vote of Thanks to the Militia in the same terms.†

On being disembodied the Establishment became reduced to 607 under the Act, ‡ passed in December, 1801.

On the 15th of July, 1802, a Circular was issued calling for a statement of the plan for the regimental establishments in the various counties, as the quota had been again increased by the new Act.§ The rank of Captain-Lieutenant was abolished, Field Officers being no longer allowed companies; the former were to rank as Lieutenants, and all supernumerary Lieutenants were to be commissioned as Ensigns.

A Circular, dated the 8th of November, 1802, was issued to the Lords-Lieutenant directing them to report the progress made in reorganizing the Militia of their counties. In compliance with this order Earl Fitzwilliam, in a letter dated Milton, 10th January, 1803, states that at a General Meeting held on the 22nd of December, 1802, the number liable to serve in each Wapentake was fixed, and they only had to be balloted for.‖

---

* Lords' Journals, Vol. XLIII., p. 526.
† Commons' Journals, Vol. LVII., pp. 303-4; and Parliamentary History, Vol. XXXVI., p. 463.
‡ 42 George III., c. 12 (see Appendix M).
§ Idem, c. 90 (see Appendices L and M).
‖ Internal Defence (Home Office), 1803, Vol. XXXV., No. 35.

CHAPTER IV.

FROM 1803 TO 1814.

EMBODIED FROM 11TH MARCH, 1803, TO 24TH JUNE, 1814.

CONTENTS.—Establishment increased to 809.—Regiment embodied.—Ordered to York.—Supplementary Men called out in July.—Regiment proceeds to Colchester.—Encamps on Elmstead Heath.—Orders in case of Invasion.—Two Companies Equipped as Rifles.—Officers' Dress in 1804.—Alarm Beacons in Yorkshire.—Encampment at Coxheath.—Quartered at Feversham and Ospringe.—Quota again reduced in 1805.—Quota increased in 1807.—Standing Orders issued by Col. Bryan Cooke in 1809.—The White Rose of York conferred as a Badge 1811.—Regiment Embarked for Ireland, December, 1811.—The Battalion of Detachments of Militia.—Quarters in Ireland.—Warrant to hold Courts-Martial.—Volunteers into the Army, 1805-1814.—Regiment returns to England, May, 1814.—March from Plymouth to Doncaster.—Letter from the Lord-Lieutenant.—Disembodied 24th June.—Thanks from Secretary of State and Commander-in-Chief.—Vote of Thanks from Parliament.—Pay of Disembodied Staff.—Establishment of the Regiment.

1803.—IN accordance with the Circular of the 15th of July, 1802, Earl Fitzwilliam, in a letter dated Milton, the 27th of January, 1803, submitted the following establishment for the West Riding regiments, which was approved of and carried into effect. Each of the three regiments to have one Grenadier, 1 Light Infantry, and 8 Battalion Companies of 81 men each, the 1st and 2nd West York to have 27 Sergeants, 27 Corporals, and 810 privates; with this exception, the establishment of each regiment was 1 Colonel, 1 Lieutenant-Colonel, 2 Majors, 10 Captains, 12 Lieutenants, 8 Ensigns, 1 Adjutant, 1 Paymaster or Regimental Clerk, 1 Surgeon, 1 Quartermaster, 26 Sergeants, 26 Corporals, 12 Drummers, and 809 privates.*

On the 2nd of February, a Circular was issued by the Lord-Lieutenant, stating that the quota having been increased from 1,822 to 2,429 privates, the establishment of the Regiment would be 809. †

On the 10th of March, the King informed Parliament, in a Message, of his intention to call out and embody the Militia,‡ and on the 14th the Lord-Lieutenant wrote to acknowledge the receipt of a letter enclosing a Warrant, dated the 11th of March, to embody the West York Militia, which was immediately carried into effect.§ The 1st Regiment assembled at Leeds, the 2nd Regiment at York, and the 3rd Regiment at Doncaster, which latter was inspected by the Lord-Lieutenant, who expressed his high approbation at their soldierlike appearance.

A War Office Circular was addressed to the Colonels of Militia, on the 15th of March, directing that the men were to be supplied, on assembling, with the following necessaries, the charge of which would be defrayed by the public:—

SERGEANTS.	s. d.	CORPORALS, DRUMMERS AND PRIVATES.	s. d.
1 Shirt	6 6	1 Shirt	6 0
2 pairs of Socks, or 1 pair of Stockings	1 6	2 pairs of Socks, or 1 pair of Stockings	1 6
1 pair Long Gaiters	4 0	1 pair of Long Gaiters	4 0
1 Black Stock	0 9	1 Black Stock	0 9
	12 9		12 3

Each man was also to receive a cap, coat, waistcoat, breeches, and one pair of shoes; and the Colonel was authorised to order

---

* Internal Defence (Home Office), Vol. XXXV., No. 35, 1803.

† 42 Geo. III., c. 90 (see Appendices M and N).

‡ Parliamentary History, Vol. XXXVI., p. 1,173, 1,174; and Lords Journals, Vol. XLIV., pp. 204-5.

§ Internal Defence (Home Office), Vol. XXXV.

PRIVATE OF THE GRENADIER COMPANY DURING THE PENINSULA WAR.

10

the necessary accoutrements, which would be paid for by Warrant, the knapsacks being supplied from the stores.*

At the funeral of one of the Officers, on the 27th of April, the Officers were order to wear crape on their arms, "and love-ribbons on their swords."

A General Order, dated Horse Guards, the 16th of May, 1803, says that "In order that the troops may be prepared to act in the most effectual manner, and to perform the various duties of an active campaign, His Royal Highness particularly enjoins Commanding Officers of Regiments of Militia to leave in their present Quarters, or in their respective County towns, all super-fluous baggage whatsoever; the Officers must confine themselves to the *most* limited portion of baggage, and on no account are the non-commissioned officers or subalterns to be permitted to carry with them any trunks or boxes."

In accordance with an Order, dated the 19th of May, from the War Office, received on the 22nd of May, the Regiment marched from Doncaster to York in three divisions.†

		1st Division. 4 Companies.	2nd Division. 3 Companies.	3rd Division. 3 Companies.
Friday	27th May	Pontefract and Ferrybridge	—	—
Saturday	28th ,,	Tadcaster	Pontefract and Ferrybridge	—
Sunday	29th ,,	Halt	Halt	—
Monday	30th ,,	York	Tadcaster	Pontefract and Ferrybridge
Tuesday	31st ,,	—	York	Tadcaster
Wednes.	1st June	—	—	York

In March, the period of the annual training of the Militia was increased from twenty-one to twenty-eight days.‡

On the 25th of May the King informed Parliament of his intention to call out the Supplementary Militia.§

---

* Militia (Home Office), No. 38, 1802-1809.
† Militia Marching Book, Vol. XCIX, p. 175.
‡ 43 Geo. III., c. 19.
§ Parliamentary History, Vol. XXXVI., p. 1,514.

The Lord-Lieutenant, in a letter dated the 9th of June, acknowledges the receipt, on the previous night, of the Royal Warrant to draw out and embody the Supplementary Militia of the West Riding; and in another letter, dated the 10th of June, recommends that the Supplementary Men should be divided amongst the existing regiments in equal proportions, making each to consist of 1,215 privates, and to provide for this addition by increasing the number of companies from ten to twelve, with the necessary officers and non-commissioned officers. This proposal being approved of in a letter, dated Downing Street, the 11th of June, was carried into effect.*

A letter from the Clerk of General Meetings, dated Wakefield, the 23rd of June, says that on receipt of His Majesty's Proclamation of the 26th of May, a General Meeting was held to order 1,214 men, or half the quota of 2,429,† to be balloted for, which had already been partly done, and the last sub-division would be completed by the 9th of July. The men were ordered to assemble at Leeds, York, and Doncaster, the head-quarters of their regiments, previous to marching to join them. From a subsequent letter it appears that at a General Meeting held at Wakefield, on the 5th of July, the Supplementary Men were ordered to assemble at the head-quarters of their respective regiments on Thursday the 14th of July.‡

In June, Orders were issued from the War Office, directing that recruiting parties were to be sent out when considered expedient, and that recruits were to be sent to the head-quarters of the Regiment as often as it was thought necessary.§

The alarm-posts of the different regiments in the district were fixed as follows (Brigade Orders, Beverley, the 22nd of June):—The 5th Dragoon Guards and 3rd West York Regiment on their respective parades at York: at Hull, a detachment of Artillery on the east side of the North Bridge, the 1st and 2nd West York Regiments on the Dock side of George

---

* War Office Militia Letter Book (England), Vol. II., pp. 16, 23.
† 42 Geo. III., c. 90 (see Appendices M and O).
‡ Internal Defence (Home Office), Vol. XXXV., No. 35.
§ Militia Marching Book, Vol. XCIX., pp. 209-211.

Street and Charlotte Street: at Scarborough, four companies of the **East** York Regiment in Castle Yard; and four companies of the same Regiment in **Church Street, Whitby**.

On the 8th **of July a Route was received, dated the 5th of July**, for the Regiment to march from **York to Colchester, and** encamp **on Elmstead Heath**.*

			1st Division. 4 Companies.	2nd Division. 3 Companies.	3rd Division. 3 Companies.
Monday	11th July		Tadcaster	—	—
Tuesday	12th	,,	Pontefract and Ferrybridge	Tadcaster	—
Wednes.	13th	,,	Doncaster	Pontefract and Ferrybridge	Tadcaster
Thursday	14th	,,	Retford and Moorgate	Doncaster	Pontefract and Ferrybridge
Friday	15th	,,	Newark	Retford and Moorgate	Doncaster
Saturday	16th	,,	Grantham	Newark	Retford and Moorgate
Sunday	17th	,,	Halt	Halt	Halt
Monday	18th	,,	Stamford	Grantham	Newark
Tuesday	19th	,,	Stilton, Norman Cross & Yaxley	Stamford	Grantham
Wednes.	20th	,,	Huntingdon and Godmanchester	Stilton, Norman Cross & Yaxley	Stamford
Thursday	21st	,,	Cambridge	Huntingdon and Godmanchester	Stilton, Norman Cross & Yaxley
Friday	22nd	,,	Linton and Havervill	Cambridge	Huntingdon and Godmanchester
Saturday	23rd	,,	Halstead and Heddingham	Linton and Havervill	Cambridge
Sunday	24th	,,	Halt	Halt	Halt
Monday	25th	,,	Colchester	Halstead and Heddingham	Linton and Havervill
Tuesday	26th	,,	—	Colchester	Halstead and Heddingham
Wednes.	27th	,,	—	—	Colchester

A Proclamation, dated **the 14th of** June, states that Militiamen who had **not** hitherto **joined** their regiments, and were therefore

---

* Militia Marching Book, Vol. **XCIX.**, pp. 231, 251.

Deserters, would be Pardoned if they joined before the 14th of July.*

On the 29th of July an inlying Piquet was ordered to mount every night at sunset, consisting of two captains, five subalterns, and 300 rank and file. The heavy baggage of regiments was ordered to be placed in Depôts appointed in each District; that of Major-General Lord Southampton's Brigade being at Hertford.

The Supplementary quota of men had been meanwhile raised, and a draft of 349 shortly after joined the Regiment at Colchester. Two of the divisions were encamped at Elmstead Heath almost immediately on their arrival, and were brigaded with the 1st West York and East York Militia; the third division was encamped on Colchester Hill. Amongst fifty-six officers of one of the regiments there were but two tents, and they were obliged to bivouac in the open air amidst innumerable snakes, with which the place was infested. In the course of an hour 200 of these reptiles are said to have been killed by the pioneers in clearing away the heath. Huts of wood were erected for the married men.†

The troops were marched almost daily into the country towards the sea, by Lord Southampton, and posted on advantageous positions, which they would probably have occupied had the French effected a landing on the Essex coast. The Light Companies of the three Yorkshire Regiments were under the command of Major Lee, of the 1st West York, and when marching out formed an Advance Guard. The strictest regulations were observed in the camp: suspicious persons and foreigners asking questions from soldiers were ordered to be taken up and brought before the senior officer in camp; and the drill was pursued with unwearied attention. At the latter part of August, the Brigade was inspected on the Heath by the Duke of York, attended by the Duke of Cambridge, Lieut.-General Craig, who commanded the district, and a numerous suite of General Officers. His Royal Highness was pleased to express, through Lord Southampton, who commanded the Yorkshire Brigade, his thorough approbation

---

* *London Gazette*, 1803.
† Sheardown's Origin and Services of the 3rd West York Light Infantry.

of the steadiness both of the officers and men, and for the great correctness of **the** evolutions and alertness of the three **Yorkshire** Regiments.

A Circular, dated the 22nd of August, was issued, directing that all correspondence relating to the Militia should be addressed to the Secretary of State for the Home Department.*

A chain of night signals was established along the coasts of **Essex**, Suffolk, Norfolk, and Cambridge; and in **October the** expectation of a descent was so great that Lord Southampton issued orders that no officer should leave the camp for more than two hours at a time. **Bâtt horses** were allowed to **each regiment,** two for the carriage of **ammunition, one for the medicine chest,** one for entrenching tools, **with which** they were provided, and one for camp kettles. Waggons and horses were provided and kept in readiness along the coast, for the purpose of conveying the sick, and women and children into the interior of the country; and preparations **were made** for sending away all the heavy baggage of the Regiment, spare arms, and stores, so that they might not be encumbered in their movements.†

The Regimental Orders of the 12th of October, 1803, state that "Colonel Cooke **is** informed by Lord Southampton **that** should the enemy land, **and** the Regiment be ordered **to** March, no Officer will be allowed to take any baggage on any of the Waggons." "No Officer or **Man on any account to leave the** Camp till further Orders, but be ready to turn out **at a Moment's** warning, **tho' to go to rest as usual.**"

In October two companies of the Regiment were equipped as Rifles, at the suggestion **of** Colonel **Sir** George Cooke, by the following authority:—

"HORSE GUARDS, *Oct.* **3rd, 1803.**

"Sir,

"I have done myself the honor **to submit** your letter of the 30th ult., with its enclosures, herewith returned, to the consideration of the Commander-in-Chief, and am directed to acquaint you that His Royal Highness does not object to the proposal trans-

---

* Internal Defences (Home Office), **Vol.** XXXV., No. 35.
† Sheardown's Origin and Services of the 3rd West York Light Infantry.

mitted by Colonel Cooke, of the 3rd West York Regiment of Militia, to Major.-Gen. Lord Southampton, that Captains Dewar and Hawkes' Companies be formed into Companies of Riflemen, and remain attached to the 3rd West York Regiment of Militia.

"I have, &c.,

"HARRY CALVERT, A.G.

"LIEUT.-GEN. SIR JAMES CRAIG, &c."

The Yorkshire Brigade, composed of the 1st and 3rd West York and the East York Regiments, was inspected on the 16th of October by Major-General Lord Southampton, under whose command they were; and he reported that the men were all "strong, active, and well-behaved."

A Warrant, dated the 22nd of November, was issued to supply them with 176 rifle-barrelled muskets, and 176 side-arms, and again on the 11th of May, 1804.*

On the 24th of November the Regiment went into winter quarters at Colchester Barracks, together with the 1st West York and East York Militia, by order of Lieut.-General Sir J. H. Craig. Notwithstanding the lowness of the ground at Elmstead, the Brigade, whilst under canvas, had very little sickness. The superior discipline and fine appearance of the Yorkshire Brigade was the theme of universal praise.

In this year the Regiment gave 544 Men to the regular Army, and 19 to the Navy; 3 were condemned to serve in the Army in the Gold Coast Corps, and 1 in the Navy.

In Regimental Orders dated Colchester, the 1st of December, 1803, it is stated that, "The Colonel having observed that there is not that uniformity in the dress of the Officers that there ought to be, he requests that all officers will appear on parade in blue pantaloons, half-boots, hair powdered, and their cues and caps; Officers for Duty to appear in cocked hats, white breeches, and long boots."

On the 28th of December a detachment of 32 men was sent to Braintree, where they remained for several months.†

---

* Ordnance Entry Book (Home Office).
† Militia Pay Lists (3rd West York), 1803.

1804.—The following **Regimental Order, dated the 12th of February,** describes the dress of the Officers **at this period:—**

"Regimental Coat complete, **ditto White Cloth or** Kersymere **Waistcoat,** White leather **or Kerseymere Breeches,** Full Boots, Cocked Hat and Feather, Hair **cued and neatly cut and powdered,** White Doeskin Gloves, Black Silk Handkerchief invariably tied behind, Sash, Regimental Great Coat when necessary, Regulation Sword and Knot, Gorget, White Buff Leather **Sword-belt and Breast-plate, except for Mounted** Officers.

"The **Caps and Blue Pantaloons at present in use are to be** laid aside, and **are in future only to be worn in Camp, and upon the march; it** may **become a subject of future consideration** whether they should **be worn in the event of** actual service."

In consequence **of the threatened French** Invasion, **beacons** were established **round the coast, and to** some of the principal inland **places, to give the** alarm **in the event** of the expected foe appearing.

A letter from the Vice-Lieutenant, B. **Frank,** Esq., dated Campsall, **18th February,** 1804, states that the **beacons were about to be reduced, only** keeping up those which would convey the most immediate **intelligence** to the **great towns within the Riding, being sent on from thence by the** Postmasters by express. **The letter also enclosed a copy of the Proceedings of the General Meeting of Lieutenants held at Leeds on the 16th of February,** of which **the following is an extract:—**

"ORDERED. **That the Chief Constables do dismiss from the** Beacons meant **to** be continued **one man from each Beacon,** leaving only **three as** guards.

"RESOLVED. **That in order to supply the place of Beacons in the more Westerly part of the Riding, among the Moors and** Mountains, **the** Communication **of the Alarm of Invasion be by express** from **one Post to** another, according **to** the following **arrangement:—**

"**1st** Line, **from Leeds to Otley, thence to Skipton, and thence to** Lord Ribblesdale at Grisburn.

"2nd Line from Skipton **to Settle.**

"3rd Line, from Leeds to Wetherby, thence to Knaresborough, **and thence to** Ripon.

"4th Line, Doncaster to Bawtry.

"And that the several Postmasters be also Directed to promulgate the alarm."*

Owing to an alarm given by the accidental lighting of some of the Beacons on the night of the 14th of August, 1805, and in the early morning of the 15th, the following corps assembled and marched for Doncaster, Selby, and other appointed places for rendezvous:— Southern Regiment of Yeomanry Cavalry, Infantry—(Volunteers), Rotherham, Sheffield, Staincross, Wath Wood, Doncaster, Ecclesfield, and Thorne.†

The Yorkshire Brigade was inspected, on the 22nd of May, by Major General Lord Southampton, upwards of 1,100 rank and file being present.

Orders were issued, dated 23rd of July, by Lieutenant-General Sir J. Craig, who commanded the District, directing the Yorkshire Brigade, consisting of the 1st, and 3rd West York and the East York regiments, in all 3,168 rank and file, under the command of Major-General Lord Southampton, to March from Colchester to Coxheath Camp on the 26th of July, where they arrived the same day.‡

The troops encamped at Coxheath in August consisted of the Yorkshire Brigade, commanded by Major-General Lord Southampton; Major-General Baird's Brigade, consisting of the East and West Norfolk and Royal Bucks Militia, of about 2,741 rank and file from Ipswich, and Major-General Finch's Brigade composed of the 2nd Battalion of the 1st and 3rd Foot Guards, a large body of horse and garrison artillery, and a regiment of cavalry, the whole under the command of Lord Chatham.

At the various reviews and field-days, the 3rd West York was particularly distinguished by Lord Southampton for their steadiness in marching and in going through the various manœuvres.

In Regimental Orders dated Coxheath Camp, the 29th of July, the Regiment was directed to march as follows into Winter Quarters on the 2nd and 3rd of November:—890 men

---

* Internal Defence (Home Office), No. 67.   † Idem, No. 91.
‡ Militia Marching Book, Vol. XCIX., p. 418.

to Faversham Barracks, 320 men to Ospring Barracks, any remaining above this number to be billeted in Faversham. They were accordingly ordered by General Dundas to march there on the 28th of October.*

The Regiment was inspected at Faversham on the 18th of December by Brigadier-General Coote Manningham, the effective strength being upwards of 1,100 privates. A detachment, consisting of one captain and 95 men, was stationed at Sheerness, and six men at the Coxheath and Wrotham Beacons. The inspecting Officer reported that "the Regiment is a very fine one, and well attended to."

1805.—An Act† was passed on the 10th of April directing that the number of men exceeding the original quota should be allowed to volunteer into the army, one Sergeant and one Corporal being allowed with every 20 men at a bounty of ten guineas; and if four-fifths of the number required from any regiment should volunteer at once no more were to be taken. A circular letter, dated Whitehall, the 15th of April, states that as the number of privates, according to the last return, was 1,030, 281 privates, and 14 corporals, being at the rate of one for every 20 men, would be allowed to enlist into the regular Army.‡

During this month 244 men volunteered into the Army from the companies quartered at Faversham.

In May the Regiment marched from Faversham to Chatham to relieve the Foot Guards; and in June they were stationed at Ashford, in Kent, until October, when they marched to Hull, and occupied the barracks in Lime Street. A detachment was sent to Scarborough.

By a Circular, dated the 12th of July, the number of Subalterns was ordered to be reduced to twelve Lieutenants and eight Ensigns,§ and the number of men to be reduced to the

---

* Militia Pay Lists (3rd West York), 1804.
† 45 Geo. III., c. 31 (see Appendix L).
‡ War Office Militia Letter Book, and Militia (Home Office), No. 38, 1802-1809.
§ Internal Defence (Home Office), No. 91.

original quota of 2,429* for the West Riding, or 809 for the Regiment by volunteering into the regular Army.

The only Route contained in the War Office Militia Marching Book for the year is one dated the 31st of October, addressed to the Officer commanding the Detachment of the 3rd West York Militia on arrival at Gravesend, ordering him to proceed to Hull by the following route to join the Regiment :—†

Monday	4th Nov.	Greenwich
Tuesday	5th ,,	Highgate
Wednesday	6th ,,	Hatfield
Thursday	7th ,,	Stevenage
Friday	8th ,,	Biggleswade
Saturday	9th ,,	St. Neots and Eaton
Sunday	10th ,,	Halt
Monday	11th ,,	Huntingdon and Godmanchester
Tuesday	12th ,,	Stilton and adjacent
Wednesday	13th ,,	Deepings
Thursday	14th ,,	Bourn and Folkingham
Friday	15th ,,	Sleaford
Saturday	16th ,,	Lincoln, with the Bail a Close
Sunday	17th ,,	Halt
Monday	18th ,,	Brigg and Redbourn
Tuesday	19th ,,	Halt
Wednesday	20th ,,	Hull

1806.—In January, 1806, it appears that some of the men of the Regiment had charge of the Beacons in Lincolnshire, and two privates from the detachment at Scarborough were ordered to attend the Beacons at Scamer and Stow, in the vicinity of that town. Extra pay was allowed for this service.

On the 8th of April a detachment of about 100 men was sent to York, returning on the 17th.

On Tuesday the 29th of April the Regiment left Hull for Durham and Darlington, in three divisions, by the subjoined route, the two first divisions going to Durham, and the third to Darlington :—‡

---

* Fixed by 42 Geo. III., c. 90 (see Appendices M and N).
† Militia Marching Book (N. S.), Vol. I., p. 139.   ‡ Idem, p 165.

	1st Division. 4 Companies.	2nd Division. 3 Companies.	3rd Division. 3 Companies.
Tuesday 29th April,	Beverley	—	—
Wednes. 30th ,,	Weighton and Pocklington	Beverley	—
Thursday 1st May ,,	York	Weighton and Pocklington	Beverley
Friday 2nd ,,	Easingwold and Thormanby	York	Weighton and Pocklington
Saturday 3rd ,,	Northallerton	Easingwold and Thormanby	York
Sunday 4th ,,	Halt	Halt	Halt
Monday 5th ,,	Darlington	Northallerton	Easingwold and Thormanby
Tuesday 6th ,,	Durham	Darlington	Northallerton
Wednes. 7th ,,	—	Durham	Darlington

On the 3rd of May the detachment at Scarborough marched to Durham by order of Lieut.-Gen. Vyse, where they arrived on the 6th. On the 7th the first division marched for Newcastle, being followed on the 8th by the remainder from Durham, and the three companies stationed at Darlington—all arriving at their destination on the 9th of May. A detachment, consisting of the two Rifle Companies, was sent to Whitburn and Monkwearmouth, which place they quitted on the 5th of June, and rejoined the Regiment the following day at Newcastle. On the 5th of June a detachment of forty men was sent from head-quarters to Carlisle, arriving there on the 7th.

On the 31st of July the greater portion of the Regiment—nearly 600 men—went to Sunderland, but it does not appear how long they remained there, probably only a day or two, as on the 6th of October the whole Regiment, consisting of 831 men, marched from Newcastle to Sunderland, where they arrived the following day. The detachment at Carlisle left there on the 11th, and joined the Regiment at Sunderland on the 14th of same month.* As the number of men still exceeded the original quota, an Act was passed in July to suspend the ballot for two years, except for supplying vacancies.†

---

* Militia Pay Lists (3rd West York), 1806.
† 46 Geo. III., c. 91 (see Appendices M and N).

Major-General **Cockburn** inspected the Regiment **on the** 18th of October, 762 **rank and file being** present under **arms.** The Inspecting Officer states, "The Regiment is in very good order. At the Inspection they performed the eighteen Manœuvres with the greatest precision"; he also said that the Regiment "is very fit for service and in high order."

1807.—The Regiment was again inspected by the same officer on the 30th of April, 728 privates being present under arms.

On the 13th of August an Act* was passed to allow the Militia to volunteer into the regular Army, **provided the** establishment was not thereby reduced below three-fifths. **If five-sixths of the** number allowed to volunteer **was completed within thirty days, no** more were to be taken. **The bounty offered was ten guineas for seven** years, or fourteen **guineas for** unlimited service. The strength of the Regiment then being 823 **rank and file, the quota allowed** to volunteer was 313—or 261, (being five-sixths) **if given within thirty** days—leaving 510 or three-fifths of the establishment. **A period of three** days' volunteering **was directed** to be held every three months until the quota was completed. **The following is** the conclusion of a Circular on the subject sent **to the** Lord-Lieutenant, and dated Whitehall, the **17th of August :—** †

"**His** Majesty, **entirely** relying on **your zeal and** attachment to His Service, has commanded me to **recommend the** execution **of this** important Law to your best **exertions, and to express his** confident Persuasion that from the Spirit **and Enterprise** of His **Militia** Soldiers, seconded by the encouraging countenance of the Officers of that important Branch **of the** public Force, His Regular and disposable **Army** will receive an immediate Augmentation equal to the pressing Exigencies of the Public Service **and** to the Expectation **of the** Legislature.

"I have, &c.,
"Hawkesbury."

---

* 47 Geo. III., c. 57 (see Appendix **L**).
† War Office Militia Letter Book, Vol. **I.**, pp. 337-40.

THIRD WEST YORK LIGHT INFANTRY.

The Militia was at the same time increased by an Act*
passed on the 14th of August, by the addition of three-fourths
of the original quota, or 1,822 for the West Riding, or 607 to
the Regiment. Under this Act, from the 1st of September, 1807,
to the 18th of March, 1808, 26,085 men were enrolled in England and Wales, only 3,129 being principals, and 22,956 substitutes. In the West Riding the proportion was 73 principals and 1,274 substitutes, or 1,347 men. The amount
paid as bounty for substitutes varied from £45 in Monmouth
to £10 in the Isle of Wight. In Yorkshire the amount varied
in each Riding; being £30 7s. in the East Riding, £29 8s. in
the West Riding, and £40 in the North Riding.†

The Regiment left Sunderland for Liverpool in October by the
subjoined route, in three divisions:—‡

		1st Division. 4 Companies.	2nd Division. 3 Companies.	3rd Division. 3 Companies.
Monday	12th Oct.,	Durham	———	———
Tuesday	13th „	Auckland	Durham	———
Wednes.	14th „	Barnard Castle and Bowes	Auckland	Durham
Thursday	15th „	Kirkby Stephen	Barnard Castle and Bowes	Auckland
Friday	16th „	Sedbergh and adjacent	Kirkby Stephen	Barnard Castle and Bowes
Saturday	17th „	Kirkby Lonsdale	Sedbergh and adjacent	Kirkby Stephen
Sunday	18th „	Halt	Halt	Halt
Monday	19th „	Lancaster	Kirkby Lonsdale	Sedbergh and adjacent
Tuesday	20th „	Garstang and adjacent	Lancaster	Kirkby Lonsdale
Wednes.	21st „	Preston	Garstang and adjacent	Lancaster
Thursday	22nd „	Ormskirk	Preston	Garstang and adjacent
Friday	23rd „	Liverpool	Ormskirk	Preston
Saturday	24th „	———	Liverpool	Ormskirk
Sunday	25th „	———	———	Halt
Monday	26th „	———	———	Liverpool

* 47 Geo. III., c. 71 (see Appendix M).
† Commons' Journals, Vol. LXIII., pp. 613-14.
‡ Militia Marching Book (N. S.), Vol. I., p. 257.

Orders were received from the War Office, dated the 20th of October, directing that the newly-balloted men were to march from Doncaster to join the head-quarters of the Regiment at Liverpool or elsewhere.* On the 29th of October a detachment of 134 men was sent to Chester, where they arrived the following day.

The Lord-Lieutenant, in a letter dated the 11th of November, submits the following establishment proposed by him for the increased strength of the regiments, and explains that he considered it better to permit the trifling disparity of numbers in the three regiments than to disturb the old distribution of the Riding, and gives the establishment of the regiments as follows :— †

	Old Establishment.	New Establishment.	Total.
1st West York	810	618	1,428
2nd West York	810	606	1,416
3rd West York	809	598	1,407
	2,429	1,822	4,251

The regiments, however, were always much below this establishment, owing to the number of Volunteers they had given under the first-named Act. Colonel Cooke therefore, on the 28th of November, wrote to the Secretary of State, proposing that the establishment of the Regiment should be 12 companies, containing 56 sergeants, 56 corporals, 27 drummers, and 1,135 privates.‡ In reply, a letter dated Whitehall, the 2nd of December, directed him to submit it for approval through the Lord-Lieutenant, which having been done, on the 8th of December, His Majesty's approval of it was notified on the following day.

Under the recent ballot, 589 men were added to the Regiment.

---

* Militia Marching Book (N. S.), Vol. I., p. 266.
† Internal Defence (Home Office), No. 123.
‡ Idem.

THIRD WEST YORK LIGHT INFANTRY. 101

Soon after arriving at Liverpool, four companies were sent to Chester, where they remained until April the following year, when they returned to Liverpool. In this year 753 men volunteered into the Army.

1808.—On the 21st of March the Lord-Lieutenant appointed a second Lieut.-Colonel and a second Major. These appointments were approved by the King, although in excess of the Establishment, as the rank and file numbered over 1,100.

On the 7th of May three companies returned from Liverpool to Chester, one of which went back to Liverpool in September.

On the 30th of May 190 men were sent from Liverpool to Manchester, where they arrived on the 1st of June, and on the 12th returned to Liverpool. The Regiment was inspected at Liverpool on the 15th of September, by Major-General Champagne.

Orders were received, dated the 27th and 31st of October, directing the eight companies at Liverpool to proceed in three divisions to Cambridge, Huntingdon, Godmanchester, and Stilton, the two companies at Chester also proceeding to Stilton.*

		1st Division. 4 Companies	2nd Division. 3 Companies.	3rd Division, 1 Company.	4th, or Chester Division. 2 Companies.
T	3rd Nov.	Wigan			
F	4th ,,	Bolton	Wigan		
S	5th ,,	Manchester	Bolton	Wigan	
S	6th ,,	Halt	Halt	Halt	
M	7th ,,	Macclesfield	Manchester	Bolton	
T	8th ,,	Leek	Macclesfield	Manchester	
W	9th ,,	Ashbourne	Leek	Macclesfield	
T	10th ,,	Derby	Ashbourne	Leek	Nampwich
F	11th ,,	Loughborough	Derby	Ashbourne	Newcastle-under-Lyne
S	12th ,,	Leicester	Loughborough	Derby	Uttoxeter
S	13th ,,	Halt	Halt	Halt	Halt
M	14th ,,	Uppingham	Leicester	Ashby-de-la-Zouch	Burton
T	15th ,,	Stilton and adjacent	Uppingham	Leicester	Ashby-de-la-Zouch

* Militia Marching Book (N. S.), Vol. I., pp. 412, 415, 417.

	1st Division. 4 Companies.	2nd Division. 3 Companies.	3rd Division. 1 Company.	4th, or Chester Division. 2 Companies.
W 16th Nov.	Huntingdon and Godmanchester	Stilton and adjacent	Uppingham	Leicester
T 17th ,,	Cambridge	Huntingdon and Godmanchester	Stilton and adjacent	Uppingham
F 18th ,,	———	———	———	Stilton and adjacent

The first division, of 334 men, and the third division, of 238 men, remained at Stilton.

The second division, of 251 men, arrived at Uppingham on the 16th of November, and on the following day went to Peterborough.

A few days later the Regiment proceeded to Norman Cross Barracks, where they remained until May, 1809. Two companies were sent to Peterborough, and were joined by two others in March the following year; detachments being stationed at Oundle and Sawtry. The arms of the Regiment then consisted of fifty-two pikes, 132 rifles, and 1,065 muskets.

The Regiment supplied the full quota* to the Regular Army, viz., 313, or 264 for limited and 49 for unlimited service, all of whom volunteered previous to the 1st of June.

1809.—An Act† was passed on the 13th of March, directing that where the number of men exceeded three-fifths of the present establishment (or less than two-fifths of the establishment in August, 1807,) two-fifths were to be allowed to enlist.

A Circular, dated Whitehall, the 23rd of March, states that the quota of Volunteers required from the Regiment for the Army is 340, or 283 provided they volunteer within thirty days. Of this number 201 volunteered, viz., 32 for unlimited service, and 169 for seven years.

A General Order, dated Horse Guards, 28th March, directs that Officers of Fusilier and Light Infantry Regiments, and of flank companies, are to wear wings in addition to epaulets.

The Regiment was inspected, at Norman Cross, on the 10th of

---

* Under the 47 Geo. III., c. 57 (see Appendix L).
† 49 Geo. III., c. 4 (see Appendix L).

May, by Major-General Williams, 567 privates being present under arms.

The **Standing Orders of** the Regiment were issued by Colonel Bryan Cooke, **from** Norman Cross Barracks, **in May,** 1809; the following **is a** copy of the Introduction:—

"The utility of **a** Compilation of STANDING ORDERS, forming a permanent and invariable system for the interior economy and guidance **of a** Regiment, is universally admitted, **and cannot be** better evinced, than by its having been **uniformly adopted by** those Regiments esteemed **the** best **in His Majesty's Service.** Indeed, a fixed plan of **discipline, and a settled rule of conduct,** by which every man may **know to a certainty what his duty is, and what may be expected from him, seems, if** not indispensably necessary, **at least to be highly** desirable, where persons **are** placed in a situation **so** totally different from modes of **common life, and in which the** observation **of form,** and of the **most** minute circumstances, even **of** ceremony, is **so** essentially **requisite, as not to** be departed from without danger. **With this view,** Colonel **Bryan Cooke has** issued **the** following **Orders, which are to** be at all times strictly complied **with and adhered to. The** Colonel **cannot omit this opportunity of expressing to the Regiment,** that, **next to the great object to which he is bound by his duty, as well as inclination (viz., that of establishing and maintaining the most perfect discipline in the Regiment), there is nothing he has more at heart than the interest of each individual of it. He** assures **the men under his command, that the** strictest **justice** shall **on every occasion be done to them; and he** promises **them** every **attention to their comfort and ease, as far as is** consistent **with his duty and their situation. The young, the ignorant, and** even **those in the first stages of swerving from their duty,** shall ever be objects **of lenity and advice, and every other means will be** adopted **to save a young** man **from the disgrace of** Public **Punishment. It is his wish, that** the System of **the Regiment may be conducted** with **as little severity or** hardness **as possible; yet he cannot** avoid holding **out the certainty of the severest Punishments to the dishonest and incorrigible, which,** though **it** cannot **reclaim them, may prove** examples of terror to deter others.

"Principles of honour, and a sense of their duty, will, he feels confident, lead the Officers to assist him in his endeavours to form the Regiment, and keep it on the best principles of discipline and subordination; and he trusts that they will not only themselves avoid deviating, in the smallest degree, from the following Regulations, but that they will be particularly careful not to permit any deviation from them in others. If Officers go through their business in a careless manner, and are inattentive to their duty, the same will instantly pervade every other part of the Regiment: its discipline will, in spite of all efforts of the Commanding Officer, become relaxed—confusion and discredit must be the inevitable consequences. Punishments, then, must wear the appearance of injustice, when a man can plead the example of his Superiors in justification of his own misbehaviour.

"On the other hand, the conduct of the Officers, in the most ready obedience to all Orders, in the most unremitting attention to their duty, will not only ensure the same exactness and regularity from the Non-commissioned Officers and private Men, and deprive them of every possibility of excuse; but will also, to a certainty, have the effect of impressing them with an esteem, affection, and confidence, from whence the most beneficial effects must flow."

The following is a list of the Necessaries with which every man had to be provided:—

3 Shirts	1 Clothes Brush
3 pairs of Worsted or Yarn Socks	3 Shoe Brushes
2 pairs of Shoes	Black-ball
2 pairs of Breeches	2 Combs
1 pair of Black Cloth Gaiters	1 Sponge
1 pair of Worsted or Yarn Mitts, during the Winter	1 Turnscrew and Worm
	1 Brush and Picker
1 pair of Russia Linen Trousers	1 Razor, and
1 Black Stock and Clasp	Articles for Cleaning his Arms and Accoutrements
1 Forage Cap	

At the end of May the Head-quarters, with four companies, was at Stowmarket, two at Needham, four at Thetford, and two at Ixworth. On the 10th of June the whole Regiment went to Woodbridge Barracks, with detachments at Aldborough and

Colonel Bryan Cooke, M.P.
1803.–1812.
As Lieutenant in the Royal Horse Guards (Blues)
1775.–1785.

Hollesley Bay. Orders dated the 16th of June and the 13th of July directed that the recruits were to join the Regiment at Woodbridge, from time to time, as the Colonel should judge expedient.*

In May † the Militia was ordered to be increased by one-half the original quota, the men to be raised by beat of drum, and after a fixed date by ballot, a fine of £40 being inflicted on every parish for every man deficient. This raised the establishment again to 1,135 privates. From May, 1809, when the Act was passed, to the 24th of October, 1813, 46,030 were raised by beat of drum, viz., 43,611 men and 2,419 boys; the following being the number raised for the Regiment—1809, May to December, 59; 1810, 175; 1811, 12; 1812, 57, and 13 boys; 1813, 38.‡

The Regiment was inspected on the 9th of October, and on the 10th the Head-quarters, with ten companies, was established at Ipswich, with two companies at Harwich, to which latter place another company was sent in November. From July to December detachments were stationed at Aldborough and Hollesley Bay, and small parties at Shotly Gate and on the east bank of the Deben.

Previous to the year 1809 the disembodied Militia received their pay and allowances from the Receiver-General of the Land Tax for each County, and the embodied Regiments received their pay from the Secretary-at-War, who, from this time, issued the pay for the whole force.§

1810.—On the 10th of March the whole Regiment was quartered at Harwich Barracks; on the 10th of April, the head-quarters were at Chelmsford, with two companies at Harwich; on the 25th April, the head-quarters and ten companies were at Colchester, two remaining at Harwich; in May the head-quarters were moved to the latter place.

In consequence of riots and disturbances being apprehended, a large body of troops was ordered to London and its vicinity. On the 10th of April the Regiment was sent from Harwich to Chelmsford, and was ordered to be held in readiness to proceed

---

* Militia Marching Book (N. S.), Vol. II., pp. 35, 57.
† 49 Geo. III., c. 53 (see Appendices M and O).
‡ Commons' Journals, Vol. LXIX., pp. 636-7.
§ Clode's Military Forces of the Crown, Vol. I., p. 292.

to London if required. The Cambridge Militia was quartered at Hampstead and Highgate, the Cornwall Militia in Kentish Town, the Westmoreland at Hackney, and the North York at the Mint, Tower Hill. The troops returned to their quarters between the 21st and the 25th of April.*

On the 30th of April, the Regiment was inspected at Harwich Barracks by Major-General Robinson, 671 privates being present under arms. The Inspecting Officer states in his report that, "as a body of men, they may be considered as very superior in point of size and make;—are of a good appearance and a serviceable age;—none too old, or too young."

A Warrant, dated the 10th of June, 1810, was issued for accoutrements for fifty-three sergeants, twenty-three drummers, and 1,050 rank and file, including swords for sergeants and drummers, a pair of new Colours, and twelve drums.

It appears from the Regimental Orders of the 29th of June, that there was a parade for company drill every Sunday morning at seven o'clock; the Light Infantry and Rifle companies were drilled separately. Any soldier found more than a mile from barracks without a pass or working ticket was punished with a month's drill.

Orders were received, dated the 9th of July, for one captain, four subalterns, nine sergeants, five drummers, and twenty rank and file, to go from Harwich to Doncaster, to receive the newly balloted men, and remain there until further orders.†

In compliance with a General Order, dated the 23rd of August, a detachment of fifty rank and file marched, on the 25th, at six o'clock, for Little Holland, and another of 100 rank and file proceeded at the same time to Walton-on-the-Naze, as working parties, to assist the Royal Engineers, where they were encamped, and remained until they were withdrawn on the 1st of November.

In Regimental Orders of the 7th of October, one of the privates is ordered to wear his jacket turned until further orders —the sign of a bad character.

---

* Commander-in-Chief (Home Office), No. 5.
† Militia Marching Book (N. S.), Vol. II., p. 130.

On the 13th of October the Officers were ordered to wear powder on their hair.

On Tuesday, the 13th of November, the Regiment marched to Colchester, the Rifle companies acting as front and rear guard. The Regiment was inspected by Major-General Sir J. C. Sherbrooke, K.C.B., on the 20th of November, 736 privates being present under arms.

1811.— In Regimental Orders, dated the 6th of March, the officers of the Rifle company are directed always to wear pantaloons of patent stocking web of the same colour as their jackets, the other officers to wear Navy-blue pantaloons of the same material, or white cloth or cassamere; the mounted officers might wear blue should they prefer it.

A detachment was ordered to march to Clackton on the 16th of March, as a working party to assist the Royal Engineers. On the 17th of April a party was ordered to be sent from Colchester to Doncaster to bring the newly-balloted men to head-quarters.*

On the 28th of March the Paymaster sent a subscription of nearly £40 from the Officers and men of the Regiment for the relief of English prisoners in France.

In April, 1811, an Act † was passed, by which the Militia was again reduced to the original quota by volunteering into the Army, and was called upon to furnish 6,856 men to the Regular Army annually, viz., 5,714 from England and Wales, and 1,142 from Scotland, to be replaced by voluntary enlistment, the number in any one county not to exceed one-seventh of the quota, any deficiency in the establishment so caused to be supplied by voluntary enlistment.

On the 1st of May volunteering was commenced for the Army for eight days, and from the 23rd of May to the 30th of May the men were permitted to volunteer into any regiment of the Line except the 60th, 98th, 99th, 100th, and 101st Regiments; the volunteers were not to be above thirty-five years of

---

* Militia Marching Book (N. S.), Vol. II., p. 171.
† 51 Geo. III., c. 20 (see Appendices L, M and N).

age, or under five feet four inches in height. Sergeants and corporals, in the proportion of one of each rank for every twenty men, were received in the Line according to their rank, but were necessarily attested as privates; the men received a bounty of ten guineas on enlisting for limited, or fourteen for unlimited service; and they took their clothing for the current year with them, except the great coats. The volunteers were sent to Stowmarket.

On the 8th of May two men of the Regiment were sentenced by a General Court-Martial to serve in the Royal African Corps. At this period men were frequently condemned to serve abroad, in the Army, for desertion.

On the 23rd of May the Regiment was inspected, 646 privates being present under arms. Major-General Payne reported that the Regiment had a "very excellent appearance on the day of Inspection," and "performed their movements in the Field with great Precision and steadiness." "The Regiment consists of young stout men, equal to any service."

On the 29th of June a detachment marched, at four o'clock, for Holland Marsh, and another detachment at the same time for Walton-on-the-Naze; a third detachment marched for Harwich Barracks on the 12th of July, all as working parties to assist the Royal Engineers at the above-named places.

The Regimental Orders of the 12th of July state that the Commanding Officer having been informed that several clubs exist in the Regiment, in which, amongst other things, non-commissioned officers are in the habit of mixing with the privates, abolishes all such clubs and societies, and strictly forbids the formation or continuance of anything of the kind without the permission of the Colonel or Lieutenant-Colonel.

Volunteering into the Line commenced on the 16th of July, and closed on the 19th, at a reduced bounty of ten guineas for unlimited, and six guineas for seven years. It appears to have been the custom to suspend the evening parades during the periods of volunteering, and that discipline was relaxed to give the men "an opportunity of spending their Bounties."

Major-General Montgomery inspected the Regiment on the 23rd of July, on Lexdon Heath.

A Circular was issued from the Horse Guards, dated the 5th of July, 1811, offering a bounty of two guineas to every non-commissioned officer and private who should volunteer for Ireland under the Interchange Act. The Circular concluded thus:—

" His Royal Highness has therefore commanded me to express his entire reliance that the confidence which he has thus reposed in the Energy and Patriotism of the Militia will not be found to have been in any Degree misplaced, and that they will most readily avail themselves of this Opportunity of extending the Field on which their Services are henceforth to be displayed, and of rendering themselves to the United Kingdom, what they have so long been to Great Britain, a never-failing Resource on every Occasion of Difficulty and Danger."

By a War Office Circular, dated July, additional pay was granted to Lieut.-Colonels, Majors, and Captains, who extended their service to any part of the United Kingdom. No increase was, however, allowed to Lieutenants or Surgeons, and non-commissioned Officers of Militia Regiments in Great Britain, upon being transferred to Ireland, but they were placed upon the Irish Establishment, and paid in Irish currency, the same as Regiments of the Line.

The Interchange Act was passed in July * to enable the English Militia to serve in Ireland, and the Irish Militia in England, on their volunteering to do so, each man receiving a Bounty of two guineas. Not more than one-fourth of the former, or one-third of the latter was to serve at the same time. No regiment was to serve for a longer period than two years in succession, or to serve again until a period of six years (from the last date of serving) for the former, and four years for the latter, except in case of invasion. In December, 1813, these regulations were abolished,† the Militia being allowed to volunteer to serve anywhere in the United Kingdom, without limit as to time.

Queues were ordered to be dispensed with, and the men's hair cropped, by a General Order dated the 29th of July; but

---

* 51 Geo. III., c. 118, 1st July, 1811.
† By the 54 Geo. III., c. 10.

by a subsequent Circular, dated the 5th of August, Colonels of Militia were authorised to retain the queues, or cut the hair short like the Regular Army.

On the 3rd of August the Colonel ordered that the use of Hair Powder by the officers should be discontined until further orders.

The Regiment marched in two divisions for Chatham, Brompton, and Gillingham;* the first division on Monday, the 5th of August, with the band and staff sergeants and six companies; the remaining six companies, with the sick, started on Tuesday.

			1st Division.	2nd Division.
Monday	5th	Aug.	Malden and Heybridge	
Tuesday	6th	„	Billericay Barracks and Town	Malden
Wednesday	7th	„	Gravesend and Northfleet	Billericay
Thursday	8th	„	Chatham	Gravesend
Friday	9th	„		Chatham

A detachment of the Regiment was stationed in the barracks, the remainder being in quarters at Brompton and Gillingham. In accordance with a Route received, 650 non-commissioned officers and rank and file were ordered to march in two divisions for Sheerness, the remainder of the Regiment remaining at Chatham Barracks. The first division, of five companies, marched on Wednesday, the 14th of August, and the second, consisting of four companies, on the following day, at 4 a.m., three companies remaining at Chatham.

The Regiment was authorised to bear the White Rose of York, as a Badge by the following Letter, received on the 30th of August:—

"HORSE GUARDS, 26th *August*, 1811.

"Sir,

"I have the honour to acquaint you, by direction of the Commander-in-Chief, that His Royal Highness, the Prince Regent, in the Name and on behalf of His Majesty, has been pleased to approve of the White Rose being worn as a Badge by the 3rd West York Regiment of Militia.

"I am to request that you will cause this Letter to be entered

---

* Militia Marching Book (N. S.), Vol. II., p. 223.

in the General Order Book of the Regiment, in order that it may be referred to when occasion may require.

"HARRY CALVERT, Adjutant-General.
"COLONEL COOKE, or Officer Commanding
3rd West York Militia."

By a General Order, dated the 8th of September, assistant-surgeons who held subaltern's commissions were directed to do duty in the former capacity only.

A Circular, dated Whitehall, the 17th of September, was sent to the Lord-Lieutenant stating that an Act* having been passed during the last Session to reduce the Militia to the original quota, that from and after the 24th of September, the establishment was to be reduced by two companies.† The two junior companies, Captain M'Adams' and Captain Wrathers', were accordingly drafted into the other ten companies, the establishment being reduced to 809, as directed by War Office Circular, dated the 12th of October.

The Second Half-yearly Inspection took place at Sheerness, on the 14th of October, only 373 privates being present under arms. The Inspecting Officer, Major-General Hope, reported that "The men of the Regiment are stout and able for any duty; they appear older in general than most Militia Regiments, but serviceable in every respect." His Royal Highness, the Duke of Clarence, also inspected the Regiment on the 7th of November, expressed his approbation of their appearance, and desired all men under punishment to be liberated and forgiven.

A private was tried by Regimental Court-Martial on the 3rd of December, for disrespectful and insolent behaviour to Lieutenant Midgley, in the execution of his duty on the Dock Guard, on the night of the 2nd inst. He was sentenced to 100 lashes, all of which were inflicted. This was considered at that time a very mild punishment.‡

---

* 51 Geo. III., c. 20 (see Appendices M and N).
† War Office Militia Letter Book.
‡ During the latter part of the last century, and as late as the year 1812, 500 or 1,000 lashes were often inflicted for the most trivial offences. At Jersey, in 1808, several men who had attempted to desert were sentenced to 1,000 lashes each. The number five was slowly counted between each

Orders were received from the Horse Guards, dated the 21st of November, for the Regiment to be held in readiness to proceed to Ireland. The Regiment was relieved by the Sussex Militia, and embarked at Sheerness, at eight o'clock on the 28th December, on board the following transports:—

	Sergeants.	Corporals.	Drummers.	Privates.	Women and Children.	Total.
The *Dawson*, No. 399*	14	12	9	165	51	251
The *Royal Brittain*, No. 344	7	7	5	160	26	205
The *Nerovah*, No. 99	7	7	4	134	23	175
The *Peace*, No. 144	7	6	4	133	21	171
Total ...	35	32	22	592	121	802

lash; the punishment consequently occupied three hours and thirty minutes.

In 1812 a General Order limited the number of lashes which could be inflicted by a Regimental Court-Martial to 300, and after the year 1832 more than 500 or 600 were seldom inflicted. So severe was the flogging, that men were often disabled for life, and sometimes died under the infliction. The following description will enable the reader to form some idea of the brutality of the old flogging with the cat-o'-nine-tails:—

"Henley, for desertion, received 200 lashes only. Acute inflammation followed, and the back sloughed. When the wounds were cleaned, and the sloughed integuments removed, the backbone and part of the shoulder-bone were laid bare. Another man was taken down, at the recommendation of the medical officer, after he had received 229 lashes, and sent to the hospital, where he died in eight days, his back having mortified."

A popular author (Mr. Southey, "Esprielli's Letter," 1807) thus describes the principal military punishments of this country:—"The martial laws of England are the most barbarous which, at this day, exist in Europe. The offender is sometimes sentenced to 1,000 lashes. A surgeon stands by to feel his pulse during the execution, and determines how long the flogging can be continued without killing him. When human nature can stand no more, he is remanded to the prison (hospital), his wound—for from the shoulders to the loins it leaves him one wound—is dressed, and, as soon as it is sufficiently healed to be opened in the same manner, he is brought out to undergo the remainder of his sentence."†

---

* With the Head-quarters Grenadiers and Rifle Companies, Staff, Band, and Sick.

† The Military Miscellany, by **Henry Marshall** (1846), pp. 115-317. This work gives an interesting account of the Recruiting of the Army, and Military Punishment.

The Regiment was under the command of Lieutenant-Colonel W. B. Cooke, and eight captains, eleven subalterns, and four staff officers, embarked at the same time. Major Benson, the surgeon, and four subalterns, remained at Chatham in charge of the men who did not extend their services to Ireland—viz., 5 sergeants, 5 corporals, 2 drummers, and 111 privates, in addition to one captain and one subaltern, recruiting at Doncaster, Leeds, and Sheffield. The detachment at Chatham was sent to Sheerness, and in January, 1812, to Dover, from which place they were sent to Bristol, to join the Battalion of Detachments of Militia stationed there.*

This "Battalion of Detachments of Militia" was formed at the end of September, 1811, and was composed of the men who declined to extend their services in those regiments which had volunteered for Ireland. The Battalion was commanded by Colonel the Marquis of Salisbury, and was formed of detachments from the following regiments, which are placed in the order they appear in the Pay Lists for December in 1811, 1812, and 1813, and in September, 1814, in which month the battalion was broken up.†

Year. 1811.	Year. 1812.	Year 1813.	Year. 1814.
East Norfolk	East Norfolk	Cumberland	Cumberland
Warwick	Warwick	Lancashire	2nd Lancashire
Leicester	Leicester	East Middlesex	3rd Lancashire
West Middlesex	West Middlesex	Berks	Carmarthen
Westminster	Westminster	Carmarthen	2nd Somerset
Dumfries	Dumfries	Monmouth	Berks
North Hants	North Hants	Carnarvon	Cheshire
Hertford	Hertford	South Lincoln	South Lincoln
Northampton	Northampton	North Gloucester	North Lincoln
Montgomery	Montgomery	Bucks	Monmouth
East Kent	East Kent	Leicester	North York
Nottingham	Nottingham	Northampton	Bucks
Westmoreland	Westmoreland	Northumberland	Cambridge
Carnarvon	Carnarvon	Cambridge	Shropshire

* Militia Marching Book (N. S.), Vol. II., p. 247.
† See Militia Pay Lists of Battalion of **Detachments of Militia** in the Public Record Office.

Year. 1811.	Year. 1812.	Year. 1813.	Year. 1814.
Northumberland	Northumberland	Shropshire	Edinburgh
2nd Surrey	2nd Surrey	Edinburgh	East Essex
……	Merioneth	East Norfolk	1st Somerset
……	Cornwall	East Essex	Bedford
……	3rd West York	Oxford	Oxford
……	……	Somerset	West Essex
……	……	East Kent	Derby
……	……	West Essex	Wilts
……	……	West Suffolk	Forfar
……	……	3rd West York	2nd West York
……	……	……	Renfrew
……	……	……	East Middlesex
Total, Dec. 24th, 1811: 16 Detachments.	Total, Dec. 24th, 1812: 19 Detachments.	Total, Dec. 24th, 1813: 24 Detachments.	Total, Sept. 24th, 1814: 26 Detachments.

The strength of the Battalion on the dates mentioned in each year was:—

	1811.	1812.	1813.	1814.
Sergeants	15	25	15	26
Corporals	17	20	10	32
Drummers	6	8	6	12
Privates …	301	399	283	484
Total …	339	452	314	554

In December, 1811, the Battalion was stationed at Bristol (at which place the detachment of the 3rd West York received orders to join them from Dover, where they had been sent on the 1st of January, 1812); they left Bristol on Saturday, the 6th of June, 1812, for Sheerness, arriving there on Friday, the 19th of June;* from January to March, 1813, they were stationed at Dover; and from April, 1813, to September, 1814, at Sheerness.

The officers of the Regiment with the detachment, were: Major Benson, Captain Dacre, Lieutenants Straubenzie, Wright-

---

* Militia Marching Book (N. S.), Vol. II., p. 288.

son, Turton, Ensigns Leaf, Hardy, and Ensign and Surgeon Hardy. Lieutenant Mather joined in April, and Captain Courtney in September. The following was the number of the officers with the detachment on the 24th of December in 1812, 1813, and June, 1814, in which month the detachment left the Battalion to proceed to Doncaster, in order to be disembodied with the rest of the Regiment.

	Majors.	Captains.	Lieuts.	Ensigns.	Surgeons.	Total.
1812	1	1	4	2	1	9
1813	—	1	5	—	1	7
1814	1	1	5	—	1	8

The volunteers into the Regular Army in this year* numbered 206—viz., 163 for limited, or seven years' service, and 43 for unlimited, being 14 short of the quota—viz., 220.

1812.—The transports arrived at Monkstown on the 14th of January, having experienced very bad weather. During the night of the 7th, the *Nerovah* parted company with the other vessels when off the Isle of Wight, and was not again seen during the passage. The men landed on the 15th, and proceeded to Cork, where the baggage had been sent on the previous evening, in charge of a party from each ship.

An Order, dated War Office, the 10th of March, was sent to the Officer Commanding the detachment at Doncaster, to cause the recruits to march to Liverpool, and embark for Dublin.†

Prizes were given for good shooting. On the 19th of April it was announced in Regimental Orders that "the best shot of each Company during the season would receive a Prize of a shirt or a pair of shoes."

While the Regiment was stationed in Ireland, the price of provisions being very high, the extra expense incurred for such articles as meat, potatoes, bread, and oatmeal, was allowed to be charged, provided they were within certain limits, which were periodically fixed according to the state of the markets. The

---

* Under the 51 Geo. III., c. 20 (see Appendix L).
† Militia Marching Book (N. S.), Vol. II., p. 255.

limits fixed when the Regiment first landed in Ireland, and again shortly before they left, are here given :—

	Meat per Pound.	Potatoes per Stone.	Bread per Pound.	Oatmeal per Pound.
August, 1813	7½	7	3½	4
„ 1814	7½	6	2¾	3

Major-General Graham inspected the Regiment on the 1st of May, 739 effective privates being present.

Volunteering into the Line and Foot Guards (any Regiment except the 60th) was ordered to take place on the 4th and 5th of May; and, if the quota was not then completed, a further period of seven days was allowed. Should the quota be then incomplete, the volunteering was to re-commence on Thursday, the 4th of June, to continue for three days, and be repeated for a like period of three days, until the prescribed number be furnished. This method was universally adopted.

The bounty of fourteen, and ten guineas, for men who enlisted for unlimited and limited service respectively, was paid, one-half on attesting, and the remainder on joining the Recruiting Depôt or Regiment. In the event of the full quota not being obtained, recruits who subsequently joined were allowed to be taken at a reduced bounty of ten, and six guineas, according as they enlisted either for limited or unlimited service. The men took with them their clothing, with the exception of great-coats and regimental appointments. Men who volunteered into the 95th Regiment, or other Rifle Corps, were to leave their clothing for the year behind, provided they had other clothes to proceed in.

In May the Regiment received orders to proceed to Fermoy, which was afterwards changed to Middleton, where they marched on the 8th, but only remained two days, returning to Cork on the 13th, where the sick and the married had remained.

One or two of the companies were always held in readiness to turn out at a moment's notice; and on the 25th of May the senior subaltern and a portion of the piquet were ordered to be in readiness to attend the High Constable.

The Commander of the Forces inspected the Regiment on the 18th of August, and expressed his entire approval of their appearance. Major-General Samuel Graham made the usual half-yearly inspection on the 3rd of October, 517 privates being present under arms.

In this month five officers and one sergeant proceeded to England from Cork to vote at the Parliamentary Election.

The fourth period of volunteering into the Regular Army commenced on the 24th of December, and continued during the two following days, the men being permitted to join any Regiment of the Foot Guards or Line, with the exception of the 60th, 98th, 99th, 100th, and 101st. The men who were serving in the Regiment on the 11th of April, 1811 (the date of the Act), were allowed a bounty of fourteen guineas for unlimited, and ten guineas for limited service. All those who joined after that date received either ten or six guineas, according to whether they enlisted for unlimited or limited service. In this year 89 men volunteered,* or 19 short of the required number of 108. Of those, 71 volunteered for limited, and 18 for unlimited service.

1813.—On the 13th of February three companies were sent to Spike Island, and one to Cove Barracks. On the 24th of February the Staff and Head-quarters moved to Cove Barracks, the Light Company to Carlisle Fort, and the Grenadiers to Camden Fort. Four companies, with the recruits and sick, remained at Cork. A detachment was also stationed at Hawlbowling.

On the 23rd of February an Order was sent from the War Office to the Officer Commanding the York district, directing the recruits of the Regiment to proceed from Doncaster to Bristol, and embark for Cork, to join their Regiment.† The garrison at Cork at this time consisted only of the Regiment and four men of the Royal Artillery.

The Regiment was inspected on the 17th of May, by Major-General Graham.

On the Regiment leaving Cork Major-General Graham, in

---

* Under the 51 Geo. III., c. 20 (see Appendix L).
† Militia Marching Book (N. S.), Vol. II., p. 312.

Garrison Orders, expressed in very flattering terms his approbation of the conduct of the officers and men during the thirteen months they were under his command.

Brigade Order.

"COVE, 29*th May*, 1813.

"Major-General Graham begs to express his approbation of the appearance under arms made this day by the 3rd West York at all the Ports in the Harbour, and observes with much satisfaction a continuance of that attention in all ranks to the duties required by them. He regrets that the Service at present required of the Corps prevents his witnessing their performance of Field Exercises and manœuvering in a body, but directs that no opportunities to practice such may be omitted in the detachments of the different stations where there is ground to allow it to be done; and that they will continue the Ball firing, at which they seem at present to be so expert. The Major-General begs that Major Dacre will accept his thanks as Commanding Officer, and offer the same to the Captains and Officers commanding companies, for the attention they have bestowed on their respective companies, which is shown by the smallness of the debts, and the ample supply and good quality of the necessaries now worn by the soldiers."

Volunteering into the Regular Army commenced on the 13th of July and two following days; those for the Foot Guards were not to be above 35 years of age, or under five feet seven inches in height, or five feet four inches for the Line. For the Royal Waggon Train, Volunteers had to be at least 18 years of age, and from five feet two to five feet four inches in height, the bounty being eleven guineas for unlimited, and seven guineas for limited service.

There were very few desertions at this period, especially in Ireland, the number being in 1808, 15; 1809, 9; 1810, 13; 1811, 5; 1812, 1; 1813, 3; and 1814, 0.

In May, 1813, a private was tried by Regimental Court-Martial for absenting himself from his guard without leave, and being drunk on duty, for which he was sentenced to receive 200 lashes, of which number 197 were inflicted. The discipline of the Regiment appears to have been remarkably good, and this is almost the only record of a severe punishment during the many years they remained embodied.

The rank of Colour-Sergeant was first created in this year by a General Order, dated Horse Guards, the 6th of July.

In July an Act* was passed, directing the Militia to be increased by one-half the original quota, to be raised by beat of drum; one-seventh of the establishment being allowed to volunteer into the Army.

A Circular, dated the 1st of August, 1813, was addressed to the Commandants of Regiments of Local Militia, ordering them to employ their permanent staff in recruiting for the Regular Militia. No man was to be received under five feet four inches, or above 32 years of age, but growing lads between seventeen and nineteen might be accepted, provided they were not less than five feet two inches in height. Each recruit was paid a bounty of ten guineas, and two guineas was allowed for all expenses, viz., £1 2s. to the bringer, six shillings to the recruiting officer of the Regular Militia, half a guinea to the Adjutant of Local Militia, half a crown for medical examination, and one shilling for attesting.

On the 19th, 20th, and 21st of October volunteering from the British Militia into the Regular Army was ordered to take place; and in a Circular to the Commanding Officers of Militia, dated Whitehall, the 6th of October, Lord Sidmouth says, "Sensible as you must be of the importance of increasing the disposable Forces of the Country at the present moment, His Royal Highness feels assured that you will do everything in your power to give full effect to the Attainment of so highly desirable an object."

A Circular from the Horse Guards dated the same month states that "The Commander-in-Chief persuades himself, from his experience of the spirit which has in every instance distinguished the Militia when their Services have been required, that, aided by the zeal of their officers, the Approaching Volunteering will add considerably to the present disposable Force, an object of the greatest importance at this Crisis; and which he is assured will receive the warmest support of everyone, who, laying aside

---

* 53 Geo. III., c. 81 (see Appendices L, M, and O).

partial considerations, truly feels for the welfare of his Country, and is interested in the success of the cause in which His Majesty's Arms have hitherto borne so distinguished a part."

The Regiment was inspected on Tuesday, the 19th of October, by Major-General Crowjoy, 455 privates being present under arms.

The detachments at Camden, Carlisle Fort, Spike Island, Haulbowling, and Monkstown were relieved, on Tuesday, the 2nd of November, by the Oxford Militia, and proceeded to Cove and Middleton; where the head-quarters were established the following day.

In a Circular, dated Whitehall, the 25th of November, it is stated that the non-commissioned officers and privates who volunteer for service in any part of Europe, *as Militia*,* were to receive a bounty of eight guineas, and the same pay as the Regular Army; and for every company of 100 men a commission in the Regular Army would be given to the captain, lieutenant, and ensign, or if less than 100 men volunteered, for 50 men a captain's, 30 men a lieutenant's, and 20 men an ensign's commission would be given, with a bounty of two guineas to each man in addition to the ordinary bounty. The rank of the officers to be temporary for nine months, and then be made permanent. On the 2nd of December the Colonel and every officer present with the Regiment stepped forward on parade, and declared their willingness to serve in any part of Europe as Militia officers, and with their own men. Lord Sidmouth, in a letter to Colonel Cooke, dated Whitehall, the 6th of December, 1813, states that no offer to serve abroad as Militia will be accepted unless the numbers amount to 80 or upwards, and "His Royal Highness has at the same time Commanded me to express to you the great satisfaction with which he observes that so large a proportion of the officers of the Regiment under your Command have tendered their services abroad at this important conjuncture."

On the 24th of December the Regiment proceeded from Middleton to Fermoy, with detachments at Mitchelstown, Ballyduff, Lismore, and Kilworth Mountain; the heavy baggage and sick

---

* Under the 54 Geo. III., c. 1, and c. 20 (see Appendix L).

being left at the former place, to which the Regiment returned on the **22nd** January.

In **this year of the quota of 114** volunteers required **for** the Army, **76 volunteered for limited and** 16 for unlimited service, **or** 92 in all, **leaving 82 short of the quota.*** The number of volunteers **obtained from the Militia during the last ten years of** the War amounted to 110,932, **or, on an average, upwards of** 11,000 a-year. The number of volunteers in each **year** being—†

1805.	1806.	1807-8.	1809-10.	1811.	1812.	1813, to Sept.	1814, from Sep. 13 to Dec. 1814.
13,580	2,968	29,108	23,885	11,453	9,927	8,834	11,177

1814.—On **the 7th of February,** detachments were **sent to** Mitchelstown and Ballyduff; **small** parties **were also stationed** for a time at **Lismore and** Kilworth Mountain. Volunteering into the Regular Army commenced on the **4th of April,—only one** volunteered **for limited** and eight for unlimited **service,** being **143 short of the quota of the** 152 men required.‡ **The number** to be enlisted from the Regiment this year was 152, an **ensign's** commission being given **with every** 50 men; but, by **a Circular** dated Whitehall, **the 24th** of March, the bounty was ordered to be reduced, after the 4th of **April, from sixteen** to twelve guineas for unlimited service, and from **twelve to** eight guineas for limited **service.** The Cornwall, **Devon, and Welsh** Militia were **allowed** to volunteer for **the corps of Sappers and Miners. Recruiting by** beat **of drum was ordered to be discontinued by a Circular dated** Whitehall, the 18th **of April.**

The following Warrant **was issued to the Commanding Officer,** to enable him to assemble Courts-Martial :—

" *By His* **Royal Highness** *the Prince* **Regent** *of the United King-*
   dom of Great Britain *and Ireland.*

"GEORGE P. R.

"**Whereas an Act has been made and passed in** this present

---

* Under the 54 Geo. III., c. 1 (see Appendix L).
† Commons' Journals, Vol. LXIX., p. 635, Appendix 5.
‡ Under the 51 Geo. III., c. 20, and 53 Geo. III., c. 81 (see Appendix L).

Sessions of Parliament, for Punishing Mutiny and Desertion, and for the better Payment of the Army and their quarters, from and after the 24th day of March, 1814, until the 25th day of March, 1815: and whereas by the Acts for the better Ordering of the Militia Forces, in that part of the United Kingdom called Great Britain, It is enacted 'that the Officers of the Militia and Private Militia Men shall, during the time of their being embodied and drawn out, be subjected and made liable to all such Articles of War, Rules and Regulations, as shall be then by Act of Parliament in force, for the Discipline and good Government of any of His Majesty's Forces in Great Britain. And whereas the Militia of the County of York (West Riding) is by His Majesty's Order at present embodied and drawn out, We have therefore thought fit hereby, in the name and on the behalf of His Majesty, to authorise and direct you, from time to time, to call, assemble, and hold General Regimental Courts-Martial, and to be President of the same, or to nominate and appoint some Field Officer belonging to the Regiment under your Command to that Duty, which Courts-Martial are to be constituted according to the Act of Parliament first mentioned, and to meet at such time, or times, as you shall appoint, for taking cognizance and awarding punishment for such Mutiny, Desertion, false Musters, and other Crimes, as have happened, or shall happen, in the Corps under your Command. And we do hereby, in the name and on the Behalf of His Majesty, further authorise and empower the said Courts-Martial, to hear and examine all such Matters and Informations, as shall be brought before them, touching the misbehaviour of any Non-Commissioned Officer or Soldier, by Mutiny, Desertion, false Muster, or otherwise, as aforesaid, and to proceed in the Trial of such Offenders, and in giving of Sentence, and awarding Punishment, according to the powers and directions contained in the said first-mentioned Act of Parliament and Articles of War, which are hereunto annexed. And for so doing this shall be your Warrant, which shall continue in force until the said 25th day of March, 1815, unless the Corps shall be previously disembodied, in which case, this Warrant shall be in force only to the day of disembodying inclusive. Given at our Court at Carlton House, this 25th day of March, 1814, in the Fifty-fourth year of His Majesty's Reign.

"By Command of His Royal Highness the **Prince** Regent, **in the** Name and **on** the behalf of His Majesty,

"SIDMOUTH.

"**To** the Colonel of His Majesty's 3rd West York Regiment of Militia, or to the Lieut.-Colonel or Major of the said Regiment, for the time being."

On Thursday, the **5th of May, the Regiment** marched from Middleton to Cove, to embark **for England.** On the departure of **the Regiment from** Ireland, **Lieut.-Gen.** Sir **John** Hope issued **the** following **observations upon Major.-Gen.** Graham's **Report** upon the **half-yearly inspection of the** Regiment at **Cork, in May** :—

"The **Commander of the Forces is** happy **to** avail himself of another opportunity, **before** the departure of the 3rd West **York from Ireland, to express the** high **sense he entertains of the Conduct of the Regiment** during its continuance **in the Country, and he** requests the Officers of the Corps will accept his **acknowledgments** for that **uniform attention to their** respective **duties, which has so** invariably **maintained the** excellent discipline and Character **of the** Battalion **since it has** served **on this** Establishment."

On **the 6th of** May, **the** Regiment **embarked, under the** command **of Major** Brooksbank, **with six captains, sixteen** subalterns, five staff officers, and **544** non-commissioned officers and **men, on** board the following ships :—

Ships.		Sergts.	Corps.	Drumrs.	Privates.	Women and Children.
No. 17 *James*	(Head-quarters, Sick, &c.)	10	4	7	106	37
Letter A. G. *William*	„	2	5	3	50	29
„ A. Y. *Laurel*	„	2	1	2	57	7
„ F. X. *Lavinia*	„	2	3	—	41	17
„ D. Y. *Rosehill*	„	5	6	2	86	25
„ H. Y. *Elizabeth*	„	5	4	3	78	14
„ A. C. *Fox*	„	3	3	2	52	13
		29	26	19	470	142

The Regiment disembarked at Plymouth on the 19th of May, and was quartered in the Stone House Barracks. On the 27th and 28th of May the Regiment marched in two divisions to Bristol, according to the following route; but on the first Division arriving there on Saturday, the 4th of June, an order was received for them to proceed, on the following Monday, to Doncaster, where they arrived on Wednesday and Thursday, the 22nd and 23rd of June, and joined the detachment from Sheerness (of the men who did not extend their services to Ireland), who had marched from that place on the 8th, and arrived at Doncaster on the 21st of June.

		1st Division.	2nd Division.
Friday	27th May	Ivy Bridge	
Saturday	28th ,,	Ashburton	Ivy Bridge
Sunday	29th ,,	Halt	Halt
Monday	30th ,,	Exeter	Ashburton
Tuesday	31st ,,	Cullomton	Exeter
Wednesday	1st June	Wellington	Cullomton
Thursday	2nd ,,	Bridgewater	Wellington
Friday	3rd ,,	Cross and Axbridge	Bridgewater
Saturday	4th ,,	Bristol	Cross and Axbridge
Sunday	5th ,,	Halt	Halt
Monday	6th ,,	Sodbury and Wickwar	Bristol
Tuesday	7th ,,	Tetbury and Minchinghampton	Sodbury and Wickwar
Wednesday	8th ,,	Gloucester	Tetbury and Minchinghampton
Thursday	9th ,,	Tewksbury and Upton	Gloucester
Friday	10th ,,	Worcester	Tewksbury and Upton
Saturday	11th ,,	Bromsgrove	Worcester
Sunday	12th ,,	Halt	Halt
Monday	13th ,,	Birmingham	Bromsgrove
Tuesday	14th ,,	Tamworth and adjacent	Birmingham
Wednesday	15th ,,	Burton-on-Trent	Tamworth and adjacent
Thursday	16th ,,	Derby	Burton-on-Trent
Friday	17th ,,	Alpeton and adjacent	Derby
Saturday	18th ,,	Chesterfield	Alpeton and adjacent
Sunday	19th ,,	Halt	Halt
Monday	20th ,,	Sheffield	Chesterfield
Tuesday	21st ,,	Rotherham	Sheffield
Wednesday	22nd ,,	Doncaster	Rotherham
Thursday	23rd ,,		Doncaster

It having been decided to disembody the Militia, the following Royal Warrant was sent for that purpose to the Lord Lieutenant of the West Riding:—*

"*In the Name and on the Behalf of His Majesty.*

"GEORGE P.R.

"Whereas, by Warrant under Our Royal Sign Manual, bearing date the eleventh day of March, in the forty-third year of Our Reign, We did, for the weighty and lawful Causes therein recited, order you to draw out and embody all the Militia of the West Riding of the County of York under your direction, *and to hold the same in readiness to March to such parts within this Kingdom, as might be judged proper to assign them*, under the Command of such General Officer or Officers as We should be pleased to appoint over them, and to obey such further Orders as should be judged Necessary for the Safety and Defence of this Kingdom. And Whereas a Definitive Treaty of Peace between this Country and France has been signed: We, being most desirous to take the first opportunity of relieving Our faithful subjects from the heavy Burthens and Expenses occasioned by the War; Our Will and Pleasure is, and We do hereby Order you, with all convenient speed, to Cause the Militia of Our said West Riding of the County of York to be Disembodied, and to Issue all the Necessary and proper Directions on your part for returning the said Militia, under the Order of their Commanding Officers, to their respective parishes and places of abode, where they are to remain subject to the same Orders and Directions, as they were by Law subject and liable to before they were drawn out and embodied as aforesaid. And for so doing this shall be your Warrant. Given at Our Court at Carlton House, the Third day of June, 1814. In the fifty-fourth year of Our Reign.

"By the Command of His Royal Highness The Prince Regent, in the Name and on Behalf of His Majesty,

"SIDMOUTH.

"*To Our Lieutenant of the West Riding of Our County of York, or, in His absence, to the Deputy-Lieutenants of the said West Riding.*"

---

* War Office Militia Letter Books.

On the receipt of this Warrant, the Lord-Lieutenant wrote to Colonel Cooke as follows:—

"GROSVENOR SQUARE,
"*June* 17*th*, 1814.

"Sir,

"Having received a Warrant, date June 3rd, 1814, under the sign manual of His Royal Highness the Prince Regent, commanding me to disembody, on the 24th of this month, such part of the West Riding Militia as shall then be within the said Riding, in obedience to the commands of the said Warrant, I have to direct you to disembody, on the 24th inst., the 3rd Regiment of West Riding Militia under your command.

. . . .

"It is a gratifying part of my duty to acquaint you that His Royal Highness has commanded me to communicate to you, and through you to the officers, non-commissioned officers, and drummers of the 3rd Regiment West Riding Militia, the high sense which he entertains of your, and of their conduct, and of the zeal and spirit which you and they have manifested on so many occasions since the Regiment has been embodied.

"I have, &c.,
"WENTWORTH FITZWILLIAM.

"COL. COOKE, *or Officer Commanding, Doncaster.*"

Colonel Bryan Cooke, in a letter* to the War Office, dated Doncaster, the 23rd of June, says that part of the Regiment had arrived from Plymouth the previous day, and that the remainder was expected to arrive during the day; and having received a letter from the Lord-Lieutenant the previous evening, ordering the Regiment to be disembodied on the 24th, according to a Warrant dated the 3rd of June; he had taken upon himself to keep the men and await instructions as to whether the officers and men were to receive the allowances usually granted on being disembodied; and also whether 276 recruits, who joined on the 22nd of June, were entitled to their marching guinea. The

---

* Internal Defence, No. 311 Y.

directions for **disembodying the** Regiment, and granting **the** usual allowances, **were received later in the** day (23rd). **And** the **reply to the above letter, dated the 25th** of June, **authorised** the **payment of** the marching **guinea to** the **recruits. The** Regiment was consequently disembodied on Friday, **the** 24th **of June,** having been embodied for eleven **years** and three months.

The following Circular was issued, **giving** full instructions for **carrying** out the Order to Disembody the Militia :—

Circular, No. 230.

"**WAR OFFICE,** 16*th June,* 1814.

"**Sir,**

"**His** Royal Highness the Prince Regent having been **pleased,** in the name **and on behalf of** His Majesty, **to** sign **orders for** disembodying the Militia **of** the County **of** York with **all** convenient speed, **I** am commanded by His Royal Highness to express **to you** the very great satisfaction which His Royal Highness has received from the exemplary and meritorious ser**vices of the** Corps of Militia of that County under your com**mand**; and to acquaint you that His Royal Highness is pleased to grant the following allowances, on this occasion, to the Officers and Men hereinafter mentioned.

"To each Subaltern, **and to the Surgeon's** Mate, **if any, an** allowance will be made equal **to two** Months' Pay, **from the day** of Disembodying exclusive; **which, being granted to them in** this shape, will not interfere with the Receipt **of Half Pay, nor** of any other Allowance, to which they **are entitled, or may here**after obtain, from Government. Officers **holding Two Appointments** are, however, to receive the Allowance **for one of** them only.

"The Adjutant, Paymaster, Surgeon, and Quarter-Master, are **not** to have the Allowance of two Months' Pay, it being intended that **they shall be** retained on **Duty, and receive** certain rates **of Pay,** commencing from the Day subsequent to that **of the Disembodying, inclusive, which** rates shall be communicated to you **as** soon as they shall have been determined upon.

"**In pursuance of the Prince** Regent's Orders signified **to the** Lord-Lieutenant of the West Riding **of** the County of York, **by**

Lord Viscount Sidmouth, and communicated by his Lordship to this Department, to retain upon the disembodied Establishment of your Regiment, the number of Sergeants, Corporals, and Drummers, allowed by the Act of the 42nd Geo. 3rd, cap. 90, sect. 83, viz., one Sergeant and one Corporal to every thirty Private men, with an additional Corporal for every surplus of fifteen men or upwards, and one Drummer per Company, with an addition of one Drummer for each flank Company of Regiments or Battalions consisting of Five or more Companies, such Sergeants, Corporals, and Drummers, as exceed that number, in each rank, are to be immediately discharged: and in the Execution of this part of His Royal Highness' Instructions, I am commanded to desire your most particular attention, that no Sergeant or Corporal be retained who is not in every respect fit for Service, and qualified for the active Duties of a Non-commissioned Officer, nor any Drummer who is not an able-bodied young Man. Such of the Sergeants to be discharged, as may be deemed deserving of the Out-Pension under The Prince Regent's Warrant dated 28th February, 1814, and such of the Corporals and Drummers as may have a claim to the Pension under the General Militia Laws, are to receive an advance of Marching Allowance, at One Shilling and Tenpence per Diem, sufficient to carry them to London, reckoning Ten Miles for a Day's March, without Halting Days, a Report thereof being made to the Agent, by whom the men will be further subsisted according to their respective Ranks, until they can pass an examination before the Chelsea Board. Each Non-commissioned Officer and Drummer, who shall be discharged, and not recommended for the Chelsea Pension, and each Private Man who shall be disembodied, is to be allowed a Bounty equal to Fourteen Days' Pay, reckoned from the Date of Discharge, or of disembodying, exclusive; and His Royal Highness is further graciously pleased to permit such Non-commissioned Officers and Men to take with them the Clothing of the Current Year, and also their knapsacks.

"The Non-commisioned Officers and Drummers retained on the Disembodied Establishment are of course not to receive the Fourteen Days' Bounty; and as the said Non-commissioned

Officers and Drummers are to wear their present clothing only until Christmas next, you will be pleased to take immediate steps for delivery on the 25th December, 1814. The clothing for them to be ready for delivery on the 25th December, 1814. The clothing for each Rank is to consist of a Cap, Cockade, Feather, or Tuft, Plate and Cap Case, a Coat, a Waistcoat, a Pair of Breeches, and a pair of Military Shoes. Instructions will be given in due time as to the Provision of Clothing for the Privates of the Disembodied Establishment.

"Before the disembodying, you will cause an exact Muster to be taken by the Regimental Paymaster, of the several Companies of the Corps; you will also see that all the Quarters be duly cleared, and take especial care that the Accounts of the Men be made up, and all their just pretensions completely satisfied to the time of their being dismissed.

"Care is to be taken that the Arms, Accoutrements, and Great Coats for the number of Men of which your Regiment is to consist when disembodied, be all collected in order to be lodged in the manner directed by the Act above referred to.

"The Tents, and whatever Arms you may have beyond the said Establishment, are to be delivered to such person as the Board of Ordnance shall appoint to receive them. The supernumerary Accoutrements, and the Great Coats of the Non-commissioned Officers and Drummers to be discharged, as also those not wanted for the use of the Privates of the disembodied Establishment, together with any serviceable Camp Necessaries that remain in the possession of the Corps, are to be sent to such place as shall be pointed out by the Storekeeper-General, to whom Inventories thereof should be sent; and the Commanding Officer will, of course, be responsible that the Arms, &c., are left in the best possible state. As all the absent Officers and Men on Furlough have been ordered to join before the Day of disembodying, it is expected that the claims of every Individual in the Corps shall be finally settled by the Paymaster; but as some few cases may possibly occur in which the non-attendance of Officers and Men may be unavoidable, the Paymaster is in such cases, and also in the cases of Men who are necessarily absent from the Corps on account of Sickness, to transmit to the Agent a Statement shewing the Names of the Persons absent, the balance due to each individual, and the stations at which they are to be found, in order that their claims may be settled upon their own application to the Agent, without difficulty or delay; a Duplicate of which Statement is to be sent to the Superintendents for Military Accompts.

"The Paymaster is to send to the Superintendents for Military Accompts, an Estimate (with a Duplicate thereof for the use of the Agent) of the Sums that will be required on the present occasion, distinguishing the proportion for each Head of Service. He is to give Credit in his last Pay List for the Unclaimed Effects and Credits of Deceased Men and Deserters, annexing a State thereof to the said Pay List. The Allowances of the Captains are to be issued only up to the Day of disembodying inclusive.

"The Paymaster is to balance his final Accounts exactly with the Agent.

"It being proposed that the Charge of the Pay, Clothing, Contingencies, and allowances to reduced Subalterns, &c., and of the dis-embodied Militia, shall in future be defrayed under the Superintendence of this Office, the appointment of Battalion Clerk will not be revived; and the Financial concerns of the Corps, when disembodied, will be carried on by the Paymaster, who is to be retained as before-mentioned. Instructions as to the transmission of Estimates, and as to the mode of preparing and rendering the Accompts for these Services, will be given to the Paymaster with as little delay as possible.

"I cannot conclude this Letter without expressing, through you, the satisfaction which I feel in having the honour of signifying on the present occasion, the Prince Regent's gracious Approbation of the Services of the Officers, Non-commissioned Officers, Drummers, and Private Men, belonging to his Majesty's Militia Forces.

"I have the honour to be, &c.,

"PALMERSTON.

"COLONEL COOKE, *3rd West York Regt.*
"*of Militia, Doncaster.*"

The Commander-in-Chief expressed his thanks to the Militia for the services they had rendered during the war, in the following General Order:—

"HORSE GUARDS, 24th *June*, 1814.

"The Re-establishment of Peace having enabled His Royal Highness the Prince Regent, in the name and on the behalf of His Majesty, to direct the disembodying of the Militia Forces, the Commander-in-Chief, previous to their return to their respective counties, desires thus publicly to offer to them his best acknowledgments for the Zeal and Perseverance with which they have, during a long and eventful War, shared with the Regular Army in every Military Duty which has fallen within their Province.

"From the Gallant and Patriotic Spirit displayed by the Militia were now derived, at the most critical periods of the War, the means of reinforcing the disposable Force of the Country—a measure which most essentially contributed to its Military Renown, by placing the British Army foremost in those Confederate Bands, which resisted the unbounded Ambition and overwhelming Power of the late Ruler of France, and, by their Bravery and Discipline, under the direction of Divine Providence, rescued that Country from Tyranny and Oppression, and restored to Europe the blessing of Peace.

The Commander-in-Chief feels personally indebted to the Militia Forces for the ready and Cheerful Obedience with which they have at all times received His Commands; and he requests that, with these heartfelt Expressions of Approbation, they will, collectively and individually, accept his warmest wishes for their Welfare and Happiness.

"FREDERICK, Commander-in-Chief."

Both Houses of Parliament passed a Vote of Thanks to the Militia for their services during the war—the House of Lords on Tuesday, the 5th, and the House of Commons on the 6th of July—in the same terms as the vote in 1803.*

---

* Lords' Journals, Vol. XLIX., p. 1,038, and Commons' Journals, Vol. LXIX., p. 438; and Parliamentary Debates, Vol. XXVIII., pp. 535-6, 621.

A Circular (No. 232), dated War Office, **the** 22nd of June, fixed the following rates of pay for the Staff of the Disembodied Militia:—

	Per Diem.	
	s.	d.
Adjutant	8	0
Paymaster in Corps consisting of three Companies and upwards	6	0
Ditto of two Companies	5	0
Ditto of one Company	4	0
Surgeon ,, ...	6	0
Quartermaster in Corps of an Establishment exceeding 360 Privates	5	0
Ditto not exceeding ditto	3	0
Sergeant-Major in Corps consisting of two or more Companies	1	10
Sergeant ,, ,, ,,	1	6
Corporal ,, ,, ,,	1	2
Drum-Major in Corps consisting of three or more Companies	1	6
Drummer	1	0

The arms, accoutrements, and other regimental stores were to be in charge of the Quartermaster, and **the Staff was to** be under his command in the absence **of the Adjutant. The** Surgeon **was to** attend the Staff and **provide medicines, for** which he received **an allowance.**

The establishment of the Regiment, when disembodied in June, 1814, **was** fixed **at 1** colonel, 1 lieutenant-colonel, 2 **majors, 10 captains, 12** lieutenants, **8** ensigns, **1** adjutant, **1 surgeon, 1** quartermaster, **1** paymaster, **1** sergeant-major, **26** sergeants, **27 corporals, 1** drum-major, **11** drummers, and **809** privates. **The arms of the** Regiment **then** consisted of **31 pikes,** 132 rifles, **14 fusils, and 723 muskets.**

CHAPTER V

FROM 1814 TO 1852.

DISEMBODIED PERIOD.

CONTENTS.—Bugles **to be worn** by Light Infantry and Rifles.—Part of **the** Militia Embodied, June, 1815 to February, 1816.—Uniform of Regimental Staff. — Training Suspended 1814-19. — The Training at **Doncaster,** 1820, **and** Pontefract, 1821.—Training at Doncaster, 1825.— **Sergeants** armed with Fusils instead of Pikes, 1830.—Green Tufts **to be worn by** Light Infantry.—Sir Robert Peel's Protest on the **Gold Lace** Question.—The Last Training at Pontefract, 1831.— Regiment Recommended to be made Light Infantry.—Order of Precedence of Militia Regiments previous to 1833.—Numbers as finally decided.— Staff Reduced, 1835.—Ordered **to be** completed, 1845.—Regiment to wear Silver instead **of** Gold **Lace.—The** Contingent Fund.—Captain **and** Adjutant Rawson.

1814.—**By General Order, dated Horse Guards, the 27th of December,** Assistant-Surgeons **were** appointed **to rank** with Lieutenants, **and** Hospital Assistants with Ensigns. Another General Order, dated the 28th **of** December, directs that all the caps of Light **Infantry** and **Rifle Regiments, or Companies, are to have a** bugle **horn,** with **the number of the regiment below it, instead of** the **brass plate worn by the rest of the Infantry.**

1815.—In consequence of **Napoleon** having escaped from **Elba early in this year, the war was** renewed.

A Circular, dated Whitehall, **the** 25th **of April, 1815, orders that** recruiting **by beat of drum,** which **had been suspended in April the previous year, was to be commenced immediately, in** consequence of an Order by the Prince Regent in Council; and the following amount of levy money would be allowed :—

		£	s.
To the Recruit { On being attested		1	1
On final approval at Head-quarters		2	2
On joining the Corps when embodied		1	1
To the Officer and Party, on final approval, to cover all expenses, and to be distributed in such manner as the Commandant shall direct... ...		1	1
Total Levy Money		5	5

The recruits, immediately upon their enlisting, were examined and attested in the usual manner, and sent to Head-quarters weekly, or oftener if necessary, for the purpose of being finally approved by the Adjutant and Surgeon of the Regiment; after which they received the second portion of their bounty, and were allowed to go home, the fourth guinea being paid on their first assembling for training or embodiment, in which latter case a second guinea was granted, under the 121st section of the General Militia Act, for the purchase of necessaries. Each recruit was entitled to pay and marching money for the days occupied in going to and from head-quarters. The non-commissioned officers and drummers, when employed in recruiting, received the same pay and allowances as when embodied.

A Warrant, dated Carlton House, the 16th of June, was issued, ordering a portion of the Militia of the following counties to be embodied :—

Durham	1st West York	South Gloucester
Flint	Devon (East, North and South Regiments)	Southampton (South)
Glamorgan		1st Surrey
Hereford	Middlesex (East and West Regiments)	City of London (East and West Regiments)
Stafford		
Sussex	Norfolk (West Division)	Tower Hamlets (1st and 2nd Regiments)
Worcester	West Kent	
East York		

The following thirteen regiments, not having been disembodied in 1814, were also serving:—

Berks	South Lincoln	1st Lancashire
Bucks	1st Somerset	2nd Lancashire
Cambridge	2nd West York	East Suffolk and Wiltshire
Carmarthen	Cheshire	
Derby		

The Denbigh, East and West Essex, 3rd Lancashire, Monmouth and Brecon, Westminster, North York, and a number of Scotch and Irish Regiments, were also embodied.

The arms of the Infantry of the Army were directed to be browned, by a General Order, dated Horse Guards, the 22nd of July.

Recruiting was discontinued, in compliance with a Letter received from Whitehall, dated the 27th of July.

1816.—In January a number of regiments were disembodied, under a Warrant dated the 15th of that month; the remainder, including the 1st and 2nd West York, were disembodied in February and March, under a Warrant issued for that purpose, dated the 27th of February.

By an Act * passed on the 22nd of June, the Training of the Militia was authorised to be dispensed with for this year; and an Order in Council, dated the 1st of July, was issued, suspending the training accordingly.†

In consequence of there being a considerable number of regimental necessaries in the Public Stores, the War Office issued a Circular, dated the 21st of October, stating that the following Articles would be supplied to the Permanent Staff of the disembodied Militia, at the rates named, viz.:—Shoes, per pair, 4s. 9d.; shirts, 4s. 2d. each; half-stockings, 8s. 6d. per dozen; stock and clasps, 8d. each; sergeant's grey trousers, 10s. per pair; private's ditto, 7s.; sergeant's half-gaiters (grey), 2s. 5d.; private's ditto, 1s. 7d.; private's ditto (black), 2s. 2d.; serge drawers, 2s. 7d.; sergeant's blue forage cap, with oilskin top, 2s. 6d.; private's ditto, 1s. 8d.

---

* 56 Geo. III., c. 64 (see Appendix L).
† *London Gazette*, 1816, p. 1,296.

1817.—By a General Order, dated the 10th of May, the Uniform of Paymasters, Quartermasters, Surgeons, Assistant-Surgeons, and Veterinary Surgeons, was fixed as follows:—" Coat: long, plain, single-breasted, without epaulettes or wings, with buttons, cuffs, and collar (embroidered, laced, or plain), the same as the uniform of their respective regiments. Cocked hats: the Paymaster and Quartermaster to wear the Regimental looping, &c.; the former not to wear a feather. The hat of the Surgeon, Assistant-Surgeon, and Veterinary Surgeon is to be plain, with a black silk button and loop; no feather. The Appointments and other Articles of Dress to be according to the Regimental Pattern. The sword-belt to be worn under the coat. No sash."

The office of Agent-General for Militia, Local Militia, and Volunteers, ceased on the 24th of June. All future payments were ordered to be made by the "Paymaster-General of His Majesty's Forces," by a War Office Circular (No. 360), dated the 11th of June.

An Act* was passed on the 30th of June, authorising the Training of the Militia to be suspended in any year by an Order in Council; and the non-commissioned officers and men were ordered to be reduced to one sergeant and one corporal to every forty men; one drummer to every two companies, with an additional drummer for each flank company.

A War Office Circular (No. 369), dated the 31st of July, ordered that all the new waistcoats, breeches, and great-coats belonging to the Militia should be returned to the Storekeeper-General, London, with a view of serving them out to the Line that year, only sufficient for one company being retained.

The Training was dispensed with by an Order in Council, dated the 15th of July.†

1818.—The Lord-Lieutenant received a Circular, dated Whitehall, the 8th of April, stating that it had been judged expedient to dispense with the Training and Exercise of the Militia for that

---

* 57 Geo. III., c. 57.
† *London Gazette*, p. 1,569.

year, and that an Order in Council, dated **the 6th instant, to** that effect had **been issued.***

1819.—The establishment of non-commissioned **officers and** drummers was reduced from **the numbers** fixed in 1802, **by 42 Geo. III., c. 90, to those fixed in 1817;** and from the 24th of April the **number to** be retained on permanent pay, **when not in** actual **service,** was fixed by War Office Circular (No. 411), dated **the** 12th of March, **at** twenty sergeants, **twenty corporals, and** seven drummers.

A Letter, dated Whitehall, **the 8th of April, was** sent to **the** Lord-Lieutenant, informing him that **the Training** and Exercise for that year had **been** dispensed with by **an Order in Council,** dated the 3rd **instant.†**

1820.—**The Militia was called out for Training and Exercise** in this year by **a** War Office Circular (No. 429), dated **the 5th of May.** The officers and men were to receive the same **pay** and allowances during the training as when embodied. The officers **received** ninepence per mile for travelling expenses, from their **place of** residence within the county, or from the border of **the county nearest** to the place they happen **to** be when summoned **to attend.** The men **received** the usual marching allowance **from the** place from **which they** proceeded **to** join, **provided such place was not more distant than the parish** for **which they were enrolled; the same allowance being made to** officers **and men on being** dismissed.

The Regiment, numbering 572 **effective privates, assembled** at **Doncaster for** twenty-eight days' **Training, from the 20th of May to the 16th of June.**

The non-commissioned officers **and men received the** following **clothing and** necessaries, which **were returned into store at the termination of the** Training (such small articles as shoe-brushes, &c., **being provided** by the Regulated Stoppages from their pay, **and were taken away** by them **when** dismissed):—1 coat, 1 waistcoat, 1 pair **of grey trousers, 1 pair of** short grey gaiters, 1 pair **of shoes, 1 cap, 1** shirt, **1 pair of** short stockings, 1 stock **and clasp, 1 turnscrew, 1 worm, 1 picker, 1** brush, **1 knapsack.**

---

* *London Gazette*, pp. 633-4, 1,215.   † Idem, pp. 609, 713, 950, 1,175.

The establishment of non-commissioned officers was increased to the original numbers fixed, in 1802, by the 42 Geo. III., c. 90, viz.: one sergeant and one corporal to every thirty privates; one drummer to every company, with an additional drummer for each flank company in regiments of five or more companies. These extra men were not to be retained on the Permanent Staff, but to be dismissed at the end of the Training with the others. (War Office Circular, No. 430, the 6th of May.) On the expiration of the period for which they were enrolled, the men were entitled to their clothing and necessaries, provided they had attended three Trainings of the Regiment. The actual cost of altering the clothing was allowed, provided the expense did not exceed two shillings and sixpence a suit. (War Office Circular, No. 433, the 2nd of June.)

1821.—The Militia was called out for Training this year, and on the 26th of May the Regiment, numbering 710 effective privates, went to Pontefract for twenty-one days' Training, being dismissed on the 15th of June.

1822.—A War Office Circular (No. 460), dated the 18th of February, directs that Militiamen who enlisted into the Regular Army were not to be allowed to join their regiments until their period of service in the Militia had expired, and any man doing so was to be given up to his regiment; and, if they failed to give themselves up to some officer when their Militia service was completed, they were treated as deserters.

The Regiment was not assembled for Training, an Order in Council, dated the 28th of February, having been issued to dispense with the Training of the Militia for that year.*

1823.—The Training of the Militia was suspended by an Order in Council, dated the 3rd of April.†

In consequence of the opinion expressed by the Committee of the House of Commons appointed to prepare the Estimates for the disembodied Militia, a War Office Circular, dated the 5th of November, directed that vacancies amongst Quarter-

---

* *London Gazette*, 1822, p. 385.   † Idem, 1823, pp. 537, 1,113.

masters were not to **be filled up, the** duties being undertaken by the **Paymasters; a Quartermaster-Sergeant, at 1s. 10d. per diem,** being **appointed to assist him.**

1824.—**An Order** in **Council, dated the 10th of March, suspended the Training of the Militia for this year.***

1825.—**The** Regiment assembled **at** Doncaster **for twenty-eight days'** Training and Exercise, from the 21st **of May to the 17th of June,** with 658 privates.

1826.—The Training **of the** Militia **was suspended by an Order in Council, dated the 15th of** February.†

1827.—**An Order in Council, dated the 14th of March, suspended the Training of the Militia for this year.**‡

1828.—**A War Office Circular (No. 625),** of the **24th of** December, **was sent to Commandants of** Militia Regiments, stating **that the** Permanent **Staff of Militia** would **probably be** shortly reduced, **and** the **Paymasters, Quartermasters, and Surgeons** dispensed **with.**

The Training **was** suspended by **an Order in Council, dated the** 13th **of** February. §

1829.—**Another War Office Circular (No. 629), dated the 31st of January, fixed the retiring** allowance as follows.—For **officers who had** served in the embodied Militia **for**—

	(Per Diem).		
	10 years and upwards. s. d.	3 years and under 10 years. s. d.	Under three years. s. d.
Paymasters	6 0	5 0	4 0
Surgeons	6 0	5 0	4 0
Quartermasters	5 0	3 6	3 0
Surgeons appointed since disembodiment, or Assistant-Surgeons who had served as such when embodied... ...	5 0	4 0	3 6

Quartermaster **appointed since** disembodiment, **but who** served **ten years as** Sergeant **when em**bodied, 2s. per diem.

---

* *London Gazette,* 1824, p. 417.   † Idem, 1826, p. 361.
‡ Idem, 1827, pp. 689, 1,510.   § Idem, pp. 313, 1,551.

These officers, like Militia Subalterns receiving disembodied pay, were liable to be called upon to join their regiments when required. The sums given for full ten years' service was the same as the disembodied allowance of the respective ranks. The Training of the Militia was suspended by an Order in Council, dated the 18th of March.*

The Permanent Staff of the Regiment was reduced, under an Act † passed on the 13th of April, to one Adjutant, one Sergeant-Major, twenty Sergeants, one Drum-Major, and seven Drummers, which, by War Office Circular (No. 635), dated the 11th of May, which was ordered to take effect from the 25th of June.

The ballot for the Militia was first suspended under this Act, which was continued annually.

In consequence of disturbances in September, the Magistrates of Doncaster, called upon the Adjutant for the assistance of the Military by the following Warrant :—

"We, the undersigned William Hurst, Esq., Mayor, John Wright. Esq., George Clarke Walker, Esq., and John Branson, Esq., His Majesty's Justices of the Peace for the Borough and Soke of Doncaster, in the county of York, finding, upon the examination on oath, of Louis Keyzor, Thomas Tymms, and Daniel Bishop, that a body of Men, to the number of 400 and upwards, have assembled in a riotous manner in Doncaster, aforesaid, and the lives and property of His Majesty's Subjects are thereby endangered, and having further found that the Civil Force and Power are wholly inadequate to protect the lives and preserve the property of His Majesty's liege Subjects in Doncaster aforesaid, do hereby require the immediate presence and aid of such Military Force and Power as by law His Majesty's Justices of the Peace are entitled to claim for His liege subjects.

"Given under Our Hands and Seals at the Town Clerk's Office in Doncaster, the 14th day of September, 1829.

"W. HURST, Mayor,
"JOHN WRIGHT,
"G. O. WALKER,
"J. BRANSON.

" To CAPTAIN RAWSON, *Adjutant of the 3rd West York Militia.*"

---

* *London Gazette*, pp. 549, 1,237.   † 10 Geo. IV., c. 10.

1830.—The Training of the Militia was suspended by an Order in Council, dated the 28th of June.*

The Sergeants were ordered to be armed with **Fusils** instead of Pikes, by a Horse Guards' Circular dated the **31st of July**.

Another Circular, dated **the 2nd of** August, directs that Light **Infantry Regiments are to wear green tufts** instead of a feather, **and that the Bands** are to be dressed in **white, with regimental** facings.

Sir Robert Peel wrote to the King **on the 8th of** August, and also to Lord Hill, the Commander-in-Chief, urging them **to reconsider the question, of depriving the** Militia **of the** right **of wearing gold lace, as he strongly objected to such a policy.** A General Order, dated the **25th of September,** directed that for the future gold **lace alone was to be worn by the** Regular **Army, the** regimental **pattern lace remaining unaltered.** Previous to this, **gold and silver lace was worn** indiscriminately **by the** Regular **Army and** Militia.

A **Circular,** dated the 30th of **December, was** issued, stating **that an Order in Council, of** the 27th inst., directed that Men **should be** balloted **for** to complete the Militia.† This was **the last occasion of the Militia** being completed by ballot.

1831.—A Circular, **dated** Whitehall, the 10th of January, **was sent** to the Lord-Lieutenant, directing him to call **out the Militia of the** West Riding for training:—

"**His** Majesty's Government, having **taken into consideration the present state of** the Militia, have deemed **it expedient that the men now** enrolled therein, except **those** whose term of **service will** expire before the 20th of November **next,** should forthwith be assembled for the purpose of Annual Training **and** Exercise for the period of twenty-eight days."

The men were to be assembled **as** early **in** February or the succeeding **month as** possible. A subsequent Circular, dated **the 21st of January,** directs that if there was no probability **of the number of men being** sufficient to form at least two com-

---

* *London Gazette*, pp. 1,393, 1,417, 1,441.
† Idem, pp. 2,713-14.

panies of 60 each, the Training was to be dispensed with until after the ballot.*

The Lord-Lieutenant, in a letter dated the 23rd of January, states that the 1st West York will assemble for Training at Doncaster, the 2nd at York, and the 3rd at Pontefract on the 10th of February.†

The Regiment assembled on the 10th of February, for twenty-eight days' training, and proceeded to Pontefract, with only 195 effective privates. The Lord-Lieutenant issued the following Warrant to the Colonel, to enable him to make provision for moving the Regiment to Pontefract.

"[West Riding of Yorkshire.]

"*To His Majesty's Justices of the Peace, acting in and for the said Riding.*

"I, His Majesty's Lieutenant for the County of York (West Riding), do hereby, in exercise of the power and authority in me for that purpose vested by the laws now in force relating to the Militia, order and direct you, or any one of you, to whom these presents shall come, to issue your Warrant to the Chief Constables, Petty Constables, or other Officers of the several Parishes or Places from, through, or near to which the Staff of the Third Regiment of West York Militia shall have to pass, on its march from the Head-Quarters of the said Regiment at Doncaster, on Monday, the seventh day of February next, to the Town of Pontefract, both in the said Riding (at which latter place the said Regiment is now under Orders to Assemble for the purpose of being Trained and Exercised for Twenty-eight days, commencing the Tenth of February next), requiring them to provide sufficient carriages and horses to convey the Arms, Clothes, Accoutrements, Ammunition, and other Stores of the said Regiment, with able Men to drive such carriages, and to provide Quarters for the Men on the March, and otherwise

---

* War Office Militia Letter Book, Vol. VII., pp. 245, 271-2.
† War Office Militia Letter Book, Vol. VII., p. 283.

Colonel George Cholmley. 1820 1850.
From a Portrait taken in 1830.

UNIV. OF
CALIFORNIA

as there shall be occasion, for which this shall be your Warrant,

"Given at Harewood House, the Twenty-sixth of January, One Thousand Eight Hundred and Thirty-one.

"HAREWOOD.

"*To* COLONEL CHOLMLEY, 3rd *West York Militia, Doncaster.*"

The establishment of non-commissioned officers and drummers was again temporarily increased during the Training (War Office Circular, No. 705, 2nd February) to the original numbers allowed at the Training of 1820, the extra men not being retained on the Permanent Staff, but returning home with the remainder of the men; the number of the disembodied Staff remaining as before.

The Subalterns and Staff Officers who received the reduced (not retired) allowance had to attend the Training, except in case of duly-certified sickness. In the event of the Paymaster being unable to attend, or of the place being vacant, four shillings per diem was allowed to the officer appointed to perform his duties. The above-named Circular also points out that under the 35th Section of the Mutiny Act, all men who had enlisted into the Regular Army or East India Company's Service, and were still serving in Great Britain, were (if their period of Militia engagement had not expired), to be required to attend the Training.

On the 19th of March the Lord-Lieutenant wrote to the Secretary of State recommending that the 3rd West York should be made a Light Infantry Regiment; but the reply from Lord Melbourne, dated Whitehall, the 31st of March, states that "it is not deemed advisable to allow any addition of Light Infantry to be made to the Militia Department." *

1832.—An Order in Council, dated the 14th of March, suspended the Training of the Militia for this year.†

A Return made in April, shows that seven Lieutenants and one Assistant Surgeon were in receipt of disembodied allowance.

---

* War Office Militia Letter Book, **Vol.** VIII., p. 28.

† *London Gazette*, 1832, **pp. 593, 617, 916.**

1833.—An Order in Council, dated the 3rd of April, suspended the Training of the Militia for this year.*

Previous to this year the Order of Precedence of Militia regiments was determined by Counties—the numbers being decided by ballot; and where there were several regiments in a County they took rank according to their County rank or numbers. Until the latter part of the last century regiments were generally known by the name of their Commanding Officer. This system of balloting was probably resorted to in order to try and allay any jealousy that might exist between regiments claiming the same position; for as most were raised in considerable numbers at the same periods—many even on the same day—it became almost impossible to decide which had the right to take precedence of another.

A large number were first raised in 1758 and 1759; these received a considerable addition in 1778, in consequence of the American War. The Irish regiments were next raised in 1793, the Scotch, and a number of Supplementary regiments in 1797.

In 1759 regiments serving together decided their relative rank for the time being by ballot.† In 1778 the rank of all the regiments in England and Wales was first decided by ballot, with the exception of a few too small to form a battalion; No. 4 being drawn for the West York Regiments. These numbers were changed annually, or remained in force only during the War. In 1780 the West York Regiments were No. 27. A Meeting of the Lords-Lieutenant of England and Wales was held at St. Alban's Tavern, on the 28th of April, 1781, to decide by lot the precedence of their several Counties, from the 1st of May, 1781, to the 1st of May, 1782, when the West York Regiments became No. 26.‡ A similar Meeting being held for the same purpose on the 7th of May the following year, when they became No. 28.§ Another Meeting was held at the same place, on the 2nd of March, 1793, to determine the precedence of the Counties during the War, when the West York

---

* *London Gazette,* 1833, pp. 665, 729, 926.   † See page 22.
‡ *London Gazette,* 1781.   § Idem, 1782.

were numbered 39*, and consequently remained in force until Peace was concluded in 1802. The numbers were next altered on the 11th of June, 1803, at a Meeting of the Lords-Lieutenant at the Horse Guards, when they became No. 32.† This was the last occasion of the numbers being decided by Counties; and they remained in force until the year 1833, when all the regiments of the United Kingdom were numbered separately, by order of William IV., who, instead of having the regiments balloted for indiscriminately, had them first classified according to the period at which they were first raised. The Scotch regiments were numbered in a separate List down to the year 1803; and the Irish regiments were also numbered by themselves previous to the year 1833.

On Thursday, the **28th of February, 1833,** the King gave a grand Military banquet at St. James's Palace, to which the Lords-Lieutenant of Counties and the Colonels of Militia were invited. After dinner His Majesty, in an appropriate speech, informed his guests that the object of the Meeting was to settle, permanently, the point of precedence among the regiments of Militia. Regular balloting glasses were then produced, and the names of the regiments were put into the glasses in three divisions, and drawn in that order. The first division contained the 47 regiments raised before the peace of 1763; the second contained the 22 regiments raised between the peace of 1763 and the peace of 1783; and the third contained the 60 regiments raised for the revolutionary war; the total being 129, including all the regiments of the United Kingdom, English, Welsh, Irish and Scotch.‡

The following Circular was in consequence sent to the Lords-Lieutenant of Counties :—§

WHITEHALL, 30*th April,* 1833.

"My Lord,

"I have the honour to notify to your Lordship that an

---

* Annual Register, Vol. XXXV., p. 13.
† *London Gazette,* 1803, p. 710.
‡ *Naval and Military Gazette,* 1833, pp. 36, 69.
§ Militia, No. 9, pp. 41-3.

Order has been issued by His Majesty in Council to dispense with the Training and Exercise of the Militia in the present year.

"I have likewise to inform your Lordship that His Majesty having been pleased to direct that the several Regiments, Battalions, and Corps of Militia should be numbered by the drawing of Lots, in order to determine finally and permanently their Precedency; and that a Drawing of Lots for that Purpose having taken place at the Palace at St. James's, in the presence of His Majesty, and several Lords-Lieutenants of Counties, and Colonels of Militia Regiments, No. —— was drawn for the ———.

"I have the honor to be, &c.,

"MELBOURNE."

LIST OF 47 REGIMENTS OF MILITIA RAISED BEFORE THE PEACE OF 1763.

3rd West York	...	1	South Devon	...	25
Huntingdon	...	2	Leicestershire	...	26
Durham	...	3	Northumberland	...	27
Rutland	...	4	Pembroke	...	28
1st West York	...	5	South Lincoln	...	29
Cheshire	...	6	Hertford	...	30
Berkshire	...	7	Monmouth and Brecon	...	31
North Lincoln	...	8	Flint	...	32
Cumberland	...	9	Wiltshire	...	33
West Suffolk	...	10	East Suffolk	...	34
2nd Surrey	...	11	Buckingham	...	35
East York	...	12	Warwick	...	36
North Hants	...	13	West Kent	...	37
East Essex	...	14	Cornwall	...	38
North Devon	...	15	West Norfolk	...	39
1st Somerset	...	16	East Norfolk	...	40
Westmoreland	...	17	East Devon	...	41
Bedford	...	18	Dorset	...	42
West Essex	...	19	South Hants	...	43
1st Surrey	...	20	Glamorganshire	...	44
2nd West York	...	21	1st Lancashire	...	45
North York	...	22	Denbigh	...	46
South Gloucester	...	23	2nd Somerset	...	47
Carmarthen	...	24			

THIRD WEST YORK LIGHT INFANTRY.   147

LIST OF 22 REGIMENTS OF MILITIA RAISED BETWEEN THE PEACE OF
1763 AND THE PEACE OF 1783.

Northampton	...	... 48	Nottingham	...	... 59
East Kent ...	...	... 49	Merioneth ...	...	... 60
Radnor	...	... 50	Anglesea ...	...	... 61
Oxford	...	... 51	Derbyshire	...	... 62
Hertford	...	... 52	Isle of Wight	...	... 63
Sussex	...	... 53	Cardiganshire	...	... 64
Shropshire	...	... 54	East Middlesex	...	... 65
Westminster	...	... 55	Stafford	...	... 66
Carnarvonshire	...	... 56	Worcester ...	...	... 67
Montgomery	...	... 57	Cambridgeshire	...	... 68
West Middlesex	...	... 58	North Gloucester	...	... 69

LIST OF 60 REGIMENTS OF MILITIA RAISED FOR THE
REVOLUTIONARY WAR.

Carlow	...	... 70	Wicklow ...	...	... 92
Fermanagh	...	... 71	Roscommon	...	... 93
Kirkcudbright and Wigton	...	... 72	Clare	...	... 94
Berwick, Haddington, Linlithgow and Peebles		} 73	Londonderry	...	... 95
			Ross, Caithness, **Sutherland** and Cromarty ...		} 96
Lanarkshire	...	... 74			
Armagh ...	...	... 75	1st Tower Hamlets ...		... 97
Inverness, Banff, Elgin and Nairn ...		} 76	King's County	...	... 98
			Wexford ...	...	.. 99
North Down	...	... 77	Dublin City	...	... 100
Fife	...	... 78	Cavan	...	... 101
Antrim	...	... 79	Donegal ...	...	... 102
Tyrone	...	... 80	Limerick City	...	... 103
Dumfries, Roxburgh and Selkirk ...		} 81	Queen's County	...	... 104
			Forfar and Kincardine		... 105
South Mayo	...	... 82	London	...	... 106
2nd Tower Hamlets...		... 83	Kerry	...	... 107
Tipperary ...	...	... 84	Louth	...	... 108
Longford ...	...	... 85	Dublin County	...	... 109
Perth	...	... 86	Cork City ...	...	... 110
South Cork	...	... 87	Leitrim	...	... 111
Kildare ...	...	... 88	South Down	...	... 112
Aberdeen ...	...	... 89	2nd Lancashire	...	... 113
Stirling, Dumbarton, Clackmannan and Kinross		} 90	Westmeath	...	... 114
			Ayr	...	... 115
Galway ...	...	... 91	North Cork	...	... 116

Argyle and Bute	...	... 117	Sligo	... ...	... 124
Cornwall and Devon Miners		... 118	3rd Lancashire	...	... 125
Meath	... ...	... 119	Edinburgh County and City		... 126
North Mayo	...	... 120	Kilkenny ...	...	... 127
Monaghan ...	...	... 121	Waterford ...	...	... 128
———	... ...	... 122	Renfrew	... ...	... 129
Limerick County	...	... 23			

1834.—The Training was again suspended by an Order in Council, dated the 19th of March.*

In this year the Permanent Staff of every regiment of Militia was inspected, with a view to effect a reduction in the numbers by discharging those who, by age or service, were unfit for further military duty. The Regimental Staff was inspected for this purpose on the 8th of July, by Colonel Sir M. McCreagh, I.F.O.†

1835.—An Order in Council, dated the 1st of April, suspended the Training of the Militia for this year.

The Militia Staff was further reduced by one-third,‡ the drum-majors and drummers being reduced. By an Order in Council, dated the 9th of September,§ seven sergeants of the Regiment were ordered to be reduced, the same to take effect from the 10th October, as directed by a War Office Circular, dated the 16th of September. The number of sergeants in the Regiment was thus reduced to twelve, and one sergeant-major. The vacancies thus caused were not filled until 1852, when the numbers had dwindled to eight.

1836.—In pursuance of the same Act, empowering His Majesty to order the Arms and Stores of the Militia to be delivered over to the Ordnance Department, a Circular, dated Whitehall, the 7th of January, was sent from the Home Office to the Lord-Lieutenant, requesting him to direct that the Arms, Accoutrements, and other Stores of the three Regiments of the West Riding, should be immediately returned to the Ordnance Depôt

---

* *London Gazette*, 1834, pp. 501, 535, 563, 719.
† See Parliamentary Return (House of Commons), No. 201, 1835.
‡ By the 5 & 6 William IV., c. 37.
§ *London Gazette*, 1835, pp. 623, 661, 691, 1,718, 1,739, 1,757.

at Hull, sufficient Arms being retained for one-half of the Permanent Staff.

The Contingent Allowance was increased from sixpence to one shilling for each private borne on the establishment, by the Pay and Clothing Act of that year, by War Office Circular, No. 802, dated the 30th of August.

In accordance with a Circular, dated the 3rd of September, the Lord-Lieutenant informed the Colonel, in a Letter, dated Harewood House, the 4th of September, that the King had been pleased to command that the Uniform of the Officers of the Militia of the United Kingdom should in future be laced in silver, and that in Royal Regiments silver embroidery, instead of lace, was to be worn. The Regiment had hitherto worn gold lace.

1845.—The whole Staff of the Disembodied Militia was inspected in this year. The Regimental Staff was inspected, on the 11th of October, by Lieutenant-Colonel Trevor, of the 59th Regiment, who was appointed to inspect the Staff of the several Regiments in Yorkshire, from which it appears that, out of ten sergeants, six had served in the Regiment between forty-one and forty-eight years. By a War Office Circular (No. 954), dated the 1st of December, the Staff of the Regiment was fixed at one adjutant, one sergeant-major, and ten sergeants, in consequence of Her Majesty having ordered the Militia Staff of the Militia to be completed, in Great Britain, to the numbers fixed by the 5 & 6 William IV., c. 37. Those who were reported at the inspection unfit for further service were replaced by picked Sergeants, who were Pensioners of Chelsea Hospital, residing in the district.

1846.—A number of Circulars were issued relating to the manner in which the Staff-Sergeants would be reduced and placed on the Chelsea Hospital Pension List. The non-commissioned officers in Great Britain were pensioned from the 25th, and those in Ireland from the 8th of September.

A Memorandum, for the information of the Adjutant or Acting-Paymaster of the Staff of the Militia of Great Britain and Ireland, gives the following rules, &c. :—

PAY OF DISEMBODIED MILITIA, PER DIEM.

	s.	d.
Adjutant	8	0
Sergeant-Major, having been a Sergeant-Major in a Provisional Battalion of Militia	2	6
Sergeant-Major, in Corps consisting of not less than two Companies	1	10
Sergeant, having been a Colour-Sergeant in a Provisional Battalion of Militia	2	0
Sergeant	1	6

Sixpence per diem was deducted from the pay of every Sergeant when absent on furlough, except in case of sick-leave.

The Commanding Officer had power, by law, to grant leave to the Adjutant or Sergeants for any period not exceeding three months. During the absence of the Colonel from the United Kingdom, the command devolved upon the next senior officer. In the absence of the Adjutant, the command of the Staff devolved upon the Sergeant-Major, or, if also absent, on some Sergeant appointed by the Commanding Officer.

The Contingent Allowance was sixpence per annum for every private borne upon the establishment, the same to be expended in repair of arms, &c., postage, stationery, &c.

In cases where full clothing was provided by the Colonel, the allowance for each suit was:—

	£	s.	d.
Sergeant-Major	5	12	1
Sergeant	3	0	0

Those appointed subsequently to the 1st of June, 1829, were entitled to a complete suit every four years; those appointed before that date being entitled to a new suit biennially, receiving 2s. 6d. per month during the third and fourth year. The actual expense of carriage and packing was allowed, in addition to the charges for altering, provided the latter item did not exceed 2s. per suit.

Pensioners of Chelsea or Kilmainham Hospitals received their pay in addition to their pensions, provided it had been granted for services other than in the Militia.

1848.—From a Return, made in compliance with a War Office Circular (No. 953), dated the 5th of November, 1845, it appears that the unexpended balance of the Contingent Fund of the Regiment amounted to upwards of £700. The amount received the six following years averaged about £80, and from 1832 to 1836, £40, and subsequently about £20. In consequence of the Regiment being so seldom assembled for Training at that period, there was generally a surplus every year, ranging from about twelve shillings to fifteen or twenty pounds, or sometimes more. A Return made to the War Office, dated the 21st of February, 1848, shows that the balance had accumulated, on the 1st of January, to £1,181 16s. 8d.

1849.—A War Office Circular, dated the 17th of January, states that the investigation into the state of the unexpended balances of the Contingent Allowance granted to Militia Regiments showed that in many cases the rules laid down in the Pay and Clothing Acts had not been attended to, as in some cases it had been applied to increase the income of the officers and non-commissioned officers; and orders that for the future the balance is to form a Stock-Purse for the Contingent Expenses of the Regiment; the Colonel, as hitherto, being responsible that it was properly expended.

1850.—Captain and Adjutant Rawson died on the 18th of July, and his duties then devolved on the Sergeant-Major, who received an extra allowance of 6d. per diem, under authority from the War Office, dated the 25th of July.

Captain Rawson joined the Regiment, as Ensign, in the year 1798, and the following year received a commission in the 35th Regiment, in which he served throughout the war; being re-appointed as Adjutant of his old Regiment in August, 1827.

CHAPTER VI.

FROM 1852 TO 1856.

EMBODIED FROM 26TH MAY, 1854, TO 30TH JUNE, 1856.

CONTENTS.—Militia raised by Voluntary Enlistment, 1852.—Four New Regiments formed in Yorkshire.—Disembodied and Retired Allowances to Officers.—Regiment made Light Infantry. — Establishment Increased.—The Training, 1853 and 1854.—Regiment Embodied and sent to Berwick.—Embarks for Dublin.—Volunteers required for Regular Army.—The Depôt.—Regiment Volunteers for Foreign Service.—Coatees changed for Tunics.—Order of Precedence of Militia Regiments Revised.—Presentation of New Colours.—Regiment Embarks at Belfast for England.—Royal Warrant to Disembody the West York Militia.—Thanks of the Queen and Parliament.

1852.—By an Act* passed on the 30th of June, to Consolidate and Amend the Laws relating to the Militia in England, a considerable change was effected. The men were ordered to be raised by voluntary enlistment to serve for five years, the quota being fixed at 80,000 men for England and Wales, 50,000 to be raised in 1852, and 30,000 in 1853, at a bounty not exceeding £6. The quota to be provided by each county was fixed by an Order in Council, and by the same means the ballot might be put in force to raise the required numbers, provided it could not be done by voluntary enlistment. No man over thirty-five years of age was, however, liable.

---

* 15 & 16 Vict., c. 50.

An Order in Council, dated the 30th of June, was issued, fixing the quota to be raised in each County; that for Yorkshire being 8,199, distributed as follows :—*

	1852.	1853.	Total.
West Riding	3,760 ...	2,284 ...	6,044
North Riding and City of York	733 ...	445 ...	1,178
East Riding ...	608 ...	369 ...	977
	5,101	3,098	8,199

This distribution was amended by an Order in Council, dated the 16th of October, by including the City of York with the West instead of the North Riding, as it had always been hitherto, thus making the numbers :—

	1852.	1853.	Total.
West Riding and City of York	3,885 ...	2,361 ...	6,246
North Riding	608 ...	368 ...	976
East Riding	608 ...	369 ...	977
	5,101	3,098	8,199

From the year 1802 until the passing of this Act the quota for the County (not including the Supplementary Men raised from time to time as occasion required) was 3,904, viz., three regiments in the West Riding, the first and second of 810 each, and the third 809 ; one regiment in the North Riding of 911, and one in the East Riding containing 564. To provide for the above increase, three additional regiments were formed in the West Riding ; the 4th West York Supplementary Regiment being revived and two new ones raised.

An Artillery Regiment was also formed in 1860, of 256 men from the North Riding, 257 from the East Riding, and 26 from

---

* *London Gazette*, pp. 1,915-6, and 2,722.

the West Riding, or a total of 539 men. The establishment of each Regiment was as follows:—

	West Riding. Six Regiments.	North Riding. One Regiment.	East Riding. One Regiment.		
1st West York	1,040	720	720		
2nd West York	1,036	...	...		
3rd West York	1,036	...	...		
4th West York	1,036	...	...		
5th West York	1,036	...	...		
6th West York	1,036	...	...		
Total	6,220	720	720	=	7,660
Artillery Regiment	26	256	257	=	539
Total	6,246	976	977	=	8,199

The Annual Training was reduced from twenty-eight to twenty-one days, Her Majesty having the power to reduce or extend the time by an Order in Council; such period not to exceed fifty-six, or be less than three days.

The Secretary at War was authorised to make regulations, which were to be laid before Parliament within twenty-one days.

The Regulations, dated the 16th of August, made by the Secretary of War, fixed the age of recruits from eighteen to thirty-five; volunteers over that age might be accepted if the surgeon certified them to be fit for duty for five years; or any man discharged from the Regular Army with a good character, after three years' service, could be accepted up to forty-five. The height was fixed at five feet four inches. Ten shillings of the bounty was payable on enrolment, and £1 1s. during each successive training, the balance of 5s. being paid at the termination of the fifth training; when embodied it was paid to them quarterly.

By a War Office Circular (No. 1,129), dated the 9th of September, Companies were ordered to be, as a general rule, about eighty strong; the permanent staff to consist of one adjutant, one sergeant-major, (in corps of not less than two companies) one sergeant to each company, one drummer to every two companies, with an extra drummer to each flank company in regiments of five companies and upwards. When the

Regiment was called out for Training, sergeants and corporals were to be added from the men to the extent of one of each rank to every forty men, one drummer to each company, with an additional one to the two flank companies.*

By another Act,† passed on the 30th of June, 1852, all Subalterns who were serving when their regiments were last disembodied, in 1814–1816, were granted a Disembodied or Retired Allowance, at the following rates per diem:—lieutenants, 2s. 6d.; ensigns, 2s.; surgeons' mates and assistant-surgeons, 2s. 6d. This, however, was not given to officers on full pay, or to any who had sufficient property or income to qualify for the rank of Captain; and they had to attend the Annual Training, except those on the Retired Allowance. The Paymasters, Quartermasters, and Surgeons reduced in 1829 were also allowed to retire on Allowances.

On the 1st of October a number of Subaltern Officers, who had been receiving the Disembodied Allowance since the close of the war in 1814, retired on the Allowances at the above rates.

The Dress Regulations, issued from the War Office on the 10th of September, directed that the uniform of the officers was to be the same as the existing patterns for the Army, silver lace being substituted for gold.

Every man received two shirts and two pairs of half-stockings, if he required them, the cost (2s. for the former, 10d. the latter) being defrayed by the public. If the men were allowed to take them away at the end of the Training, they were to produce them at each subsequent Training, or be provided with others, and put under stoppages for the amount.

The enrolment of men for the Regiment commenced on the 25th of September, and before the 31st of December the full quota of 1,036 had been obtained.

The addition of two Sergeants to the Permanent Staff, to act as Paymaster-Sergeant and Quartermaster-Sergeant respectively, was approved by the War Office on the 9th of December.

---

* See War Office Circular, No. 1,132, dated 22nd October.
† 15 & 16 Vict., c. 74.

The following Letter was sent from the Home Office to the Lord-Lieutenant:—*

"WHITEHALL, 18*th* December, 1852.

"My Lord,

"I have had the honor to lay before the Queen your Lordship's letter of the 15th instant, recommending that the Third West York Regiment of Militia should be made a Light Infantry Corps; and I have to inform your Lordship that Her Majesty has been Graciously Pleased to direct that that Corps shall be formed into a Light Infantry Regiment.

"I have the honor, &c.,

"S. H. WALPOLE.

"*The* EARL OF HAREWOOD, &c., &c., *Harewood House, Leeds.*"

Some dispute having arisen as to the liability of Militia Officers to pay stamp duty on their Commissions, a Circular, dated Whitehall, the 12th of November, was sent to the Lords-Lieutenant, enclosing a copy of the opinion of the Law Officers of the Crown, who stated: "We think that the Commissions of Officers in the Militia are not liable to duty, whatever may have been the construction of the word 'Army' used in the Stamp Act. The Commissions of Militia Officers are not granted by Her Majesty, or by any person duly authorized by Her, but by the Lord-Lieutenant, under the provisions of an Act of Parliament; and the veto of Her Majesty as to granting such Commissions makes no difference in the matter."

1853.—On Tuesday, the 15th of February, a General Meeting of the Lieutenantcy was held at the Court House, at Leeds, to consider the accommodation required for Depôts for the Head-quarters of the several Regiments.†

By a Circular, dated Whitehall, the 5th of March, the following twenty-seven new Regiments were authorised to be raised: 2nd Cheshire, 2nd Cornwall, 2nd Derby, Devon Artillery, 2nd Durham, Durham Artillery, Essex Artillery, Kent Artillery,

---

* See also *London Gazette*, 1st February, 1853, p. 264.
† Idem, p. 202.

4th, 5th, 6th, 7th Lancashire, and Lancashire Artillery, 4th and **5th Middlesex, Norfolk Artillery, Northumberland** Artillery, Hants **Artillery, 2nd and 3rd** Stafford, Suffolk Artillery, **3rd Surrey, Sussex Artillery, 2nd Warwick, 4th,** 5th, and 6th West York.

A letter, dated Whitehall, **the 10th** of March, **1853, to the** Lord-Lieutenant, gives the establishment of **the West** Riding Militia, **in six** regiments, as follows : **1 colonel, 1 lieutenant-colonel, 1** major, 10 captains, 10 lieutenants, **10 ensigns, 1 adjutant, 1** surgeon, 1 assistant-surgeon, 1 quartermaster, **1 sergeant-major,** 34 sergeants, **34** corporals, **7 drummers, 1,036 privates ; the 1st** West York to have 1,040 **privates ; and, as no more full colonels** were to **be appointed, the new** regiments **were to have a lieutenant-colonel and two majors.**

A subsequent **Circular, dated the 29th of** March, states **that** if the Lord-Lieutenant **thinks it** for the good of the service **that a** regiment **should have a** full Colonel, one may be appointed, **who** should **be a** landed proprietor **of** influence and position, **to stand in** the **same position** towards his regiment as a General Officer, **the Colonel of a Line** Regiment; but the rank to be **honorary, and not to** take actual and **detailed** command **either** during training or when embodied, **but to** assist the Lord-Lieutenant in correspondence **and general superintendance.**

Up to the year 1852, the Commanding Officer of this and most other large regiments was always a full Colonel, with one Lieutenant-Colonel and one Major. Since then the rank of Colonel has, in most cases, been only honorary; the Commanding Officers of all regiments only holding the rank of Lieutenant-Colonel, and two Majors being appointed instead of one. All full Colonels appointed previous to this year, retained their rank.

From the 1st of January to the 31st of March, 118 recruits were obtained, and nine between then and the 30th of June; making a total of 1,063.

Previous to this year, Militiamen who enlisted into the Regular Army without the permission of their Commanding Officer, were liable to be imprisoned for six months; but the Mutiny Act was altered in this year, to put them under stoppage of a penny a day for eighteen months instead.

A Circular, dated Whitehall, the 23rd of May, 1853, was sent to the Lords-Lieutenant of Counties, representing that great diversity prevailed regarding the fees on Commissions, varying from £10 10s. to £1 1s. for a Colonel's, and other ranks in proportion; in the West Riding the fee being one guinea for a Subaltern's, and an additional guinea for each step in rank, making five guineas for a Colonel's. The new scale proposed was, two guineas for Field Officers and one guinea for other Officers.*

The Regiment was assembled at Doncaster on Wednesday the 25th of May, for twenty-eight days' Training, on which day the first Volunteer sergeants and corporals were appointed. Two sergeants, twenty-five corporals, and seventeen privates were sent from the 21st and 28th Regiments, to assist in drilling the men. The Regiment was inspected by Colonel M. J. Slade, I.F.O., on the 18th of June; 1,154 men were enrolled, and the number present consisted of thirty-two Officers, twenty-eight sergeants (including thirteen staff), seven drummers, and 877 rank and file; 800 privates being present under arms.

The following extract is taken from the Regimental Orders of that day: "The Commanding Officer has much pleasure in making it known to the Officers, Non-commissioned Officers and Men of the Regiment, the great satisfaction expressed by the Inspecting Officer, at the appearance and steadiness of the Regiment under Arms this morning, who expressed his conviction that nothing but great exertion on the part of the Officers and Non-commissioned Officers and Men of the Regiment, as well as that of the Non-commissioned Officers and Men of the 21st and 28th Regiments who have acted as Drill Instructors, combined with great willingness, intelligence, and zeal on the part of the Men, could in so short a period have brought the Regiment into that state of perfection he was so much gratified to find it in." In Regimental Orders of the 20th of June, the Commanding Officer states that he "cannot allow the Officers, Non-commissioned Officers and Men of the Regiment to disperse to their several places of abode without expressing his deep sense of the grati-

---

* Parliamentary Papers (House of Commons), No. 998, 1853; and 404, 1862.

fication it has afforded him to witness the very great efficiency that the Regiment has attained in the short period they have been together, as well as the orderly and general good conduct of the men in Quarters, the first of which has been so fully borne testimony to by the Lord-Lieutenant of the County and the Inspecting Field Officer, and the latter by the Mayor and inhabitants of the Town of Doncaster.

"These good impressions the Commanding Officer sincerely hopes will not be effaced by any irregularity on the part of the men during these, the two last days of the period of training; but that they will leave that impression behind them on the minds of the inhabitants of Doncaster that they may receive a hearty welcome at the next period of Training, and that the 3rd West York may be reported of as second to no Militia Regiment in England, both for steadiness under Arms, and General Good Conduct."

The number of buglers was increased to one per Company, by War Office Circular, No. 318, dated the 16th of September. Assistant-Surgeons had formerly held Subalterns' Commissions in their regiments, but a War Office Circular, dated the 26th of October, directs that for the future they are no longer to do so, but are to take rank with Lieutenants, according to the date of their Commissions.

A new edition of the Standing Orders of the Regiment was published this year.

1854.—The Regiment assembled at Doncaster for twenty-eight days' training and exercise on the 18th of April, and was inspected by Colonel M. J. Slade, I.F.O., on the 12th of May, the number on parade being thirty-two officers, thirty-five sergeants (including twenty staff), ten drummers, and 877 rank and file.

"The Inspecting Officer was pleased to express his extreme gratification at the General Appearance and the Steadiness of the Regiment under Arms as well as their precision of movement on parade. The Commanding Officer feels that he has been much assisted in bringing the Regiment to so satisfactory a state, by the attention and zeal the Officers and Non-commissioned Officers have shown in the performance of their duties. He is desirous also of taking this opportunity of expressing how much he feels indebted to the Drill Instructors from the 1st Battalion Grenadier Guards for the great assistance they have afforded the Regiment."

On the last day of the Training, the 14th of May, a telegram was received from the War Office, directing that the Regiment should remain ten days longer for training.

From the 16th of May two sergeants and one drummer per company were authorised in addition to the sergeant-major, quartermaster-sergeant, and paymaster-sergeant.

A War Office Circular, dated the 27th of May, directed that Militiamen might be released for the purpose of enlisting into the Line, without repaying the bounty.

A letter from the Secretary of State for War, dated the 17th of June, 1854, states that he does not deem it expedient to sanction the pay of colour-sergeants in the Embodied Militia: but a subsequent letter, dated the 19th of July, approves of one of the sergeants allowed for every 100 rank and file being borne as colour-sergeant, at 2s. 4d. a-day.

A letter from the War Office, dated the 22nd of May, was received, stating that a Warrant would be prepared and sent to the Lord-Lieutenant, directing him to draw out and embody the 3rd West York Regiment of Militia, on the 26th of May; which having been done, the Regiment was ordered to proceed by rail, on the 27th of May, from Doncaster to Berwick. On the Regiment being embodied, the establishment was increased by a paymaster, one colour-sergeant to each company, and four sergeants, and four corporals for every 100 rank and file.

The clothing of regiments still continued to be provided by the Commanding Officers, the following sums being allowed for the various ranks by War Office Circular, dated the 21st of June, 1854:—

	Sergeants. £ s. d.	Corporals and Drummers. £ s. d.	Privates. £ s. d.
Suit of coatee, trousers and boots for battalion companies ...	2 18 0	1 17 9	1 12 0
Ditto, for flank companies	2 18 6	1 18 9	1 13 0
Or suit of tunic, trousers and boots	3 1 6	1 19 11	1 14 2
Ditto, for flank companies	3 2 0	2 0 11	1 15 2

This sum included two pairs of **boots for each** sergeant, and **one** for all other ranks, supplied annually whilst embodied. **The chacos were issued triennially; those for the** sergeants at a cost **of 8s. 6d. and privates 7s. 6d. A pair of fatigue trousers, at 7s. 6d., was** allowed **on joining, and also a stock, at 9½d.; but both these** articles **had to be kept up afterwards by the men** as necessaries. One shilling **per suit was** allowed for altering, **and** the clothing **did not** become the man's property until **it had been worn for one year.**

A **Letter was received from the Horse Guards, dated the 29th of** July, 1854, ordering **the Regiment to be held in** readiness to proceed from Berwick to **Dublin viâ Liverpool.**

A Memorial **was presented by the Mayor,** Sheriff, **and inhabitants** of Berwick-upon-Tweed, **to Viscount** Hardinge, the **Commander-in-Chief, stating that the "** Memorialists have **heard** with **deep regret the order which has** been received for the **sudden removal of the 3rd West** York Militia from the Barracks **of this Town." That the officers** of the Regiment had **by their gentlemanly deportment** and urbanity of manners secured the **esteem of all classes, and** that the best understanding existed **between the** Regiment generally **and the people. The Memorialists** were therefore hopeful that, **if it** could **be** done **with** justice to **the Service,** the **order for the** Regiment's removal **might be cancelled, or that their place** might **be supplied with** another **Corps.**

The **Regiment left Berwick in two divisions for Dublin; the** left **wing proceeding by rail, viâ Liverpool, on Wednesday, the 2nd of August, and arriving at Richmond Barracks on the 4th; the Head-quarters and right wing leaving on the 3rd, and arriving on the 5th of August, on board the steam ship** *Princess.*

The other regiments quartered **in Dublin were** the 3rd and **7th** Dragoon Guards, 56th **and 60th** Foot, and Cambridge and **Northampton Militia.**

A War Office **Circular, dated the** 1st of September, ordered **the bayonet** belt to **be altered to a waist belt.**

Major-General **Cochrane inspected the Regiment on the 23rd October.**

By a Circular from the **Home** Office, **dated Whitehall, the**

M

9th of November, the rank of second-lieutenant was abolished, officers thenceforth being appointed as ensign in the Militia, both in the Infantry and Artillery.

In consequence of the large number of Embodied Militia which it was found necessary to keep in billets, owing to the want of sufficient Barrack accommodation, the lodging allowance to be paid to innkeepers was increased from one halfpenny to three-halfpence per man, or from threepence halfpenny to tenpence halfpenny a week.

The following Circular on the subject of Volunteers for the Army was issued from the War Office, dated the 20th of November:—

" Sir,

" The rapid augmentation of the Regular Army being at this moment of urgent importance, it has become necessary to call upon all embodied as well as disembodied Militia Regiments to give as many Volunteers as possible to the Regiments of Guards and Line, and to the Royal Marines.

" In taking this step the Government is aware that the efficiency of your Regiment will for a time be considerably impaired by the sudden loss of a large proportion of highly trained men, whom you will have to replace by raw recruits; but at this moment the maintenance of the efficiency, for immediate service, of Regiments raised especially for home duty, important as it is, must yield to the necessity of strengthening to the utmost that portion of Her Majesty's Forces which are engaged in the operation of war abroad; and upon an occasion like the present I am confident that the same spirit which has induced you to devote yourself so successfully to the formation of the Regiment under your Command will secure to the Government your assistance and co-operation in strengthening Her Majesty's Regular Forces by drafts from your Regiment.

" It is intended to limit the demand thus to be made on Militia Regiments to twenty-five per centum on their strength, amounting in the case of the 3rd West York Regiment to 259. Recruiting parties will be forthwith directed to proceed to your head-quarters in order to recruit Volunteers.

" It is proposed to give a priority to the Recruiting parties from those Regiments which have a County Connection with your Regiment, provided such Regiments form a part of the force under Lord Raglan's orders; but men will be at liberty to join other Regiments, or the Marines if they prefer it.

"The Guards will be allowed to send parties to Regiments generally, their standard not enabling them to obtain enough recruits from any corresponding number of Militia Regiments. The Marines will likewise send parties.

"All these parties will be recalled immediately the number to be raised shall have volunteered.

"The men will be offered a bounty exceeding by £1 the augmented bounty authorised for ordinary recruits, namely £1 in addition to £6, or £7 in all.

"Though the limit of 25 per cent. is placed on the number of men whom the recruiting parties will be empowered to raise, any larger number of men will be accepted provided you are willing, with a view to further the public service in this emergency, to consent to their discharge.

"The General Commanding-in-Chief, sensible of the great exertions which have been made by Militia Officers to bring their Regiments to their present high state of efficiency, and of the sacrifice which they are now called upon to make, has authorised me to state that he is prepared to place at your disposal for any officer in your regiment whom you may wish to name, an Ensigncy in the Line without purchase for the first seventy-five men who shall Volunteer from your Regiment, and have been passed and accepted in the Regulars, or Marines, and another for the second seventy-five, and a third Ensigncy for a third seventy-five, if the strength of your Regiment enables you to give them.

"You will take the necessary measures in your County to recruit your Regiment again to its numbers after it shall have been reduced by Volunteering to the Line.

"I have the honour, &c.,

"SIDNEY HERBERT.

"COLONEL LOFTUS, 3rd West York
  Regiment of Militia."

In Regimental Orders, dated Dublin the 23rd of November,

the Commanding Officer gives notice that he will **not** allow any **man** to enlist except into those Regiments serving **or about to serve under Field Marshal Lord Raglan.** In November **and** December 196 **men** Volunteered into **the** Regular Army, the majority into **the Royal** Artillery, Grenadier Guards, and **97th Regiment.**

A Letter **was received from the Colonel of the** 19th Regiment, dated Walmer, **29th November, 1854, stating that as** his was a Yorkshire **Corps, and being very much in want of men** owing to its loss **in the** Crimea, he hoped **that the Colonel would** assist in upholding the character of Yorkshiremen, **by** encouraging Volun**teers into the** Line to join his Regiment.

In December a Horse **Guards'** Circular was issued, stating **that if the required** quota **of** twenty-five per cent. of Volunteers **into the Regular Army was not** furnished on the day specified, seven days more would be allowed, and this period would be repeated **if** necessary. The men were to be under thirty years of age, and the standard height was fixed at five-feet six inches for the Guards, five feet five and a-half inches for the Cavalry, and five feet four inches for the Infantry.

A Depôt was erected **at Doncaster, in St. J**ames Street South, in the year 1815, **at** a cost **to the West Riding of** £925, including £103 for the purchase **of the ground. The premises were con**verted into a Lock-Up **and residence for a Superintendent of the** West Riding Constabulary in **1854, when Belle-Vue, the present** Depôt, was purchased for **the sum of £3,000; £616 19s.** 8d. being spent in converting it.

In April, 1856, **the** Regimental Stores were still kept in the premises which had been taken in March, **1854, as a** Hospital; **and** nothing had then **been** done to the new Depôt, nor had it **been** handed over to the Regiment.

1855.—By an Act* passed **on the 23rd** of December, 1854, Her Majesty was enabled to accept **the** services of the Militia out of the United Kingdom, for the vigorous prosecution **of the**

---

* 18 Vict., c. 1. This Act is similar to the 54 Geo. III., c. 1, and c. 20, passed in 1813.

war; but not more than three-fourths of the actual establishment was to serve abroad; and the men who volunteered were to be re-enrolled for five years. The following Circular on the subject was received at Dublin on the 16th of January :—

"WAR DEPARTMENT, 15th Jan., 1855.

"Sir,

"In pursuance of an Act which has recently received the Royal Assent, intituled 'An Act to enable Her Majesty to accept the Services of the Militia out of the United Kingdom, for the Vigorous Prosecution of the War,' I am Commanded by the Queen to signify to you Her Royal pleasure that you should without loss of time assemble the Corps under your command, and ascertain what number of Officers, Non-Commissioned Officers, Drummers, and Private Men thereof may be disposed to extend their services as Militia to certain parts and places out of the United Kingdom, (that is to say) to Gibraltar, Malta, and the Ionian Islands, under the Provisions and subject to the Rules, Regulations, and Restrictions of that Act, and subject to such Rules and Regulations as Her Majesty may think fit to appoint.

"And I have to request that after fully explaining to every Non-commissioned Officer and Man of the Regiment under your Command the conditions of the said Act under which they may volunteer for service out of the United Kingdom, you will then transmit to the Right Honorable Sidney Herbert, Her Majesty's Secretary at War, a nominal list of Officers, and a certified statement of the number of Non-commissioned Officers, Drummers, and Private men who, in pursuance of the said Act, shall voluntarily offer to extend their services (under the Provisions of the said Act) to such parts and places out of the United Kingdom as are hereinbefore mentioned, (that is to say) to Gibraltar, Malta, and the Ionian Islands.

"I have the honor, &c.,
"NEWCASTLE.

"To the Officer Commanding
"The Third West York Regiment of Militia."

On volunteering under the above Act, the men were released

from their existing engagement, and re-enrolled for a further period of five years, according to the following form :—

"I, ———, No. ———, of the ——— Regiment of Militia, do hereby declare, That, on being released from my previous Militia Engagement, I am willing to serve in the Militia for a term of Five Years; and further, I do, of my own free Will and Consent, volunteer to serve out of the United Kingdom.
(Signed)   "———."

The Commanding Officer had to certify in each case that he had explained to the man that the offer was purely voluntary.

The men had to take the following oath :—

"I, ———, do sincerely promise and swear, That I will be faithful and bear true Allegiance to Her Majesty Queen Victoria, and that I will faithfully serve in the Militia for the Term of Five Years in [the United Kingdom, Gibraltar, Malta, *or* the Ionian Islands], unless I shall be sooner discharged."

The following Regulations regarding the number who would be permitted to serve abroad, and the pay and allowance which would be granted, were issued from the War Office :—

"WAR OFFICE, 15th *Jan.*, 1855.

" Sir,

"In transmitting for your information the accompanying Copy of the Act of Parliament, authorizing Her Majesty to accept the services of the Militia out of the United Kingdom, I have the honor to acquaint you that the following will be the conditions under which the voluntary offers of the Militia to serve out of the United Kingdom will be accepted :—

"1.—Only three-fourths of the Actual Establishment of any Regiment can be allowed to serve out of the United Kingdom. The companies proceeding abroad will consist of ninety rank and file each, and the remainder of the Regiment will form an embodied Depôt at the County Head-Quarters.

" 2.—The establishment of the companies proceeding abroad will consist as follows :—

" One Lieut.-Colonel, one Major ; one Captain and two Subalterns per Company ; one Paymaster, one Adjutant, one Quartermaster, one Surgeon, one Assistant-Surgeon, one Sergeant-Major, one Quartermaster-Sergeant, one Paymaster-Sergeant, one Armourer-Sergeant, one Hospital-Sergeant, one Orderly-Room Clerk ; five Sergeants per Company, including Colour-Sergeants ; one Drum-Major, two Drummers, per Company ; five Corporals and eighty-five Privates per Company.

" 3.—If the Regiment is Commanded by an Officer of the rank of Colonel in the Militia, there will be no objection to his proceeding with the Regiment, retaining his pay of £1 2s. 6d. as such ; but he can only rank with the Officers of Her Majesty's Regular Forces as a Lieut.-Colonel of Militia.

" 4.—The pay and allowances of Officers, Non-Commissioned Officers and Men, will be the same as in the Line, so far as may be applicable to the Militia Forces.

" The non-effective allowance to Field Officers is not admissible in Militia Regiments ; but the allowance of 3s. a-day to the Commanding Officer, and contingent allowance to the Captain at the regulated rate, will be admitted.

" The Mess allowance granted to Officers of Embodied Regiments of Militia in the United Kingdom will not be admissible at stations abroad where the allowance is not issued to Officers of Line Regiments.

" 5.—Clothing for the Non-Commissioned Officers and Men will be provided under the Regulations already issued to Embodied Regiments of Militia ; and compensation in lieu of clothing, whenever liable to be claimed, will be allowed, under such Regulations as may be fixed for the Infantry of the Line.

" 6.—Such Militiamen as may wish to volunteer for service out of the United Kingdom, will be required to make a declaration that, of their own free will and consent, they do so volunteer ; and that such offer is to be purely voluntary, should be particularly explained to each man, as pointed out in Clause 3 of the Act ; and that, on their being released from their previous engagement in the Militia, they will take the oath prescribed in the accompanying form, to serve for five years in the United Kingdom, Gibraltar, Malta, or the Ionian Islands.

"7.—The following Bounty will be allowed for each man who may volunteer for such extended service, and take the prescribed oath to serve out of the United Kingdom, viz. :—

£2 to the man on volunteering and taking the oath;
£1 to be laid out in providing him with extra necessaries;
£5 to be issued to him at the rate of £1 a-year, or 5s. quarterly.

£8 total.

"The issue of the Annual Bounty will be subject to the same Regulations as that granted to Militiamen serving in the United Kingdom.

"I have to request, therefore, that on the receipt of the Order from the Secretary of State referred to in the First Clause of the Act, you will fully explain to the Non-commissioned officers and men of the Regiment under your Command the above-recited conditions, under which they may volunteer for service out of the United Kingdom, and that you will then transmit to me a nominal List of the Officers, and a certified statement of the number of men who are prepared to offer their services under the provisions of the Act, with a view to the issue of such further instructions as may be necessary for carrying the offers of service into effect.

"I have the honor, &c.,

"SIDNEY HERBERT.

"*Officer Commanding 3rd West York Regiment of Militia.*"

The following Letter on the subject was sent to the Secretary of State for War by the Commanding Officer :—

1st (3rd West York) Militia.

"DUBLIN, 7th March, 1855.

"Sir,

"With reference to your communication marked pressing $\frac{123,374}{36}$ 29th January, and $\frac{123,374}{89}$ of the 17th ultimo, I have the

UNIV. OF
CALIFORNIA

Colonel Ferrars Loftus, 1852-1870.
in the Undress Uniform of the Regiment, 1852-56.

honor to enclose a **Return of the** Different Ranks willing to **go abroad,** and to report **that the full number of 540 rank and file of the** 1st **(3rd West York) Regiment of Militia under my command** have **volunteered to serve** in the Militia **out of the** United **Kingdom, and are ready to embark for Foreign Service on** the conditions promulgated in the **Circular dated War Office,** 15th January, 1855, $\overline{\dfrac{\text{K}}{\text{Militia.}}}$

$\overline{71}$

"I have the honor, &c.,

"FERRARS LOFTUS, Colonel,

"Commanding 3rd West York Militia."

The following **reply was received to the** above letter :—

(*Pressing.*) "WAR OFFICE, 13*th March*, 1855.

"Sir,

"In reply to your letter of the 7th Instant, **I am** directed to acquaint you, **that** the Secretary of State has approved of the **offer made by you on the part** of the Regiment under your Command, **to volunteer for service out of the** United Kingdom, **being accepted; and I am accordingly to transmit to you the necessary documents to enable you to carry your offer of Service into** effect, under **the terms set forth in the Circular Letter of the 15th Ultimo. I am again to point out to you the necessity of explaining to each man, that his offer to serve out of the United Kingdom is purely voluntary. I am to add that a** Battalion for service abroad **is not to exceed six companies, and a** sufficient number of men **beyond those volunteering must be left for** the **Depôt at home; and further, that no man should be allowed to volunteer for service abroad, who is not** certified to be medically fit for such service.

"You will be pleased **to report the number of** non-com- **missioned officers and men who have taken the oath.**

"I have the honor, &c.,

"B. HAWES.

"*The Officer* Commanding *3rd West York Militia.*"

A War Office Circular, dated the 22nd of March, states that all correspondence for the future will be carried on by the War Office instead of the Home Office, and a similar communication was made to the Deputy-Lieutenants on the 17th of March, the following year.

Some doubt having been expressed as to whether the men who were enrolled prior to the 12th of May, 1854, under previous Acts, were liable to be kept embodied for more than fifty-six days a-year, a Circular was issued from the War Office, dated the 27th of March, 1855, directing that such men should be re-attested for the remaining period of their five years' engagement, receiving an additional bounty of £1; those who declined to be re-attested to be sent to their homes, but to be called up for fifty-six days' training annually.

A War Office letter, dated the 29th of March, in reply to one of the 23rd inst., approved of the men being attested for Foreign service at once.

In consequence of the above circular 310 men declined to be re-attested, and were therefore sent to their homes from Dublin on the 3rd of April, as disembodied men. Of the remainder 157 accepted the extra bounty of £1 to be re-attested,—289 men who had joined subsequent to the 12th of May (the date of the amended Act, under which they were enlisted) were consequently liable to serve.

Colonel Loftus, in a letter to the War Office, dated the 6th of April, 1855, states, in reply to the letter authorizing the attestation of the men who volunteered for foreign service, that in consequence of the number of men who had availed themselves of permission to go home, having been enrolled previous to the 12th of May, 1854, there were not a sufficient number left, in his opinion, to serve abroad.

Of the men enrolled in England and Wales previous to the 12th of May, 1854, 16,269 were disembodied in consequence of declining to be re-attested, and 11,909 accepted the extra £1 bounty, and were re-attested. Scotland and Ireland were not affected by the Act.*

---

* Parliamentary Return (House of Commons), No. 353, 1855.

On Thursday, the 3rd of May, 1855, the Regiment was moved from Dublin to Waterford, which place they left on Wednesday, the 5th of September, for the camp at the Curragh, where they formed part of the Second Brigade, being relieved by the Dublin County Militia.

On the 12th of June a detachment of two companies was sent from Waterford to New Ross, where they remained until the 5th of September, when they joined the Regiment at the Curragh.

A communication was received from the War Department, dated the 8th of June, 1855, stating that as it had been represented to Lord Panmure that the men called up for only fifty-six days in the year would be but of little service in Embodied Regiments, while the men themselves will be interrupted in their ordinary pursuits, by having to attend for such training, such men might, if they had not been re-attested on or before the 1st of June, be with their own consent released from further service, and discharged altogether from the Militia.

On the 11th of October 99 men were struck off the strength of the Regiment in accordance with this regulation. Thirty-six men were discharged in consequence of their wives and families becoming chargeable to their parishes.

A Circular Letter was sent to Commanding Officers of Militia Regiments, dated War Department, the 26th of July, 1855, informing them that after the 1st of April, 1856, the clothing, arms, and appointments, would be provided for the Regular Army and Militia by the Government, instead of by the Officers commanding Regiments. From the earliest times until now it had been the custom for the Colonel to supply the clothing and equipment of his regiment, for which he received a fixed sum for every man on the establishment, which was known as "off reckonings."*

Double-breasted tunics, instead of the old coatee with swallow-tails, were worn for the first time on Sunday, the 5th of August, 1855. The *Waterford Daily Express* remarks that in marching to church on that day "they presented a very striking appearance."

From 1853 to 1856 the officers wore epaulets, and those of

---

* Clode's Military Forces of the Crown, Vol. II., Appendix W.W., p. 568.

the flank companies, wings; the men of the Grenadiers and Light Infantry Companies had a grenade and bugle, respectively, on the collar, the others a white rose. A black waist-belt and white shoulder-belt, with plate, chain, and whistle, was worn, the sash being tied round the waist. A single-breasted blue frock-coat was worn for undress. In 1857 a single-breasted tunic, double-breasted blue frock coat, and white waist-belt was adopted, the sash being worn over the shoulder, and cross-belts were discontinued.

A General Order (No. 650) was issued from the Horse Guards, dated the 9th of August, stating that the large increase of the Militia, and the organisation of a portion of that Force as Artillery, having rendered it necessary to determine the precedence of the New Regiments recently enrolled, a Board of Militia Officers was ordered to assemble in the Camp at Aldershot, for the purpose of declaring the precedence, alphabetically, of the Militia Artillery, and of determining, by lot, the numbers of the new Regiments of Infantry as well as those of three old Regiments which appeared to claim the same numbers.

The numbers for the Artillery were fixed as follows:—

1. Antrim
2. Armagh
3. Berwick, Haddingtonshire*
4. Cork, West
5. Cork City*
6. Cornwall and Devon Miners*
7. Devon
8. Donegal
9. Dublin City
10. Durham
11. Edinburgh City
12. Fife*
13. Forfar and Kincardine*
14. Galway
15. Glamorgan
16. Hampshire
17. Isle of Wight*
18. Kent
19. Lancashire
20. Limerick City*
21. Londonderry
22. Norfolk
23. Northumberland
24. Pembroke*
25. Suffolk*
26. Sussex
27. Tipperary*
28. Tyrone
29. Waterford*

Since then three new regiments have been added, viz., the Yorkshire in 1860, and the Argyle and Bute,* and the Carmarthen* in 1861. The latter regiment appears to have displaced the Pembroke as the 24th Regiment, which is now, together with the Yorkshire and Argyle and Bute Regiments, without a number.

Out of the 129 regiments of Infantry, the numbers of which were

---

* These thirteen old regiments were formerly Infantry, and were mostly changed into Artillery corps in 1853. The remaining nineteen regiments are new, and were raised as Artillery.

REGIMENTAL BADGES.
Half Size.

1. Officer's Chaco Plate, Gilt Star and Crown, Silver Bugle and White Rose, worn from 1853 to 1857.

2. Officer's Cross Belt Plate, Gilt Plate, with Garter and White Rose (Silver), worn from 1811 to 1852.

3. Cross Belt Plate, Chain and Whistle (Silver), worn on Cross Belt by Officers of Light Infantry Regiments, from 1853 to 1857.

THIRD WEST YORK LIGHT INFANTRY.   173

fixed in 1833, only twenty-two changes were effected, and six new
numbers were added, the following alterations being made :—

1833.	1855.	CAUSE OF ALTERATION.
Number.		
4. Rutland	5th **West York***	See No. 14.
13. North Hants	Essex Rifles	See No. 122.
14. East Essex	Rutland	See No. 13.
15. North Devon	South **Mayo**	Amalgamated with the other Devon Regiments, 1853.
28. Pembroke	5th **Middlesex***	Pembroke made Artillery.
31. Monmouth & Brecon	Monmouth	Brecon separated, see No. 132.
34. East Suffolk	2nd **Derby***	Suffolk made Artillery.
43. South Hants	2nd Durham*	Amalgamated with North Hants, 1853.
52. Hereford	Sussex	See No. 110.
53. Sussex	2nd Warwick*	See No. 52.
58. West (now 2nd) **Middlesex**	2nd Stafford*	See No. 63.
63. Isle **of Wight**	2nd **Middlesex**	Isle of Wight made Artillery.
73. Berwick and Haddington	3rd Stafford*	Berwick and Haddington made Artillery.
78. **Fife**	2nd Lanark*	Fife **made** Artillery.
82. South Mayo	6th Lancashire*	See No. 15.
84. Tipperary	4th Lancashire*	Tipperary made Artillery.
103. Limerick City	2nd Royal Cheshire*	Limerick City made Artillery.
105. **Forfar** & Kincardine	2nd South Tipperary*	Forfar and Kincardine made Artillery.
110. Cork City	Hereford	Cork City made Artillery.
118. Cornwall and Devon Miners	3rd Surrey*	Cornwall and Devon made Artillery.
122. ———	Hampshire	———
128. Waterford	4th South Middlesex*	**Waterford** made Artillery.
130. ———	7th **Lancashire***	
131. ———	2nd **Cornwall***	
132. ———	Brecon	New numbers added.
133. ———	4th **West York***	
134. ———	6th **West York***	
135. ———	5th **Lancashire***	

* These nineteen regiments were all new, the greater number having been raised in **1853.**

Of the twenty-two changes thus made, eleven were **caused** by **regiments being made Artillery** Corps; two regiments— viz., the **North Devon and South** Hants—were amalgamated **with the other** regiments **of their respective** counties (six additional **places were** added, **increasing the numbers** from 129 to 135); **and** eight regiments changed places, in **consequence** of some confusion **having** arisen by several claiming **the same number,** viz.:—

	1833	1855.		1833.	1855.
	From No.	to No.		From No.	to No.
Rutland	4	14	Hereford	52	110
North Hants	13	122	Sussex	53	52
Essex Rifles	14	13	West (2nd) Middl.	58	63
Brecon	31	132	South Mayo	82	15

At the present time, **five** places have become vacant, **viz.,** No. 14, by Rutland being amalgamated with the Northampton, in 1860; No. 24, by the Carmarthen **Fusiliers** being made **Artillery, in 1861;** No. 72, by the Kirkcudbright and Wigtown being **amalgamated, the Kirkcudbright with** the Dumfries, and the **Wigtown with the Ayr;** No. 117, **by the Argyle** and Bute being **made Artillery, in 1861; and** No. 131, **by the** 2nd Cornwall being **amalgamated with the Cornwall Rangers.**

On **the 15th of August, the Colonel wrote from Waterford,** stating **that, having obtained a number of recruits, he had no** doubt **the required** number **of men were willing to serve abroad;** **and requested** permission **to re-commence** attesting **the men for that purpose. A** reply **was received from the** War Department, **dated the** 12th of October, **stating that "As there is no** immediate **prospect of the Services of Militia Regiments** being **required abroad, Lord** Panmure cannot **at present issue an** Order **for the** attestation **of the** Volunteers of your **Regiment."**

On Thursday, the **23rd of** August, the Regiment received new Colours, to replace those which had been in **use** since 1810. The Colours, having **been consecrated** by the **Very Rev.** E. N. Hoare, Dean of Waterford, **were** presented by Miss Loftus, the daughter of the Colonel, who spoke **as follows:—***

---

* The *Waterford Daily Express.*

"Soldiers of the 3rd West York Militia,—I have a great honour conferred on me in being selected to present these Colours to the Regiment under my father's command. In doing so, I feel confident they will never be deserted. Wherever they are, there you will be, to protect your Queen and country. We are now unfortunately at war, and it is possible you will be called upon to serve, for the protection of your country, out of the United Kingdom; and I am sure you will, one and all, come forward, and follow these Colours, which I have now the honour of presenting to you."

A Letter from the Horse Guards, dated the 29th of December, authorised Captain Flood to do duty with the Turkish Contingent in the Crimea, and to be reported as "absent on duty."

1856.—The following General Order was issued to Regiments in Ireland :—

General Order.

"ADJUTANT-GENERAL'S OFFICE, DUBLIN,
7th January, 1856.

"The exemplary conduct, order, and regularity of the Regiments of Irish Militia, on the occasion of their embarking lately, at Kingstown and Cork, for England, and of the English Regiments of Militia, on their disembarking to replace them, have been mentioned in the most favourable terms by Major-General Cochrane, commanding the Dublin District, and by Major-General Mansel, commanding the Cork District.

"The General Commanding has had great satisfaction in receiving and communicating to the Field-Marshal Commanding-in-Chief the reports to which he refers, and which are so creditable to the state of discipline of these Corps, to the exertions of the Officers in Command of them, and to the Departmental Officers under whose immediate superintendence the arrangements for the departure and reception of thirty-one Regiments were made, and this service carried into effect.

"By Order of the General Commanding,

"G. E. HILLIER, Major,
"A.A.G. for the D.A.G."

Regiments of Militia embarked for England.	Regiments of Militia disembarked in Ireland.
Antrim	Bedford
Armagh	Cambridge
Cambridge	Cheshire
Cavan	Cumberland
Clare	**Devon, 1st**
Cork, **North**	Kent, West
Dublin City	Lancashire, 4th
Galway	Lancashire, 5th
Kerry	Lincoln, South
Limerick County	Middlesex, 4th
Northampton	Norfolk, **West**
Roscommon	Northampton
Tyrone	Nottingham
Westmeath	Somerset, 2nd
	Warwick, 2nd
	York, West, 1st
	York, West, 3rd

On the 8th of April, **1856**, the Regiment was relieved by the 2nd Somerset Militia, **and moved** from the Curragh by rail to Belfast.

The Regiment was inspected, at Belfast, by Major-General Gough, C.B., on the 21st of May.

A Letter was received from the Quartermaster-General's Office, dated the 10th of May, ordering the Regiment to be held in readiness to move, at the shortest notice, to Richmond Barracks, Dublin, until required to embark for Liverpool.

Orders were received by telegraph for the Regiment to embark at Belfast for Fleetwood, in two divisions; the first division, with Head-quarters, on the evening of the 29th of May, on board the *Prince Patrick;* and the second division, on Friday, the 30th of May, on board the *Royal Consort*. The Regiment arrived at Doncaster on the following day, and was quartered in billets, previous to being disembodied, which took place on Monday, the 30th of June, in accordance with the following Royal Warrant:—

"VICTORIA R.

"Whereas, by Warrant under Our **Royal** Sign-Manual, bearing date the twenty-fourth **day** of May, **1854, in** the seventeenth

Year of Our Reign, We did, for the weighty and lawful causes therein recited, order you to draw out and embody the Third West York Regiment of Militia, of the County of York (West Riding), under your direction, and to hold the same in readiness to march to such parts within this Kingdom as might be judged proper to assign to them, under the Command of such General Officer or Officers as We should be pleased to appoint over them, and to obey such further Orders as should be judged necessary for the safety and defence of this Kingdom; and whereas a Definitive Treaty of Peace has been signed, We, being most desirous to take the first opportunity of permitting the Officers, Non-Commissioned Officers and Men, who have voluntarily undertaken the obligation of Militia Service, to return to their Homes, and of relieving Our faithful subjects from the heavy burdens and expenses occasioned by the War, Our Will and Pleasure is, and We do hereby order you, with all convenient speed, to cause the said Militia of Our said County of York (West Riding) to be disembodied, and to issue all the necessary and proper directions on your part for returning the Men of the said Militia, under the orders of their Commanding Officers, to their respective Parishes and Places of Abode, where they are to remain subject to the same orders and directions as they were by law subject and liable to before they were drawn out and Embodied as aforesaid; and for so doing this shall be your Warrant.

"Given, at Our Court at St. James's, this eighteenth day of June, in the nineteenth Year of Our Reign.

"By Her Majesty's Command,

"PANMURE.

"*To Our Lieutenant of the West Riding of Our County of York; or, in his Absence, to The Deputy-Lieutenants of the said County.*"

When disembodied, on the 30th of June, the Regiment consisted of 38 officers, 41 sergeants, 21 drummers, and 657 rank and file. Up to the 24th of July, 1856, 2,380 men had been enrolled in the Regiment.

Extract from General Order No. 669.
"HORSE GUARDS, *9th June,* 1856."

"The Militia Forces having been directed to be disembodied, the Field-Marshal Commanding-in-Chief, previously to their return to their Counties, desires to offer to the Officers, Non-Commissioned Officers and Men, his best acknowledgments for the zeal and discipline which they have shown during the whole period of their service. They have not only performed every duty which fell to their share with the cheerful obedience of good soldiers, but they have, in large numbers, gallantly volunteered into the Line, at the most critical period of the War; and, by thus reinforcing the British Army before Sebastopol, have essentially contributed to its success.

"Several Regiments having volunteered their services for the garrisons of the Mediterranean, the offers of ten were accepted, thereby liberating an equal number of Regiments of the Line to proceed to the Crimea.

"The Field-Marshal has received constant reports from General Officers, at home and abroad, of the excellent state of discipline of the Militia Regiments generally; and, at this moment of their returning to their homes, he desires to express to the Officers, Non-Commissioned Officers and Private Soldiers, of every regiment embodied during the War, his thanks for their good conduct, and his best wishes for their welfare and happiness."

The following extracts are taken from the Circular Letters addressed to the Colonel, dated War Department, 20th June, 1856:—

"Sir,
"Her Majesty having been pleased to sign Orders for Disembodying the Third West York Regiment of Militia, of the County of York (West Riding), with all convenient speed, I am commanded to express to you the very great satisfaction which Her Majesty has received from the exemplary service of the said Corps under your Command, and to acquaint you that Her Majesty is pleased to grant the follow-

ing allowances on the occasion to the Officers and Men hereinafter mentioned."

To each Subaltern an allowance equal to six months' pay, and to the Surgeon and Assistant-Surgeon an allowance equal to one year's pay, from the day of Disembodiment exclusive.

The Men received the balance of their bounty for the current year, together with an allowance of fourteen days' pay, part of which was retained until the Men joined at the next Training.

The Adjutant and Permanent Staff did not receive any allowance, as they remained on pay all the year round.

" I cannot conclude this letter without expressing, through you, the satisfaction which I feel in having the honor of signifying, on the present occasion, Her Majesty's Gracious approbation of the Services of the Officers, Non-Commissioned Officers, Drummers, and Private Men, belonging to the Regiment under your Command.

"I have the honor, &c.,

" PANMURE."

Circular
K
3rd West York
233

" WAR DEPARTMENT, 20th June, 1856.

" My Lord,

" I have the honor of transmitting herewith a Warrant which Her Majesty has been pleased to issue for the disembodying of the Regiment of Militia of the County of York (West Riding) named in the Margin, and I am commanded to signify to you Her Majesty's Pleasure that it should be carried into execution on the 30th June, 1856, provided the Regiment shall be in the said Riding at that period, or, if not, as soon after as the Public Service will admit of its being sent there.

3rd
West
York.

" It is a very gratifying part of my duty to state that Her Majesty has, at the same time, Commanded me to communicate, through you, to the Officers, Non-Commissioned Officers, Drummers, and Private Men, the high sense She entertains of their Conduct, and of the zeal and spirit which they have manifested since they have been embodied, &c.

"PANMURE.

"*To Her Majesty's Lieutenant of the County of York, West Riding.*"

The following Copy of the Thanks of the House of Commons was received by the Regiment:—

"HOUSE OF COMMONS,
"*Jovis 8° die Maii,* 1856.
"*Operations of the Late* War.

"Resolved, Nemine Contradicente,

"That the Thanks of this House be given to the Officers of the several Corps of Militia which have been embodied in Great Britain and Ireland during the Course of the War, for the zealous and meritorious services which they have rendered to their Queen and Country at home and abroad.

"Resolved, Nemine Contradicente,

"That this House doth highly approve and acknowledge the services, at home and abroad, of the Non-Commissioned Officers and Men of the several Corps of Militia which have been embodied in Great Britain and Ireland during the Course of the War; and that the same be communicated to them by the Colonels or Commanding Officers of the several Corps, who are desired to thank them for their meritorious conduct.

"Ordered,

"That Mr. Speaker do signify the said Resolutions respecting the Militia, by Letter, to Her Majesty's Lieutenant of each County, Riding, and Place in Great Britain, and to his Excellency the Lord-Lieutenant of that part of the United Kingdom called Ireland."

The House of Lords passed a similar Vote of Thanks to the Militia for their services rendered during the War.*

---

* Parliamentary Debates, Vol. CXLII., pp. 182, 204-5, and 216-237.

CHAPTER VII.

FROM 1857 TO 1875.

EMBODIED FROM 1st OCTOBER, 1857, TO 2nd MAY, 1860.

CONTENTS.—Royal Warrant to Embody the Regiment.—Regiment sent to Aldershot.—Thence to Carlisle, Ashton-under-Lyne, and Tynemouth.—Volunteers supplied to the Army.—Establishment when Embodied.—Militia made liable to serve in all parts of United Kingdom.—Regiment Disembodied.—Recruiting from the Militia.—Scheme for dividing the Riding between the Six Regiments.—Training Suspended, 1861.—Establishment reduced to 700 Privates, 1864-7.—Alteration in Uniform.—Formation of the Militia Reserve.—Property Qualification Abolished.—Honorary Rank.—Reserve and Auxiliary Forces.—Commissions in the Line offered to Subalterns.—Establishment of Brigade Depôts.—Rank of Ensign abolished for that of Sub-Lieutenant.—Clothing of Men changed from Red Tunics to Scarlet Kerseys.—White Rose to be worn on Uniform.—The Annual Training 1862-1875.

1857.—After the Regiment had been disembodied on the 30th of June, 1856, they were not again assembled until re-embodied fifteen months later, a letter having been received from the War Office, dated the 11th of March, 1857, stating that it had been judged expedient by Her Majesty's Government not to assemble the Militia for training until after the 1st of September.

A Return, dated the 18th of May, 1857, gives the number of deserters from the Regiment, from the 25th of September, 1852, as 139; during the same period 2,614 men were enrolled, and 547 volunteered into the Army.

On the 25th of August an Act was passed authorising the Militia to be embodied; this Act was continued annually until the 25th of March, 1861, when it expired.*

---

* 20 & 21 Vict., c. 82 ; 21 Vict., c. 4 ; and 21 & 22 Vict., c. 86.

On the occasion of the Queen and the Prince Consort passing through Doncaster on their way to Scotland, on the 28th of August, the Regimental Staff formed the Guard of Honour at the Railway Station.

On the 5th of September, 1857, the Lord-Lieutenant wrote to inform the Colonel that he had that day received a communication from Lord Panmure stating that the 3rd West York Militia was to be drawn out and embodied with as little delay as possible, and suggesting that the 1st of October would be a convenient day for the assembly of the Regiment. In Regimental Orders of the 12th of September, it is stated that authority had been received from the Lord Lieutenant to embody the Regiment on that date.

The following is a copy of the Warrant :—

VICTORIA REG.

" We, considering that the Military operations in which We are engaged in India render it necessary to send a large part of Our Regular Forces abroad, deem it proper to provide without delay additional means for the Military service at home.

" Our will and pleasure therefore is, and We do hereby in pursuance of the Acts for the better ordering the Militia Forces in that part of Our United Kingdom of Great Britain and Ireland called England, and especially of an Act passed in the last Session of Parliament entitled An Act to Authorise the Embodying of the Militia, Order you, with all convenient speed, to draw out and embody, at such place as you shall judge most convenient, The Third Regiment of Militia of the West Riding of Yorkshire under your direction, or such a portion of the same as We may from time to time direct under the hand of one of our principal Secretaries of State, and that you do cause the same to be held in every respect ready to march as occasion shall require to such parts within this Kingdom as We shall judge proper to assign them, and to be put under command of such General Officer or Officers as We shall be pleased to appoint over them, and to obey such further Orders as shall be judged necessary for the safety and defence of this Kingdom, and for so doing this shall be your Warrant.

"Given at Our Court at St. James's this 1st day of September, 1857, in the twenty-first year of Our Reign.

"By Her Majesty's Command,

"PANMURE.

" *To Our Right Trusty and Well-beloved Cousin* WILLIAM THOMAS SPENCER, *Viscount* MILTON, *Lord-Lieutenant of the West Riding of Our County of Yorkshire, or, in his absence, to the Deputy-Lieutenants of the said County.*"

The Regiment was consequently embodied, at Doncaster, on the 1st of October, 1857, the strength being thirty-three officers and 704 non-commissioned officers and men; 423 were absent, the enrolled strength being 1,127.

On Friday, the 16th of October, the Regiment furnished a Guard of Honour to Her Majesty the Queen at the Railway Station, consisting of one captain, two subalterns, and 100 rank and file.

On Wednesday evening, the 11th of November, the Regiment moved from Doncaster to Aldershot by rail, where they arrived early the following day, and were quartered as follows: Headquarters and two companies (252 rank and file) in S. T. and V. Lines, South Camp, and eight companies (507 rank and file) in the East Block of the Permanent Barracks. One captain, one subaltern, and the assistant-surgeon, were left in Doncaster, with three sergeants and twenty-five rank and file who refused to be re-attested, and were therefore discharged as their periods of service expired. The Regiment formed part of the 2nd Brigade (which in December became the 3rd Brigade), which was composed of the 15th and 96th Regiments, 4th Lancashire, Berks, Dumfries, Sherwood Foresters (Nottingham), South Down, and Louth (Rifle), Regiments of Militia. The 15th Regiment was afterwards relieved by the 2nd Battalion of the 6th Regiment, and the 96th by the 67th Regiment. The City of Dublin and Donegal Militia also formed part of the Brigade.

A War Office Letter, dated the 25th of April, was received, stating that the services of a paymaster were to be dispensed with the services of such an officer not being considered necessary.

1858.—On the 20th of February the old "Brown Bess" muskets were replaced by the Enfield Rifle.

In March the Regiment occupied Q. and R. Lines, and in September the Head-quarters were moved to T. V. and Z. Lines, South Camp. The Regiment was inspected at Aldershot, on the 18th of May, by Major-General Lawrence, C.B., commanding the 3rd Brigade; 603 privates being present under arms.

By an Act* passed on the 2nd of August, which remained in force until the 2nd of August, 1861, the Militia was allowed to serve abroad on the same terms as under the Act passed in 1854.

On Monday, the 27th of September, the Regiment left Aldershot for the north, four companies proceeding from Farnborough to Ashton-under-Lyne, consisting of 276 rank and file; three companies to Tynemouth, of 214 rank and file; and the Head-quarters, with three companies to Carlisle, with 276 rank and file, all arriving at their destination the same day. The last-named detachment was inspected by Lieut.-General Sir Harry Smith, G.C.B., on the 7th of October. The Regiment was inspected on the 11th of December, by Colonel Wilbraham, A.A.G., at Carlisle, 204 privates being present under arms and 473 on detachment.

One company was sent from Ashton-under-Lyne, on the 17th of December, to Stockport, for target practice, returning on the 7th of January.

In January and March, 1858, 132 men volunteered into the Line; during the remainder of the year 108 more volunteered, making a total of 240 men.

The Revised Instructions issued from the Horse Guards for carrying on the volunteering from the Embodied Militia to the Regular Army in December, 1857, and January and August, 1858, fixed the quota to be supplied at seventeen per cent. of the effective rank and file on the 1st of January, 1858, which for the Regiment, was 135—184 volunteered. The volunteering was to be kept open, if necessary, for a period of three days, and if the required number of Volunteers was not furnished at once, the volunteering was to be subsequently re-opened until

---

* 21 & 22 Vict., c. 85.

the quota was completed. The men received a bounty of £2 (which was afterwards increased to £3), and were allowed to reckon one-half of their embodied Militia service, rendered while over the age of eighteen, as a part of Line service, to entitle them to pensions and other advantages, such as good-conduct pay, &c., provided they had completed six months' Militia service.

An Ensign's commission in the Line for every seventy-five men was offered by War Office Circular dated the 19th of August, 1858, for officers under twenty-three years of age, to complete the 2nd Battalions of certain Regiments.

Another Circular, dated the 30th of August, increased the number of men necessary to obtain a commission in any Regiment of the Line, Artillery or Engineers, to 100; and a subsequent one, dated the 30th of March, 1859, says that unless the numbers required are completed by the 15th of April, 1859, no commissions will be given.

The Establishment of the Regiment, when embodied, was fixed by Horse Guards' Circular, dated the 17th of December, 1858, as follows: One colonel, one lieut.-colonel, one major, ten captains, ten lieutenants, ten ensigns, one paymaster, one adjutant, one quartermaster, one surgeon, one assistant-surgeon, one sergeant-major, one quartermaster-sergeant, one paymaster-sergeant, one hospital-sergeant, one orderly-room clerk, ten colour-sergeants, forty-three sergeants, one drum-major, twenty-one drummers, fifty-four corporals, and 1,036 privates.

1859.—On the 3rd of January the detachment of three companies went from Tynemouth to Carlisle, an equal number being sent from the latter place to Tynemouth.

The first half-yearly inspection took place at Carlisle, by Colonel Wilbraham, A.A.G., on the 21st of May; only 201 privates were present on parade, 453 being on detachment.

The four companies at Ashton-under-Lyne moved on the 3rd of June to Sunderland; the Head-quarters with three companies moving at the same time from Carlisle to Newcastle-on-Tyne, where they were joined the same day by the three companies from Tynemouth.

An Act* was passed on the 13th of August, similar to the Interchange Act of 1811, to allow the Militia to serve in any part of the United Kingdom, and in the Channel Islands; and for the future Men were ordered to be enlisted to serve in Great Britain and Ireland; previous to this they were only enlisted to serve in their respective divisions of the United Kingdom.

On the 16th of August, two companies moved from Sunderland to Newcastle-on-Tyne; two companies at the latter place proceeding to Sunderland, and on the 31st of August one company from Sunderland and Newcastle exchanged quarters. All the above changes were made for the purpose of carrying on target practice.

A War Office Circular, dated the 17th of September, allowed one quartermaster, one orderly-room clerk, one additional sergeant as acting hospital sergeant, one drum or bugle-major, and one sergeant-instructor of musketry.

The Regiment was inspected on the 25th of October by Lieut.-General Sir J. L. Pennefather, K.C.B.

Colours were reduced in size this year, fringe being added, and a crown and lion substituted for a spear head on the staff.

1860.—Under the authority of War Office Circular, $\frac{\text{A Militia}}{406}$, dated 21st February, men re-enrolled after five years' service were to receive ten shillings gratuity.

On the 12th of March, three companies at Sunderland went to Carlisle. One company was sent from Newcastle to Sheffield on Saturday the 7th April, and another proceeded on the same day from Sunderland to join Head-quarters at Newcastle.

On Tuesday the 24th of April, the three companies at Carlisle, and the company at Sheffield proceeded to Doncaster, where they were joined the following day by the Head-quarters and six companies from Newcastle.

A Royal Warrant was received, dated the 5th of April, 1860, similar to the one dated the 18th of June, 1856,† stating that Her Majesty had been graciously pleased to sign orders for

---

* 22 & 23 Vict., c. 38.   † See pages 176, 177

disembodying the Militia, &c. The Regiment was therefore disembodied at Doncaster on the 2nd of May, the strength then being 36 officers, 50 sergeants, 16 drummers, and 831 rank and file.

The Badge of the Regiment—"the White Rose" of York—which was conferred by the Prince Regent in 1811, was approved by Her Majesty this year; a Memorandum, dated War Office, the 15th of August, 1860, being forwarded to the Regiment by order of the Lord-Lieutenant in a letter from the Clerk of Lieutenancy, dated the 25th of August, and ordered to be deposited with the other Regimental Records at Headquarters.

A War Office Circular, dated the 14th of June, 1860, addressed to the Officers Commanding Militia Regiments, and signed by Sidney Herbert, on the subject of recruiting the Regular Army from the Militia, was issued, from which the following are a few extracts:—

"It is most important to the efficiency of the Militia, as a Reserve Force upon which dependence can be placed in case of national danger, that it should be raised from among men of settled habits and fixed residence within the county to which the regiment belongs." . . . . . "And who by leaving the Militia for the Line after receiving the Militia bounty, disorganise the Militia, while they enter the Army at an increased and unnecessary expense to the public." . . . .

"Stringent orders have been issued prohibiting any Line, or other Recruiting Parties, from attempting in future in any way to induce Miltiamen to leave their respective regiments, in order to enlist in Her Majesty's Regular Forces, or Marines: Militiamen having no more right to do so than men of one Line Regiment have to enlist in another without the consent of their Commanding Officer. Such a proceeding on their part amounts to desertion, and will expose them to the penalties attached to that offence, a liability which every opportunity should be taken to make known. Volunteers, therefore, who may be anxious to enlist in the Regular Army, should apply for permission to their Commanding Officer, who will exercise their discretion as to granting their request, bearing in mind the policy of granting conditional releases to men who are bent on enlisting, and over whose movements, except during the one month's training, they have little or no practical control. In such cases I shall be prepared, on your recommendation, to give you a covering authority for the release of any such men to whom you may think it right to grant the indulgence. But it is to be clearly understood that in all such cases the men will be required to refund 18s. 6d., to cover the bounty and other expenses incurred on their enrolment; also any balance of bounty they may have received in advance on account of their first engagement, if re-attested for a second."

A Letter was received from the **Clerk of Lieutenancy**, dated **Leeds, the 14th of July, 1860**, stating that the Lord-Lieutenant had received a communication from the Secretary of State for War, relative to the division of the Riding into Recruiting Districts for the Militia, and suggesting that a meeting of the Commanding Officers and Adjutants of the several Regiments of the Riding should be arranged to settle the question. The following scheme was the result of the two meetings held; but this proposed arrangement has never been carried into effect:—

" At a General Meeting of Lieutenancy, held under the sanction of Her Majesty's principal Secretary of State for War, in the Grand Jury Room, at the Town Hall, in Leeds, on Wednesday, the 24th day of October, 1860, for the purposes directed by Section I. of the 23rd and 24th Victoria, Cap. 120.*

---

* " The Lieutenant of each County, Riding, and Place in *England* shall, as soon as conveniently may be after the passing of this Act, when required or authorised so to do by One of Her Majesty's Principal Secretaries of State, summon a General Meeting of the Lieutenancy of such County, Riding, or Place, and such Lieutenant, together with Three or more Deputy-Lieutenants, or in the Absence of the Lieutenant, or, if his Office be vacant, any Five or more Deputy-Lieutenants, may at such General Meeting, or at an Adjournment thereof, alter all or any of the appointed Sub-divisions within such County, Riding, or Place, or constitute new Sub-divisions therein, in such Manner as may appear to them convenient for the Execution of this Act and other Acts in relation to the Militia (the Act of the Session holden in the Fifteenth and Sixteenth Years of Her

"The Right Honourable the Earl FitzWilliam, Lord-Lieutenant, in the Chair.

"Resolved,

"1. That, as there are now three Regiments added to the three formerly existing in the Riding, it is desirable to discontinue the former divisions, and to divide the Riding afresh.

"2. That a new arrangement should include, as nearly as may be, one-sixth part of the Riding for each Regiment—not in area only, but also in reference to population.

"3. That for this purpose a Committee be appointed to consider and report thereon, five to be a quorum; such Committee to be formed in the following manner, viz.: a Deputy-Lieutenant to be appointed by the Deputy-Lieutenants in each Petty Sessional Division, to be a Member of the Committee; and that the Clerk of Lieutenancy do communicate with the Deputy-Lieutenants in each Petty Sessional Division, requesting them to proceed herein, and to report to him.

"4. That this Meeting do now adjourn to the call of the Lord-Lieutenant, to consider and determine on the Report of the Committee.

"FitzWilliam, Chairman."

The following were the details fixed by the Committee at their second meeting:—

"Town Hall, Leeds, 21st Dec., 1860.

"At a Meeting of the Committee appointed in pursuance of the Resolution passed at the General Meeting of the 24th October last, the Rev. J. A. Rhodes in the Chair,

"Resolved,

"1. That the following division of the Riding be adopted as a basis on which to arrange the Sub-divisions, viz.:—

"For the First Regiment of Militia (Head-Quarters, Pontefract).—The Wapentake of Agbrigg (excepting the Borough of

---

Majesty, Chapter Fifty, Section Ten, notwithstanding), and the Lieutenant shall report the Result of every such Meeting, and the Description of the Sub-division of such County, Riding, and Place, whether altered or constituted at such Meeting, or otherwise, to the Secretary of State."

Huddersfield); the Wapentake of Staincross; the Wapentake of Osgoldcross.

"For the Second Regiment (Head-Quarters, York).—The City and Ainsty of York; the Wapentake of Barkston Ash; one-half of the Borough of Bradford; one-half of the Borough of Huddersfield.

"For the Third Regiment (Head-Quarters, Doncaster).—The Wapentake of Strafforth and Tickhill.

"For the Fourth Regiment (Head-Quarters, Leeds).—The Wapentake of Skyrack; that part of the Borough of Leeds which is in the Wapentake of Morley.

"For the Fifth Regiment (Head-Quarters,* Knaresborough.)—The Wapentake of Claro; the Wapentake of Staincliff; the Wapentake of Ewcross; one-half of the Borough of Bradford.

"For the Sixth Regiment (Head-Quarters, Halifax).—The Wapentake of Morley (except the Borough of Bradford, and that part of the Borough of Leeds which is in this Wapentake); one half of the Borough of Huddersfield.

"2. That the Clerk of Lieutenancy communicate with the Deputy-Lieutenants acting within each of the above-named Six Divisions, requesting them to ascertain what would be the most convenient places within such Divisions respectively for holding Sub-division Meetings, and to fix the limits of the Sub-divisions accordingly, subject to confirmation by the adjourned General Meeting.

"J. A. RHODES, Chairman."

1861.—A Letter from the Clerk of Lieutenancy, dated Leeds, the 1st of April, states that the Regiment is not to be called out for Training this year.

1862.—The recruits of the Regiment assembled on the 24th of April, for fourteen days' preliminary drill, at Doncaster; the remainder assembled on the 8th of May, for twenty-one days' Training. Colonel Goodwyn, C.B. (41st Foot) inspected the Regiment on the 26th of May, the strength being: twenty officers, forty-three sergeants, fourteen drummers, and 816 rank

---

* This arrangement contemplates the possibility of the Head-quarters of the Regiment being removed to Skipton.

and file; 764 privates being present under arms. The Regiment was dismissed on the 28th of May.

A War Office Circular, dated the 30th of April, 1862, Militia, directs that Militia officers, both captains and subalterns, proceeding to the School of Musketry, are to receive the pay of their rank and travelling expenses, &c.

$\frac{A}{687}$

Orders were issued from the Horse Guards, dated the 12th of February, directing that Companies were to stand on parade according to the seniority of the captains, from flanks to centre, the senior captain on the right, the next senior on the left, and so on.

1863.—The Regiment assembled for twenty-one days' Training on the 22nd of April, at Doncaster, the recruits having assembled for fourteen days' preliminary drill on the 8th of April. The inspection took place on the 11th of May, by Lieutenant-General Sir G. A. Wetherall, K.C.B., the numbers present being: seventeen officers, forty sergeants, thirteen drummers, and 759 rank and file; 689 privates being present under arms. The Regiment was dismissed the following day.

1864.—On the 4th of April the recruits assembled at Doncaster for fourteen days' preliminary drill, and were joined, on the 18th of April, by the remainder of the Regiment, for twenty-one days' Training.

At the inspection by Colonel Campbell, C.B., I.F.O., on the 3rd of May, the Regiment mustered fifteen officers, forty-one sergeants, eleven drummers, and 863 rank and file; 803 privates being present under arms. The men were dismissed on the 8th of May.

A War Office Letter, dated the 23rd of August, ordered that the Regiment was not to be recruited above 700, with 10 volunteer sergeants and 30 corporals.

Great-coats with detached capes were sanctioned in General Orders, on the 28th of April.

1865.—The preliminary drill of the recruits who were called out on the 24th of April, was reduced to seven days this year, the Training being increased from twenty one to twenty-seven days, so that the actual period remained the same.

The Regiment assembled on the 1st of May at Doncaster, and was inspected on the 25th of May by Colonel G. W. P. Bingham, C.B., A.A.G., Manchester. The numbers present at the inspection were fifteen officers, thirty-seven sergeants, eleven drummers, and 759 rank and file; 692 privates being present under arms. The Regiment was dismissed on the 27th of May.

A War Office Letter, dated the 18th of January, directed that soldiers might be transferred to the Militia after eighteen instead of twenty years' service, the subsequent service in the Militia to count the same as Line service to complete the qualifying period for pension.

A Circular Memorandum, dated Horse Guards, the 10th of June, directs that companies are to be designated in the Infantry by letters from A to M (excluding J), for all purposes of interior economy.

1866.—The Regiment assembled for twenty-seven days' Training at Doncaster, on the 16th of April, the recruits having assembled for seven days' preliminary drill on the 9th of April. At the inspection by Colonel Budd, 1st Battalion 14th Foot, on the 10th of May, the following numbers were present:—fourteen officers, thirty-six sergeants, eleven drummers, and 614 rank and file; 556 privates being present under arms. On the 12th of May the Regiment was dismissed.

By War Office Circular (No. 971, Militia), dated the 20th of August, stripes, similar to the good-conduct stripes worn in the Line, were ordered to be worn on the right arm above the cuff by re-enrolled men, one for each period of re-engagement.

On the 31st of December, steel scabbards, instead of black leather, were sanctioned for all officers by Horse Guards' Memorandum.

1867.—The recruits were called up for fourteen days' preliminary drill on the 13th of May, and the Regiment assembled for twenty-seven days' Training at Doncaster on the 27th of May. On the 18th of June the Regiment was inspected by Colonel

H. Bingham, C.B., I.F.O., and was dismissed on the 22nd of June. The strength at the inspection was eighteen officers, thirty-six sergeants, eleven drummers, and 637 rank and file; 562 privates being present under arms.

In March the undress double-breasted blue frock-coat was abolished, and the present blue patrol jacket substituted, and the Bands, which had been dressed in white coatees or tunics, with regimental facings, since 1830, were ordered to wear red tunics. (G. O. Nos. 21 and 22).

The Militia Reserve Act* was passed on the 20th of August, which authorised one-fourth of the quota of the United Kingdom, or 30,000 men, to be enlisted for five years, receiving one pound per annum in addition to their Militia Bounty, for which they became liable to be drafted into any regiment of the Regular Army in case of war.

The pay of the men was increased by twopence a-day from the 1st of April, by War Office Letter, dated the 20th of August.

The Regiment was ordered to be recruited up to its full strength of 1,036 privates, by War Office Letter, dated the 16th of October.

In consequence of the Fenian disturbances this year, a guard of one orderly-sergeant and one drummer was ordered by War Office Letter, dated the 17th of October, to remain on duty at the Depôt night and day, to protect the stores. On the 23rd of March, 1869, the guard was dispensed with.

On the 30th of December, Snider breech-loading rifles were supplied to the Permanent Staff.

1868.—The Regiment was assembled for twenty-seven days' Training at Doncaster, on the 18th of May, the recruits having joined on the 4th of May for fourteen days' preliminary drill. Colonel H. Bingham, C.B., I.F.O., inspected the Regiment on the 10th of June, consisting of fourteen officers, thirty-six sergeants, eleven drummers, and 645 rank and file; 565 privates being present under arms. On the 13th of June the Regiment was dismissed.

---

* 30 & 31 Vict., c. 111.

In September the tunic of the Infantry of the Army was altered, by the buttons being removed from the cuffs and skirts, the latter being made plain, like the Royal Artillery, and the former braided with lace; the present full-dress, lace, sash and belts, &c., were at the same time sanctioned (General Order No. 79).

The first men for the Militia Reserve, to the number of eighteen, were enrolled on the 10th of June; three more subsequently joined.

1869.—On the 26th of April the Regiment assembled at Doncaster for twenty-seven days' Training, the recruits having been called out on the 12th of April for fourteen days' preliminary drill. The Regiment was inspected by Colonel A. Wombwell, A.I.R.F., on the 19th of May; strength,—eighteen officers, thirty-six sergeants, eleven drummers, and 658 rank and file; 552 privates being present under arms. The Regiment was dismissed on the 22nd of May.

Lodging allowance was granted, during Training, to officers when not provided with quarters, at the following rates:—field officers commanding Infantry or Artillery battalions, 4s. per diem; other field officers, 3s.; captains, 2s. 3d.; subalterns, 2s.; surgeons, 3s.; assistant-surgeons, 2s; quartermasters being increased from 10s. to 14s. a-week, or the same as for subalterns.

By War Office Circular, dated the 23rd of April, 1869, the pay of Militia officers was made the same as officers of the Line, with 4s. mess allowance per diem. If in Public Quarters, half lodging allowance was authorized to be given to provide furniture, &c. Exchanges to other regiments were sanctioned, officers retaining the date of their commissions in the Service.

Officers were allowed to retain their rank and wear the uniform of their regiments on retiring after fifteen years' service, ten of which had been in the Militia; and a step of honorary rank was granted to field officers after twenty years' service, of which fifteen had been in the Militia; captains after twenty years' service, of which ten had been in the Militia; lieutenants after twenty years' service, of which ten had been in the Militia.

A War Office **Letter, dated the 17th** of March, ordered that **if the number of men enrolled exceeded** 1,000, **recruiting was to be suspended.**

An Act* was passed on the 13th of May which abolished the property **qualification** for officers, and allowed the Militia to be put **under the** command of General Officers when assembled for Training, and during which period officers of **the** Regular Army might also be attached to assist, **or** to make **up the** number required.

In May a General Order **was issued (No. 55)** directing **that the** sergeant-major **and quartermaster-sergeant were** to **wear the** chevrons below **the elbow, the other sergeants above.**

In June a **new pattern chaco** was adopted, smaller **in size,** with a curb chain, **and** lace for officers, by G. O. No. 65.

The Articles **of War were** altered this year **to** allow the Commanding Officers **of** Regiments to impose fines for drunkenness.

Previous to this year Special Circulars were issued by the **War** Office on each subject to each branch of the Reserve Forces, **but on the** 19th of April a series of " Reserve Forces Circulars " **were commenced,** which were issued complete, for all **the Reserve Forces, and have** since been continued quarterly.

1870.—The recruits assembled at Doncaster for fourteen days' preliminary drill on the 18th of April; **the** Regiment assembled on the 2nd of May for twenty-seven days' preliminary drill. **Eight** officers from the **Line, viz., two from the 4th, four from the** 22nd, and **two from the 100th** Foot, **were attached to the Regiment for the Training. The inspection took** place on the 25th of May, by Colonel Wombwell, **A.A.G., the strength** being (exclusive of **the** eight **subalterns** from the Line) fourteen officers, thirty-seven **sergeants, nine** drummers, and 748 rank and file ; **674** privates being present under arms. The Regiment was dismissed on the 28th of May.

A War Office Circular, dated the 16th of April, states that **a Commission will** be given for every hundred Militia Reserve **men** when called out for **active** service.

* 32 Vict. c. 13.

On the 28th of April the waterproof cloak at present in use was approved by General Order No. 28.

Another Circular, dated the 25th of June, sanctions honorary rank being conferred whilst serving, but which was not to confer higher command.

Schools of Instruction for Officers of the Reserve Forces were established by a War Office Circular (Special), dated the 29th of August.

On the 1st of September, 1,034 Snider breech-loading rifles were received, to replace the Enfield muzzle-loader.

1871.—The Regiment assembled for twenty-seven days' training at Doncaster on the 8th of May, the recruits having assembled for twenty-eight days' preliminary drill on the 10th of April. The Regiment was inspected on the 31st of May by Col. Nason, A.A.G., the strength being nineteen officers, thirty-four sergeants, nine drummers, and 798 rank and file (exclusive of four subalterns from the 14th Regiment); 723 privates were present under arms. On the 3rd of June the Regiment was dismissed.

A Letter was received from the War Office, dated the 9th of August, and again on the 30th of December, ordering every endeavour to be made to complete the full quota of the Regiment.

The Regulation of the Forces Act,* which was passed on the 17th of August, transferred the command of the Militia from the Lords-Lieutenant of Counties to the Crown; the Officers from this time being commissioned by the Sovereign instead of by the Lord-Lieutenant of their county. The Preliminary Drill for recruits was authorised to be extended to a period not exceeding six months.

On the 20th of October the clothing for the Permanent Staff was ordered to be made up at Head-quarters for the future.

1872.—On the 26th of February the recruits assembled for fifty-five days' preliminary drill at Doncaster, but did not

---

* 34 & 35 Vict., c. 86.

attend the Training, being dismissed on the 20th of April, after having been inspected by Colonel Nason, A.A.G., on the 17th of April. The Regiment assembled for twenty-seven days' training on the 20th of May, and was encamped for the first time on the Race Common. The Regiment was inspected by Colonel Nason, A.A.G., on the 12th of June, the strength being seventeen officers, thirty-four sergeants, ten drummers, and 639 rank and file (exclusive of one subaltern from the 2nd Battalion 8th Foot and three sergeants from the 73rd Foot); 526 privates being present under arms. The Regiment was dismissed on the 15th of June.

On the 5th of January a General Order (No. 5) directs that pantaloons and high boots are to be worn instead of booted overalls or Wellington boots. This order was made applicable to mounted Officers of Infantry the following month by G. O. No. 18, which also approved of a sabretache being worn, and altered the mess jacket to the pattern now worn.

An Order in Council, dated the 5th of February, notified the transfer of the command of the Militia from the Lords-Lieutenant to the Crown, under the Regulation of the Forces Act. Under this Circular all Subalterns, unless they had served for one year in the Regular Army, had to pass an examination within a fixed period after their appointment; and, except under very exceptional circumstances, no Subaltern was to be promoted to the rank of Captain, unless he had served for three Trainings, or been in the Regular Army; and the subjects of examination for each rank were laid down, which all had to pass before promotion, up to the rank of Major. Honorary Colonels were also authorised to be appointed to regiments.

Commissions in the Line were offered to Subalterns of the Militia who had served two Trainings, and were between nineteen and twenty-two years of age, at the rate of one per annum for every regiment of ten companies.

Dating from the 22nd of February, 1871, adjutants were to hold their appointments for five years only.

This was also the first year in which Militia regiments were allowed to encamp for Training instead of being quartered in billets.

A War Office Circular (Special), dated the **24th of** February, directs that the **Militia are to wear** good-shooting badges, the same as the Line.

By a War Office Circular, dated the 28th of May, the title of the Militia, **Yeomanry, and Volunteers,** was changed from " Reserve " to " Auxiliary" Forces ; the Pensioners and Army Reserve being styled " Reserve Forces."

1873.—The recruits assembled at Doncaster, on the 7th of April, for fifty-five days' preliminary drill, **and were** joined by the remainder of the Regiment on the **2nd of June for** twenty-seven days' Training. The Regiment **was encamped on the Race Common, and was inspected** on the 25th **of** June by Colonel Lightfoot, C.B., commanding the 7th Brigade Depôt, the strength being **twenty-one** officers, thirty-three sergeants, eight drummers, and **727 rank and file ;** 535 privates being present under arms. The Regiment was dismissed on the 28th of June.

By Auxiliary **Forces** Circular, **dated** the 1st **of** January, no candidate is eligible **for a commission as** Lieutenant in the Militia if above thirty **years of age, or as** Captain if over thirty-five years. Officers who have served upwards of three years in the Regular **Army may be** appointed Lieutenants up to thirty-five years, or a **Captain up to forty years of age, provided they** held that **rank, or passed the qualifying examination for pro-motion.**

A Circular, **dated** the 21st of April, contains a Warrant, dated the 8th of April, stating that the Queen had sanctioned the formation of Brigade Depôts of Militia, **Yeomanry, and** Volunteers, as now established.*

The Regiment was **brigaded with the 65th (North** Yorkshire) **and 84th (**York and **Lancaster)** Regiments, **and a 2nd** Battalion **was added to** the Regiment, which has not **yet** been raised. The

---

* The **Committee which organised** the scheme **of** Brigade Depôt Centres presented **their** first **Report on the** 22nd of February, 1872, this was followed by **a** supplementary **report, dated the** 4th **of** July ; the final report, in which the present **organisation was completed,** being dated the 21st of February, **1873.**

Fourth Administrative Battalion West York Rifle Volunteers and 2nd West York Rifle Volunteers were also attached to the brigade, the whole forming the 7th Sub-district, under the command of Colonel Lightfoot, C.B., of the 84th Regiment.

The Regulations relating to honorary rank, which were first issued in a Letter to the Lords-Lieutenants, dated the 23rd of April, 1869, were revised. Officers, after fifteen years' service, ten of which had been in the Militia, were to retain their rank and wear the uniform of their regiment on retirement; and a step in rank was given to field officers, except colonels, after twenty-five years' service, of which fifteen had been in the Militia; to captains after twenty years' service, fifteen of which had been in the Militia; and to lieutenants after twenty years' service, ten of which had been in the Militia.

By another Circular (Special), dated the 28th of May, the rank of second lieutenants, cornets, and ensigns was abolished in the Auxiliary Forces; officers being appointed as sub-lieutenants, to serve for two years on probation, and provided they had then passed the necessary examination, were promoted to lieutenants, their commissions being antedated to the date of their first commissions.

Two important Circulars were issued on the 22nd of November, and the 5th of December, which, under the authority of the New Act, extended the period of service in the Militia, and the Militia Reserve, from five to six years, from and after the 8th of December.

A Royal Warrant, dated the 20th of September, was also issued abolishing (nominally) the stoppage for the rations of bread and meat.

1874.—By Circulars, dated the 22nd of January and the 5th of March, 1874, the stoppage for Militiamen was reduced to threepence per diem.

A scarlet patrol jacket was approved in General Orders (No. 65) in September, but was only in existence a short time, being abolished in August the following year by General Order No. 57.

On the 13th of April the recruits assembled for fifty-five days' preliminary drill at Doncaster. The Regiment assembled for twenty-seven days' Training on the 8th of June, the whole being encamped on the Race Common, where the recruits had been since the 1st of June. The Regiment was inspected by Colonel Lightfoot, C.B., commanding the 7th Brigade Depôt, on the 2nd of July, the men being dismissed on the 4th of July. The strength at the inspection was twenty-two officers, forty-four sergeants, nine drummers, and 701 rank and file; 544 privates being present under arms.

On the 1st of April a War Office Circular was issued revising the Regulations for Examination for Promotion, which added the Standing Orders of the Regiment to the subjects of examination.

By War Office Circular (Special) dated the 25th of February, the red tunic was abolished, and was replaced by a scarlet cloth frock for sergeants, and Kersey frock for privates; which were issued at the commencement of the Training, together with one pair of blue tweed (instead of black cloth) trousers for both ranks.

On the 7th of May a new pattern Badge for the Glengarry caps of the men was approved.

In May the first step was taken towards forming 2nd Battalions to Militia Regiments, under the New Organisation Scheme, by a War Office Circular (Special), dated the 13th of May, which added a second battalion to four regiments, and increased twelve regiments by two companies, or batteries, and four by one company, or battery.

By a Circular (Special), dated the 11th of May, an addition of one sergeant and one corporal was authorised; making four sergeants (including Staff) and four corporals per company.

This was the last year in which shell jackets were worn by the men for undress.

A Circular, dated the 25th of July, ordered the uniform of sub-lieutenants to be the same as lieutenants, with a star on the collar of the tunic instead of a crown; previous to this sub-lieutenants were not permitted to wear lace.

1875.—The recruits were assembled for fifty-five days' preliminary drill on the 5th of April. The Regiment assembled for twenty-seven days' Training on the 31st of May, and was

REGIMENTAL BADGES.
Half Size.

1. Chaco Plate, Universal Pattern, worn by Rank and File. 2. Officer's Chaco Plate, 1857-75. 3. Forage Cap Plate, for Rank and File, 1874. 4. Old Forage Cap Plate for Rank and File, 1853-73. 5. Full Dress Waist Belt Plate, for Infantry Officers of Line and Militia, 1868-75. 6. Embroidered Forage Cap Badge, worn by Officers, 1853-75. 7. Officer's Waist Belt Plate, 1857-75. 8. Universal Pattern Button, for Army and Militia, 1873-75. 9. Regimental Button, worn from about 1810 to 1852. 10. Regimental Button, 1853-75. 11. Drummer's Lace, Regimental Pattern—white with green border and diagonal red stripe. 12. Drummer's Lace, Universal Pattern—white with red crown, 1873-75

encamped on the Race Common. On the 24th of June the Regiment was inspected by Colonel Lightfoot, C.B., commanding 7th and 8th Brigade Depôts; 409 privates being present under arms.

On the 29th of March a Circular (Special) was issued, in accordance with a Warrant dated the 24th of March, under which Adjutants who were appointed previous to the 22nd of February, 1871, were offered a higher rate of retired allowance provided they accepted the terms before the 1st of October. This was done with a view of completing the new Brigade Depôt Scheme, by appointing officers who were on the full pay of their Regiments, and for five years only. The following were the rates offered:—

	Per Diem.	
	s.	d.
Under five years as Adjutant...	7	0
After five years and under ten years...	8	0
After ten years and under fifteen	9	0
Fifteen years' service as such...	10	0

On the 30th of June, the White Rose was authorised to be worn on the collar of the Kersey frocks, in consequence of the Regimental pattern buttons having been abolished throughout the Army, except for officers, and a universal pattern, bearing the Royal Arms, having been adopted; all Regiments entitled to special Badges being permitted to wear them in this manner, instead of, as hitherto, upon their buttons.

COLOURS.

It was formerly the custom for regiments to bear the Arms of their County, County Town, Lord Lieutenant, or Colonel, on their Regimental Colour. The Regimental Colour in 1798 was bottle green, with the Arms of the Colonel, Sir George Cooke, Bart., on a shield in the centre, surrounded by a wreath, with a rose, thistle, and shamrock underneath, and " V. Regiment West York Militia;" changed to " III." Regiment in 1800. They appear to have afterwards been dark green, with the words " III. Regiment West York Militia," in gold letters on a shield with crimson ground, surrounded with a wreath of oak leaves *proper* and spangles.

FIRST REGIMENT OF MILITIA.

The Colours of Infantry are of Silk. The Royal, or First Colour of every Regiment is the Great Union, the Imperial Colour of the United Kingdom of Great Britain and Ireland, in which the Cross of St. George is conjoined with the Crosses of St. Andrew and St. Patrick, on a blue field, with the Imperial Crown in the centre, and the number of the regiment in gold Roman characters underneath.

The Regimental, or Second Colour is of the same colour as the facings of the regiment, with the Union, 12 inches square, in the upper canton, except in those regiments which are faced with red, white, or black; in those regiments which are faced with red, or white, the Second Colour is the Red Cross of St. George, in a white field, and the Union in the upper canton. In those regiments which are faced with black, the Second Colour is the St. George's Cross, with the Union in the upper canton; the three other cantons black. The number of the regiment is embroidered in gold Roman characters in the centre.

The Regimental Colours also bear the devices, distinctions and mottoes, which have been conferred by Royal Authority; the whole ensigned with the Imperial Crown. *Second* Battalions carry the same Colours as First Battalions, with the addition of " II. Batt." on a scroll below the Union-wreath.

Those regiments which have a Royal, County, or other title, bear such designation on a red ground, in a circle within the Union-wreath of roses, thistles, and shamrocks. The number of the regiment in gold Roman characters in the centre.

In those regiments which bear any ancient badge, the badge is on a red ground in the centre, and the number of the regiment in gold Roman characters underneath. The Royal, or other title, being inscribed on a circle within the Union-wreath.

Previous to the year 1859 Colours were 6 feet flying, and 5 feet 6 inches deep on the pike, which was surmounted by a spear-head; but in this year they were reduced in size to 3 feet 9 inches flying, and 3 feet on the pike, exclusive of the fringe (about 2 inches deep), which was then added; the Royal Crest—a Crown and Lion *passant gardant* being substituted for the spear-head. The fringe of the First or Royal Colour is gold and crimson; and of the Second, gold combined with the same colour as the flag itself. The cords and tassels are crimson and gold mixed, and are 3 feet long.

The Colours now in use by the Regiment are of the large pattern, with spear-head, and without fringe, having been presented in 1855; and with this exception they are precisely the same as the illustration at the beginning of this volume, which is according to the new pattern, the Badges, &c. remaining unaltered.

APPENDIX A.

SUCCESSION OF OFFICERS

of

THE REGIMENT.

FROM 1758 TO 1875.

RANK AND NAME.	DATE OF APPOINTMENT.	REMARKS.
HONORARY COLONEL.		
Ferrars Loftus	25th April, 1870	From Colonel Commanding
COMMANDANTS.		
Colonel William Thornton	1758-1763	To Colonel, 2nd West York
,, Sir George Cooke, Bt.	27th Feb., 1797	Resigned 15th May, 1803
,, Bryan Cooke	16th May, 1803	Resigned 22nd Feb., 1812
,, Wm. Bryan Cooke	23rd Feb., 1812	From Lt.-Col., res. 7th Dec. 1819
,, George Cholmley	27th Jan., 1820	From Lt.-Col., re. 29th Aug. 1850
,, George Lane Fox	31st Aug., 1850	Resigned 17th Sept., 1852
,, Ferrars Loftus	18th Sept., 1852	Res. 24th Ap. 1870. To Hon.Col.
Lieut.-Colonel **Commandant,** Edward Prothero	25th April, 1870	From Lieut.-Col. Hon. rank of Colonel, 12th Sept. 1870
LIEUT.-COLONELS.		
Daniel Lascelles	1758-1763	
Peter Auriol H. Drummond	27th Feb., 1797	Died 21st March, 1799
John Cooke	1st April, 1799	From Maj., res. 24th May, 1803
George Wroughton	30th May, 1803	From Maj., res. 16th June, 1806
John Vincent	17th June, 1806	From Major, res. 24th Oct. 1811
William Marshall	21st Mar., 1808	From Major, res. 5th June, 1811
William Bryan Cooke	25th Oct., 1811	Promoted to Col. 23rd Feb. 1812
George Cholmley	26th May, 1812	Promoted to Col. 27th Jan. 1820
Stamp Brooksbank	22nd May, 1820	From Major, res. 9th Jan. 1822
Francis Dacre	10th Jan, 1822	From Maj., res. 27th Feb., 1846
John Barnett	28th Feb., 1846	Died at Dublin, 23rd Feb., 1855
Edward Prothero	20th Mar., 1855	Promoted to Lt.-Col. Commdt., 25th April, 1870

LIEUT.-COLONELS—Con.	DATE OF APPOINTMENT.	REMARKS.
Thomas John Stannard MacAdam	14th Mar., 1871	Honorary Rank } Now
John Kendall	30th July, 1873	Honorary Rank } serving

MAJORS.		
William Tuffnell Joliffe	1758-1763	Died 21st April, 1797
John Cooke	27th Feb., 1797	Prom. to Lt.-Col. 1st Apr., 1799
George Cooke	25th June, 1798	From Capt., res. 6th Jan., 1799
George Wroughton	7th Jan., 1799	From Capt., **prom. to** Lt.-Col., 30th May, **1803**
John Tunnadine Vincent	1st May, 1799	From Capt., prom. to Lt.-Col. 17th June, 1806
William Mordaunt Milner	20th June, 1803	From Capt. 1st W. Y. M., resigned 13th Oct., 1803
Hugh Blaydes	19th Oct., 1803	From Capt., res. 24th Mar.,1807
William Marshall	17th June, 1806	From Capt., prom. to Lt.-Col. 21st Mar., 1808
James Richardson Collins	22nd Mar., 1807	From Capt., died 22nd June, 1810
Godfrey Higgins	21st Mar., 1808	**Reappointed.** From Capt., res. 6th Dec., 1811
Robert Haggard Benson	30th Oct., 1811	From Capt., cshd.1st Oct., 1813
Francis Dacre	15th May, 1812	From Capt., prom. to Lt.-Col. 10th Jan., 1822
Stamp Brooksbank	17th Nov., 1813	From Capt., prom. to Lt.-Col. 22nd May, 1820
Christopher Clarke	22nd May, 1820	From Capt., died 1851 (?)
William Duncombe (afterwards Baron Feversham	9th Jan., 1823	Resigned 27th Feb., **1846**
Charles Stapleton	28th Feb., 1846	Resigned 1852
Henry Dixon	17th April, 1851	Resigned 1852
Ralph Creyke	26th Nov., 1852	Resigned 21st Feb., **1855**
Edward Prothero	2?nd Feb., 1855	From Capt. and Adjt., prom. to Lieut.-Col. 20th Mar., 1855
Thomas John Stannard MacAdam	20th Mar., 1855	Honry. Lt.-Col. 14th **Mar.,** 1871
Thomas **William** *Kinder*	22nd Mar., 1870	Honorary Rank on Retirement
John Kendall	25th May, 1870	Honry. Lt.-Col. 30th July, 1873
Francke Muckleston Allen	20th Nov., 1872	Honorary Rank } Now
John Boham Chantrell	1st Jan., 1873	Honorary Rank } serving
Frederick Durham	15th Mar., 1873	Honorary Rank on Retirement
Frank Henry Eadon Eadon	29th Mar., 1873	Honorary Rank on Retirement
John Henry Manwaring	12th April, 1873	Honorary Rank. Now serving

CAPTAINS.		
Sir Cecil Wray, Bart.	1758-1763	Resigned 30th Mar., **1762**
Mann Horsfield		
Walter Wade		Resigned 29th April, 1761
Josias Morley		

APPENDIX A.]   THIRD WEST YORK LIGHT INFANTRY.   205

CAPTAINS—*Continued.*	DATE OF APPOINTMENT.	REMARKS.
Henry Duncombe	} 1758-1763	
William Weddal		
William Meeke		
George Cooke	28th Feb., 1797	Prom. to Major 25th June, 1798
Bryan William Darwin Cooke	1st Mar., 1797	Resigned 24th April, 1798
George Wroughton	2nd Mar., 1797	Prom. to Major 7th Jan., 1799
John Tunnadine Vincent	3rd Mar., 1797	Prom. to Major 1st May, 1799
John Saville Poljambe	4th Mar., 1797	Resigned 31st March, 1799
Robert Tomlinson	5th Mar., 1797	Resigned 24th Oct., 1803
Thomas Copley	6th Mar., 1797	Resigned 10th April, 1801
William Walbank Childers	25th April, 1798	From Capt.-Lt., res. 20 Jan.1801
Sir Charles Kent, Bart.	18th June, 1798	Resigned 13th Jan., 1800
Leonard W. Childers	7th Jan., 1799	Resigned 24th May, 1803
Thomas Gresham	1st April, 1799	From Capt.-Lt., res. 24 Oct. 1803
Timothy Ramsden	24th Jan., 1800	From Lieut., died April, 1802
Hugh Blaydes	1st June, 1800	Prom. to Major 19th Oct., 1803
George Waugh	25th June, 1800	Displaced 7th July, 1804
James Richardson Collins	15th April, 1801	Appointed Paymaster 28th Dragoons, 6th April, 1802
Hugh Massey	5th April, 1802	Resigned 30th April, 1806
Godfrey Higgins	1st Nov., 1802	Resigned 24th April, 1805
William Marshall	16th Nov., 1802	Prom. to Major 17th June, 1806
James Richardson Cullins	23rd April, 1803	Prom. to Major 22nd Mar., 1807
Henry Richard Wood	28th April, 1803	Resigned 13th April, 1804
Henry Magill	29th April, 1803	From Lieut. See *Adjutants* (*Brevet Rank*)
The Hon. Martin Bladen Hawke	20th June, 1803	Resigned 10th Jan., 1805
George Stinton	5th July, 1803	Resigned 26th Feb., 1807
John E. Dewar	6th July, 1803	Resigned 24th June, 1806
Thomas Hudson, Jun.	2nd Nov., 1803	From Lt., res. 24th July, 1805
John Macpherson Brackenbury	25th Nov., 1803	Resigned 5th April, 1806
Francis William Barlow	18th Mar., 1804	Resigned 6th Nov., 1804
William Gell	12th May, 1804	Resigned 24th June, 1804
Robert Mogg	10th July, 1804	Resigned 18th May, 1808
Robert Haggard Benson	1st Sept., 1804	Prom. to Maj. 30th Oct., 1811
George Sampson	25th Feb., 1805	Resigned 24th April, 1806
Francis Dacre	30th May, 1805	Prom. to Maj. 15th May, 1812
Francis Ingram	20th May, 1806	Resigned 4th Jan., 1810
Christopher Marriott	21st May, 1806	Resigned 31st May, 1807
Christopher Clarke	26th June, 1806	From Lieut., promoted to Major, 22nd May, 1820
James Hook	10th July, 1807	To 9th Gar. Bat. 23rd May,1808
George Brown	14th Aug., 1807	Resigned 1st June, 1810
Nathaniel Milner	22nd Oct., 1807	Resigned 8th Sept., 1808
John Nicholas Bourke	23rd Oct., 1807	Resigned 13th Aug., 1808
Stamp Brooksbank	24th Dec., 1807	Prom. to Maj. 17th Nov., 1813
Henry Preston	31st Dec., 1807	Resigned 1st Dec., 1809
Frederick Gulston	7th March, 1808	Resigned 24th April, 1808
William F. Butler	13th May, 1808	Never joined
Edward Birmingham	12th June, 1808	Resigned 10th Dec., 1809
Stephen Donelan	8th July, 1808	From Lieut. 1st W. York Militia
Anthony Allison	29th July, 1808	Brev.-rank (see *Adj.*). To Wakefield Local Mil. 7th May,1809
Charles Thorley	6th Sept., 1808	Res. 24th Dec. 1809. To East Essex Militia

CAPTAINS—Continued.	DATE OF APPOINTMENT.	REMARKS.
Henry Courtney	1st Oct., 1808	Resigned 1824
Charles Bourryan Luard	25th Dec., 1808	Resigned May, 1825
John Bainbridge	24th Jan., 1810	Resigned 6th Aug., 1853
John Tennant	11th Feb., 1810	From Ens., res. 20th Oct., 1811
James Cuff Blake	16th Feb., 1810	Resigned 9th May, 1813
Philip MacAdam	28th Feb., 1810	From Lieut., resigned 1846
Thomas Wrather	27th June, 1810	From Lieut., died May, 1839
Charles Stapleton	26th June, 1812	Prom. to Major 28th Feb., 1846
Chas. Frederick Clavey Palmer	16th July, 1813	Res. 28th Dec., 1815. To 1st West York Militia
Butler Rolla Langford	25th Dec., 1813	Resigned 21st July, 1814
Benjamin Midgeley	28th May, 1814	From Lt.-Brevet Rank. To Wakefield Local Militia, 12th Apl., 1815 (see Adjutants)
Sir John Hayford Thorold, Bt.	27th Oct., 1818	Resigned May, 1820
Sir Joseph Copley, Bart.	22nd Nov., 1819	Resigned 6th June, 1825
Jonathan Layborn	7th June, 1820	From Ens., res. 23rd Feb., 1831
William Read Vincent	2nd July, 1827	From Lt., res. 20th Nov., 1830
Charles Thellusson	5th Nov., 1827	Resigned after 1839
William Rawson	15th March, 1831	Brevet Rank, died 18th July, 1850 (see Adjutants)
Hugh Bleades	27th Feb., 1832	Died
William Stainforth	28th Feb., 1846	Resigned 1852-1853
Thos. John Stannard MacAdam	28th Feb., 1846	Prom. to Maj. 20th March, 1855
William Hepworth	28th Feb., 1846	Resigned 1853
Seymour Stewart Thellusson	28th Feb., 1846	Resigned 21st February, 1854
Edward Prothero	17th July, 1852	Prom. to Major 22nd Feb., 1855 (see Adjutants)
Duncan Littlejohn	25th Nov., 1852	To 5th W. Y. Mil. 5th Nov., 1854
William Garforth	21st Feb., 1853	Resigned 3rd July, 1855
John Crossley Sutcliffe	21st Feb., 1853	Resigned 1st August, 1854
Thomas Shearburn	26th Feb., 1853	Resigned 8th July, 1859
William Waite	30th April, 1853	From Lt., res. 30th Sept., 1859
Jeremiah Bourne Faviell	2nd May, 1853	Resigned 23rd Nov., 1855
John Kendall	12th May, 1853	From Lieut., prom. to Major 25th May, 1870
Edward Chivers Bower	24th May, 1853	From Lt., res. 12th Jan., 1859
Robert Dudley Baxter	21st Feb., 1854	From Lt., res. 1st Feb., 1855
John Boham Chantrell	22nd May, 1854	From Lt. Hon. Rank of Major 1st Jan., 1873
Edward Nicholson	20th July, 1854	From Lieut. (see Paymasters)
Maurice Rodgers	11th Aug., 1854	From Lt., res. 1st Sep., 1854
Frank Henry Eadon Eadon	2nd Sept., 1854	From Lt., ret. with Hon. Rank of Major 29th Mar., 1873
Thomas Marshall	1st Feb., 1855	From Lt., died 6th March, 1864
Alexander Hamilton Robson	14th Mar., 1855	Died 15th May, 1871 (see Adjutants)
John Henry Manwaring	20th Mar., 1855	From Lieut., Hon. Rank of Maj. 12th April, 1873
John Charles Flood	4th July, 1855	Removed 23rd October, 1858
Frederick Durham	24th Nov., 1855	From Lt., ret. with Hon. Rank of Major, 15th March, 1873
Francke Muckleston Allen	13th Jan., 1859	From Capt. Carnarvon Militia Hon. Rank of Major 20th Nov., 1872

APPENDIX A.]   THIRD WEST YORK LIGHT INFANTRY.   207

CAPTAINS—Continued.	DATE OF APPOINTMENT.	REMARKS.
Thomas William **Kinder**	11th Feb., 1859	Ret. 3rd March, 1870.—Hon. Rank of Major
Douglas Loftus	9th July, 1859	Ret. with Rank of Capt. 22nd Mar.,1871 (see Ens. June,1854)
Ferrars Compton **Clarges** Loftus	20th Oct., 1859	From Lieut., retired with rank of Captain, 12th April, 1871
Gerald Rochfort	13th June, 1864	From Lieut., retired with rank of Captain, 5th May, **1870**
James Redfern Bottomley	12th Mar., 1870	From Lieut. (see Instructors **of** Musketry) Now serving
William Greaves Blake	2nd May, 1870	From Lieutenant. Now serving
Henry William Barlow	20th July, 1870	**Late** Captain Royal Engineers. Now serving
John Straker Wilson	15th April, 1871	**From** Lieut., res. 1st June, 1872
Michael Curry	15th April, 1871	**Late** Capt. 81st Regiment. Now serving
The Hon. Frederick *Charles Howard*	*17th Sept.,* 1871	(*See Adjutants*)
George Alfred Raikes	1st June, 1872	From Lieutenant ⎫ Now
John Taylor Winnington	11th April, 1873	From Lieutenant ⎬ serving
Grenfell Todd Naylor	21st Feb., 1874	From Lieutenant ⎭

CAPTAIN-LIEUTENANTS.

William Walbank **Childers**	1st March, 1797	Prom. to Capt. 25th Ap., 1798
George Augustus Cooke	14th June, 1798	Resigned 29th Jan., 1799
Thomas Gresham	30th Jan, 1799	From Lieut., promoted to Capt. 1st April, 1799
Peter Cotes	*1st April,* 1799	*From Lieut. Retired H.P., 23rd April,* 1802 (see Adjutants)

LIEUTENANTS.

Walter Vavasour	⎫	Resigned 29th June, 1761
George Thompson	⎪	
William Nowel	⎪	
William Foster	⎪	
Henry Scott	⎬ 1758 to 1769	Resigned 30th March, 1762
Samuel Wand	⎪	Quarterm. Lieut.2nd West York, 22nd October, 1763
George Hassell	⎪	
John Wiltus	⎪	
James Morley	⎪	
George Iveson	⎪	From Ensign
Edward Norton	⎪	
Peter Cotes	⎭ 1st Mar., 1797	*Prom. to Capt.-Lieut.* 1st *Apl.* 1799 (see Adjutants)
Thomas Gresham	2nd Mar., 1797	Promoted to Captain-Lieutenant 30th January, 1799
Timothy Ramsden	3rd Mar., 1797	**Prom. to** Capt. 24th Jan., 1800
Thomas Wild	5th Mar., 1797	**Resigned** 24th Mar., 1799
Thomas Elston	6th *Mar.*, 1797	(*See Paymasters*), *died* 18*th, Aug.*, 1822
Benjamin Robinson	7th Mar., 1797	Res. 24th Jan., 1804 (*see* Surgeons)

FIRST REGIMENT OF MILITIA; OR, [APPENDIX A.

LIEUTENANTS—*Continued.*	DATE OF APPOINTMENT.	REMARKS.
John Brookfield	8th Mar., 1797	Resigned 24th May, 1798
John Rickard	9th Mar., 1797	Resigned 13th May, 1800
Thomas Carnelley	10th Mar., 1797	Resigned 24th May, 1800
John Bolderick	11th Mar., 1797	Resigned 24th April, 1800
Theobald Dillon	12th Mar., 1797	To Lieut. 2nd West York Militia 13th April, 1798
William Salmon	14th April, 1798	From Ens., res. 24th Aug., 1798
Richard Womack	18th June, 1798	From Ensign. To 1st Royal Scots 27th Aug., 1799
Thomas Hudson, Jun.	19th June, 1798	From Ensign, prom. to Capt. 2nd Nov., 1803
Samuel Turner	20th June, 1798	From Ens., res. 24th Oct., 1798
George Parker	21st June, 1798	From Ens., res. 24th July, 1798
Joseph Fowler	22nd June, 1798	*From Ens., displaced 24th Oct., 1799 (see Assistant-Surgeons)*
William Lowther Rutter	23rd June, 1798	From Ens., res. 24th Mar. 1800
Henry Watkins	24th June, 1798	Resigned 24th March, 1800
Richard Littlewood	25th June, 1798	Resigned 24th Feb., 1799
Henry Magill	*25th June,* 1798	To *Capt. 29th April,* 1803 (see *Adjutants*)
Henry Bower	10th July, 1798	Resigned 24th March, 1800
James Wetherherd	1st Sept., 1798	Resigned 24th Nov., 1799
William Rawson	1st April, 1799	From Ensign. To 35th Regt. 18th August, 1799
Edward Conroy	1st April, 1799	To 6th West India Regt. Mar. 1802
George Marshall	1st May, 1799	To 82nd Regt. 24th Feb., 1800
Hector J. McLaine	2nd May, 1799	Resigned 10th April, 1801
Thomas Wilson	24th Feb., 1800	To 34th Regt. 2nd May, 1805
William Fozard	5th Mar., 1800	Resigned 24th May, 1800
Joseph Wagster	6th Mar., 1800	From Ensign. Died 17th June, 1804. Killed in a duel
Thomas Jones	17th May, 1800	Resigned 22nd Dec., 1800
Thomas Brockell	25th May, 1800	Resigned 31st August, 1803
George Walker	26th May, 1800	Resigned 31st May, 1803
James Winskill	*24th July,* 1800	*From Ensign. Died 24th April,* 1803 (see Quartermasters)
John Armer	1st July, 1801	*From Ensign,* res. 24th *June,* 1803 (see Assist.-Surgeons)
William Fozard	15th Mar., 1803	Reappointed. Adjut. Maidstone Volunteers, 7th Jan., 1805
Thomas Langhorne	30th Mar., 1803	From Ens., res. 24th May, 1804
George Armitage	31st Mar., 1803	From Ens., res. 27th July, 1804
Patrick Conroy	1st April, 1803	From Ens., to 6th West India Regt., 27th August, 1803
Charles Strawbenzie	30th May, 1803	Resigned 24th Oct., 1803
John Horne	20th June, 1803	Resigned 16th April, 1804
George Mitchell	25th June, 1803	Resigned 24th Nov., 1804
George Vincent	26th June, 1803	From Ens. To 2nd Lieutenant Gunner Drivers, 1st Sep., 1804
Alexander Ward	27th June, 1803	Resigned 24th April, 1804
Thomas Wrightson	11th July, 1803	Resigned 23rd Aug., 1808 (see Quartermasters)
John Leaming Firth	14th July, 1803	Resigned 24th July, 1804
Levett Broadley Parkins	7th Aug., 1803	Resigned 9th July, 1804

APPENDIX A.]   THIRD WEST YORK LIGHT INFANTRY.   209

LIEUTENANTS—*Continued.*	DATE OF APPOINTMENT.	REMARKS.
— Donabal	8th Aug., 1803	Never joined
William Thomas	17th Aug., 1803	From Ensign to 67th Regt., 12th Nov., 1807 (see Asst.-Surg.)
Anthony Allison	18th Aug., 1803	From Ens., prom. to Capt. 29th July, 1808 (see Adjutants)
Randolph Crewe	26th Sept., 1803	Reappointed. To 58th Regiment, 6th September, 1804
John Goulden	29th Oct., 1803	From **Ens.**, displ. 25th Ap. 1807
William Hudson	31st Oct., 1803	From **Ens.**, res. 24th Feb. 1805
Richard Hudson	1st Nov., 1803	From Ens. To 40th **Regt., 26th** April, 1809
Charles Woodcock	2nd Nov., 1803	From Ens., **res. 1st Dec.,** 1807 (see Assist.-Surgeons)
Robert Shaw...	3rd Nov., 1803	From **Ens.** To 51st Regt., 25th August, 1807
James Coward	4th Nov., 1803	From Ens., res. 24th Aug. **1804**
Samuel Worthington	5th Nov., 1803	From Ens., res. 14th Feb. **1805**
Hugh Parker...	7th Nov., 1803	From Ens. Died 20th Nov. **1827**
Thomas Sharpe	7th Nov., 1803	From Ens., res. 24th July, **1805**
George Van Straubenzee	8th Nov., 1803	Resigned 24th July, 1805
James Emmerson	31st Dec., 1803	Resigned 24th July, 1805
Christopher Tallon	16th Jan., 1804	From Ens. res. 24th Nov., 1807
John Read Vincent	3rd May, 1804	From Ensign. To Ensign 24th Regiment, 14th Sept., 1804
John Lambert	4th May, 1804	From Ens., **res.** 24th Feb., 1805
William Fisher	5th June, 1804	From Ens., **res.** 23rd Jan., 1808
Christopher Clarke	26th June, 1804	From Ens., promoted to Cap., 26th June, 1806
John Robins	17th Aug., 1804	Resigned 24th October, 1804
William Jewitt	2nd Jan., 1805	Resigned 24th April, 1805
William Wild	29th Jan., 1805	From **Ens., res.** 14th Dec., 1807
Benjamin Midgeley	25th Feb., 1805	Qrtr.-Master, *promoted to Cap.* 28th *May*, 1814
John Rothwell Marsden	9th Aug., 1806	From Ensign. To 4th Reg., 9th April, 1809
Joseph Hubert Kighley	6th Aug., 1807	From **Ens.** To 53rd Reg., 19th May, 1808
John Armstead Braddell	14th Sept., 1807	From **Ens.** To 36th Reg., **15th October,** 1807
Ralph Marshall	5th Nov., 1807	From **Ens.** To 10th Reg., 3rd February, 1808
John Doddington **Forth**	8th Dec., 1807	From Ens., **res.** 22nd July, 1808
James Dixon	9th Dec., 1807	From Ens., res. 16th Mar., 1810
Thomas Wrather	10th Dec., 1807	From Ensign, promoted to Cap. 27th June, 1810
George White	11th Dec., 1807	From **Ens., res.** 3rd Dec., 1808
George Ramsden	12th Dec., 1807	Resigned 1809
Hugh Stafford Donnellan	8th April, 1808	From Ensign. To 82nd Foot, 19th May, 1808
Nicholas **Higgins**	8th April, 1808	From Ens., res. 9th April, 1810
John Shaw	25th May, 1808	From Ens. To 34th Foot, 7th Dec., 1809
William Small	26th May, 1808	*From Ens., res.* 9th *Nov.*, 1809 (see Assistant-Surgeons)
Charles Straubenzee	21st June, 1808	Retired 1st October, 1852

P

LIEUTENANTS—*Continued*	DATE OF APPOINTMENT.	REMARKS.
Edward Jonathan Priestley ...	5th Sept., 1808	To 33rd Foot, 12th April, 1809
George Pearson Dawson ...	6th Sept., 1808	*From Ens., died* 23rd Dec., 1829 (see Assistant-Surgeons)
John Mather ...	4th Dec., 1808	From Ensign, resigned 1852-3
Philip MacAdam ...	22nd April, 1809	From Ens., promoted to Capt. 28th February, 1810
James Gordon Ogle	5th May, 1809	From Ens. To 33rd Foot, 9th May, 1811
William Handley	6th May, 1809	From Ens. To 48th Foot, 25th August, 1809
John Watson	19th May, 1809	From Ens., res. 3rd Oct., 1809
Thomas Burroughs	28th Oct., 1809	From Ens., died 19th June, 1811
Thomas Mathison	19th Nov., 1809	From Ens., res. 24th May, 1810
John Jeffryes...	14th Feb., 1810	From Ens., died 17th Aug., 1827
John Augustus Mathison ...	15th Feb., 1810	From Ensign. To 77th Foot, 8th May, 1811
Robert Standish Peppard ...	31st Mar., 1810	From Ens., res. 24th Feb., 1812
Thomas Vokes	31st Mar., 1810	From Ens., died 2nd Feb., 1831
James Marshall	27th June, 1810	From Ensign. To 4th Foot, 16th May, 1811
William Greaves	27th June, 1810	From Ens., res. 9th Oct., 1810
Thomas Wrightson	31st Oct., 1810	From Ens., ret. 1st Oct., 1852
Thomas Buxton Vincent ...	31st Oct., 1810	From Ens., ret. 1st. Oct., 1852
George Turton	30th June, 1811	From Ens. To 33rd Foot, 27th May, 1812
William Midgeley	27th Aug., 1811	From Ens. To 1st Foot, 19th December, 1811
Thomas Norton ...	28th Aug., 1811	From Ens. To 86th Foot, 12th August, 1813
Frederick Atherstone ...	6th Mar., 1812	From Ens., died 25th Sept. 1819
Thomas Eyre ...	7th Mar., 1812	From Ens. To 34th Foot, 7th April, 1813
William Read Vincent ...	8th Mar., 1812	From Ens., promoted to **Capt.**, 2nd July, 1827
Charles Toriano Houlton ...	19th July, 1812	Resigned 1852-3
Leonard Leaf ...	16th July, 1813	From Ens., retired 1st Oct. 1852
Thomas Gee	13th Sept., 1813	From Ensign. To Lieutenant 49th Foot, 12th May, 1814
John Atkinson	23rd June, 1814	*Brevet Rank* (see Quartermasters)
John Lockwood Harrison ...	11th July, 1825	From Ens., retired 1st Oct., 1852
Henry Whitaker	15th Mar., 1831	*From Ensign, res.* 1852-3 (see Paymasters)
William Waite	15th Mar., 1831	From Ens., promoted to Capt. 30th April, 1853
Edmd. FitzEustace Robinson	27th Feb., 1832	Resigned 1853
Jestin Homfray ...	22nd Nov., 1838	Resigned 1852-3
Frederick Augustus Laughton	28th Feb., 1846	Resigned
John Kendall	26th Oct., 1852	Prom. to Capt. 12th May, 1853
Edward Chivers Bower ...	4th Nov., 1852	Prom. to Capt. 24th May, 1853
Robert Dudley Baxter ...	4th Nov., 1852	Prom. to Capt. 21st. Feb., 1854
Stephen Holdforth ...	4th Nov., 1852	Resigned 21st February, 1854
John Boham Chantrell ...	25th Nov., 1852	Prom. to Capt. 22nd May, 1854
Edward Nicholson ...	25th Nov., 1852	Promoted to Captain 20th July, 1854 (see Paymasters)
Maurice Rodgers	25th Nov., 1852	Prom. to Capt. 11th Aug., 1854

THIRD WEST YORK LIGHT INFANTRY.

LIEUTENANTS—Continued.	DATE OF APPOINTMENT.	REMARKS.
Frank Henry Eadon **Eadon**	21st Dec., 1852	Prom. to Capt. 2nd Sept., 1854
Thomas Marshall	9th March, 1853	Prom. to Capt. 1st Feb., 1855
John Henry Manwaring	10th March, 1853	Prom. to Capt. 20th Mar., 1855
William Manley Eastwood	19th March, 1853	Resigned 31st July, 1854
Cockcroft Sutcliffe	19th March, 1853	Resigned 10th Aug., **1855**
Theophilus Smith	21st Feb., 1854	From Ens., res. 15th Aug., **1854**
Frederick Durham	21st Feb., 1854	From Ensign, prom. to Capt. 24th Nov., 1855
Ferrars Compton Clarges Loftus	22nd May, 1854	From Ensign, prom. to Capt. 20th Oct., 1859
Henry Neville Cotton Thurston	11th Aug., 1854	From Ensign. To **7th Foot**, 22nd Dec., 1854
Francis Patrick Smith	11th Aug., 1854	From Ens., res. 19th Mar., **1855**
Walter Henry Hinde	29th Aug., 1854	From Ens., res. 15th Dec., **1854**
William Greaves Blake	29th Aug., 1854	From Ens. To 89th Foot, **27th** Feb., 1856
Henry Dickinson Wilkinson	2nd Sept., 1854	From Ensign, res. March, 1865
Humphrey Brook Firman	12th Jan., 1855	From Ens., res. 30th Sept., 1857
Gerald Rochfort	12th Jan., 1855	From Ensign, promoted to Capt. 13th June, 1864
Robert John Bell	1st Feb., 1855	From Ensign. To 37th Foot, 7th March, 1856
Kynaston Walter **Smith**	20th March, 1855	From Ens., died 27th Aug., 1857
Alfred Andrew Pinson	20th March, 1855	From Ensign. To 16th Foot, 30th April, 1856
William Armit	11th Aug., 1855	From Ens., removed 10th March, 1859
Arthur Joliffe **Tufnell**	24th Nov., 1855	From Ensign. To 93rd Foot, 15th May, 1857
John Forbes **Mosse**	18th March, 1856	From Ensign. To **18th Foot**, 21st May, 1858
Athelstane Owen **Powell**	18th March, 1856	**From Ens., rem. 27th June, 1862**
Edward Landon	30th May, 1856	**From Ensign, res. 8th Jan., 1858**
John George Smith **Willcocks**	17th Aug., 1857	From Ens., Adjt. 47th Lanc. Vol. 3rd Nov., 1860 (see I. of M.)
Michael Thunder	1st Oct., 1857	From Ensign. To 21st Foot, 28th Jan., 1859
William Goodman **Gatliff**	19th Oct., 1857	From Ens., **res. 22nd June, 1858**
John Cadman	18th Jan., 1858	From Ens., **res. 29th June, 1866**
Chamberlin Wm. J. Walker	18th June, 1858	From Ens., **res. 1st June, 1860**
Joe Drury Bottomley	23rd June, 1858	From Ens. To Royal Marines, 11th Sept., 1859
Joseph Henry Palmer	17th March, 1859	From Ens., died 26th Jan., 1864
Gordon, James Douglas	26th April, 1859	From Ens., **res. 5th Sept., 1860**
Thomas Bolger	20th Oct., 1859	From Ens., **res. 26th June, 1860**
Frederick Arthur **Verner**	20th Oct., 1859	From Ens., rem. 27th June, 1862
George Campbell	8th Sept., 1860	From Ensign. To 79th Foot, 29th July, 1862
Edward Henry Saunders	8th Sept., 1860	From Ensign. To **5th Lancers**, 2nd July, 1861
William Parkin Brown	8th Sept., 1860	From Ens., rem. 27th June, 1862
Robert Harry M'Loghlin	23rd Nov., 1860	From Ens., res. 12th April, 1867
Thomas Walter Lambert	24th June, 1862	From Ens., res. 28th April, 1864
James Redfern Bottomley	24th June, 1862	From Ensign, promoted to Capt. 12th Mar., 1870 (see **I. of M.**)

FIRST REGIMENT OF MILITIA; OR, [APPENDIX A.

LIEUTENANTS—Continued.	DATE OF APPOINTMENT.	REMARKS.
Frederick Alfred Roberts	24th June, 1862	From Ens., rem. 10th July, 1866
John Robert Clarke	24th June, 1862	From Ens., res. 20th April, 1863
Stephen Vincent Folch	28th April, 1863	Removed 17th August, 1868
William Alexander Browne	19th March, 1866	Died 14th September, 1867
William Vernon	29th June, 1866	Resigned 27th May, 1870
John Straker Wilson	10th April, 1867	Prom. to Capt. 15th April, 1871
William Greaves Blake	27th June, 1868	**Prom. to** Capt. 2nd May, 1870
George Alfred Raikes	1st July, 1869	**Prom. to** Capt. 1st June, 1872
John Taylor Winnington	20th July, 1870	Prom. to Capt. 11th April, 1873
Edward Douglas Prothero	8th Sept., 1870	Resigned 14th June, 1871
John Bull	13th Jan., 1871	(See Quartermasters) Now servg
Grenfell **Todd** Naylor	11th April, 1871	Prom. to Capt. 21st Feb., 1874
William Henry Thomas	5th July, 1871	Now serving
Egremont Eadon Shearburn	7th July, 1871	To Lieut. 9th Royal Lancers, 22nd May, 1874
Harry Wetherell Rowden	6th April, 1872	To Lt. 99th Foot, 2nd Dec. 1874
Thos. Archibald Fisher Hall	24th July, 1872	Resigned 29th March, 1873
Edward Bowen	31st July, 1872	Now serving
Frank John de Vie Beamish	5th Feb., 1873	Resigned 22nd June, 1875
John Matson Vincent	24th Sept., 1873	From Sub-Lt. 3 Sept., 1875 ⎫
John Edmond Groom	21st Feb., 1874	From Sub-Lt. 3 Sept., 1875 ⎬ Now serving
William Noble Bennett	29th May, 1874	From Sub-Lt. 3 Sept., 1875 ⎭

ENSIGNS.

	DATE OF APPOINTMENT.	REMARKS.
Joseph Ostler		
Christopher Wharton		
Richard Dawson, Jun.		Adjutant
David Swails		
Richard Clapham		
Richard Taylor		Surgeon
Miles Staveley		
Philip Sands		Capt. 2nd West York, 24th May, 1775
William Sands	⎫	
Richard Dewes	⎪	
Isaac Webster	⎬ 1758 to 1763	
John Wilks	⎪	
John Horner	⎪	
John Allinson	⎪	
— Sheppard	⎭	
John Veavers		Res. 30th Mar., 1762, Capt 2nd West York, 13th May, 1778
George Iveson		Promoted to Lieutenant
Richard Burton		**Ens.** 2nd W. Y., 22 Oct., 1763
Samuel Wiggins		To Lieutenant 2nd West York, 22nd October, 1763
Richard Womack	1st March, 1797	**Prom.** to Lieut. 18th June, 1798
Thomas Hudson, Jun.	2nd March, 1797	Prom. to Lieut. 19th June, 1798
George Marshall	3rd March, 1797	Prom. to Lieut. 1st May, 1799
Samuel Turner	4th March, 1797	Prom. to Lieut. 20th June, 1798
Theobald Dillon	4th March, 1797	Prom. to Lieut. 12th Mar., 1797
William Salmon	3rd March, 1798	Prom to Lieut. 14th Apr., 1798

APPENDIX A.] THIRD WEST YORK LIGHT INFANTRY. 213

ENSIGNS—Continued.	DATE OF APPOINTMENT.	REMARKS.
George Parker	21st **April,** 1798	Prom. to Lieut. 21st June, 1798
Joseph Fowler	25th **April,** 1798	*Prom. to Lieut.* 22nd June, 1798 (see Assistant-Surgeons)
William Lowther Rutter	6th **May,** 1798	Prom. to Lieut. **23rd** June, 1798
James Winskill	18th **June,** 1798	*Prom. to Lieut.* 24th July, 1800 (see Quartermasters)
William Rawson	10th Sept., 1798	**Prom.** to Lieut. 1st April, 1799
John Armer	1st April, 1799	***Prom.*** to Lieut. 1st July, 1801 (**see** Assistant-Surgeons)
John C. Gilbert	2nd **April,** 1799	Never joined
Joseph Wagster	15th **Aug.,** 1799	Prom. to Lieut. 6th Mar., 1800
John Carfrae	5th **March,** 1800	Resigned 24th October, 1800
Randolph Crewe	6th **March,** 1800	Resigned 24th December, **1801**
Charles Eyre	24th **June,** 1800	Displaced March, 1803
John Harrison Sellers	1st **July,** 1800	Displaced 24th September, 1800
George Russell Sladden	24th **July,** 1800	Resigned 24th December, 1800
Thomas Langhorne	25th **Aug.,** 1800	Prom. to Lieut. 30th Mar., 1803
George Armitage	1st Dec., 1800	Prom. **to** Lieut. 31st Mar., 1803
Patrick Conroy	24th April, 1801	Prom. to Lieut. 1st April, 1803
George Vincent	1st August, 1801	Prom. to Lieut. 26th June, 1803
William Thomas	20th *June,* **1803**	*Promoted to Lieut.* 17th *Aug.,* 1803 (see Asst.-Surgeons)
Anthony Allison	27th **June,** 1803	*Promoted to Lieut.* 18th *Aug.,* 1803 (see Adjutants)
John Goulden	28th June, 1803	Prom. to Lieut. 29th Oct., 1803
Tyras Redhead	11th July, 1803	Displaced 24th July, 1803
William Hudson	12th July, **1803**	Prom. to Lieut. 31st Oct., 1803
Richard Hudson	13th July, 1803	**Prom. to** Lieut. 1st Nov., 1803
Charles Woodcock	14th *July,* 1803	***Promoted to*** *Lieut.* 2nd *Nov.,* 1803 (see Assist.-Surgeons)
Robert Shaw	25th **July,** 1803	Prom. to Lieut. 3rd Nov., 1803
Hugh Parker	17th **Aug.,** 1803	**From** Quartermaster, promoted to Lieut. 7th Nov., 1803
Thomas Sharpe	18th **Aug.,** 1803	**Prom. to** Lieut. 7th **Nov., 1803**
James Coward	27th **Aug.,** 1803	Prom. **to** Lieut. 4th Nov., 1803
Samuel Worthington	28th Aug., **1803**	Prom. to Lieut. 5th Nov., 1803
Christopher Tallon	21st Oct., **1803**	Prom. to Lieut. 16th Jan., 1804
John Read Vincent	12th Nov., 1803	Prom. to Lieut. 3rd May, 1804
John Lambert	16th **Jan.,** 1804	Prom. to Lieut. 4th May, 1804
William Fisher	8th **Feb.,** 1804	Prom. to Lieut. 5th June, 1804
Christopher Clarke	23rd **May,** 1804	**Prom. to** Lieut. 26th June, 1804
Robert Heptinstall Stringer	18th **Aug.,** 1804	**Never** joined
John Rencher	14th **Oct.,** 1804	**Resigned** 24th Jan., 1805
William Wild	15th **Oct.,** 1804	**Prom. to** Lieut. 29th Jan., 1805
Archibald Davis	25th **Feb.,** 1805	Resigned 24th May, 1805
George M'Kenzie	26th **Feb.,** 1805	Resigned 24th March, 1806
Nathaniel Moore	8th **April,** 1805	Resigned 24th May, 1806
John Rothwell **Marsden**	23rd **April,** 1805	**Prom.** to Lieut. 9th Aug., 1806
John Alderson	7th **June,** 1805	Resigned 24th June, 1806
Adam Gregory	11th **June,** 1805	To 29th Foot, 12th June, 1806
William Booth	18th **Aug.,** 1805	Resigned 24th March, 1806
Joseph **Hubert** Kighley	19th **Aug.,** 1805	Prom. to Lieut. 6th Aug., 1807
John Armsted Braddell	29th **Sept.,** 1805	**Prom. to** Lieut. 14th Sept., 1807
Ralph Marshall	28th **Mar.,** 1806	**Prom.** to Lieut. 5th Nov., 1807
Richard Hill	5th **June,** 1806	**Died 19th June,** 1807

ENSIGNS—*Continued.*	DATE OF APPOINTMENT.	REMARKS.
John Doddington Forth	22nd Nov., 1806	Prom. to Lieut. 8th Dec., 1807
Benjamin Sigston	5th Dec., 1806	Resigned 24th Nov., 1807
James Dixon	31st Dec., 1806	Prom. to Lieut. 9th Dec., 1807
Thomas Wrather	13th May, 1807	Prom. to Lieut. 10th Dec., 1807
George White	18th July, 1807	Prom. to Lieut. 11th Dec., 1807
Nicholas Higgins	6th Aug., 1807	Prom. to Lieut. 8th Apr., 1808
Bowes Higgins	14th Sept., 1807	Never joined
Hugh Stafford Donnellan	2nd Nov., 1807	Prom. to Lieut. 8th Apr., 1808
Richard Joshua Peat	8th Dec., 1807	To 92nd Foot, 2nd Aug., 1808
John Shaw	15th Dec., 1807	Prom. to Lieut. 25th May, 1808
William Small	21st Dec., 1807	Prom. *to Lieut. 26th May*, 1808 (see Assist.-Surgeons)
Edward Jonathan Priestley...	5th Jan., 1808	Prom. to Lieut. 5th Sept., 1808
George Pearson Dawson	18*th Jan.*, 1808	*Prom. to Lieut. 6th Sept.*, 1808 (see Assist.-Surgeons)
John Mather	21st Feb., 1808	Prom. to Lieut. 4th Dec., 1808
Philip MacAdam	29th Mar., 1808	Prom. to Lieut. 22nd Apr. 1809
John Garbut	31st Mar., 1808	To 84th Foot, 23rd May, 1808
James Gordon Ogle	8th April, 1808	Prom. to Lieut. 5th May, 1809
William Handley	25th April, 1808	Prom. to Lieut. 6th May, 1809
John Watson	12th June, 1808	Prom. to Lieut. 19th May,1809
Thomas Burroughs	13th June, 1808	Prom. to Lieut. 28th Oct., 1809
Thomas Mathison	28th July, 1808	Prom. to Lieut. 19th Nov., 1809
Patrick Græme	2nd Aug., 1808	To 18th Foot 10th Feb., 1809
John Jeffryes	30th Aug., 1808	Prom. to Lieut. 14th Feb.,1810
Thomas Wood	5th Oct., 1808	Resigned 24th March, 1809
John Augustus Mathison	4th Dec., 1808	**Prom. to Lieut.** 15th Feb., 1810
Robert Standish Peppard	19th Mar., 1809	**Prom. to** Lieut. 31st Mar., 1810
Thomas Vokes	21st April, 1809	**Prom. to** Lieut. 31st Mar., 1810
James Marshall	29th May, 1809	Prom. to Lieut. 27th June, 1810
William Greaves	29th May, 1809	Prom. to Lieut. 27th June, 1810
Thomas Wrightson	2nd June, 1809	Prom. to Lieut. 31st Oct., 1810
John Tennant	5th Aug., 1809	Prom. to Capt. 11th Feb., 1810
Thomas Buxton Vincent	24th Nov., 1809	Prom. to Lieut. 31st Oct., 1810
Timothy Raper	19th Feb., 1810	Resigned 10th Jan., 1811
George Turton	10th July, 1810	Prom. to Lieut. 30th June, 1811
William Midgeley	29th Sept., 1810	Prom. to Lieut. 27th Aug., 1811
Francis Travers	19*th Oct.*, 1810	*Resigned* 31*st August*, 1811 (see Assistant-Surgeons).
Thomas Norton	31st Dec., 1810	Prom. to Lieut. 28th Aug., 1811
Samuel Hardy	24th Feb., 1811	Resigned 12th April, 1812
Thomas Eccles	25th Feb., 1811	Resigned 31st August, 1811
Frederick Atherstone	4th April, 1811	Prom. **to Lieut.** 6th Mar., 1812
Thomas Eyre	14th April, 1811	**Prom. to Lieut.** 7th Mar., 1812
Charles Thomas Bourke	31st May, 1811	Never joined; res. 25 July, 1811
William Read Vincent	10th Aug., 1811	Prom. to Lieut. 8th Mar., 1812
Leonard Leaf	7th Jan., 1812	**Prom. to Lieut.** 16th July, 1813
Thomas Gee	3rd Feb., 1812	**Prom. to** Lieut. 13th Sept., 1813
William Hawkes	7th April, 1812	Died 31st March, 1823
Jonathan Layborn	15th May, 1812	**Prom. to** Capt. 7th June, 1820
Henry Hebden	7th July, 1812	To 2nd Garrison Battalion, 25th May, 1815
Robert Mann	8*th July,* 1812	*Retired* 1*st Oct.,* 1852 (see Assistant-Surgeons)
William Atkin	1st Sept., 1812	To 88th Foot, 12th May, 1814

APPENDIX A.] THIRD WEST YORK LIGHT INFANTRY. 215

ENSIGNS—Continued.	DATE OF APPOINTMENT.	REMARKS.
Richard Blacklin	2nd Sept., 1812	To 1st Foot, 18th July, 1815
John Lockwood Harrison	25th July, 1813	Prom. to Lieut. 11th July, 1825
Robert Caley	13th Sept., 1813	Never joined; res. 16 Sept., 1813
Edward Bracken	17th Oct., 1813	Resigned 19th May, 1820
Leonard Leaf	10th July, 1817	
William Markham Oddie	11th July, 1817	Resigned 27th May, 1820
Thomas Gee	7th June, 1819	Resigned 9th March, 1831
Frederick William Chambers	25th July, 1821	Serving in May, 1839
John William Sturges	8th Oct., 1822	*Resigned 19th April, 1827* (see Paymasters)
Henry *Whitaker*	20th Feb., 1827	*Promoted to Lieut.* 15th March, 1831 (see Paymasters)
William Waite, Jun.	22nd Jan., 1831	Prom. to Lieut. 15th Mar., 1831
Thomas Richard Dunhill	17th Sept., 1846	Resigned 1853 (?)
Theophilus Smith	4th Jan., 1853	Prom. to Lieut. 21st Feb. 1854
Frederick Durham	8th Jan., 1853	Prom. to Lieut. 21st Feb. 1854
Ferrars Compton Clarges Loftus	19th March, 1853	Prom. to Lieut. 22nd May, 1854
Henry Neville Cotton Thurston	24th March, 1853	Prom. to Lieut. 11th Aug. 1854
Francis Patrick Smith	12th April, 1853	Prom. to Lieut. 11th Aug. 1854
Walter Henry Hinde	12th April, 1853	Prom. to Lieut. 29th Aug. 1854
Cotterell Scholefield	25th April, 1853	Resigned 30th June, 1854
William Greaves Blake	2nd May, 1853	Prom. to Lieut. 29th Aug. 1854
Henry Dickinson Wilkinson	18th May, 1853	Prom. to Lieut. 2nd Sept. 1854
Henry William Heaton	24th Mar., 1854	To 14th Foot, 22nd Dec., 1854
Thomas Orton Howorth	10th June, 1854	To 44th Foot, 29th Dec., 1854
Douglas Loftus	17th June, 1854	To Gren. Guards, 13th Feb. 1855
Humphrey Brook Firman	3rd Aug., 1854	Prom. to Lieut. 12th Jan. 1855
Gerald Rochfort	11th Aug., 1854	Prom. to Lieut. 12th Jan. 1855
Robert John Bell	11th Aug., 1854	Prom. to Lieut. 1st Feb. 1855
Thomas Nixon	2nd Sept., 1854	Resigned 3rd Nov., 1854
Alfred Augustus James	31st Oct., 1854	Resigned 31st Oct., 1854
Kynaston Walter Smith	31st Oct., 1854	Prom. to Lieut. 20th Mar., 1855
Edward Gould Hasted	17th Nov., 1854	To 57th Foot, 2nd March, 1855
Albert Andrew **Pinson**	21st Nov., 1854	Prom. to Lieut. 20th Mar. 1855
William Armit	20th Dec., 1854	Prom. to Lieut. 11th Aug. 1855
Arthur Joliffe Tufnell	12th Jan., 1855	Prom. to Lieut. 24th Nov. 1855
Allan Ramsey Spence	27th Jan., 1855	Removed 29th Dec., 1855
William Augustus Tighe	1st Feb., 1855	**Never joined** Removed 1859
Andrew James Watson	1st Feb., 1855	**Died**, at Dublin, 15th Dec. 1855
John Forbes Mosse	17th Mar., 1855	Prom. to Lieut. 18th Mar. 1856
Athelstan Owen Powell	20th Mar., 1855	Prom. to Lieut. 18th Mar. 1856
Edward Landon	5th May, 1855	Prom. to Lieut. 30th May, 1856
John Geo. Smith Willcocks	5th May, 1855	Prom. to Lieut. 17th Aug., 1857 (see Instructors of Musketry)
Michael Thunder	24th May, 1855	Prom. to Lieut. 1st Oct., 1857
William Goodman Gatliff	3rd Aug., 1855	Prom. to Lieut. 19th Oct., 1857
Thomas Barff	20th Sept., 1855	Resigned 14th Feb., 1856
John Cadman	30th Nov., 1855	Prom. to Lieut. 18th Jan., 1858
William **Pickard**	1st Feb., 1856	Resigned 30th Sept., 1857
North Gatliff	15th Feb., 1856	Resigned 10th Nov., 1857
Chamberlin Wm. **Jervoise** Walker	15th Feb., 1856	Prom. to Lieut. 18th June, 1858
Edward Wright **M'Creary**	19th Feb., 1856	Resigned **26th Feb., 1858**
Lorenzo Nickson **Mosse**	18th Mar., 1856	Resigned **30th Sept., 1857**

216 FIRST REGIMENT OF MILITIA; OR, [APPENDIX A.

ENSIGNS—*Continued*.	DATE OF APPOINTMENT.	REMARKS.
Joe Drury Bottomley	30th May, 1856	Promoted to Lieut. 23rd June 1858 (see I. of M.)
Adolphus William Murray	19th Oct., 1857	Resigned 11th July, 1858
William Samuel Bennett	19th Oct., 1857	Resigned 18th March, 1858
Joshua Paul Barker..	24th Nov., 1857	Never joined. Removed 13th March, 1858
Joseph Henry Palmer	24th Nov., 1857	**Prom.** to Lieut. 17th Mar., 1859
Thomas Bolger	26th Dec., 1857	**Prom. to** Lieut. 20th Oct., 1859
Gordon James Douglas	17th Mar., 1858	Prom. to Lieut. 26th April, 1859
Henry Pyne Hiffernan	7th April, 1858	Appointmt. canc. 26th Oct., 1858
James Macguire Manjin	7th April, 1858	Resigned 16th April, 1859
Frederick Arthur Verner	7th April, 1858	Prom. to Lieut. 20th Oct. 1859
George Campbell	7th April, 1858	Prom. to Lieut. 8th Sept., 1860
Edward Henry Saunders ...	18th June, 1858	Prom. to Lieut. 8th Sept., 1860
William Parkin Brown	27th June, 1858	Prom. to Lieut. 8th Sept., 1860
Robert Henry M'Loghlin	31st Jan., 1859	Prom. to Lieut. 23rd Nov., 1860
Thomas Walter Lambert	17th Mar., 1859	Prom. to Lieut. 24th June, 1862
James Redfern Bottomley ...	26th April, 1859	Prom. to Lieut. 24th June, 1862
Frederick Alfred Roberts ...	8th June, 1859	Prom. to Lieut. 24th June, 1862
John Robert Clarke	19th June, 1859	Prom. to Lieut. 24th June, 1862
W. Lisle Blenkinsop Coulson	20th Oct., 1859	To 25th Foot 16th March, 1860
George William Hoyle... ...	8th June, 1860	Never joined. Removed 9th Aug., 1864
SUB-LIEUTENANTS.		
John Matson Vincent ...	24th Sept., 1873	Promoted to Lt. 3rd Sept., 1875
Cuthbert Johnson Baines ...	11th Oct., 1873	Never joined, res. 11 Feb., 1874
John Edmond Groom ...	21st Feb., 1874	Promoted to Lt. 3rd Sept., 1875
John Stanley Lightfoot ...	13th April, 1874	Now serving
William Noble Bennett ...	29th May, 1874	Promoted to Lt. 3rd Sept., 1875
Arthur Barré Phipps	3rd March, 1875	}
Herbert Sturges Barlow ...	13th March, 1875	} Now serving
Philip Bower MacAdam ...	14th April, 1875	}

REGIMENTAL STAFF.

PAYMASTERS.	DATE OF APPOINTMENT.	REMARKS.
Thomas **Elston** ...	23rd April, 1798	Died 18th Aug., 1822 (see Lieutenants, 1797)
John William **Sturges**	28th Dec., 1822	Resigned 19th April, 1827 (see Ensigns, 1822)
Henry **Whitaker**	20th April, 1827	Resigned 1852-3 (see Ensigns, 1827, and Lieuts., 1831
Edward Nicholson	20th July, 1854	(See Lts., 1852, & Capts., 1854)
INSTRUCTORS OF MUSKETRY.		
John Geo. Smith Willcocks...	8th Jan., 1858	To Adjt. 47th Lanc. R.V., 3rd Nov., 1860 (see Ensigns, 1855, and Lieuts., 1857)

INSTRUCTORS OF MUSKETRY—Continued.	DATE OF APPOINTMENT.	REMARKS.
James Redfern Bottomley ...	21st May, 1867	(See Ensigns,1859, Lieuts.1862, and Capts. 1870)

ADJUTANTS.

Richard Dawson, Jun.	13th Feb., 1759	(See Ensigns, 1759)
Peter Cotes ...	25th March,1798	Ret. H.P. 23rd April, 1802 (see Lts. 1797, Capt.-Lts. 1799)
Henry Magill	13th July, 1798	Retired F.P. 20th Dec., 1813 (see Lts. 1798, Capts. 1803)
Anthony Allison	11th Sept., 1803	To Wakefield Loc. Mil. 7th May 1809 (see Ens. and Lieuts. 1803, and Capts. 1808)
Benjamin Midgeley ...	21st Dec., 1813	To Wakefield Loc.Mil.12thApr., 1815 (see Quarterm. 1804, Lts. 1805, and Capts. 1814)
Henry Magill	30th May, 1815	Reap. Retired 6th Aug., 1827. Died 20th Nov., 1828
William Rawson ...	7th August, 1827	**Died** 18th July, 1850 (see Captains 1831, also Ens. 1798, and Lieuts. 1799)
Edward Prothero ...	17th July, 1852	**From** Capt. 14th Foot, prom. to Major 9th Feb., 1855
Alexander Hamilton **Robson**	14th Mar., 1855	**From** Capt. 3rd Foot. Died 15th May, 1871
The Hon. Fred. Chas. Howard	17th Sept., 1871	(See Capts. 1871). Now serving

QUARTERMASTERS.

Samuel Wand	8th Oct., 1759	(**See** Lieuts. 1758-1763)
James Winskill	25th Mar., 1798	**Died** 24th April, 1803 (see Ensigns 1798, and Lieuts. 1830)
Hugh Parker	25th June, 1803	Resigned (Quartermaster) 16th August, 1803 (see Ensigns and Lieutenants 1803)
Thomas Wrightson	17th Aug. 1803	Res. (Q.-M.) 27th Sept., **1804.** (see Lieuts. 1803)
Benjamin Midgeley	28th Sept., 1804	Promoted to Adjutant 21st Dec. 1813 (see Adjutants)
John Atkinson	25th Jan., 1814	Died 3rd Apr. 1842 (see Lieuts. 1814)
John Bull ...	4th Sept., 1854	(See Lieuts. 13th Jan., 1871)

SURGEONS.

Richard Taylor ...	1758—1763	Ensign 1758-1763
Benjamin Robinson ...	25th Mar., 1798	Resigned 24th Jan., 1804 (see Lieuts. 1797)
John Hardy ...	25th **Jan., 1804**	Died 22nd Oct., 1836
John Lister ...	28th **Sept., 1852**	Resigned 16th Aug., 1854
Thomas Guy ...	22nd **Aug., 1854**	From Assist.-Surg., resigned 30th April, 1868
Lawrence Kiernan ...	1st **May, 1868**	Now serving

FIRST REGIMENT OF MILITIA. [APPENDIX A.

ASSISTANT-SURGEONS.	DATE OF APPOINTMENT.	REMARKS.
Joseph Fowler	25th April, 1798	Displaced 24th Oct., 1799 (see Ens. and Lieuts. 1798)
John Armer	1st April, 1799	Resigned 24th June, 1803 (see Ens. 1799, and Lieuts. 1801)
William Thomas	20th June, 1803	To Assist.-Surg. 67th Foot, 12th Nov., 1807 (see Ens. and Lieuts. 1803)
Charles Woodcock	14th July, 1803	Resigned 1st Dec. 1807 (see Ens. and Lieuts. 1803)
William Small	21st Dec., 1807	Resigned 9th Nov., 1809 (see Ens. 1807, and Lieuts. 1808)
George Pearson Dawson	18th Jan., 1808	Died 23rd Dec., 1829 (see Ens. and Lieuts. 1808)
Francis Travers	28th Sept., 1810	Resigned 31st Aug. 1811 (see Ens. 1810)
Robert Mann	25th Aug., 1812	Retired 1st Oct. 1852 (see Ensigns, 1812)
Thomas Guy	31st May, 1854	Prom. to Surg., 22nd Aug. 1854
Richard Hayes Perry	22nd Aug., 1854	Removed 10th July, 1866
Charles Henry Lister	9th Oct., 1867	Resigned 10th June, 1874

AGENTS.		
Messrs. Thos. William Maude " Rolleston & Hammond	1758–1763 1797	Downing Street, Westminster Horse Guards, afterwards Palace Yard
John Humphrey, Esq. Messrs. Edward Taylor & Co.	6th April, 1812	(Irish Agents) Mountjoy Sq., Dublin
" Cox & Co. Sir E. R. Borough, Bt.	May, 1854	Craig's Court, Charing Cross
Armit & Co.	August, 1854	(Irish Agents) Dublin

NOTE.—From the year 1853 no full Colonels have been appointed, but since 1870 the Commanding Officers of regiments have been made Lieutenant-Colonels Commandant, and Honorary Colonel of their regiment on retirement.

The Rank of Captain-Lieutenant was abolished in 1802 by the 42 George III., c. 90, previous to which the Field Officers were (nominally) Captains of Companies, and as such they received the pay; the senior Subaltern of the Colonel's company being a Captain-Lieutenant, or Senior Subaltern, of the regiment until the year 1778, when a Royal Warrant was issued, dated the 26th of March, conferring on them the rank of Captain (Militia Home Office, 1775-88, No. 4).

The appointment of Ensigns in the Militia was suspended in July, 1860.

The rank of Ensign was abolished and Sub-Lieutenants first appointed in May, 1873.

Instructors of Musketry were first appointed in 1853.

Assistant-Surgeons were styled also Surgeons' Mates down to the year 1814.

The names of the officers of the Regimental Staff appointed to serve with the rank of Captain, or Subalterns, or holding commissions as such, and all officers holding the Honorary Rank of Lieutenant-Colonels and Majors are printed in italics.

APPENDIX B.

ALPHABETICAL LIST OF OFFICERS

OF

THE REGIMENT.

FROM 1758 TO 1875.

ALDERSON, JOHN.—Ensign 7th June, 1805; Resigned 24th June, 1806.

ALLEN, FRANCKE MUCKLESTONE.—2nd Lieutenant Royal Carnarvon Rifle Militia 20th October, 1852; 1st Lieutenant 29th March, 1854; Captain 29th August, 1856; Captain 3rd West York Light Infantry 13th January, 1859; Honorary Major 20th November, 1872. Now serving

ALLISON, ANTHONY.—Ensign 27th June, 1803; Lieutenant 18th August, 1803; Adjutant 11th September, 1803; Brevet Captain 29th July, 1808; Adjutant Wakefield Local Militia 7th May, 1809.

ALLINSON, JOHN.—Ensign 1758-63.

ARMER, JOHN.—Ensign and Assistant-Surgeon 1st April, 1799; Lieutenant 1st July, 1801; Resigned 24th June, 1803.

ARMIT, WILLIAM.—Ensign 20th December, 1854; Lieutenant 11th August, 1855; Removed 10th March, 1859.

ARMITAGE, GEORGE.—Ensign 1st December, 1800; Lieutenant 31st March, 1803; Resigned 27th July, 1804.

ATHERSTONE, FREDERICK.—Ensign 4th April, 1811; Lieutenant 6th March, 1812; (Received Militia Disembodied Allowance from 25th June, 1815); Died 25th September, 1819.

ATKIN, WILLIAM.—Ensign 1st September, 1812; Ensign 88th Foot 12th May, 1814; Lieutenant 11th January, 1821; Retired H.-P. 25th August, 1821; Died 21st August, 1852.

ATKINSON, JOHN.—Private 5th March, 1798 ; Corporal 25th March, 1798 ; Sergeant 25th September, 1798; Sergeant-Major 28th September, 1804 ; Quartermaster 25th January, 1814 ; Brevet-Lieutenant 23rd June, 1814 ; Died 3rd April, 1842.

BAINBRIDGE, JOHN.—Captain 24th January, 1810; Resigned 6th August, 1853.

BAINES, CUTHBERT JOHNSON.—Sub-Lieutenant 11th October, 1873 ; Resigned 11th February, 1874. Never joined.

BARFF, THOMAS.—Cornet 1st West York Yeomanry 1848; Ensign 3rd West York Light Infantry 20th September, 1855 ; Resigned 14th February, 1856.

BARKER, JOSHUA PAUL—Ensign 24th November, 1857 ; Never joined ; Removed 13th March, 1858.

BARLOW, FRANCIS WILLIAM.—Captain 18th March, 1804 ; Resigned 6th November, 1804.

BARLOW, HENRY WILLIAM.—Cadet Royal Military Academy, Woolwich, 1837 to 1840 ; 2nd Lieutenant Royal Engineers 16th December, 1840; 1st Lieutenant 15th November, 1843 ; 2nd Captain 31st August, 1851 ; 1st Captain 14th March, 1855 ; Resigned 1st May, 1857 ; Captain 3rd West York Light Infantry 20th July, 1870. Now serving. Served in Canada from September, 1842, to May, 1843.

BARLOW, HERBERT STURGES.—Sub-Lieutenant 13th March, 1875. Now serving.

BARNETT, JOHN.—Ensign 71st Foot 25th November, 1813; Lieutenant 23rd November, 1815 ; appointed to 87th Foot 22nd February, 1816 ; Exchanged back to 71st Foot 30th May, 1816 ; H.-P. 1818 ; Lieutenant 23rd Foot 18th February, 1819 ; H.-P. 61st Foot 12th September, 1822 ; Retired 1836 ; Lieutenant-Colonel 3rd West York Light Infantry 28th February, 1846. Died at Linen Hall Barracks, Dublin, 23rd February, 1855. Was present at the Battle of Waterloo, 18th June, 1815, as Ensign ; Served in Belgium and France 1815-19 ; Waterloo Medal.

BAXTER, ROBERT DUDLEY.—Lieutenant, 4th November, 1852 ; Captain 21st February, 1854 ; Resigned 1st February, 1855 ; Died 20th May, 1875.

BEAMISH, FRANK JOHN DE VIE.—Lieutenant 5th February, 1873 ; Resigned 22nd June, 1875 ; Served as a Volunteer with 1st Zouaves before Paris 1870-1871. Present at the Engagements of Clamart, **Vilesey,** and Chatillon, Slightly wounded. **French** Military **Medal.**

BELL, ROBERT JOHN.—Ensign 11th **August,** 1854; **Lieutenant 1st February, 1855;** Ensign 37th **Foot 7th** March, **1856; Died on board the** *Argo,* 12th **May, 1858.**

BENNETT, **WILLIAM** SAMUEL.—Ensign **19th October, 1857;** Resigned 18th March, **1858.**

BENNETT, WILLIAM NOBLE.—Ensign 6th Tower Hamlets Rifle **Volunteers 5th June,** 1872; Lieutenant 19th February, **1873;** Resigned **29th May, 1874; Sub-Lieutenant** 3rd West **York Light** Infantry **29th May, 1874; Lieutenant 3rd** September, 1875; **(Ante-dated 29th May, 1874); Now serving.** Captain's **Certificate from School of** Instruction, dated Chelsea **Barracks, 31st October, 1872.**

BENSON, **ROBERT HAGGARD.—Captain 1st** September, 1804; **Major 30th October, 1811; Cashiered 1st** October, 1813.

BIRMINGHAM, EDWARD.—Captain 12th June, **1808;** Resigned 10th **December,** 1809.

BLACKLIN, RICHARD.—Ensign 2nd September, 1812; (Received Militia Disembodied Allowance from 24th December, 1814), Ensign 1st Foot 18th July, **1815;** Lieutenant 13th July, 1820; Captain 8th August, 1833; **Retired H.-P.** (Unattached) 6th February, 1846, Major **9th** November, 1846; Lieutenant-**Colonel 20th** June, 1854; Colonel 1st November, **1858; Died 18th May, 1867. Waterloo** Medal; Military **Knight of Windsor (Royal Foundation).**

BLAKE, JAMES CUFF.—**Captain 16th** February, **1810;** Resigned **9th May, 1813.**

BLAKE, WILLIAM GREAVES.—Ensign 2nd May, **1853;** Lieutenant 29th August, 1854; Ensign **89th Foot** 27th February, 1856; Cornet 2nd **Royal** North British (Scots Greys) Dragoons 17th July, 1857; **Lieutenant 6th** Dragoon Guards (Carabineers) 3rd March, 1858; Lieutenant 9th (Queen's Royal) Lancers 21st March, 1861; Retired **26th** April, 1864; Re-appointed Lieutenant **3rd** West York Light **Infantry 27th June,** 1868; Captain 2nd May, 1870; Now serving. **Served with** the 6th Dragoon Guards in **Oude and the Trans-Gogra** District in 1858-59; and was present at **the Action** of Doondiakera, affair of Churda, taking of the Fort of Mujudia, and Action at Bankee under Lord Clyde. Medal. In India from March, 1858, to July, 1861.

BLAYDES, HUGH.—Captain 1st June, 1800; Major 19th October, 1803; Resigned 24th March, 1807.

BLEADES, HUGH.—Captain 27th February, 1832. Died.

BOLDERICK, JOHN.—Lieutenant 11th March, 1797; Resigned 24th April, 1800.

BOLGER, THOMAS.—Ensign 26th December, 1857; Lieutenant 20th October, 1859; Resigned 26th June, 1860.

BOOTH, WILLIAM.—Ensign 18th August, 1805; Resigned 24th March, 1806.

BOTTOMLEY, JOE DRURY.—Ensign 30th May, 1856; Lieutenant 23rd June, 1858; 2nd Lieutenant Royal Marines 11th September, 1859; 1st Lieutenant 3rd September, 1862; Retired with rank of Captain 1st August, 1873. Changed his name to Drury 15th January, 1866.

BOTTOMLEY, JAMES REDFERN.—Ensign 26th April, 1859; Lieutenant 24th June, 1862; Instructor of Musketry 21st May, 1867; Captain 12th March, 1870; Now serving. First Class Certificate from School of Musketry (Fleetwood), dated Hythe 6th October, 1866.

BOURKE, JOHN NICHOLAS.—Captain 23rd October, 1807; Resigned 13th August, 1808.

BOURKE, CHARLES THOMAS.—Ensign 31st May, 1811; Resigned 25th July, 1811; Never joined; Ensign 48th Foot 14th June, 1811; Lieutenant 27th August, 1813; (Lieutenant in Army from 20th May); Retired H.-P. 3rd October, 1814; Resigned March 1834.

BOWEN, EDWARD.—Lieutenant 31st July, 1872; Now serving.

BOWER, HENRY.—Lieutenant 10th July, 1798; Resigned 24th March, 1800.

BOWER, EDWARD CHIVERS.—Lieutenant 4th November, 1852; Captain 24th May, 1853; Resigned 12th January, 1859; Captain 1st West York Yeomanry 9th May, 1864; Resigned 24th February, 1872.

BRACKEN, EDWARD.—Ensign 17th October, 1813; (Received Militia Disembodied Allowance from 25th June, 1815); Resigned 19th May, 1820. Died 16th May, 1825.

BRACKENBURY, JOHN MACPHERSON.—Captain 25th November, 1803; Resigned 5th April, 1806.

BRADDELL, JOHN ARMSTED.—Ensign 29th September, 1805; Lieutenant 14th September, 1807; Ensign 36th Foot 15th October, 1807; Lieutenant 25th May, 1809; Retired H.-P., 3rd August, 1811; Resigned December, 1846.

BROCKELL, THOMAS.—Lieutenant 25th May, 1800; Resigned 31st August, 1803.

BROOKFIELD, JOHN.—Lieutenant 8th March, 1797; Resigned 24th May, 1798.

BROOKSBANK, STAMP.—Captain 24th December, 1807; Major 17th November, 1813; Lieutenant-Colonel 22nd May, 1820; Resigned 9th January, 1822.

BROWN, GEORGE.—Ensign 8th Foot 17th December, 1803; Lieutenant 21st March, 1805; Retired October, 1806; Captain 3rd West York Light Infantry 14th August, 1807; Resigned 1st June, 1810.

BROWN, WILLIAM PARKIN.—Ensign 27th June, 1858; Lieutenant 8th September, 1860; Removed 27th June, 1862.

BROWNE, WILLIAM ALEXANDER. — Lieutenant 19th March, 1866. Died at Conisbro', near Doncaster, 14th September, 1867, from injuries received by falling into a well in the dungeon in Conisbro' Castle, on the 27th June.

BULL, JOHN.—Ranks and Non-Commissioned Officer 81st Regiment 7th January, 1831 to 8th October, 1852; Sergeant-Major 3rd West York Light Infantry 9th October, 1852; Quartermaster 4th September, 1854; Lieutenant 13th January, 1871; Now serving. Served abroad at Gibraltar from May, 1836, to 1840; West Indies, from January, 1840, to September, 1843; and in Canada, from September 1843, to July, 1848.

BURROUGHS, THOMAS.—Ensign 13th June, 1808; Lieutenant 28th October 1809; Died 19th June, 1811.

BURTON, RICHARD.—Ensign 1758-1763; Ensign 2nd West York 22nd October, 1763; Lieutenant 14th May, 1774.

BUTLER, WILLIAM F.—Captain 13th May, 1808. Never joined.

CADMAN, JOHN.—Ensign 30th November, 1855; Lieutenant 18th January, 1858; Resigned 29th June, 1866.

CALEY, ROBERT.—Ensign 13th September, 1813; Resigned 13th September, 1813. Never joined.

CAMPBELL, GEORGE.—Ensign 7th April, 1858; Lieutenant 8th September, 1860; Resigned 27th June, 1862; Ensign 79th Foot 29th July, 1862; Ensign 77th Foot 2nd November, 1866; Lieutenant 2nd September, 1868. Now serving.

CARFRAC, JOHN.—Ensign 5th March, 1800; Resigned 24th October, 1800.

CARNELLY, THOMAS.—Lieutenant 10th March, 1797; Resigned 24th May, 1800.

CHAMBERS, WILLIAM FREDERICK.—Ensign 25th July, 1821. Serving in May, 1839.

CHANTRELL, JOHN BOHAM.—Lieutenant 25th November, 1852; Captain 22nd May, 1854; Honorary Major 1st January, 1873. Now serving.

CHILDERS, WILLIAM WALBANK.—Captain-Lieutenant 1st March, 1797; Captain 25th April, 1798; Resigned 20th January, 1801. Afterwards ordained, and became Rector of Beeford and Vicar of Cantley, near Doncaster, and Prebendary of Ely. Died 8th February, 1833.

CHILDERS, LEONARD W.—Captain 7th January, 1799; Resigned 24th May, 1803; Captain Doncaster Volunteers 15th October, 1803; Died 24th January, 1826.

CHOLMLEY, GEORGE.—Cornet 7th (Queen's Own) Light Dragoons, 11th June, 1801; Lieutenant 12th May, 1803; Captain 18th April, 1805; Major 27th April, 1809; (and Assistant Adjutant-General) Retired 7th May 1812; Lieutenant-Colonel 3rd West York Light Infantry 26th May, 1812; Colonel 27th January, 1820; Resigned 29th August, 1850. Three Medals for Sahagun and Beneventi.

CLAPHAM, RICHARD.—Ensign 1758-1763.

CLARKE, CHRISTOPHER N.—Ensign 23rd May, 1804; Lieutenant 26th June, 1804; Captain 26th June, 1806; Major 22nd May, 1820; Died 1851. (?)

CLARKE, JOHN ROBERT.—Ensign 19th June, 1859; Lieutenant 24th June, 1862; Resigned 20th April, 1863.

COLLINS, JAMES RICHARDSON.—Captain 15th April, 1801. Paymaster 28th Dragoons 6th April, 1802; Placed on H.-P. 1802 (the Regiment being disbanded); Re-appointed Captain

3rd West York Light Infantry 23rd April, 1803 ; Major 22nd March, 1807 ; Died 22nd June, 1810.

CONROY, EDWARD.—Lieutenant 1st April, 1799 ; Ensign 6th West India Regiment, 11th December, 1802 ; Lieutenant 6th August, 1803 to 1804.

CONROY, PATRICK.—Ensign 24th April, 1801 ; Lieutenant 1st April, 1803 ; Ensign 6th West India Regiment 27th August. 1803 ; Lieutenant 26th July, 1804 ; Lieutenant 4th Foot 13th February, 1805 ; Retired H.P. 1814 ; Died at Moshill, Co. Roscommon, 5th July, 1835.

COOKE, SIR GEORGE, Bart. (succeeded as Seventh Bart. 4th March, 1769).—Cornet Royal Horse Guards (Blues) 18th April, 1766 ; Retired April, 1770 ; Captain North York Militia 5th September, 1789 to 1794 ; Colonel 3rd West York Light Infantry 27th February, 1797 ; (Brevet-Colonel in the Army for as long as the Regiment should remain embodied, 18th August, 1798) ; Resigned 15th May, 1803 ; Lieut-Colonel Doncaster Volunteers, 15th October, 1803 ; Died 2nd June, 1823.

COOKE, JOHN.—Ensign Grenadier Guards 4th June, 1781 ; Lieutenant and Captain 28th November, 1787 ; Exchanged to Captain 45th Foot 14th July, 1790 ; Retired 26th October, 1790 ; Major 3rd West York Light Infantry 27th February, 1797 ; Lieut.-Colonel 1st April, 1799 ; Resigned 24th May, 1803.

COOKE, GEORGE.—Captain 28th February, 1797 ; Major 25th June, 1798 ; Resigned 6th January, 1799.

COOKE, BRYAN WILLIAM DARWIN.—Ensign Grenadier Guards 16th April, 1782 ; Lieutenant and Captain 13th June, 1789 ; Exchanged to Captain 15th Foot, 1st December, 1792 ; Exchanged to H.-P. Independent Companies 22nd December, 1792 ; Captain 3rd West York Light Infantry 1st March, 1797 ; Resigned 24th April, 1798 ; Captain Doncaster Volunteers, 15th October, 1803 ; Died 26th April, 1824.

COOKE, GEORGE AUGUSTUS (eldest son of Sir George Cooke, Bart.).— Captain-Lieut. 14th June, 1798 ; Resigned 29th January, 1799 ; Ensign 1st Foot Guards (Grenadiers), 29th March, 1799 ; Lieutenant and Captain 23rd April, 1800 ; Retired

H.-P. 1802 ; Exchanged back to F.-P. 25th December, 1802 ; Retired 31st July, 1806 ; Died 5th May, 1808.

COOKE, BRYAN.—Cornet Royal Horse Guards (Blues) 22nd March, 1775 ; Lieutenant 6th May, 1781 ; Retired 14th June, 1784 ; Lieut.-Col. West York Yeomanry (Northern Regiment), 13th August, 1794 ; Colonel 3rd West York Light Infantry 16th May, 1803 ; Resigned 22nd February, 1812 ; was M.P. for Malton, from 1797 to 1812 ; Died 18th November, 1821.

COOKE, SIR WILLIAM BRYAN, Bart. (second son of Sir George Cooke, Bart., succeeded to the title as Eighth Bart. 2nd June, 1823).—Ensign 1st Foot Guards (Grenadier) 15th October, 1803 ; Lieutenant and Captain 25th June, 1807 ; Retired 26th May, 1808 ; Lieut.-Colonel 3rd West York Light Infantry 25th October, 1811 ; Colonel 23rd February, 1812 ; Resigned 7th December, 1819 ; Died 24th December, 1851.

COPLEY, THOMAS.—Captain 6th March, 1797 ; Resigned 10th April, 1801.

COPLEY, SIR JOSEPH, Bart. (succeeded as Third Bart., 11th April, 1801).—Captain 22nd November, 1819 ; Resigned 6th June, 1825 ; Died 21st May, 1838.

COTES, PETER.—Ensign 56th Foot 1st February, 1788 ; Lieutenant 30th July, 1791 ; Captain H.P. 1795-99 ; Lieutenant 3rd West York Light Infantry 1st March, 1797 ; Adjutant 25th March, 1798 ; Captain-Lieutenant 1st April, 1799 ; Retired H.P. 23rd April, 1802.

COULSON, WILLIAM LISLE BLENKINSOP.—Ensign 20th October, 1859 ; Ensign 25th Foot 16th March, 1860 ; Lieutenant 23rd August, 1861 ; Captain 4th December, 1866 ; (Aide-de-Camp to Major-General Macdonell) ; Now serving.

COURTNEY, HENRY.—Ensign 65th Foot 26th February, 1799 ; Lieutenant 10th May, 1799 ; Captain 5th West India Regiment 4th June, 1801 ; Exchanged to 32nd Foot 9th July, 1801 ; Exchanged to 47th Foot 9th July, 1803 to 1808 ; Captain 3rd West York Light Infantry 1st October, 1808 ; Resigned 1824.

COWARD, JAMES.—Ensign 27th August, 1803 ; Lieutenant 4th November, 1803 ; Resigned 24th August, 1804.

CREWE, RANDOLPH.—Ensign 6th March, 1800; Resigned 24th December, 1801; Ensign 1st West York Militia 27th August, 1803; Re-appointed Lieutenant 3rd West York Light Infantry 26th September, 1803; Ensign 58th Foot 6th September, 1804; Lieutenant 29th December, 1804; Captain 29th March, 1810; Retired H.P. 25th February, 1816. (Name removed from Army List in 1822, with **several others to whom no** pay had been issued **for seven years.**)

CREYKE, RALPH.—Captain 2nd West York Militia 20th April, 1835; Major 3rd West York Light Infantry 26th November, 1852; Resigned 21st February, 1855. Died 7th February, 1858.

CURRY, MICHAEL.—Ranks, **and Non-Commissioned** Officer 81st Foot 1st September, 1838, to 1st February, 1858; Ensign 81st Foot 2nd February, 1858; Lieutenant 26th July, 1864; Adjutant 24th September, 1858, to 1st February, 1870; **Captain unattached** 19th February, 1870; Captain 3rd West **York Light** Infantry 15th April, 1871; Now serving. Certificate dated School **of Musketry,** Hythe, 6th November, 1865. **Served** throughout the Indian Mutiny from first outbreak **till the** termination in 1857-8; Served **in the** Eusoofzai Frontier Campaign in India, under Major-General Sir Sydney Cotton, K.C.B., in 1858; Abroad in **Canada 24th May, 1843 to September, 1847;** and in India from **1st July, 1853, to April,** 1865; Indian Mutiny Medal, North Western Frontier Medal **with Clasp, and Meritorious Service** Medal.

DACRE, FRANCIS.—Captain **30th May, 1805;** Major **15th May, 1812;** Lieutenant-Colonel **10th** January, 1822; Resigned 27th February, 1846.

DAVIS, ARCHIBALD.—Ensign 25th February, 1805; Resigned 24th May, **1805.**

DAWSON, RICHARD, Jun.—Adjutant 13th February, 1759; Ensign 8th October, 1759–1763.

DAWSON, GEORGE PEARSON.—Ensign and Assistant-Surgeon 18th January, 1808; Lieutenant 6th September, 1808. (Received **Militia** Disembodied Allowance from 25th June, 1814.) Died 23rd December, 1829.

DEWAR, JOHN E.—Captain 6th July, 1803; Resigned 24th June, 1806.

DEWES, RICHARD.—Ensign 1758-1763.

DILLON, THEOBALD.—Ensign 4th March, 1797; Lieutenant 12th March, 1797; Lieutenant 2nd West York Militia 13th April, 1798; Captain 15th February 1798 to 1803.

DIXON, JAMES.—Ensign 31st December, 1806; Lieutenant 9th December, 1807; Resigned 16th March, 1810.

DIXON, HENRY.—Ensign 29th Foot 20th August, 1812; Lieutenant 21st December, 1815; Lieutenant 81st Foot 24th February, 1820; Captain 21st November, 1828; Brevet-Major 23rd November, 1841; Retired on H.P. 16th June, 1843; Placed on Retired F.P. 10th May, 1844; Lieutenant-Colonel 28th November, 1854; Major 3rd West York Light Infantry 17th April, 1851; Resigned 1852; Died 27th October, 1874. Served in the Peninsula. Waterloo Medal.

DONABAL, —.—Lieutenant 8th August, 1803; Never joined; Removed previous to 1804.

DONELAN, STEPHEN J.—Ensign 1st West York Militia, 30th October, 1807; Lieutenant 23rd November, 1807; Captain 3rd West York Light Infantry 8th July, 1808; Resigned or Died subsequent to 1852.

DONNELLAN, HUGH STAFFORD.—Ensign 2nd November, 1807; Lieutenant 8th April, 1808; Ensign 82nd Foot 19th May, 1808; Lieutenant 8th March, 1810; Captain 13th March, 1827; Retired H.P. 11th December, 1828; Retired November, 1835.

DOUGLAS, GORDON JAMES.—Ensign 17th March, 1858; Lieutenant 26th April, 1859; Resigned 5th September, 1860.

DRUMMOND, PETER AURIOL H.—Lieutenant-Colonel 27th February, 1797; Died 21st March, 1799. Killed by the library steps falling upon him at his residence, Bawtry, near Doncaster.

DRURY, JOE DRURY.—(See Bottomley.)

DUNCOMBE, HENRY.—Captain 1758-1763.

DUNCOMBE, WILLIAM.—(Succeeded as Second Baron Feversham 16th July, 1841). Major 9th January, 1823; Resigned 27th February, 1846. Was M.P. for Yorkshire from 1826 to

1831, and for the North Riding from 1832 to 1841; Died 11th February, 1867.

DUNHILL, THOMAS RICHARD.—Ensign 17th September, 1846; Resigned 1853.

DURHAM, FREDERICK.—Ensign 8th January, 1853; Lieutenant 21st February, 1854; Captain 24th November, 1855; Retired with Honorary Rank of Major 15th March, 1873.

EADON, FRANK HENRY EADON.—Lieutenant 21st December, 1852; Captain 2nd September, 1854; Retired with Honorary Rank of Major 29th March, 1873.

EASTWOOD, WILLIAM MANLEY.—Lieutenant 19th March, 1853; Resigned 31st July, 1854.

ECCLES, THOMAS.—Ensign 25th February, 1811; Resigned 31st August, 1811.

ELSTON, THOMAS.—Lieutenant 6th March, 1797; Paymaster 23rd April, 1798; Died 18th August, 1822. Killed by being thrown from a gig at Bentley, near Doncaster.

EMMERSON, JAMES.—Lieutenant 31st December, 1803; Resigned 24th July, 1805.

EYRE, CHARLES.—Ensign 24th June, 1800; Displaced March, 1803.

EYRE, THOMAS.—Ensign 14th April, 1811; Lieutenant 7th March, 1812; Ensign 34th Foot 7th April, 1813; Lieutenant 21st November, 1816; Retired H.-P. 25th March, 1817; Died in London 20th June, 1821.

FAVIELL, JEREMIAH BOURNE.—Captain 2nd May, 1853; Resigned 23rd November, 1855.

FEVERSHAM, BARON.—(See DUNCOMBE, WILLIAM.)

FIRMAN, HUMPHREY BROOK.—Cornet 4th Light Dragoons 14th May, 1852; Retired 21st July, 1854; Ensign 3rd West York Light Infantry 3rd August, 1854; Lieutenant 12th January, 1855; Resigned 30th September, 1857.

FIRTH, JOHN LEAMING.—Lieutenant 14th July, 1803; Resigned 24th July, 1804.

FISHER, WILLIAM.—Ensign 8th February, 1804; Lieutenant 5th June, 1804; Resigned 23rd January, 1808.

FLOOD, JOHN CHARLES.—2nd Lieutenant 5th Fusiliers 22nd December, 1846; Lieutenant 21st May, 1850; Resigned 5th June, 1855; Captain 3rd West York Light Infantry 4th July, 1855; (Captain Turkish Contingent 1st January to August, 1856); Removed 23rd October, 1858. Served abroad from September, 1847, to December, 1853, in Mauritius, and, January to June, 1856, in the Crimea.

FOLCH, STEPHEN VINCENT.—Lieutenant 28th April, 1863; Removed 17th August, 1868.

FOLJAMBE, JOHN SAVILE.—Captain 4th March, 1797; Resigned 31st March, 1799.

FORTH, JOHN DODDINGTON.—Ensign 22nd November, 1806; Lieutenant 8th December, 1807; Resigned 22nd July, 1808.

FOSTER, WILLIAM.—Lieutenant 1758–1763.

FOWLER, JOSEPH.—Ensign and Assistant-Surgeon 25th April, 1798; Lieutenant 22nd June 1798; Displaced 24th October, 1799.

FOX, GEORGE LANE.—Colonel 31st August, 1850; Resigned 17th September, 1852.

FOZARD, WILLIAM.—Lieutenant 4th West York Militia 10th April, 1799; Lieutenant 3rd West York Light Infantry 5th March, 1800; Resigned 24th May, 1800; Reappointed Lieutenant 15th March, 1803; Adjutant Maidstone Volunteers 7th January, 1805 (Commission dated 10th November, 1804).

GARBUT, JOHN.—Ensign 31st March, 1808; Ensign 84th Foot 23rd May, 1808; Lieutenant 13th October, 1808; Died April (?), 1811.

GARFORTH, WILLIAM.—Served as a Volunteer (2nd Lieutenant) in the Hanoverian Rifle Guards from 1st April, 1835, to 30th December 1836; Ensign 97th Foot 31st December, 1836; Lieutenant 22nd March, 1839; Captain 24th June, 1844; Retired 6th February, 1846; Captain 3rd West York Light Infantry 21st February, 1853; Resigned 3rd July, 1855. Served abroad in the Ionian Isles from 31st January, 1841, to 1st May, 1844, and from 17th October, 1844, to 6th February, 1846.

GATLIFF, WILLIAM GOODMAN.—Ensign 3rd August, 1855; Lieutenant 19th October, 1857; Resigned 22nd June, 1858.

GATLIFF, NORTH.—Ensign 15th February, 1856; Resigned 10th November, 1857.

GEE, THOMAS.—Ensign 3rd February, 1812: Lieutenant 13th September, 1813; Lieutenant 49th Foot 12th May, 1814 (Temporary Rank); Retired H.-P. 1814; Retired December, 1829; Reappointed (?) Ensign 3rd West York Light Infantry 7th June, 1819; Resigned 9th March, 1831.

GELL, WILLIAM.—Captain 12th May, 1804; Resigned 24th June, 1804.

GILBERT, JOHN C.—Ensign 2nd April, 1799; Never joined; Removed before 1800.

GOULDEN, JOHN.—Ensign 28th June, 1803; Lieutenant 29th October, 1803; Displaced 25th April, 1807.

GRÆME, PATRICK.—Ensign 2nd August, 1808; Ensign 18th Foot 10th February, 1809; Ensign 44th Foot 25th February, 1810; Lieutenant 89th Foot 25th April, 1811; Died 1814.

GREAVES, WILLIAM.—Ensign 29th May, 1809; Lieutenant 27th June, 1810; Resigned 9th October, 1810.

GREGORY, ADAM.—Ensign 11th June, 1805; Resigned 24th April, 1806; Ensign 29th Foot 12th June, 1806; Lieutenant 8th February, 1808; Captain 24th November, 1814; Retired H.-P. 3rd January, 1822; Retired September, 1834.

GRESHAM, THOMAS.—Lieutenant 2nd March, 1797; Captain-Lieutenant 30th January, 1799; Captain 1st April, 1799; Resigned 24th October, 1803.

GROOM, JOHN EDMOND.—Sub-Lieutenant 21st February, 1874; Lieutenant 3rd September, 1875 (antedated to 21st February, 1874). Now serving.

GULSTON, FREDERICK.—Captain 7th March, 1808, (7th November, 1807, in the Army List); Resigned 24th April, 1808.

GUY, THOMAS.—Assistant-Surgeon 31st May, 1854; Surgeon 22nd August, 1854; Resigned 30th April, 1868.

HALL, THOMAS ARCHIBALD FISHER.—Lieutenant 24th July, 1872; Resigned 29th March, 1873. Never joined.

HANDLEY, WILLIAM.—Ensign 25th April, 1808; Lieutenant 6th May 1809; Ensign 48th Foot 25th August, 1809; Dismissed June 1811.

HARDY, JOHN.—Surgeon 25th January, 1804; Died 22nd October, 1836.

HARDY, SAMUEL.—Ensign 24th February, 1811; Resigned 12th April, 1812.

HARRISON, JOHN LOCKWOOD.—Ensign 25th July, 1813; Received Militia Disembodied Allowance from 25th June, 1815); Lieutenant 11th July, 1825; Retired on Militia Allowance 1st October, 1852.

HASSELL, GEORGE.—Lieutenant 1758–1763; Captain 2nd West York Militia October, 1763.

HASTED, EDWARD GOULD.—Ensign 17th November, 1854; Ensign 57th Foot 2nd March, 1855; Lieutenant 26th February, 1856; Captain 22nd May, 1863; Retired 15th March, 1873. Served in the Crimea from 24th September, 1854, and was present with the 57th Regiment at the bombardment and capture of Kinbourn. Served in the New Zealand War, at Taranaki, in 1861; also in the Wangariri Campaign, 1865–66; and was present at the affair at Kakaramea, also at the attack and capture of the fortified Pahs at Otapowa Ketemeri, and Meremere. Crimean, Turkish, and New Zealand Medals.

HAWKE, THE HON. MARTIN BLADEN.—Captain 20th June, 1803; Resigned 10th January, 1805.

HAWKES, WILLIAM.—Ensign 7th April, 1812; (Received Militia Disembodied Allowance from 25th June, 1815); Died 31st March, 1823.

HEATON, HENRY WILLIAM.—Ensign 24th March, 1854; Ensign 14th Foot 22nd December, 1854; Lieutenant 9th March, 1855; Retired 1860; appointed Captain and Adjutant 3rd Manchester, or 40th Lancashire, Rifle Volunteers, from 8th December, 1860 (dated 17th December), to February, 1872. Served in the Trenches before Sevastopol; Medal and Clasp.

HEBDEN, HENRY.—Ensign 7th July, 1812; Ensign 2nd Garrison Battalion 25th May, 1815; Retired H.-P. 25th December, 1816; Ensign 58th Foot 27th January, 1820; Lieutenant 7th April, 1825; Captain 13th May, 1826; Retired H.P. (Unattached) 26th April, 1827; Captain 1st West India Regiment 29th **April,** 1853; Brevet Major 23rd November, 1841; Brevet Lieutenant-Colonel 11th **November, 1851** (the last three appointments all gazetted on 29th April, **1853**); Retired May, 1853.

HEPWORTH, WILLIAM.—Captain 28th February, 1846; Resigned **1853.**

HIFFERNAN, HENRY PYNE.—Ensign **7th** April, **1858.** Never joined. Commission cancelled 26th October, **1858.**

HIGGINS, GODFREY.—Captain 1st November, **1802**; Resigned 24th April, 1805; Re-appointed Major 21st March, **1808**; Resigned 6th **December, 1811.**

HIGGINS, NICHOLAS.—Ensign 6th August, **1807**; Lieutenant 8th **April, 1808**; Resigned 9th April, **1810.**

HIGGINS, BOWES.—Ensign 14th September, **1807.** Never joined. Removed before 1808.

HILL, RICHARD.—Ensign 5th June, 1806; Died 19th June, 1807.

HINDE, WALTER HENRY.—Ensign 12th April, 1853; Lieutenant 29th **August, 1854**; Resigned 15th December, 1854.

HOLDFORTH, STEPHEN.—Lieutenant **4th** November, **1852**; Resigned 21st February, 1854.

HOMFRAY, JESTIN.—Lieutenant 22nd **November, 1838**; Resigned **1852-3.**

HOOK, JAMES.—Captain 10th July, 1807; Ensign 9th Garrison Battalion 23rd May, **1808**; Ensign 103rd Foot 19th May, **1808**; Retired H.-P. 1813; Resigned September 1830.

HORNE, JOHN.—Lieutenant 20th June, 1803; Resigned 16th April, 1804.

HORNER, JOHN.—Ensign 1758-1763.

HORSFIELD, MANN.—Captain 1758-1763.

HOULTON, CHARLES TORIANO.—Lieutenant 19th **July,** 1812; (Received Militia Disembodied Allowance from 25th June, **1815**); Resigned **1852.** (?)

HOWARD, THE HON. FREDERICK CHARLES.—Ensign and Lieutenant Coldstream Guards **13th** May, 1859; Lieutenant and Captain 11th August, **1863**; Resigned 19th July, **1866**; Cornet

Queen's Own Oxford Yeomanry 27th May, 1868; Resigned 9th February, 1872; Captain and Adjutant 3rd West York Light Infantry 17th September, 1871; Temporary Rank of Captain in the Army 25th of February, 1874. Now serving.

HOWORTH, THOMAS ORTON.—Ensign 10th June, 1854; Ensign 44th Foot 29th December, 1854; Lieutenant 9th March, 1855; Captain 18th July, 1862; Died 23rd January, 1865. Served at the siege of Sevastopol from 16th June to 1st July, including the attack on the 18th June; severely wounded; Medal and Clasp, and Turkish Medal. Served all through the Campaign of 1860, in the North of China, in the Chinese Coolie Corps; including the affairs of the 14th, 18th, and 21st September, and the Capitulation of Pekin; Medal and Clasp.

HOYLE, GEORGE WILLIAM.—Ensign 8th June, 1860; Removed 9th August, 1864. Never joined.

HUDSON, THOMAS, Jun.—Ensign 2nd March, 1797; Lieutenant 19th June, 1798; Captain 2nd November, 1803; Resigned 24th July, 1805.

HUDSON, WILLIAM.—Ensign 12th July, 1803; Lieutenant 31st October, 1803; Resigned 24th February, 1805.

HUDSON, RICHARD.—Ensign 13th July, 1803; Lieutenant 1st November, 1803; Ensign 40th Foot 26th April, 1809; Lieutenant 7th November, 1811; Retired H.-P. 21st March, 1822; Died 13th August, 1827, at Carofin, Co. Clare. Waterloo Medal.

INGRAM, FRANCIS.—Captain 20th May, 1806; Resigned 4th January, 1810.

IVESON, GEORGE.—Ensign 8th August, 1759; Lieutenant 1763; Captain 2nd West York Militia October, 1763.

JAMES, ALFRED AUGUSTUS.—Ensign Royal London Militia 27th June, 1854; Ensign 3rd West York Light Infantry 31st October, 1854; Resigned same date; Lieutenant Hampshire Militia 20th December, 1854, to March, 1857.

JEFFRYES, JOHN.—Ensign 30th August, 1808 ; Lieutenant 14th
February, 1810 ; (Received Militia Disembodied Allowance
from 25th June, 1815) ; Died 17th August, 1827.

JEWITT, WILLIAM.—Lieutenant 2nd January, 1805 ; Resigned 24th
April, 1805.

JOLIFFE, WILLIAM TUFFNELL.—Major 1758–1763.

JONES, THOMAS.—Lieutenant 17th May, 1800 ; Resigned 24th December, 1800.

KENDALL, JOHN.—Lieutenant 26th October, 1852 ; Captain 12th
May, 1853 ; Major 25th May, 1870 ; Honorary Lieutenant-
Colonel 30th July, 1873 ; Now serving.

KENT, SIR CHARLES, Bart. (Charles Egleton created 1st Bart. 3rd
August, 1782.)—Captain 18th June, 1798 ; Resigned 13th
January, 1800. M.P. for Thetford, 1784-90. Died 14th
March, 1811.

KIERNAN, LAWRENCE.—Assistant-Surgeon 1st West York Yeomanry
24th April, 1863 ; Surgeon 3rd West York Light Infantry,
1st May, 1868 ; Now serving in both regiments.

KIGHLEY, JOSEPH HUBERT.—Ensign 19th August, 1805 ; Lieutenant
6th August, 1807 ; Ensign 53rd Foot 19th May, 1808, to
July, 1809.

KINDER, THOMAS WILLIAM.—Ensign Worcester Militia 4th December,
1840 ; Lieutenant 30th January, 1846 ; Captain 9th September, 1853 ; Captain 3rd West York Light Infantry 11th
February, 1859 ; Retired 3rd March, 1870 ; (Honorary Rank
of Major 22nd March, 1870.)

LAMBERT, JOHN.—Ensign 16th January, 1804 ; Lieutenant 4th May,
1804 ; Resigned 24th February, 1805.

LAMBERT, THOMAS WALTER.—Ensign 17th March, 1859 ; Lieutenant
24th June, 1862 ; Resigned 28th April, 1864.

LANDON, EDWARD.—Ensign 5th May, 1855 ; Lieutenant 30th May,
1856 ; Resigned 8th January, 1858.

LANGFORD, BUTLER ROLLA.—Captain 25th December, 1813 ; Resigned
21st July, 1814.

LANGHORNE, THOMAS.—Ensign 25th August, 1800 ; Lieutenant 30th
March, 1803 ; Resigned 24th May, 1804.

LASCELLES, DANIEL.—Lieutenant-Colonel 1758–1763. M.P. for North allerton, 1752–1780. Died 1734.

LAUGHTON, FREDERICK AUGUSTUS.—Lieutenant 28th February, 1846; Resigned 1852.

LAYBORN, JONATHAN.—Ensign 15th May, 1812; Captain 7th June, 1820; Resigned 23rd February, 1831.

LEAF, LEONARD.—Ensign 7th January, 1812; Lieutenant 16th July, 1813 (Received Militia Disembodied Allowance from 25th June, 1815); Re-appointed Ensign (?) 10th July, 1817; Retired on Militia Allowance 1st October, 1852.

LIGHTFOOT, JOHN STANLEY.—Sub-Lieutenant 13th April, 1874; Now serving.

LISTER, JOHN.—Surgeon 28th September, 1852; Resigned 16th August, 1854.

LISTER, CHARLES HENRY.—Assistant-Surgeon 9th October, 1867; Resigned 10th June, 1874.

LITTLEJOHN, DUNCAN.—Ensign 48th Madras Native Infantry 1820; Lieutenant 1st May, 1824; Captain 5th March, 1836; Retired 13th August, 1846; Captain 3rd West York Light Infantry 25th November, 1852; Captain 5th West York Militia 5th November, 1854; Resigned 26th August, 1860.

LITTLEWOOD, RICHARD.—Lieutenant 25th June, 1798; Resigned 24th February, 1799.

LOFTUS, FERRARS.—Ensign 1st Foot Guards (Grenadiers) 1st July, 1815; Lieutenant 22nd July, 1815 (the rank of Lieutenant was granted to Ensigns in the Guards on this date); Retired H.P. 25th December, 1818; Exchanged back to F.P. 15th June, 1820; Lieutenant and Captain 20th November, 1823; Captain and Lieutenant-Colonel 27th December, 1833; Retired 29th December, 1840; Colonel 3rd West York Light Infantry 18th September, 1852; Resigned 24th April, 1870; Honorary Colonel of the Regiment 25th April, 1870. Served in Portugal from December, 1826 to May, 1828.

LOFTUS FERRARS COMPTON CLARGES.—Ensign 19th March, 1853; Lieutenant 22nd May, 1854; Captain 20th October, 1859; Retired with rank of Captain 12th April, 1871.

LOFTUS, DOUGLAS.—Ensign 17th June, 1854; Ensign and Lieutenant Grenadier Guards 13th February, 1855; Resigned 9th

November, 1858; Re-appointed Captain 3rd West York Light Infantry 9th July, 1859; Retired with rank of Captain 22nd March, 1871.

LUARD, CHARLES BOURRYAN.—Captain 25th December, 1808; Resigned 6th May, 1825.

MACADAM, PHILIP.—Ensign 29th March, 1808; Lieutenant 22nd April, 1809; Captain 28th February, 1810; Resigned 1846; Died 2nd September, 1855.

MACADAM, THOMAS JOHN STANNARD.—Captain 28th February, 1846; Major 20th March, 1855; Honorary Lieutenant-Colonel 14th March, 1871; Now serving.

MACADAM, PHILIP BOWER.—Sub-Lieutenant 14th April, 1875; Now serving.

M'CREARY, EDWARD WRIGHT.—Ensign 19th February, 1856; Resigned 26th February, 1858.

M'KENZIE, GEORGE.—Ensign 26th February, 1805; Resigned 24th March, 1806.

MCLAINE, HECTOR J.—Lieutenant 2nd May, 1799; Resigned 10th April, 1801.

M'LOGHLIN, ROBERT HENRY.—Ensign 31st January, 1859; Lieutenant 23rd November, 1860; Resigned 12th April, 1867.

MAGILL, HENRY.—Lieutenant 25th June, 1798; Adjutant 13th July, 1798; Brevet Captain 29th April, 1803; Retired F.P. 20th December, 1813; Re-appointed (?) Adjutant 30th May, 1815; Retired 6th August, 1827; Died 20th November, 1828.

MANJIN, JAMES MAGUIRE.—Ensign 7th April, 1858; Resigned 16th April, 1859.

MANN, ROBERT.—Ensign 8th July, 1812; Assistant-Surgeon 25th August, 1812 (Received Militia Disembodied Allowance from 25th June, 1815); Retired on Militia Allowance 1st October, 1852.

MANWARING, JOHN HENRY.—Lieutenant 10th March, 1853; Captain 20th March, 1855; Honorary Major 12th April, 1873; Now serving.

MARRIOTT, CHRISTOPHER.—Captain 21st May, 1806; Resigned 31st May, 1807.

MARSDEN, JOHN ROTHWELL.—Ensign 23rd April, 1805; Lieutenant 9th August, 1806; Ensign 4th Foot 9th April, 1809; Lieutenant 30th October, 1810; Died October, 1813.

MARSHALL, GEORGE.—Ensign 3rd March, 1797; Lieutenant 1st May, 1799; Ensign 82nd Foot 24th February, 1800; Lieutenant 15th August, 1804; Captain 27th October, 1808; Brevet-Major 27th May, 1825; Major 6th November, 1835; Brevet Lieutenant-Colonel 28th June, 1838; Lieutenant-Colonel 21st June, 1839; Died in Jamaica 2nd June, 1841. Knight of Hanover.

MARSHALL, WILLIAM.—Captain 16th November, 1802; Major 17th June, 1806; Lieutenant-Colonel 21st March, 1808; Resigned 5th June, 1811.

MARSHALL, RALPH.—Ensign 28th March, 1806; Lieutenant 5th November, 1807; Ensign 10th Foot 3rd February, 1808; Lieutenant 12th April, 1810; Retired H.-P. 12th June, 1823; Died in London 1st February, 1867.

MARSHALL, JAMES.—Ensign 29th May, 1809; Lieutenant 27th June, 1810; Ensign 4th Foot 16th May, 1811; Lieutenant 23rd September, 1813; Retired H.-P., 25th March, 1817; Lieutenant 77th Foot 4th March, 1818; Died in Jamaica, 1825.

MARSHALL, THOMAS.—Lieutenant 9th March 1853; Captain 1st February, 1855; Died 6th March, 1864.

MASSEY, HUGH.—Captain 5th April, 1802; Resigned 30th April, 1806.

MATHER, JOHN.—Ensign 21st February, 1808; Lieutenant 4th December, 1808; (Received Militia Disembodied Allowance from 25th June, 1815); Resigned 1852. (?)

MATHISON, THOMAS.—Ensign 28th July, 1808; Lieutenant 19th November, 1809; Resigned 24th May, 1810.

MATHISON, JOHN AUGUSTUS.—Ensign 4th December, 1808; Lieutenant 15th February, 1810; Ensign 77th Foot 8th May, 1811; Lieutenant 12th August, 1813; Retired H.-P., 25th March, 1817; Died 5th November, 1868. Served in the Peninsula with the 77th Foot, and was present at the Sieges of Ciudad Rodrigo, and Badajoz; and at the Battles of Vittoria, Pyrenees, Nive, Orthes, and Toulouse; War Medal with Seven Clasps.

MEEKE, WILLIAM.—Captain 1758-1763.

MIDGELEY, BENJAMIN.—Quartermaster 28th September, 1804; Lieutenant 25th February, 1805; Adjutant 21st December, 1813; Brevet-Captain 28th May, 1814; Adjutant Wakefield Local Militia 12th April, 1815.

MIDGELEY, WILLIAM.—Ensign 29th September, 1810; Lieutenant 27th August 1811; Ensign 1st Foot 19th December, 1811; Lieutenant 25th August, 1813; Resigned October, 1815.

MILNER, WILLIAM MORDAUNT.—Captain 1st West York Militia 1st November, 1802 (11th March, 1803 in Army List); Major 3rd West York Light Infantry 20th June, 1803; Resigned 13th October, 1803. Lieut-Col. York Ainsty Volunteers, 6th October, 1803.

MILNER, NATHANIEL.—Ensign 2nd West York Militia 2nd December, 1804–1807; Captain 3rd West York Light Infantry 22nd October, 1807; Resigned 8th September, 1808.

MITCHELL, GEORGE.—Lieutenant 25th June, 1803; Resigned 24th November, 1804.

MOGG, ROBERT.—Captain 10th July, 1804; Resigned 18th May, 1808.

MOORE, NATHANIEL.—Ensign 8th April, 1805; Resigned 24th May, 1806.

MORLEY, JOSIAS.—Captain 1758–1763.

MORLEY, JAMES.—Lieutenant 1758–1763.

MOSSE, JOHN FORBES.—Ensign 17th March, 1855; Lieutenant 18th March, 1856; Ensign 18th Foot, 21st May, 1858; Lieutenant 1st April, 1862; Captain 27th August, 1873; Now serving.

MOSSE, LORENZO NICKSON.—Ensign 18th March, 1856; Resigned 30th September, 1857.

MURRAY, ADOLPHUS WILLIAM.—Ensign 19th October, 1857; Resigned 11th July, 1858.

NAYLOR, GRENFELL TODD.—Lieutenant 11th April, 1871; Captain 21st February, 1874; Now serving.

NICHOLSON, EDWARD.—Lieutenant 25th November, 1852; Captain and Paymaster 20th July, 1854; Now serving.

NIXON, THOMAS.—Ensign 2nd September, 1854; Resigned 3rd November, 1854.

NORTON, EDWARD.—Lieutenant 1758–1763.

NORTON, THOMAS.—Ensign 31st December, 1810; Lieutenant 28th August, 1811; Resigned 11th August, 1813; Ensign 86th Foot 12th August, 1813; Resigned 1814.

NOWEL, WILLIAM.—Lieutenant 1758–1763.

ODDIE, WILLIAM MARKHAM.—Ensign 11th July, 1817; Resigned 27th May, 1820.

OGLE, JAMES GORDON.—Ensign 8th April, 1808; Lieutenant 5th May, 1809; Ensign 33rd Foot 9th May, 1811; Lieutenant 17th March, 1814; Died 12th September, 1817.

OSTLER, JOSEPH.—Ensign 8th October, 1759.

PALMER, CHARLES FREDERICK CLAVEY.—Captain 16th July, 1813; Resigned 28th December, 1815; Captain 1st West York Militia 7th December, 1815–1825.

PALMER, JOSEPH HENRY.—Ensign 24th November, 1857; Lieutenant 17th March, 1859; Died in Dublin, 26th January, 1864.

PARKER, GEORGE.—Ensign 21st April, 1798; Lieutenant 21st June, 1798; Resigned 24th July, 1798.

PARKER, HUGH.—Quartermaster 25th June, 1803; Resigned as Quartermaster 16th August, 1803; Ensign 17th August, 1803; Lieutenant 7th November, 1803; (Received Militia Disembodied Allowance from 25th June, 1815); Died 20th November, 1827.

PARKINS, LEVETT BROADLEY.—Lieutenant 7th August, 1803; Resigned 9th July, 1804.

PEAT, RICHARD JOSHUA.—Ensign 8th December, 1807; Ensign 92nd Foot 2nd August, 1808; Lieutenant 12th April, 1810; Captain 7th April, 1825; Retired H.P. 20th October, 1825; Retired January, 1827. Waterloo Medal.

PEPPARD, ROBERT STANDISH.—Ensign 19th March, 1809; Lieutenant 31st March, 1810; Resigned 24th February, 1812.

PERRY, RICHARD HAYES.—Assistant-Surgeon 22nd August, 1854; Removed 10th July, 1866.

PHIPPS, ARTHUR BARRÉ.—Sub-Lieutenant 3rd March, 1875. Now serving.

PICKARD, WILLIAM.—Ensign 1st February, 1856 ; Resigned 30th September, 1857.

PINSON, ALBERT ANDREW.—Ensign 21st November, 1854 ; Lieutenant 20th March, 1855 ; Ensign 16th Foot 30th April, 1856 ; Lieutenant 23rd March, 1858 ; Captain 7th December, 1867 ; Retired January, 1870.

POWELL, ATHELSTAN OWEN.—Ensign 20th March, 1855 ; Lieutenant 18th March, 1856 ; Removed 27th June, 1862.

PRESTON, HENRY.—Captain 31st December, 1807 ; Resigned 1st December, 1809.

PRIESTLEY, EDWARD JONATHAN.—Ensign 5th January, 1808 ; Lieutenant 5th September, 1808 ; Ensign 33rd Foot 12th April, 1809 ; Lieutenant 24th August, 1811 ; Adjutant 2nd December, 1813, to 10th May, 1815 ; Captain 2nd November, 1815 ; Retired H.P. 24th July, 1817 ; Captain 25th Foot 24th February, 1820 ; Major 31st August, 1830 ; Retired October, 1835.

PROTHERO, EDWARD.—Ensign 14th Foot 2nd October, 1835 ; Lieutenant 9th April, 1839 ; Captain 23rd December, 1847 ; Retired 16th July, 1852 ; Captain and Adjutant 3rd West York Light Infantry 17th July, 1852 (dated 11th August) ; Major 22nd February, 1853 ; Lieutenant-Colonel 20th March, 1855 ; Lieutenant-Colonel Commandant 25th April, 1870 (see *Gazette*, 27th May) ; Honorary Rank of Colonel 12th September, 1870. Now serving. Served in the West Indies and Canada from November, 1836, to August, 1841. Aide-de-Camp to the late Lieutenant-General the Hon. Sir Henry Murray, K.C.B., Commanding the Western District, from 1846 till April, 1852.

PROTHERO, EDWARD DOUGLAS.—Lieutenant 8th September, 1870 ; Resigned 14th June, 1871 ; Never joined.

RAIKES, GEORGE ALFRED.—Cadet (Private) Honourable Artillery Company 4th March, 1869 ; Sergeant-Instructor of Musketry 25th November, 1872 ; Lieutenant and Assistant-Instructor of Musketry 6th November, 1875 ; Lieutenant 3rd West York Light Infantry 1st July, 1869 ; Captain 1st June, 1872 ; Now Serving in both Regiments ; Captain's Certificate from School of Instruction, Wellington Barracks, dated 31st May, 1872 ;

First Class Certificate from School of Musketry, **dated** Hythe, 5th October, 1872; **Field Officer's** Certificate from School of Instruction, dated Chelsea Barracks, 31st October, 1872.

RAMSDEN, TIMOTHY.—Lieutenant 3rd **March, 1797; Captain 24th** January, 1800; **Died April, 1802.**

RAMSDEN, GEORGE.—Lieutenant 12th December, 1807 to 1809.

RAPER, TIMOTHY.—Ensign 19th February, 1810; Resigned 10th January, 1811.

RAWSON, WILLIAM.—Ensign 10th September, 1798; Lieutenant 1st April, 1799; Ensign 35th Foot 18th August, 1799; Lieutenant 29th March, 1804; Adjutant (1st Battalion) 5th December, 1804 to 1809; Captain 4th May, 1809; Retired H.P. 2nd July, 1818; Re-appointed Adjutant 3rd West York Light Infantry 7th August, 1827; Brevet-Captain 15th March, 1831; Died 18th July, 1850. Served at the Siege of Valetta, in Malta, 1800; at Minorca, Naples, Sicily, 1805, and Egypt, 1807; At Alexandria he led a storming party of 25 men to the attack; Present at Rosetta, Siege of Flushing, 1809, Antwerp, and had Command of Sluys, in Flanders; Was present at Waterloo, Cambray, and Paris; As Captain of the Guard he received Louis XVIII. at Ostend; Aide-de-Camp and Brigade-Major during the War.

REDHEAD, TYRAS.—Ensign 11th July, 1803; Displaced 24th July, 1803.

RENCHER, JOHN.—Ensign 14th October, 1804; Resigned 24th January, 1805.

RICKARD, JOHN.—Lieutenant 9th March, 1797; Resigned 13th May, 1800.

ROBERTS, FREDERICK ALFRED.—Ensign 8th June, 1859; Lieutenant 24th June, 1862; Removed 10th July, 1866.

ROBINS, JOHN.—Lieutenant 17th August, 1804; Resigned 24th October, 1804.

ROBINSON, BENJAMIN.—Lieutenant 7th March, 1797; Surgeon 25th March, 1798; Resigned 24th January, 1804.

ROBINSON, EDMUND FITZEUSTACE.—Lieutenant 27th February, 1832; Resigned 1853.

ROBSON, ALEXANDER HAMILTON.—Ensign 3rd Foot 25th December, 1838; Lieutenant 29th May, 1840; Captain 6th June, 1854; Captain and Adjutant 3rd West York Light Infantry 14th March, 1855. Died at Eastbourne 15th May, 1871. Served in the Gwalior Campaign, and was present at the Battle of Punniar 29th December, 1843, in Command of No. 4 Company; Medal—The Bronze Star.

ROCHFORT, GERALD.—Ensign 11th August, 1854; Lieutenant 12th January, 1855; Captain 13th June, 1864; Retired with Rank of Captain 5th May, 1870 (*Gazette* of 27th May).

RODGERS, MAURICE.—Lieutenant 25th November, 1852; Captain 11th August, 1854; Resigned 1st September, 1854.

ROWDEN, HARRY WETHERELL.—Lieutenant 6th April, 1872; Lieutenant 99th Foot 2nd December, 1874; Now serving.

RUTTER, WILLIAM LOWTHER.—Ensign 6th May, 1798; Lieutenant 23rd June, 1798; Resigned 24th March, 1800; Ensign 2nd Foot 29th April, 1800; Lieutenant 14th August, 1800. Died at Doncaster 19th December, 1805.

SALMON, WILLIAM.—Ensign 3rd March, 1798; Lieutenant 14th April, 1798; Resigned 24th August, 1798.

SAMPSON, GEORGE.—Captain 25th February, 1805; Resigned 24th April, 1806.

SANDS, WILLIAM (PHILIP?).—Ensign 1758-1763; Lieutenant 2nd West York Militia October, 1763; Captain 24th May, 1775.

SAUNDERS, EDWARD HENRY.—Ensign 18th June, 1858; Lieutenant 8th September, 1860; Cornet 5th (Royal Irish) Lancers 2nd July, 1861; Lieutenant 14th April, 1863; Captain 17th November, 1869; Exchanged to 8th (King's Royal Irish) Hussars 11th September, 1875; Now serving.

SCHOLEFIELD, COTTERELL.—Ensign 25th April, 1853; Resigned 30th June, 1854.

SCOTT, HENRY.—Lieutenant 1759; Resigned 30th March, 1762.

SELLERS, JOHN HARRISON.—Ensign 1st July, 1800; Displaced 24th September, 1800.

SHARPE, THOMAS.—Ensign 18th August, 1803; Lieutenant 7th November, 1803; Resigned 24th July, 1805.

Shaw, Robert.—Ensign 25th July, 1803; Lieutenant 3rd November, 1803; Ensign 51st Foot 25th August, 1807; Lieutenant 8th May, 1809; Superseded 8th February, 1810. Died at Leeds 17th November, 1812.

Shaw, John.—Ensign 15th December, 1807; Lieutenant 25th May, 1808; Ensign 34th Foot 7th December, 1809; Lieutenant 2nd July, 1812. Died at Portsmouth 7th March, 1824.

Shearburn, Thomas.—Captain 26th February, 1853; Resigned 8th July, 1859. Died 10th July, 1873.

Shearburn, Egremont Eadon.—Lieutenant 7th July, 1871; Lieutenant 9th (Queen's) Royal Lancers 22nd May, 1874; Now serving.

Sheppard, —.—Ensign 1759–1763.

Sigston, Benjamin.—Ensign 5th December, 1806; Resigned 24th November, 1807.

Sladden, George Russell.—Ensign 24th July, 1800; Resigned 24th December, 1800.

Small, William.—Ensign and Assistant-Surgeon 21st December, 1807; Lieutenant 26th May, 1808; Resigned 9th May, 1809.

Smith, Theophilus.—Ensign 4th January, 1853; Lieutenant 21st February, 1854; Resigned 15th August, 1854.

Smith, Francis Patrick.—Ensign 12th April, 1853; Lieutenant 11th August, 1854; Resigned 19th March, 1855.

Smith, Kynaston Walter.—Ensign 4th Royal Lancashire Militia 8th August, 1854; Ensign 3rd West York Light Infantry 31st October, 1854; Lieutenant 20th March, 1855; Died 27th August, 1857. Accidentally killed out shooting.

Spence, Allan Ramsey.—Ensign 27th January, 1855; Removed 29th December, 1855.

Stainforth, William.—Captain 28th February, 1846; Resigned 1852 (?).

Stapleton, Charles.—Ensign 2nd West York Militia, 14th September, 1803–1805; Lieutenant 1st West York Militia 29th November, 1807–1809; Captain 3rd West York Light Infantry 26th June, 1812; Major 28th February, 1846; Resigned 1851.

STAVELEY, MILES.—Ensign 1758–1763.

STINTON, GEORGE.—Captain 5th July, 1803; Resigned 26th February, 1807.

STRAUBENZEE, CHARLES (VAN?).—Ensign 3rd Foot, 28th October, 1795; Lieutenant 5th September, 1796; Exchanged to Lieutenant 92nd Foot, 12th April, 1800; Placed on H.-P. March, 1803; Lieutenant 3rd West York Light Infantry, 30th May, 1803; Resigned 24th October, 1803; Re-appointed Lieutenant F.P. 92nd Foot, 27th September, 1803 (dated 9th July); Exchanged from 92nd to 46th Foot 18th February, 1804; Captain 6th Foot, 14th December, 1804; Retired H.-P. 15th October, 1807; Re-appointed Lieutenant 3rd West York Light Infantry, 21st June, 1808; (Received Militia Disembodied Allowance from 25th June, 1815); Retired on Militia Allowance 1st October, 1852; Died 25th January, 1866.

STRAUDENZEE, GEORGE VAN.—Lieutenant 8th November, 1803; Resigned 24th July, 1805; Ensign 34th Foot, 14th November, 1805; Lieutenant 40th Foot, 16th July, 1807; Killed at Badajoz 6th April, 1811.

STRINGER, ROBERT HEPTINSTALL.—Ensign 18th August, 1804; Never joined.

STURGES, JOHN WILLIAM.—Ensign 3rd Foot (The Buffs) 20th July, 1815; Placed on H.-P. 25th February, 1816; Retired November, 1833; Ensign 3rd West York Light Infantry, 8th October, 1822; Paymaster 28th December, 1822; Resigned 19th April, 1827; Died 9th August, 1861.

SUTCLIFFE, JOHN CROSSLEY.—Captain 21st February, 1853; Resigned 1st August, 1854.

SUTCLIFFE, COCKCROFT.—Lieutenant 19th March, 1853; Resigned 10th August, 1855.

SWAILS, DAVID.—Ensign 1758–1763.

TALLON, CHRISTOPHER.—Ensign 21st October, 1803; Lieutenant 16th January, 1804; Resigned 24th November, 1807.

TAYLOR, RICHARD.—Ensign and Surgeon 1758–1763.

TENNANT, JOHN.—Ensign 5th August, 1809; Captain 11th February, 1810; Resigned 20th October, 1811.

THELLUSSON, CHARLES.—Captain 5th November, 1827; Resigned subsequently to May, 1839; Died 1856.

THELLUSSON, SEYMOUR STEWART.—Captain 28th February, 1846; Resigned 21st February, 1854.

THOMAS, WILLIAM.—Ensign and Assistant-Surgeon 20th June, 1803; Lieutenant 17th August, 1803; Assistant-Surgeon 67th Foot, 12th November, 1807; Surgeon 37th Foot, 28th July, 1814 to 25th March, 1817; (Regiment reduced and 2nd Battalion disbanded on that date).

THOMAS, WILLIAM HENRY.—Lieutenant 5th July, 1871. Now serving. Captain's Certificate dated School of Instruction, Wellington Barracks, 31st May, 1873.

THOMSON, GEORGE.—Lieutenant 1758-1763; Captain 2nd West York Militia 1763.

THORLEY, CHARLES.—Captain 6th September, 1808; Resigned 24th December, 1809; Captain East Essex Militia, 20th December, 1809 to 1811.

THORNTON, WILLIAM.—First Colonel of the Regiment 1758-1763; Colonel 2nd West York Militia, October, 1763 to February, 1772. Captain Thornton, of Thornville, near York, raised and maintained a Company of 75 men, with which he marched to Scotland, and was present at the Battle of Falkirk (17th January, 1746). He was the author of a pamphlet entitled, "The Counterpoise; being Thoughts on a Militia and a Standing Army." From 1747-54, and 1758-61, he represented the City of York in Parliament, and took an active part in the debates on the New Militia Bills. (See Parliamentary History, Vol. XIV. (1747-53), pages 1,086, 1,124, 1,128, 1,137, 1,199, 1,204, 1,318, 1,322, 1,327, and 1,355.)

THOROLD, SIR JOHN HAYFORD, Bart. (succeeded as Tenth Bart., 25th February, 1815).—Captain 27th October, 1818; Resigned May, 1820; Died, 7th July, 1831.

THUNDER, MICHAEL.—Ensign 24th May, 1855; Lieutenant 1st October, 1857; Ensign 21st Foot, 28th January, 1859; Lieutenant 22nd October, 1861; Captain 23rd October, 1867; Retired 13th April, 1875.

THURSTON, HENRY NEVILLE COTTON ; Ensign 24th March, 1853 ; Lieutenant 11th August, 1854 ; Ensign 7th Foot, 22nd December, 1854 ; Lieutenant 13th April, 1855 ; Captain 24th December, 1858 ; Exchanged to 61st Foot 25th February, 1859 ; Exchanged to 13th Foot 8th February, 1861 ; Retired April, 1862.

TIGHE, WILLIAM AUGUSTUS.—Ensign 1st February, 1855 ; Removed March, 1859 ; Never joined.

TOMLINSON, ROBERT.—Captain 5th March, 1797 ; Resigned 24th October, 1803.

TRAVERS, FRANCIS.—Assistant-Surgeon 28th September, 1810 ; Ensign 19th October, 1810 ; Resigned 31st August, 1811.

TUFNELL, ARTHUR JOLIFFE.—Ensign 12th January, 1855 ; Lieutenant 24th November, 1855 ; Ensign 93rd Highlanders, 15th May, 1857 ; Lieutenant 61st Foot, 1st October, 1858 ; Captain 16th February, 1864 ; Exchanged to 34th Foot 25th December, 1867 ; Now serving. Served with the 93rd Highlanders at the Relief of the Garrison of Lucknow in November, 1857 ; at the Defence of Cawnpore and Defeat of the Gwalior Mutineers there, and at Seria Ghat ; also present at the Action of Kalee Nuddee. Medal and Clasp.

TURNER, SAMUEL.—Ensign 4th March, 1797 ; Lieutenant 20th June, 1798 ; Resigned 24th October, 1798.

TURTON, GEORGE.—Ensign 10th July, 1810 ; Lieutenant 30th June, 1811 ; Ensign 33rd Foot 27th May, 1812 ; Retired April, 1813.

VAN STRAUBENZEE. (*See* STRAUBENZEE.)

VAVASOUR, WALTER.—Lieutenant 1758 ; Resigned 29th June, 1761 ; (Succeeded as Sixth Bart. 13th April, 1766) ; Died 3rd November, 1802.

VEAVERS, JOHN.—Ensign 1759 ; Resigned 30th March, 1762.

VERNER, FREDERICK ARTHUR.—Ensign 7th April, 1858 ; Lieutenant 20th October, 1859 ; Removed 27th June, 1862.

VERNON, WILLIAM.—Lieutenant 29th June, 1866 ; Resigned 27th May, 1870.

VINCENT, JOHN TUNNADINE.— 2nd Lieutenant Royal Marines 18th November, 1780 ; Placed on H.P. 1st September, 1783 ;

Captain 3rd West York Light Infantry 3rd March, 1797; Major 1st May, 1799; Lieutenant-Colonel 17th June, 1806; Resigned 24th October, 1811; Died 17th December, 1846.

VINCENT, GEORGE.—Ensign 1st August, 1801; Lieutenant 26th June, 1803; 2nd Lieutenant Commissary Gunner Drivers 1st September, 1804; Ensign 81st Foot, 31st May, 1805; Lieutenant 4th Foot, 7th June, 1805; Captain 5th October, 1815; Retired H.P. 25th February, 1816. Served in the Peninsular. Died at Lannion, Lower Brittany 10th March, 1845.

VINCENT, JOHN READ.—Ensign 12th November, 1803; Lieutenant 3rd May, 1804; Ensign 24th Foot, 14th September, 1804; Lieutenant 4th Foot, 18th April, 1805; Captain 29th July, 1813; Retired H.P. 25th February, 1816; Brevet Major 10th January, 1837; Major Rifle Brigade 2nd July, 1847; Retired same day; Died 13th July, 1874. Present at Fuentes d'Onor, Badajoz, Vittoria, St. Sebastian, Walcheren Expedition, 1809; Present at the Siege of Flushing. Silver Medal.

VINCENT, THOMAS BUXTON.—Ensign 24th November, 1809; Lieutenant 31st October, 1810 (Received Militia Disembodied Allowance from 25th June, 1815); Retired on Militia Allowance 1st October, 1852; Died 12th August, 1866.

VINCENT, WILLIAM READ.—Ensign 10th August, 1811; Lieutenant 8th March, 1812 (Received Militia Disembodied Allowance from 25th June, 1815); Captain 2nd July, 1827; Resigned 20th November, 1830; Died 14th March, 1862.

VINCENT, JOHN MATSON.—Sub-Lieutenant 24th September, 1873; Lieutenant 3rd September, 1875 (antedated to 24th September, 1873); Now serving.

VOKES, THOMAS.—Ensign 21st April, 1809; Lieutenant 31st March, 1810 (Received Militia Disembodied Allowance from 25th June, 1815); Died 2nd February, 1831.

WADE, WALTER.—Captain 1758; Resigned 29th April, 1761.

WAGSTER, JOSEPH.—Ensign 15th August, 1799; Lieutenant 6th March, 1800; Died 17th June, 1804. Killed in a duel with Surgeon Hardy at Ashford, Kent.

WAITE, WILLIAM, Jun.—Ensign 22nd January, 1831; Lieutenant 15th March, 1831; Captain 30th April, 1853; Resigned 30th September, 1859; To retain his rank for long service in the Regiment 8th November, 1859.

WALKER, GEORGE.—Lieutenant 4th West York Militia, 18th February, 1799; Lieutenant 3rd West York Light Infantry, 26th May, 1800; Resigned 31st May, 1803.

WALKER, CHAMBERLIN WILLIAM JERVOISE.—Ensign 15th February, 1856; Lieutenant 18th June, 1858; Resigned 1st June, 1860.

WAND, SAMUEL.—Lieutenant and Quartermaster 1759; Lieutenant 2nd West York Militia October, 1763; Captain 20th May, 1765.

WARD, ALEXANDER.—Lieutenant 27th June, 1803; Resigned 24th April, 1804.

WATKINS, HENRY.—Lieutenant 24th June, 1798; Resigned 24th March, 1800.

WATSON, JOHN.—Ensign 12th June, 1808; Lieutenant 19th May, 1809; Resigned 3rd October, 1809.

WATSON, ANDREW JAMES.—Ensign 1st February, 1855; Died at Dublin 15th December, 1855.

WAUGH, GEORGE.—Captain-Lieutenant 1st West York Supplementary Militia 3rd July, 1798; Captain 1st April, 1799; Captain 3rd West York Light Infantry, 25th June, 1800; Displaced 7th July, 1804.

WEBSTER, ISAAC.—Ensign, 1758–1763.

WEDDAL, WILLIAM.—Captain 1758–1763; Major 2nd West York Militia October, 1763.

WETHERHERD, JAMES.—Lieutenant 1st September, 1798; Resigned 24th November, 1799.

WHARTON, CHRISTOPHER.—Ensign 1758–1763; Lieutenant 2nd West York Militia October, 1763; Captain 9th April, 1774.

WHITAKER, HENRY.—Ensign 20th February, 1827; Paymaster 20th April, 1827; Lieutenant 15th March, 1831; Resigned after 1852. (?)

WHITE, GEORGE.—Ensign 18th July, 1807 ; Lieutenant 11th December, 1807 ; Resigned 3rd December, 1808.

WIGGINS, SAMUEL (JAMES?).—Ensign 1758–1763 ; Lieutenant 2nd West York Militia October, 1763 ; Captain-Lieutenant 2nd November, 1778.

WILD, THOMAS.—Lieutenant 5th March, 1797 ; Resigned 24th March, 1799.

WILD, WILLIAM.—Ensign 15th October, 1804 ; Lieutenant 29th January, 1805 ; Resigned 14th December, 1807.

WILKINSON, HENRY DICKINSON.—Ensign 18th May, 1853 ; Lieutenant 2nd September, 1854 ; Resigned March, 1865.

WILLCOCKS, JOHN GEORGE SMITH.—Ensign 5th May, 1855 ; Lieutenant 17th August, 1857 ; Instructor of Musketry 8th January, 1858 ; Adjutant 47th (St. Helen's) Lancashire Rifle Volunteers 3rd November, 1860 ; Now serving. First Class Certificate from School of Musketry, Hythe, dated 8th January, 1858.

WILKS, JOHN.—Ensign 1758–1763.

WILSON, THOMAS.—Ensign 1st West York Supplementary Militia 27th October, 1798 ; Lieutenant 22nd August, 1799 ; Lieutenant 3rd West York Light Infantry, 24th February, 1800 ; Ensign 34th Foot 2nd May, 1805 ; Lieutenant 56th Foot, 4th February, 1807 ; Retired H.P. 25th April, 1817 ; Died at Wrexham 27th October, 1827.

WILSON, JOHN STRAKER.—Lieutenant 10th April, 1867 ; Captain 15th April, 1871 ; Resigned 1st June, 1872.

WILTUS, JOHN.—Lieutenant 1758–1763.

WINNINGTON, JOHN TAYLOR.—Ensign 12th (East Suffolk) Foot, 3rd September, 1862 ; Lieutenant 9th November, 1866 ; Exchanged to 1st Royal Dragoons 8th January, 1868 ; Retired 5th May, 1869 ; Lieutenant 3rd West York Light Infantry, 20th July, 1870 ; Captain 11th April, 1873 ; Served abroad in Australian Colonies and New Zealand from 25th February, 1863, to 1st April, 1867 ; New Zealand Medal.

WINSKILL, JAMES.—Quartermaster 25th March, 1798 ; Ensign 18th June, 1798 ; Lieutenant 24th July, 1800 ; Died 24th April, 1803.

WOMACK, RICHARD.—Ensign 1st March, 1797; Lieutenant 18th June, 1798; Ensign 1st Foot, 27th August, 1799; Exchanged to Cornet 4th Light Dragoons, 19th December, 1799-1803.

WOOD, HENRY RICHARD.—Captain 28th April, 1803; Resigned 13th April, 1804.

WOOD, THOMAS.—Ensign 5th October, 1808; Resigned 24th March, 1809.

WOODCOCK, CHARLES.—Ensign and Assistant-Surgeon 14th July, 1803; Lieutenant 2nd November, 1803; Resigned 1st December, 1807.

WORTHINGTON, SAMUEL.—Ensign 28th August, 1803; Lieutenant 5th November, 1803; Resigned 14th February, 1805.

WRATHER, THOMAS.—Ensign 13th May, 1807; Lieutenant 10th December, 1807; Captain 27th June, 1810; Died May, 1839.

WRAY, Bart., Sir CECIL (succeeded as Tenth Bart., 26th January, 1752).—Captain, 1758; Resigned 30th March, 1762; Died 10th January, 1805; M.P. for East Retford from 1768 to 1775, and Westminster from 1782 to 1784.

WRIGHTSON, THOMAS.—Lieutenant 11th July, 1803; Quartermaster 17th August, 1803; Resigned as Quartermaster 27th September, 1804; Resigned 23rd August, 1808; Reappointed Ensign 2nd June, 1809; Lieutenant 31st October, 1810 (Received Militia Disembodied Allowance from 25th June, 1815); Retired on Militia Allowance 1st October, 1852.

WROUGHTON, GEORGE.—Captain 2nd March, 1797; Major 7th January 1799; Lieutenant-Colonel 30th May, 1803; Resigned 16th June, 1806.

NOTE.—This List contains 373 Officers. Of this number, 22 had previously served in the Regular Army (exclusive of Adjutants); 63 volunteered into the Army, 6 of whom subsequently rejoined the Regiment; 14 were received from, and 15 sent to, other Militia Regiments.

For the Regulations relating to the Militia Disembodied and Retired Allowances, see page 155.

APPENDIX C.

LIST OF OFFICERS APPOINTED FROM THE REGIMENT TO THE REGULAR ARMY.

TABLE No. 1.

DATE.	RANK AND NAME.	APPOINTED.	REMARKS.
1799. 29th March	Capt.-Lieut. G. A. Cooke	Ensign Grenadier Guards	Capt., Retired 31st July, 1806
,, 18th Aug.	Lieut. W. Rawson, M.	35th Foot	Capt., retired H.P. 1818. (See Table No. 5)
,, 27th Aug.	,, R. Womack	1st Royal Scots	Cornet, 4th Lt. Dgns. 19th Dec. 1799–1803
1800. 24th Feb.	,, G. Marshall, M. M.	82nd Foot	Lieut.-Col., died 2nd June, 1841
,, 29th April	,, W. L. Rutter	2nd Queen's	H.P. Dec., 1802. Regt. disbanded
1802. 6th April	Capt. J. R. Collins	Paymaster 28th Dragoons	H.P. Dec., 1802. Regt. disbanded
,, 11th Dec.	Lieut. E. Conroy	Ensign 6th West India Regiment	Lieutenant. No record after 1804
1803. 27th Aug.	,, P. Conroy	6th West India Regiment	Lieut., retired H.P. 1814
1804. 1st Sept.	,, G. Vincent	2nd Lieut.-Commis. Gunner Drivers	Capt., retired H.P. 1816
,, 6th Sept.	,, R. Crewe	Ensign 58th Foot	Capt., retired H.P. 1816
1805. 14th Sept.	,, J. R. Vincent	24th Foot	Major, retired 1847
,, 7th Jan.	,, W. Fozard	Adj. Maidstone Volunteers	No further record
,, 2nd May	,, T. Wilson	Ensign 34th Foot	Lieut., retired H.P. 1817. (See Table No. 6)
1806. 14th Nov.	,, G. Van Straubenzes	34th Foot	Lieut., died 1811
1807. 12th June	Ensign A. Gregory	29th Foot	Capt., retired H.P. 1822
,, 25th Aug.	Lieut. R. Shaw	51st Foot	Lieut., superseded 8th Feb, 1810
,, 15th Oct.	,, J. A. Braddell	36th Foot	Lieut., retired H.P. 1811
,, 12th Nov.	,, and Assist.-Surg. W. Thomas	Assistant-Surgeon 67th Foot	Surgeon, 37th Foot 1817
1808. 3rd Feb.	,, R. Marshall	Ensign 10th Foot	Lieut., retired H.P. 1823
,, 19th May	,, J. H. Kighley	53rd Foot	No record after July 1809
,, 19th May	,, H. S. Donnellan	82nd Foot	Capt., retired H.P. 1828
,, 23rd May	Capt. J. Hook	9th Garrison Battalion	Ensign, retired H.P. 1813
,, 23rd May	Ensign J. Garbut	81th Foot	Lieut., died 1811
1809. 2nd Aug.	,, R. J. Peat, M.	92nd Foot	Capt., retired H.P. 1825
,, 10th Feb.	,, P. Greano	18th Foot	Lieut., died 1814
,, 9th April	Lieut. J. R. Marsden	4th Foot	Lieut., died October, 1813
,, 12th April	,, E. J. Priestley	33rd Foot	Major, retired 1835
,, 26th April	,, R. Hudson, M.	40th Foot	Lieut., retired H.P. 1822
,, 7th May	Capt. and Adjt. A. Allison	Adjt. Wakefield Local Militia	No further record

[APPENDIX C.] THIRD WEST YORK LIGHT INFANTRY. 253

"	25th	Aug.	Lieut. W. Hardey	Ensign 18th Foot	Dismissed June, 1811
	7th	Dec.	" J. Shaw	34th Foot	Lieut., died 1824
1811.	8th	May	" J. A. Mathison, Col.	77th Foot	Lieut., retired H.P. 1817
	9th	May	" J. G. Ogle	33rd Foot	Lieut., died 1817
	16th	May	" J. Marshall	4th Foot	Lieut., died 1825
	14th	June	Ensign C. T. Bourke	43th Foot	Lieut., retired H.P. 1814
	19th	Dec.	Lieut. W. Midgeley	1st Royal Scots	Lieut., retired 1815
1812.	27th	May	" G. Turton	33rd Foot	Ensign, retired 1813
1813.	7th	April	" T. Eyre	34th Foot	Lieut., retired H.P. 1817
	12th	Aug.	" T. Norton	86th Foot	Ensign, retired 1814
1814.	12th	May	" T. Gee	Lieut. 49th Foot	Lieut., retired H.P. 1814. (See Table No. 5)
1815.	12th	April	Ensign W. Aitkin	Ensign 88th Foot	Lieut., retired H.P. 1821
	25th	May	Capt. and Adjt. B. Midgeley	Adjt. Wakefield Local Militia	No further record
	18th	July	Ensign H. Heblen	Ensign 2nd Garrison Battalion	Lieut.-Col., died 18th May, 1867
1854.	22nd	Dec.	" R. Blacklin, Col.	1st Royal Scots	Colonel, died 18th May, 1867
	29th	Dec.	Lieut. H. N. C. Thurston	7th Fusiliers	Capt., retired April, 1862
1855.	13th	Feb.	Ensign H. W. Heaton, S.	14th Foot	Capt., retired 1860
			" T. O. Howorth, S. and C.	44th Foot	Capt., died 23rd Jan., 1865
			" D. Loftus	and Lieut. Grenadier Guards	Lieut. and Capt., ret.1858. (See Table No. 5)
1856.	2nd	March	" E. G. Hasted, S. and N. Z.	57th Foot	Capt., retired 15th March, 1873
	1st	Jan.	Capt. J. C. Flood	Capt. Turkish Contingent	To August 1856. (See Table No. 3)
	27th	Feb.	Lieut. W. G. Blake	Ensign 89th Foot	Lieut., retired 1864. (See Table No. 5)
	7th	March	" R. J. Bell	37th Foot	Ensign, died 12th May, 1868
1857.	30th	April	" A A. Pinson	16th Foot	Capt., retired Jan., 1870
1858.	15th	May	" A. J. Tufnell	93rd Highlanders	Capt., now in 34th Foot
1859.	21st	May	" J. F. Mosse	18th Foot	Capt., now serving
	28th	Jan.	" M. Thunder	21st Fusiliers	Capt., retired April, 1875
1860.	11th	Sept.	" J. D. Bottomley	2nd Lieut. Royal Marines	Capt., retired 1st Aug., 1873
	16th	March	Ensign W. L. B. Coulson	Ensign 25th Foot	Capt., now serving
1861.	3rd	Nov.	Lieut. J. G. S. Willcocks	Capt. and Adjt. 47th Lanc. R. V.	Now serving
1862.	2nd	July	" E. H. Saunders	Cornet 5th Lancers	Capt., now serving in 8th Hussars
	29th	July	" G. Campbell	Ensign 79th Foot	
1874.	22nd	May	" E. E. Stocarburn	Lieut. 9th Lancers	} Lieuts., now serving
"	2nd	Dec.	" H. W. Lowden	99th Foot	

The columns of Remarks in all these Tables show the highest rank attained by each Officer; but it must be borne in mind that the services of Militia Officers, previous to the year 1815, were accepted to serve during the war only, after which they became entitled to Half-Pay. This will account for so few having obtained any high rank, as they were placed on compulsory Half-Pay on the reduction of their regiments after the Peninsular War, the 2nd Battalions of many Regiments being then disbanded.

H. K., Knight of Hanover. W., Waterloo; Medal. S., Served in Crimea before Sebastopol; Medal. C., China; Medal. N.Z., New Zealand; Medal.

REGIMENTS OF THE REGULAR ARMY TO WHICH OFFICERS HAVE BEEN APPOINTED.

TABLE No. 2.

REGIMENT.	NO. OF OFFICERS GIVEN.	YEAR.	REGIMENT.	NO. OF OFFICERS GIVEN.	YEAR.
5th (Royal Irish) Lancers	One	1861	40th (Hertfdsh., Prin. Charlotte's of W.)	One	1813
9th Queen's (Royal) Lancers	One	1874	Royal Marines, Light Infantry	One	1859
Royal Artillery (Gunner Drivers)	One	1864	51st (King's O. Lt. In., 2nd W.R.Yorks.)	One	1807
Grenadier Guards	Two	1799 and 1855	53rd (Shropshire)	One	1808
1st (Royal Scots)	Three	1799, 1811 and 1815	57th (West Middlesex)	One	1855
2nd (Queen's Royal)	One	1800	58th (Rutlandshire)	One	1804
4th (King's Own Royal)	Two	1809 and 1811	67th (South Hampshire)	One	1807
7th (Royal Fusiliers)	One	1854	77th (East Middlesex)	One	1811
10th (North Lincoln)	One	1808	79th (Cameron Highlanders)	One	1862
14th (Buckinghamshire)	One	1854	82nd (The Prince of Wales's Volunt.)	Two	1800 and 1808
16th (Bedfordshire)	One	1856	84th (York and Lancaster)	One	1805
18th (Royal Irish)	Two	1809 and 1858	86th (Royal County Down)	One	1813
21st (Royal North British Fusiliers)	One	1859	88th (The Connaught Rangers)	One	1814
24th (Second Warwickshire)	One	1864	89th (Princess Victoria's)	One	1856
25th (The King's Own Borderers)	One	1860	92nd (Gordon Highlanders)	One	1808
29th (Worcestershire)	One	1806	93rd (Sutherland Highlanders)	One	1857
33rd (Duke of Wellington's)	Three	1809, 1811 and 1812	99th (Lanarkshire)	One	1874
34th (Cumberland)	Four	1805 (Two), 1809 and 1813	47th (Lancashire Rifle Volunteers)	One	1860
			25th Light Dragoons	One	1802
35th (Royal Sussex)	One	1799	2nd Garrison Battalion	One	1815
36th (Herefordshire)	One	1807	9th Garrison Battalion	One	1808
37th (North Hampshire)	One	1856	6th West India Regiment	Two	1802 and 1803
40th (Second Somerset)	One	1809	Turkish Contingent (Infantry)	One	1856
44th (East Essex)	One	1854	Wakefield Local Militia	Two	1809 and 1815
48th (Northamptonshire)	Two	1809 and 1811	Maidstone Volunteers	One	1805

Now Disbanded.

APPENDIX C.] THIRD WEST YORK LIGHT INFANTRY. 255

LIST OF OFFICERS APPOINTED TO THE REGIMENT FROM THE REGULAR ARMY.

TABLE No. 3.

DATE.		RANK, NAME, AND REGIMENT.	APPOINTED.	REMARKS.
1797.	27th Feb.	Sir G. Cooke, Bart., late Cornet Royal Horse Guards	Colonel	Resigned 15th May, 1803
,,	27th Feb.	Capt. John Cooke, Grenadier Guards	Major	Resigned 24th May, 1803
,,	1st March	Capt. B. W. D. Cooke, Grenadier Guards	Captain	Resigned 24th April, 1798
,,	3rd March	2nd Lieut. J. T. Vincent, Royal Marines	Captain	Lieut.-Col., resigned 1811
1803.	16th May	B. Cocke, late Lieut. Royal Horse Guards	Colonel	Resigned 22nd Feb., 1812
,,	30th May	Lieut. C. Strauberzee, 92nd Foot	Lieutenant	Resigned 24th Oct., 1803. (*See* Table 5)
1807.	14th Aug.	Lieut. G. Brown, 8th Foot	Captain	Resigned 1st June, 1810
1808.	21st June	Capt. C. Strauberzee, 61st Foot	Lieutenant	Resigned 1st October, 1852. *Re-appointed*
,,	1st Oct.	Capt. H. Courtney, 47th Foot	Captain	Resigned 1824
1811.	25th Oct.	Capt. W. B. Cooke, Grenadier Guards	Lieutenant-Colonel	Col., resigned 7th Dec., 1819
1812.	26th May	Major G. Cholmley, 7th Light Dragoons	Lieutenant-Colonel	Col., resigned 29th August, 1850
1822.	6th Oct.	Ensign J. W. Sturges, 3rd Buffs	Ensign	Paymaster, resigned 19th April, 1827
1846.	28th Feb.	Lieut. J. Barnett, 23rd Foot	Lieutenant-Colonel	Died 23rd Feb., 1855
1851.	17th April	Lieut.-Colonel H. Dixon, 81st Foot	Major	Resigned 1852
1852.	17th July	Capt E. Prothero, 14th Foot	Captain and Adjutant	*Lieut.-Col. Commandant. Now serving*
,,	18th Sept.	Lt.-Col. F. Loftus, Grenadier Guards	Colonel	Resigned 24th April, 1870
,,	25th Nov.	Capt. D. Littlejohn, 48th Madras N.I.	Captain	To Capt. 5th W.Y.M. 5th Nov., 1854. (*See* Table No. 8)
1853.	21st Feb.	Capt. G. Garforth, 97th Foot	Captain	Resigned 3rd July, 1855
1854.	3rd Aug.	Cornet H. B. Firman, 4th Light Dragoons	Ensign	Lieut., resigned 30th Sept., 1857
1855.	14th March	Capt. A. H. Robson, 3rd Foot	Captain and Adjutant	*Died 15th May*, 1871
1859.	9th July	Lieut. D. Loftus, Grenadier Guards	Captain	Removed 23rd Oct., 1858. (*See* Table No. 1)
1870.	20th July	Capt. H. W. Barlow, Royal Engineers	Captain	Retired with rank of Capt. 22nd March, 1871. (*See* Table No. 5)
,,	20th July	Lieut. J. T. Winnington, 1st Dragoons	Lieutenant	Capt., now serving
1871.	15th April	Capt. M. Curry, 81st Foot	Captain	Now serving
,,	17th Sept.	Capt. the Hon. F. C. Howard, Coldstream Guards	Captain and Adjutant	Capt., now serving

REGIMENTS OF THE REGULAR ARMY FROM WHICH OFFICERS HAVE BEEN APPOINTED.

TABLE No. 4.

REGIMENT.	NO. OF OFFICERS.	YEAR.	REGIMENT.	NO. OF OFFICERS.	YEAR.
Royal Horse Guards	Two	1797 and 1803	14th (Buckinghamshire)	One	1852
1st Royal Dragoons	One	1870	23rd (Royal Welsh Fusiliers)	One	1846
4th (Queen's Own) Hussars	One	1854	35th (Royal Sussex)	*One	1827
7th (Queen's Own) Hussars	One	1812	47th (Lancashire)	One	1808
9th (Queen's Royal) Lancers	*One	1868	49th (Hertfordshire, Princess Charlotte of Wales's)	*One	1819
28th Light Dragoons	*One	1802	Royal Marines	One	1797
Royal Engineers	One	1870	92nd (Gordon Highlanders)	*One	1803
Grenadier Guards	*Five	{ 1797, 17x8, 1811, 1852, and 1859	97th (Earl of Ulster's)	One	1853
Coldstream Guards	One	1871	81st (Loyal Lincoln Volunteers)	Two	1851 and 1870
3rd (East Kent) Buffs	Two	1822 and 1855	48th Madras Native Infantry	One	1852
5th (Northumberland Fusiliers)	One	1855			

* These officers were originally appointed to the above corps (only one of the Grenadier Guards) from the Regiment. (*See* Table No. 5.)

LIST OF OFFICERS FROM THE REGIMENT WHO WERE APPOINTED TO THE REGULAR ARMY, AND SUBSEQUENTLY REJOINED THE REGIMENT.

TABLE No. 5. (See Tables Nos. 1 and 3.)

DATE.	RANK, ETC., WHEN RE-APPOINTED.	APPOINTED.	REMARKS.
1863. 23rd April	Paymaster J. R. Collins, 28th Dragoons	Captain	Major, died 22nd June, 1810
1808. 21st June	Capt. C. Straubenzee, 92nd Foot	Lieut.	Ret. 1st October, 1852
1819. 7th June	Lieut. T. Gee, 49th Foot	Ensign	Resigned 9th March, 1831
1827. 7th Aug.	*Capt. W. Rawson*, 35th Foot	Adjutant	*Brevet Capt.*, died 18th *July*, 1850
1859. 9th July	Lieut. and Capt. D. Loftus, Grenadier Grds.	Captain	Ret. with rank of Capt. 22nd March, 1871
1263. 27th June	Lieut. W. G. Blake, 9th Lancers	Lieut.	Capt., now serving

APPENDIX C.] THIRD WEST YORK LIGHT INFANTRY. 257

LIST OF OFFICERS APPOINTED TO THE REGIMENT FROM OTHER MILITIA REGIMENTS.

TABLE No. 6.

DATE.	RANK, NAME AND REGIMENT.	APPOINTED.	REMARKS.
1800. 24th Feb.	Lieut. T. Wilson, 3rd W. Y. Saptry. Regt.	Lieut.	To Ensign 34th Foot, 2nd May, 1805
,, 5th March	Lieut. W. Fozard, 4th ,, ,, ,,	Lieut., Adj. Maidstone Vols. 1805	No further record
,, 26th May	Lieut. G. Walker, 4th ,, ,, ,,	Lieut.	Resigned 31st May, 1803
,, 25th June	Capt. G. Waugh, 3rd ,, ,, ,,	Captain	Displaced 7th July, 1804
1803. 20th June	Capt. W. M. Milner, 1st W. Y. Militia...	Major	Resigned 13th October, 1803
,, 26th Sept.	Ensign R. Crewe, ,, ,, ,,	Lieut.	To Ensign 58th Foot 6th Sept., 1804
1807. 22nd Oct.	Ensign N. Milner, 2nd ,, ,,	Captain	Resigned 8th September, 1808
1808. 8th July	Lieut. S. J. Donelan, 1st ,, ,,	Captain	No record after 1825
1815. 26th June	Lieut. C. Stapleton, 2nd ,, ,,	Captain	Major Resigned.
1852. 26th Nov.	Capt. R. Croyke, ,, ,, ,,	Major	Resigned 21st February, 1855
1859. 13th Jan.	Capt. F. M. Allen, Carnarvon Militia	Captain	Hon. Major, now serving
,, 11th Feb.	Capt. T. W. Kinder, Worcester Militia...	Captain	Retired with Hon. rank of Major, 1870
1854. 31st Oct.	Ensign A. A. James, Roy. London Militia	Ensign	Res. 1854. Never joined. (See Table No. 8)
,, ,,	Ensign K. W. Smith. 4th Roy. Lanc. Mil.	Ensign	Lieut. died 27th August, 1857

REGIMENTS OF MILITIA FROM WHICH OFFICERS HAVE BEEN APPOINTED.

TABLE No. 7.

REGIMENTS.	NO. OF OFFICERS.	YEAR.	REGIMENTS.	NO. OF OFFICERS.	YEAR.
1st West York Rifles	Three	Two in 1803, one in 1808	Royal Carnarvon Rifles	One	1859
2nd West York Light Infantry	Three	1807, 1812, and 1852	4th Royal Lancashire Light Infantry	One	1854
3rd West York Supplementary Militia	Two	1800	Royal London Militia	One	1854
4th West York Supplementary Militia	Two	1800	Worcester Militia	One	1859

S

LIST OF OFFICERS APPOINTED FROM THE REGIMENT TO OTHER MILITIA REGIMENTS.

TABLE No. 8.

DATE.		RANK, NAME AND REGIMENT.	APPOINTED.	REMARKS.
1763.	October	Colonel W. Thornton	Colonel 2nd West York Militia	
,,	,,	Captain W. Weddal	Major ,, ,, ,,	
,,	,,	Lieut. G. Thompson	Capt. ,, ,, ,,	
,,	,,	Lieut. G. Iveson	Capt. ,, ,, ,,	No Records
,,	,,	Lieut. G. Hassel	Capt. ,, ,, ,,	
,,	,,	Lieut. S. Wand	Lieut. ,, ,, ,,	
,,	,,	Ensign C. Wharton	Lieut. ,, ,, ,,	
,,	,,	Ensign P. Sands	Lieut. ,, ,, ,,	
,,	,,	Ensign S. Wiggins	Lieut. ,, ,, ,,	
,,	,,	Ensign R. Burton	Ensign ,, ,, ,,	
1793.	13th April	Lieut. T. Dillon	Lieut. ,, ,, ,,	Capt. till 1803
1803.	27th Aug.	Ensign R. Crowe	Ensign 1st West York Militia	Re-appointed Lieut. 3rd W. Y. L. I., 1803
1809.	29th Dec.	Capt. C. Thorley	Capt. East Essex Militia	No record after 1811
1815.	7th Dec.	Capt. C. F. C. Palmer	Capt. 1st West York Militia	No record after 1825
1854.	5th Nov.	Capt. D. Littlejohn	Capt. 5th West York Militia	Resigned 26th Aug., 1860. (See Table No. 3)
1854.	29th Dec.	Ensign A. A. James	Lieut. Hampshire Militia	To March, 1857. (See Table No. 6)

REGIMENTS OF MILITIA TO WHICH OFFICERS HAVE BEEN APPOINTED.

TABLE No. 9.

REGIMENT.			NO. OF OFFICERS.	YEAR.
1st West York Rifles			One	1863
2nd West York Light Infantry	...	...	Ten	Nine in 1763, one in 1798
5th West York	...	...	One	1854
East Essex	...	...	One	1809
Hampshire			One	1854

APPENDIX D.

LORDS-LIEUTENANT OF THE WEST RIDING OF YORKSHIRE, FROM 1751 TO 1875.

NAME.	CUSTOS ROTULORUM.		LORD-LIEUTENANT.		REMARKS.
1. Charles, Marquis of Rockingham	8th July,	1751	18th July,	1751	
2. Francis, Earl of Huntingdon	30th Dec.,	1761	25th Feb.,	1762	
3. Charles, Marquis of Rockingham	5th Sep.,	1765	12th Sept.,	1765	10th Earl. Died 2nd Oct., 1789
4. Charles Howard, Earl of Surrey, afterwards Duke of Norfolk	23rd Oct.,	1782	11th Oct.,	1782	Re-appointed. Died 1st July, 1782. Title extinct
5. William Wentworth, Earl Fitzwilliam	21st Feb.,	1798	2nd March,	1798	10th Duke. Died 31st Aug., 1756
6. Henry, Viscount Lascelles, became 2nd Earl of Harewood, April 1820	15th Nov.,	1819	18th Nov.,	1819	Died Nov., 1841
7. James Archibald, Lord Wharncliffe	24th Dec.,	1841	29th Dec.,	1841	1st Baron, 12th July, 1826. Died 19th Dec., 1815
8. Earl of Harewood	22nd Jan.,	1846	17th Jan.,	1846	Died 22nd Feb., 1857
9. Viscount Milton, now Earl Fitzwilliam	24th March,	1857	31st March,	1857	Succeeded as 6th Earl, 4th Oct., 1857

PATENT ROLLS IN THE PUBLIC RECORD OFFICE.

1. Vol. 52, 1st Part, 25 Geo. III., p. 146: and Vol. 53, 3rd Part, Geo. III., p. 14, and 6th Part, p. 45.
2. Vol. 53, 2nd Part, Geo. III., pp. 115 and 121.
3. Vol. 53, 6th Part, 5 Geo. III., p. 184.
4. Vol. 54, 1st Part, 23 Geo. III., p. 66.
5. Vol. 54, 4th Part, 38 Geo. III., pp. 324-5.
6. Vol. 56, 1st Part, 60 Geo. III., pp. 111-2; and 6th Part, 1 Will. IV., p. 17; and 10th Part, 1 Will. IV., p. 28; Vol. 57, 10th Part, 1 Vict., p. 30; and 12th Part, 1 Vict., p. 37.
7. Vol. 57, 18th Part, 5 Vict., p. 375.
8. Vol. 59, 21st and 22nd Parts, 9th Vict.
9. Vol. 59, 3rd Part, 20 Vict.

APPENDIX E.

PROPERTY QUALIFICATION REQUIRED FOR OFFICERS OF MILITIA.

RANK.	1757.* (30 Geo. II. c. 25.) An Estate of the Yearly Value of	Or Heir-Apparent of a Person of a Yearly Estate of	1786.† (26 Geo. III. c. 107.) An Estate of the Yearly Value of	Or Heir-Apparent of a Person of a Yearly Estate of	1802. (42 Geo. III. c. 90.)	1855.‡ (18 & 19 Vic. c. 100).§ An Estate of (or Heir-Apparent of some Person) the Yearly Value of
COLONEL	£400	£800	£1,600	£2,000		£600
LIEUT.-COLONEL	300	600	600	1,200		400
MAJOR	300	600				*300
CAPTAIN	200	400	200	400		*200
	Or Younger Son of some Person of an Estate of £100		Or Younger Son of some Person of an Estate of £600			* Or Son of any Person of an Estate of like value.
LIEUTENANT	Or Son of some Person of an Estate of £200		Or Personal Estate of £1,000; or Real and Personal together of £2,000; or Son of some Person of an Estate of £100, or Personal Estate of £2,000, or Real and Personal Estate of £3,000			
ENSIGN	Or Son of some Person of an Estate of £100	£50	Or Personal Estate of £500; or Real and Personal Estate of £1,000; or Son of some Person of an Estate of £50, or Personal of £1,000, or Real and Personal Estate of £1,500	£20		

The same Qualification as required by the previous Act of 1786 (including Deputy-Lieutenants), with the exception of that for the rank of Major, which was doubled, being increased to £400 and £800—a younger son, &c., not being qualified.

The Qualification required for Subalterns was abolished 30th June, 1852, by the 15 & 16 Vic. c. 50.

* Under this Act Officers might be promoted for extraordinary merit, or in case of invasion or danger; but none higher than Captain who wanted a Property Qualification for that rank. At least one-half the amount of property to be situated within the county for which the Officer was serving. The Qualification for a Deputy-Lieutenant was the same as that for a Colonel.

† One-half of such Qualification to be situated within the county for which the Officer was serving. The Qualification for a Deputy-Lieutenant was reduced by one-half, viz., to £200, and £400.

‡ In 1852, under the 15 & 16 Vic. c. 50, Captains, or Officers of higher rank in the Regular Army or East India Company's service, might be appointed Captains or Majors; and Majors, or higher rank, Lieut.-Colonels or Colonels, without any Property Qualification; and any person qualified for the rank of Major or Lieut.-Colonel in the Militia, and having received a Commission as such, might be promoted to any higher rank. The income of Personal Estate in possession of the Officer to be deemed equivalent to the yearly value of land.

§ Under this Act the Property Qualification was made the same for all Great Britain. Formerly the qualification varied in Wales, Cumberland, Huntingdon, Monmouth, Westmoreland, Rutland, Isle of Ely, in Cambridgeshire, and such Cities and towns as are Counties within themselves. Officers of five years' service, in the Regular Army or East India Company's service, might be appointed Captains, or if a Captain, or any higher rank, might be appointed Captain or Major, and any Major or higher rank in the said Regular Forces might be appointed a Lieut.-Colonel, or Colonel, and any person qualified for the rank of Major or Lieut.-Colonel in the Militia, and having received a Commission as such, might be promoted to any higher rank without the Property Qualification. This Act did not extend to the Militia of London and Edinburgh.

All Property Qualification was abolished on the 13th of May, 1869, by the 32 Vic. c. 13.

APPENDIX F.

CHRONOLOGICAL SUMMARY

OF THE

CHANGE OF QUARTERS

OF

THE REGIMENT.

FROM 1758 TO 1875.

1758-1759
The Regiment formed at York.

1760
June	The Regiment from York to Sunderland.
September	,, ,, Sunderland to Yorkshire, viz., to Settle, Ingleton, Skipton, Leeds, Otley, Ripon, Knaresborough, Green Hammerton, and York.
December	The Detachment removed from Leeds.

1761
June	The Regiment assembled at York.
August	,, from York to Leeds.
September	,, ,, Leeds to York.

1762
June	The Regiment from York to Newcastle-on-Tyne.
August	,, ,, Newcastle-on-Tyne to Nottingham.
November	,, ,, Nottingham to York and adjacent.

1763-1796

The Regiment was disembodied and subsequently incorporated with the First and Second West York Militia.

1797

The Regiment was trained in five Divisions, viz., First and Second Divisions at Doncaster, on the 27th Feb.; Third Division at York, on 17th April; Fourth Division at Sheffield, on 12th May; Fifth Division on the 5th June.

1798

5th March	The Regiment embodied at Doncaster.
May	The Regiment left Doncaster, and was quartered in the following places in the neighbourhood :— One Company at Blyth, two Companies at Worksop, three Companies at Rotherham, one Company at Bawtry, one Company at Tickhill, one Company at Hatfield, and one Company at Thorne.
25th May	The Regiment re-assembled at Doncaster and marched to Hull; the two flank Companies were sent to Holderness to join the Grenadier and Light Infantry Battalions, and remained there till July, 1799.
July	Five Companies from Hull to Beverley, three to Burlington, and two into camp at Hilston.
October	Five Companies from Beverley, and three at Burlington to Doncaster. Two Companies from Hilston Camp to Hull.

1799

June	Eight Companies from Doncaster to Hornsea Camp. Two ,, ,, Hull to Hilston Camp.
July	Two ,, ,, Hilston to Hornsea Camp.
October	The Regiment from Hornsea Camp to Citadel Barracks, Hull.

1800

5th June	Four Companies from Hull to Durham.
	Three ,, ,, ,, Darlington.
	Three ,, ,, ,, Northallerton.
	The Regiment remained at the above places from the 13th to 22nd of June, and then marched to Sunderland.
3rd July	One Company from Sunderland to South Shields.
5th November	The Regiment from Sunderland to Berwick and Tweedmouth.
28th November	The Regiment from Berwick to Stirling, where six Companies were stationed; two Companies being sent to Falkirk, and two to Linlithgow.

1801

6th August	Six Companies from Stirling to Edinburgh Castle.
	Two ,, Falkirk ,, ,,
	Two ,, Linlithgow ,, ,,
	Two ,, Edinburgh Castle to Leith.

1802

23rd January	Eight Companies from Edinburgh Castle to Berwick.
	Two ,, Leith ,,
3rd & 4th Feb.	Five ,, Berwick to Doncaster.
	Three ,, ,, Bawtry.
	Two ,, ,, Pontefract and Ferrybridge.
12th April	Two Companies from Pontefract to Doncaster.
	Two ,, ,, Doncaster ,, Rotherham.
22nd April	The Regiment Disembodied at Doncaster.

1803

11th (?) March	The Regiment Embodied at Doncaster.
27th May	,, ,, from Doncaster to York.
11th July*	,, ,, ,, York to Colchester, and encamped at Elmstead Heath.

---

* The Regiment was increased from ten to twelve Companies in July, and remained at that number till September, 1811, when they were again reduced to ten Companies.

24th November	The Regiment from Elmstead **Heath** Camp to Colchester Barracks.
28th December	A Detachment sent to Braintree.

1804

26th July	The Regiment from Colchester **Barracks** to Coxheath Camp.
28th October	The Regiment from Coxheath Camp to Faversham, and Ospringe, with Detachment at Sheerness.

1805

May	The Regiment from **Faversham** and Ospringe to Chatham.
June	The Regiment from Chatham to Ashford.
October	,, ,, Ashford to Hull.
	Detachment sent from Hull to Scarborough.

1806

8th April	Detachment from Hull to York.
17th ,,	,, ,, York ,, Hull.
29th & 30th April	The Regiment from Hull to **Newcastle-on-Tyne**.
3rd May	Detachment ,, Scarborough to Newcastle.
	One Company ,, Newcastle to Whitburn.
	One ,, ,, ,, ,, Monkwearmouth.
5th June	Two Companies at Whitburn and Monkwearmouth to Newcastle.
	A Detachment from Newcastle to Carlisle.
6th October	The Regiment ,, ,, ,, Sunderland.
11th ,,	Detachment ,, Carlisle ,, ,,

1807

12th October	The Regiment from Sunderland to Liverpool.
	Four Companies ,, Liverpool ,, Chester.

1808

April	Four Companies from Chester to Liverpool.
May	Three ,, ,, Liverpool to Chester.
30th May	Three ,, ,, ,, ,, Manchester.
12th June	Three Companies from Manchester to Liverpool.

September	One Company from Liverpool to Chester.
3rd November	Five Companies ,, ,, ,, Stilton.
	Three ,, ,, ,, ,, Peterboro'.
10th November	Two ,, ,, ,, ,, Stilton.
,, ,,	The Regiment from Stilton to Norman Cross.
	Two Companies from Norman Cross to Peterboro'.

1809

March	Two Companies from Norman Cross to Peterboro'. Detachments at Oundle and Sawtry.
May	Four Companies and Head-Quarters at Stowmarket.
,,	Two ,, at Needham.
	Four ,, ,, Thetford.
	Two ,, ,, Ixworth.
10th June	The Regiment at Woodbridge Barracks. Detachments at Aldborough and Hollesley Bay.
October	Ten Companies from Woodbridge to Ipswich.
	Two ,, ,, ,, ,, Harwich.
November	One Company ,, ,, ,, ,,
December	Detachments from Aldborough and Hollesley Bay to Ipswich.

1810

March	The Regiment (12 Companies) at Harwich.
10th April	Ten Companies from Harwich to Chelmsford.
25th ,,	Ten ,, ,, Chelmsford to Colchester.
10th May	Ten ,, ,, Colchester ,, Harwich.
25th August	Detachments from Harwich to Walton-on-the-Naze and Little Holland.
1st November	Detachments from Walton-on-the-Naze and Little Holland to Harwich.
13th November	The Regiment from Harwich to Colchester.

1811

16th March	Detachment from Colchester to Clacton.
29th June	Detachments ,, ,, ,, Holland Marsh, Walton-on-the-Naze, and Harwich Barracks.
5th August	The Regiment from Colchester to Chatham and Brompton.

14th & 15th Aug.	Nine Companies* from Chatham to **Sheerness**.
28th December	The Regiment ,, **Sheerness** ,, Monkstown, Ireland.

1812

15th January	The Regiment from Monkstown to Cork.
8th May	,, ,, Cork to Middleton.
13th ,,	,, ,, Middleton to Cork.

1813

13th February	Three Companies from Cork to Spike Island.
,, ,,	One Company ,, ,, Cove.
24th ,,	Head-Quarters (four Companies) from Cork to Cove.
,, ,,	One (Grenadiers) Company from Cork to Camden Fort.
,, ,,	One (Light) Company from Cork to Carlisle Fort.
,, ,,	Detachments at Hawlbowline and Monkstown.
2nd November	The above four detachments relieved by **Oxford Militia**, and returned to Cove and Middleton.
3rd ,,	Head-Quarters from **Cove** to Middleton.
24th December	The Regiment from Middleton to Fermoy.
,, ,,	Detachments at Mitchelstown, Ballyduff, **Lismore**, Kilworth Mountains.

1814

22nd January	Nine Companies from Fermoy to Middleton (one Company only remaining at Mitchelstown and Ballyduff).
5th May	The Regiment from Middleton to Cove (embarked for England 6th May).
19th ,,	The Regiment landed at Plymouth.
27th & 28th May	The Regiment from Plymouth to Doncaster (arriving 23rd June).
8th June	Detachment from Sheerness to Doncaster (arriving 21st June).
24th ,,	The Regiment Disembodied.

1815-1819

Not assembled for Training.

---

* The Regiment was reduced in **September from twelve to ten Companies**.

1820

20th May to 16th June. Assembled at Doncaster for twenty-eight days' Training.

1821

26th May to 15th June. Assembled at Doncaster, and marched to Pontefract for twenty-one days' Training.

1822-1824

Not assembled for Training.

1825

21st May to 17th June. Assembled at Doncaster for twenty-eight days' Training.

1826-1830

Not assembled for Training.

1831

10th Feb. to 9th March. Assembled at Doncaster, and marched to Pontefract for twenty-eight days' Training.

1832-1852

Not assembled for Training.

1853

25th May to 21st June. Assembled at Doncaster for twenty-eight days Training.

1854

18th April to 25th May. Assembled at Doncaster for twenty-eight days' Training (increased to thirty-nine).

26th May	The Regiment was Embodied at Doncaster.
27th „	„ from Doncaster to Berwick.
2nd & 3rd August	„ „ Berwick to Dublin.

1855

3rd May   The Regiment from Dublin to Waterford.

12th June	Two Companies from Waterford to New Ross.
5th September	Eight ,, ,, ,, ,, The Curragh.
,,	Two ,, ,, ,, New Ross ,, ,,

1856

8th April	The Regiment from The Curragh to Belfast.
29th & 30th May	,, ,, Belfast to Doncaster.
30th June	,, Disembodied at Doncaster.

1857

1st October	The Regiment Embodied at Doncaster.
11th November	The Regiment from Doncaster to Aldershot.

1858

27th September	Four Companies from Aldershot to Ashton-under-Lyne.
,, ,,	Three Companies from Aldershot to Tynemouth.
,, ,,	Three Companies and Head-Quarters from Aldershot to Carlisle.
17th December	One Company from Ashton-under-Lyne to Stockport.

1859

7th January	One Company from Stockport to Ashton-under-Lyne.
3rd June	Four Companies from Ashton-under-Lyne to Sunderland.
,,	Three Companies and Head-Quarters from Carlisle to Newcastle-on-Tyne.
,,	Three Companies from Tynemouth to Newcastle-on-Tyne.

1860

12th March	Three Companies from Sunderland to Carlisle.
7th April	One Company from Newcastle-on-Tyne to Sheffield.
,, ,	One Company from Sunderland to Newcastle-on-Tyne.

24th April	Three Companies from Carlisle to Doncaster.
,,	One Company from Sheffield to Doncaster.
25th April	Six Companies from Newcastle-on-Tyne to Doncaster.
2nd May	The Regiment Disembodied at Doncaster.

1861

Not assembled for Training.

1862-1875

Assembled Annually at Doncaster for Training. (For date and number of days, see Appendix I.)

APPENDIX G.

ALPHABETICAL LIST OF PLACES

WHERE

THE REGIMENT

HAS BEEN

QUARTERED.

ENGLAND.

Aldborough, Suffolk.—Detachment stationed from June to December, 1809.

Aldershot.—Regiment stationed from 11th November, 1857, to 27th September, 1858.

Alfreton, Derbyshire.—Regiment on the march from Plymouth to Doncaster, 17th to 19th June, 1814.

Alnwick, Northumberland.—Regiment on the march from Sunderland to Berwick, 7th to 10th November, 1800.

Ashbourne, Derbyshire.—Regiment on the march from Liverpool to Norman Cross, 9th to 11th November, 1808.

Ashburton, Devon.—Regiment on the march from Plymouth to Doncaster, 28th to 30th May, 1814.

Ashby-de-la-Zouch, Leicester.—Detachment on the march from Liverpool and Chester to Norman Cross, 14th and 15th November, 1808.

Ashford, Kent.—Regiment stationed from June to October, 1805.

Ashton-under-Lyne, Lancashire.— Detachment of four Companies stationed from 27th September, 1858, to 3rd June, 1859.

Auckland, Durham.—Regiment on the march from Sunderland to Liverpool, 13th to 15th October, 1807.

Axbridge, Somerset.—Regiment on the march from Plymouth to Doncaster, 3rd and 4th June, 1814.

Barnard Castle, Durham.—Regiment on the march from Sunderland to Liverpool, 14th to 16th October, 1807.

Bawtry, W. R. Yorks.—One Company stationed in May, 1798; three Companies from February to April, 1802.

Belford, Northumberland.—Regiment on the march from Sunderland to Berwick, 8th to 11th November, 1800.

Berwick-on-Tweed, Northumberland.—Regiment stationed 10th to 28th November, 1800; Regiment on the march from Edinburgh to Doncaster, January–February, 1802; Regiment stationed from 27th May to 3rd August, 1854.

Beverley, E. R. Yorks.—Detachment of five Companies stationed from July to October, 1798; Regiment on the march from Hull to Darlington, &c., 5th to 7th June, 1800; Regiment on the march from Hull to Durham, &c., 29th April to 1st May, 1806.

Biggleswade, Bedfordshire.—Detachment on the march from Gravesend to Hull, 8th November, 1805.

Billericay, Essex.—Regiment on the march from Colchester to Chatham, 6th and 7th August, 1811.

Birmingham, Regiment on the march from Plymouth to Doncaster, 13th and 14th June, 1814.

Bishop Auckland (*see* Auckland).

Blyth, Nottingham.—A Detachment of one Company stationed in May, 1798.

Bolton, Lancashire.—Regiment on the march from Liverpool to Norman Cross, 4th to 7th November, 1808.

Boroughbridge, W. R. Yorks.—Regiment on the march from Hull to Durham, &c., 9th to 11th June, 1800.

Bourn, Lincolnshire.—Detachment on the **march from Gravesend to Hull, 14th November,** 1805.

Bowes, N. R. Yorks.—Regiment on **the** march from Sunderland to **Liverpool,** 14th to 16th October, 1807.

Bridgewater, Somerset.—Regiment on the march **from Plymouth to** Doncaster, 2nd and 3rd June, 1814.

Bristol, Somerset.—Detachment stationed from **January to June, 1812,** with the Battalion of Detachments of Militia ; Regiment on the march from **Plymouth** to Doncaster, **4th to 6th June,** 1814.

Bridlington (*see* Burlington).

Brigg (or Glanford **Bridge), Lincolnshire.—Detachment on the march from Gravesend to Hull, 18th November, 1805.**

Brompton, Middlesex.—Detachment **stationed from 9th to** 14th August, **1811.**

Bromsgrove, Worcestershire.—Regiment on the march from Plymouth to **Doncaster,** 11th to 13th June, 1814.

Burlington, E. R. Yorks.—Detachment of three Companies stationed from July to October, 1798.

Burton-on-Trent, Staffordshire.—Regiment **on the march from Plymouth to** Doncaster, 15th and 16th **June 1814.**

Cambridge.—Regiment on **the march from York to** Colchester, 21st **to** 23rd July, 1803.

Carlisle.—Head-quarters, with **three Companies, from 27th September,** 1858, **to 3rd June, 1859 ; Detachment of three Companies from 12th** March to 24th April, **1860.**

Chatham, Kent.—Regiment stationed **from 8th** to 15th August, 1811, **and Detachment from 16th August** to December, 1811.

Chelmsford, Essex.—Head-quarters and ten Companies stationed from 10th to **25th** April, **1809.**

Chester.—Detachment stationed from 29th October, **1807, to 10th** November, 1808.

Chesterfield, Derbyshire.—Regiment on the march from Plymouth to Doncaster, 18th to 20th June, 1814.

T

Clacton, **Essex.**—Detachment, March 16th, 1811, **as a** working party to assist Royal Engineers.

Colchester, Essex.—Regiment **on the march from York to** Elmstead Heath Camp, 25th **to 27th July, 1803**; Regiment stationed from 24th November, 1803, **to 26th** July, 1804; Headquarters and ten companies from 25th April to May, 1810; Regiment from **13th** November, 1810, **to August,** 1811.

Coxheath (Camp), Essex.—Regiment **from 26th** July to 28th October, 1804.

Cross, Somerset.—Regiment **on the march from Plymouth** to Doncaster, 3rd and 4th June, **1814.**

Cullompton, Devonshire.—Regiment on the march **from Plymouth to Doncaster, 31st** May to 1st June, 1814.

Darlington.—Regiment **on the march from Hull to** Sunderland, 11th to 22nd June, 1800; Regiment **on the march from** Hull to Newcastle-on-Tyne, 5th to 8th **May,** 1806.

Deeping, **Lincolnshire** (*see* Market Deeping).

Derby.—**Regiment on the march from Liverpool to** Norman Cross, **10th to** 13th November, **1803;** Regiment on the march from Plymouth to Doncaster, **16th and 17th June, 1814.**

Doncaster, W. R. Yorks.—**Permanent Head-quarters of the Regiment since 1797.** Eight **Companies stationed from October, 1798, to June, 1799;** Detachment **of five Companies from 17th February, 1802**; Regiment disembodied April, **1802**; Regiment **embodied** March, 1803—remained till 27th May, 1803; Regiment on the march from York to Colchester, **13th to 15th July, 1803;** Regiment stationed 22nd to 24th June, 1814; **disembodied** on latter date; Regiment assembled **for** Training from **20th May to 16th June, 1820**; from 21st May to 17th June, 1825; from **25th May to 18th** June, 1853; from 18th April to 26th May, **1854; embodied** 27th May, 1854; returned 31st May, **1856; disembodied** 30th June, 1856; embodied **1st** October, 1857, and remained till 11th November, 1857; returned and was disembodied **2nd May, 1860;** assembled for Training annually (except 1861) from 1860 to **1875.** (*See* Appendix I.)

Dover, Kent.—Detachment January, 1812, and from January to March, 1813, with the Battalion of Detachments of Militia.

Durham.—Regiment on the march from Hull to Sunderland, 13th to 22nd June, 1800 ; Regiment on the march from Hull to Newcastle-on-Tyne, 6th and 7th May, 1806 ; Regiment on the march from Sunderland to Liverpool, 12th to 14th October, 1807.

Easingwold, N. R. Yorks.—Regiment on the march from Hull to Newcastle-on-Tyne, 2nd to 5th May, 1806.

Eaton (near St. Neots), Huntingdonshire.—Detachment on the march from Gravesend to Hull, 9th November, 1805.

Elmstead Heath (Camp), near Colchester.—Regiment from 28th July to 23rd November, 1803.

Exeter, Devon.—Regiment on the march from Plymouth to Doncaster, 30th and 31st May, 1814.

Faversham, Kent.—A wing of the Regiment from 28th October, 1804, to June, 1805.

Ferrybridge, W. R. Yorks.—Detachment of one Company stationed from 18th February to 12th April, 1802 ; Regiment on the march from Doncaster to York, 27th to 30th May, 1803 ; Regiment on the march from York to Colchester, 12th to 14th July, 1803.

Fleetwood, Lancashire.—Regiment landed from Ireland, 31st May, 1856.

Folkingham, Lincoln.—Detachment on the march from Gravesend to Hull, 14th November, 1805.

Garstang, Lancashire.—Regiment on the march from Sunderland to Liverpool, 20th to 22nd October, 1807.

Gateshead, Durham, near Newcastle.—Regiment on the march from Sunderland to Berwick, 5th to 7th November, 1800.

Gillingham, near Chatham.—Detachment stationed from 9th to 14th August, 1811.

Glanford Bridge (*see* Brigg).

Gloucester.—Regiment on the **march from Plymouth to Doncaster,** 8th and 9th June, **1814.**

Godmanchester, Huntingdonshire.—Regiment on the march from York to Colchester, 20th to 22nd July, 1803; Detachment on the march from Gravesend to Hull, 11th November, 1805; Regiment on the march from Liverpool to Norman Cross, 16th and 17th November, **1808.**

Grantham, Lincolnshire.—**Regiment on the march from** York to Colchester, **16th to** 19th **July, 1803.**

Gravesend, Kent.—Detachment on the march to Hull, 3rd November, **1805;** Regiment on the march from Colchester to Chatham, **7th** and 8th August, 1811.

Green Hammerton, W. R. Yorks.—Detachment stationed September, 1760 to June, 1761.

Greenwich, Kent.—Detachment on the march to Hull, 4th November, 1805.

Halstead, Essex.—**Regiment on the march from York to** Colchester, 23rd **to 26th July,** 1803.

Harwich, Essex.—Detachment **of** two Companies stationed 10th October, 1809; joined by remainder of Regiment from March to 10th April, 1810; Detachment of **two** Companies from then till May, when remainder **of Regiment returned, and** remained to 13th November, 1810.

Hatfield, Hertford.—Detachment **on the march from** Gravesend to Hull, 6th November, 1805.

Hatfield, near Doncaster.—Detachment of **one** Company stationed in **May,** 1798.

Haverhill, Essex.—Regiment on the **march from** York to Colchester, **22nd to** 25th **July,** 1803.

Heddingham, Essex.—Regiment on the march from York to Colchester, 23rd to 26th July, 1803.

Heybridge, Essex, near Maldon.—Regiment on the march from Colchester to Chatham, 5th and 6th August, 1811.

Highgate, Middlesex.—Detachment on the march from Gravesend to **Hull, 5th** November, 1805.

Hilston (Camp), E. R. Yorks.—Two Flank Companies from July to October, 1798, and June and July, 1799.

Holland **Marsh**, Essex.—Detachment stationed as Working **Party, to** assist Royal Engineers, June and July, 1811.

Hollesley Bay, Suffolk.—Detachment stationed from June **to December**, 1809.

Hornsea, E. R. Yorks.—Regiment **stationed from June to October,** 1799.

Howden, E. R. Yorks.—**Regiment on the** march **from Doncaster to** Hull, May, 1798.

Hull.—Regiment **stationed from** June to October, 1798; **Detachment** of two Flank Companies from October, **1798,** to June, 1799; Regiment from October, 1799, to June, 1800; Regiment from **October, 1805, to** 29th **April, 1806.**

Huntingdon.—Regiment **on the march from** York to Colchester, 20th to 22nd July, **1803**; Detachment on the march from Gravesend to Hull, 11th November, 1805; Regiment on the march from Liverpool to Norman Cross, 16th and 17th November, 1808.

Ingleton, **W. R.** Yorks.—Detachment stationed from September, 1760, to June, 1761.

Ipswich, Suffolk.—Head-quarters and ten Companies stationed **from** 10th October, 1809, to March, 1810.

Ivy Bridge, Devon.—Regiment on the march from Plymouth **to Doncaster,** 27th and 28th **May, 1814.**

Ixworth, Suffolk.—Detachment of two Companies stationed from May to 10th **June, 1809.**

Kirkby Lonsdale, Westmoreland.—Regiment **on** the march from Sunderland to Liverpool, 17th to 20th October, 1807.

Kirkby Stephen, Westmoreland.—Regiment on the march from Sunderland to Liverpool, 15th to 17th October, 1807.

Knaresborough, W. R. Yorks.—Detachment stationed from September, 1760, to June, 1761.

Lancaster.—Regiment on the march from Sunderland to Liverpool, 19th to 21st October, 1807.

Leeds.—Detachment stationed from September, 1760, to June, 1761; Regiment from York, **August, 1761,** till Races were over; then returned to York.

Leek, Stafford.—Regiment on the march from Liverpool to **Norman Cross, 8th to 10th November,** 1808.

Leicester.—Regiment on the march from Liverpool to Norman Cross, **12th to 15th November, 1808.**

Lincoln.—Detachment on the march from Gravesend to Hull, **16th to 17th November, 1805.**

Linton, Cambridge,—Regiment on the march from York to Colchester, **22nd to 25th** July, 1803.

Little Holland, Essex.—Detachment stationed from August to November, **1810.**

Liverpool.—Regiment stationed from **23rd October, 1807,** to 3rd November, **1808.**

Loughborough, Leicestershire.—Regiment on the march from Liverpool to Norman Cross, 11th and 12th November, **1808.**

Macclesfield, Cheshire.—Regiment on the march from Liverpool to Norman Cross, **7th to 9th November,** 1808.

Maldon, Essex.—Regiment on the march from Colchester to Chatham, 5th and 6th August, 1811.

Manchester.—Detachment stationed from 30th May to 12th June, 1808; Regiment on the march from Liverpool to Norman Cross, **5th to 8th November, 1808.**

Market Deeping, Lincolnshire.—Detachment on the march from Gravesend to Hull, **13th November, 1805.**

Market Weighton.—Regiment on the march from Hull to Sunderland, 6th **to 9th June, 1800;** Regiment on the march from Hull to Newcastle, **30th April to 2nd** May, 1806.

Minching Hampton, Gloucestershire.—Regiment on the march from Plymouth to **Doncaster,** 7th and 8th June, 1814.

Monkwearmouth, Durham.—Detachment stationed from 9th **May to 5th June, 1806.**

Moorgate, near Retford, Nottinghamshire.—Regiment on the march **from** York to Colchester, 14th to 16th July, 1803.

Morpeth, Northumberland.—Regiment on the march from Sunderland to Berwick, 6th to 8th November, 1800.

Needham, Suffolk.—Detachment of two Companies from May to 10th June, 1809.

Newark, Nottinghamshire.—Regiment on the march from York to Colchester, 15th to 18th July, 1803.

Newcastle-on-Tyne.—Regiment stationed from June to August, 1762; Regiment on the march from Sunderland to Berwick, 5th to 7th November, 1800; Regiment stationed from 9th May to 6th October, 1806; Head-quarters and six Companies from 3rd June, 1859, to 25th April, 1860.

Norman Cross, Huntingdonshire.—Regiment on the march from York to Colchester, 19th to 21st July, 1803; Regiment stationed from November, 1808, to May, 1809.

Northallerton, N. R. Yorks.—Regiment on the march from Hull to Sunderland, 10th to 22nd June, 1800.

Northfleet, Kent.—Regiment on the march from Colchester to Chatham, 7th and 8th August, 1811.

Nottingham.—Regiment stationed from August to November, 1762.

Ormskirk, Lancashire.—Regiment on the march from Sunderland to Liverpool, 22nd and 23rd October, 1807.

Ospringe, Kent.—A wing of the Regiment stationed from 28th October, 1804, to June, 1805.

Otley, W. R. Yorks.—Detachment stationed from September, 1760, to June, 1761.

Oundle, Northamptonshire.—Detachment in March, 1809.

Peterborough, Northampton.—Detachment stationed from 17th November, 1808, to May, 1809.

Plymouth, Devon.—Regiment landed from Ireland, 19th May, 1814, and remained till 28th May.

Pocklington, E. R. Yorks.—Regiment on the march from Hull to Sunderland, 6th to 9th June, 1800; Regiment on the march from Hull to Newcastle-on-Tyne, 30th April to 2nd May 1806.

Pontefract.—Detachment stationed from 18th February to 12th April, 1802; Regiment on the march from Doncaster to York, 27th to 30th May, 1803; Regiment on the march from York to Colchester, 12th to 14th July, 1803; Regiment assembled for Training from 26th May to 15th June, 1821, and from 10th February to 9th March, 1831.

Preston, Lancashire.—Regiment on the march from Sunderland to Liverpool, 21st and 22nd October, 1807.

Redbourn, Lincoln.—Detachment on the march from Gravesend to Hull, 18th and 19th November, 1805.

Retford, Nottingham.—Regiment on the march from York to Colchester, 14th to 16th July, 1803.

Ripon, W. R. Yorks.—Detachment stationed from September, 1760, to June, 1761.

Rotherham, W. R. Yorks.—Detachment of three Companies stationed May, 1798; Detachment of two Companies, 12th to 22nd April, 1802; Regiment on the march from Plymouth to Doncaster, 21st and 22nd June, 1814.

Roos, Holderness, E. R. Yorks.—Detachment stationed in June, 1799.

Sawtry, Huntingdonshire.—Detachment in March, 1809.

Scarborough, N. R. Yorks.—Detachment stationed from October, 1805, to 3rd May, 1806.

Sedbergh, W. R. Yorks.—Regiment on the march from Sunderland to Liverpool, 16th to 19th October, 1807.

Settle, W. R. Yorks.—Detachment stationed from September, 1760, to June, 1761.

Sheffield.—Regiment on the march from Plymouth to Doncaster, 20th to 21st June, 1814; Detachment of one Company stationed from 7th to 24th April, 1860.

Sheerness, Kent.—Detachment stationed December, 1804; Regiment stationed from 14th August to 28th December, 1811; Detachment stationed from 19th June, 1812, to January, 1813, and from April, 1813, to September, 1814, with the Battalion of Detachments of Militia.

Skipton, W. R. Yorks.—Detachment stationed from September, 1760, to June, 1761.

Sleaford, Lincolnshire.—Detachment on the march **from Gravesend to Hull, 15th November,** 1805.

Sodbury, Gloucestershire.—Regiment on the march from Plymouth to **Doncaster, 6th and** 7th June, **1814.**

South Shields, Durham.—Detachment of two Companies from 3rd July to November, 1800.

Stamford, Lincolnshire.—Regiment on the **march from York to Colchester, 18th to 20th July, 1803.**

Stevenage, Hertford.—Detachment **on the march from Gravesend to Hull, 7th November,** 1805.

Stilton, Huntingdonshire.—Regiment on the march from York to Colchester, 19th to 21st July, 1803; Detachment on the march **from** Gravesend to Hull, 12th November, 1805; Detachment stationed November, 1808.

St. Neot's, Huntingdonshire.—Detachment **on the** march from Gravesend to Hull, **9th November,** 1805.

Stockport.—Detachment of one Company from 17th December, 1858, to **7th** January, 1859.

Stowmarket, Suffolk.—Head-quarters and four Companies from May to 10th June, 1809.

Sunderland, Durham.—Regiment stationed **from June to** September, 1760; Regiment stationed from June to November, 1800; Regiment stationed from **6th** October, 1806, to 12th October, **1807; four Companies** stationed from 3rd June, 1859; on 12th March, **1860, three Companies** sent to Carlisle; and, on 7th April, **remaining Company to Newcastle.**

Tadcaster, **W. R.** Yorks.—Regiment **on the** march from Doncaster **to** York, 28th to 31st May, 1803; Regiment on the march **from** York to Colchester, 11th to 13th July, 1803.

Tamworth, Staffordshire.—Regiment on the march from Plymouth to Doncaster, 14th and 15th June, 1814.

Tetbury, Gloucestershire.—Regiment on the march from Plymouth to Doncaster, 7th and 8th June, 1814.

Tewksbury, Gloucestershire.—Regiment on the march from Plymouth to Doncaster, **9th and** 10th June, 1814.

Thetford, Norfolk.—Detachment of four Companies stationed from May to 10th June, 1809.

Thorne, W. R. Yorks.—Detachment of one Company stationed in May, 1798.

Thormanby, N. R. Yorks.—Regiment on the march from Hull to Newcastle-on-Tyne, 2nd to 5th May, 1806.

Tickhill, W. R. Yorks., near Doncaster.—Detachment of one Company stationed in May, 1798.

Tilbury, Essex (*see* Gravesend).

Tunstall, **Holderness**, E. R. Yorks.—Flank Companies, from May to July, 1799.

Tweedmouth, near Berwick, Northumberland.—Regiment stationed from 10th to 28th November, 1800.

Tynemouth, Northumberland.—Detachment of three Companies stationed from **27th** September, 1858, to 3rd June, 1859.

Upton, Worcestershire.—Regiment on the march from Plymouth to Doncaster, **9th** and 10th **June, 1814.**

Uppingham, Rutland.—Regiment **on the** march from Liverpool to Norman **Cross, 14th to 17th** November, 1808.

Walton-on-the-Naze, Essex.—Detachment stationed **from** August to November, 1810.

Weighton (*see* Market Weighton).

Wellington, Somerset.—Regiment on the march **from** Plymouth to Doncaster, 1st **and** 2nd **June, 1814.**

Whitburn, Durham.—Detachment stationed **from 9th May** to 5th **June, 1806.**

Wickwar, Gloucestershire.—Regiment on **the march from Plymouth** to Doncaster, 6th and 7th **June, 1814.**

Wigan, Lancashire.—Regiment **on the march** from Liverpool to Norman **Cross, 3rd to 5th** November, 1808.

Woodbridge, Suffolk.—Regiment stationed **from 10th June** to 10th October, 1809.

Worksop, Nottingham.—Detachment of two Companies stationed in May, 1798.

Worcester.—Regiment on the march from Plymouth to Doncaster, 10th and 11th June, 1814.

Yaxley, Huntingdonshire, near Peterborough.—Regiment on the march from York to Colchester, 19th to 21st July, 1803.

York.—The Regiment first formed at York in 1758, and remained there till June, 1760; Detachment stationed from September, 1760, to June, 1761; end of August, 1761, Regiment to Leeds until the Races were over, and remained till June, 1762; Regiment disembodied December, 1762; Regiment on the march from Hull to Sunderland, 7th to 10th June, 1800; Regiment stationed from 30th May to 10th July, 1803; Regiment on the march from Hull to Newcastle-on-Tyne, 1st to 4th May, 1806.

WALES.

Never Quartered in Wales.

SCOTLAND.

Edinburgh Castle.—Head-Quarters and eight Companies stationed from 6th August, 1801, to January, 1802.

Falkirk, Stirling.—Detachment of two Companies stationed from November, 1800, to August, 1801.

Leith, Edinburgh.—Detachment of two Companies stationed from August, 1801, to January, 1802.

Linlithgow, Linlithgow.—Detachment of two Companies stationed from November, 1800, to August, 1801.

Stirling, Stirling.—Six Companies stationed from November, 1800, to August, 1801.

IRELAND.

Belfast, Antrim.—Regiment stationed from 8th April to 30th May, 1856.

Ballyduff.—Detachment stationed 7th February, 1814.

Camden Fort, near Cork.—Detachment of one Company stationed from 24th February to 2nd November, 1813.

Carlisle Fort, near Cork.—Detachment of one Company stationed from 24th February to 2nd November, 1813.

Cork.—Regiment stationed from 15th January, 1812, to 13th February, 1813 ; Head-quarters and four Companies from then till 24th February ; Detachment till 3rd November.

Cove.—Detachment of one Company stationed from 13th February, 1813, joined by Head-Quarters 24th February ; Regiment embarked for England 6th May, 1814.

Curragh Camp, Kildare—Regiment stationed from 5th September, 1855, to 8th April, 1856.

Dublin.—Regiment stationed from 4th August, 1854, to 3rd May, 1855.

Fermoy, Co. Cork.—Regiment stationed from 24th December, 1813, to 22nd January, 1814.

Hawlbowline, Cork.—Detachment stationed from 24th February to 2nd November, 1813.

Kilworth Mountain, Co. Cork.—Detachment stationed 7th February, 1814.

Lismore, Waterford.—Detachment stationed 7th February, 1814.

Middleton, Co. Cork.—Regiment stationed from 8th to 13th May, 1812 ; Detachment stationed from 2nd November to 5th May, 1814.

Mitchellstown, Co. Cork.—Detachment stationed 7th February, 1814.

Monkstown, Co. Cork.—Regiment landed 15th January, 1812, to 2nd November, 1813.

New Ross, Wexford.—Detachment of two Companies stationed from 12th June to 5th September, 1855.

Queenstown (*see* **Cove**).

Spike Island, Queenstown.—Detachment of three Companies stationed from 13th February to 2nd November, 1813.

Waterford, Waterford.—Regiment stationed from 3rd May to 5th September, 1855.

SUMMARY OF COUNTIES

IN WHICH

THE REGIMENT HAS BEEN QUARTERED.

ENGLAND.

Bedford.—November, 1805.

Cambridge.—July, 1803.

Cheshire.—October, 1807, to November, 1808.

Cumberland.—September, 1858, to June, 1859; March and April, 1860.

Derby.—November, 1808, and June, 1814.

Devon.—May, 1814.

Durham.—June to August, 1760; June to November, 1800; May to June, 1806; October, 1806, to October, 1807; May to August, 1854.

Essex.—July, 1803, to October, 1804; April, 1809; October, 1809, to May, 1810; August, 1810, to August, 1811.

Gloucester.—June, 1814.

Hertford.—November, 1805.

Huntingdon.—July, 1803; November, 1805; November, 1808, to May, 1809.

Kent.—October, 1804, to November, 1805; August to December, 1811; January, 1812; June, 1812, to September, 1814.

Lancashire.—October, 1807, to November, 1808; September, 1858, to June, 1859.

Leicester.—November, 1808.

Lincoln.—July, 1803; November, 1805.

Middlesex.—November, 1805; August, 1811.

Northampton.—November, 1808, to May, 1809.

Northumberland.—June to August, 1762; November, 1800; January and February, 1802; May to October, 1806; May to August, 1854; September, 1858, to April, 1860.

Nottingham.—August to November, 1762; May, 1798; July, 1803.

Norfolk.—May and June, 1809.

Rutland.—November, 1808.

Somerset.—January to June, 1812; June, 1814.

Stafford.—November, 1808; June, 1814.

Suffolk.—May to March, 1810.

Surrey.—November, 1857, to September, 1858.

Warwick.—June, 1814.

Westmoreland.—June, 1814.

WALES.

Never Quartered in Wales.

SCOTLAND.

Edinburgh.—August, 1801, to January, 1802.

Linlithgow.—November, 1800, to August, 1801.

Stirling.—November, 1800, to August, 1801.

IRELAND.

Antrim.—April and May, 1856.

Cork.—January, 1812, to May, 1814.

Dublin.—August, 1854, to May, 1855.

Kildare.—September, 1855, to April, 1856.

Waterford.—May to September, 1855.

Wexford.—June to September, 1855.

APPENDIX H.] THIRD WEST YORK LIGHT INFANTRY. 287

APPENDIX H.

ENROLLED STRENGTH OF THE REGIMENT IN EACH YEAR, FROM 1758 TO 1875.

Year and Date.	Colonel	Lieutenant-Colonels	Majors	Captains	Lieutenants	Ensigns and Sub-Lieutenants	Paymaster	Adjutants	Quartermaster	Surgeon	Assist.-Surgeons	Total Officers	Sergeants	Corporals	Drummers	Privates Effective	Privates Wanting to Complete	Remarks
1758-1764	1	1	1	1	10	10		1	1	1		33	20	20	20	460		
1798—24th Dec.	1	1	2	11	15	1	1	2	1	1		32	54	50	23	949	121	Establishment 1,050
1799—24th Dec.	1	1	2	11	12	3	1	2	1	1		29	54	60	22	542	65	Establishment 607
1800—24th Dec.	1	1	2	5	5	6	1	2	1	1	1	25	42	38	22	588	19	
1801—24th Dec.	1	1	2	6	6	5	1	2	1	1	1	29	71	56	27	816		Estab. 809; 7 Supernumeraries
1802—24th Apr.	1	1	2		23		1	2	1	1	1	26	71	52	27	811		,, 2 Supernumeraries
1803—24th Dec.	1	1	2	11	19	2	1	2	1	1	2	47	62	60	26	1,033	151	Estab. increased to 1,214
1804—24th Dec.	1	1	2	10	12	8	1	2	1	1	2	43	63	58	27	1,108	106	3 Supernumeraries
1805—24th Dec.	1	1	2	8	6	6	1	2	1	1	2	41	46	41	23	812		Establishment reduced to 809
1806—24th Dec.	1	1	2	10	14	2	1	2	1	1	2	31	46	40	22	791	18	
1807—24th Dec.	1	1	2	11	14	10	1	2	1	1	1	37	53	56	23	918	217	
1808—24th Dec.	1	1	2	10	12	9	1	2	1	1	2	47	50	49	26	908	227	
1809—25th Dec.	1	1	2	10	14	4	1	1	1	1	1	41	42	39	26	727	408	Estab. increased to 1,135
1810—25th Dec.	1	2	2	12	14		1	4	1	1	2	40	45	40	27	883	252	

ENROLLED STRENGTH OF THE REGIMENT IN EACH YEAR.—FROM 1758 TO 1875 (continued).

Year and Date	Colonel	Lieutenant-Colonels	Majors	Captains	Lieutenants	Ensigns and Sub-Lieutenants	Paymaster	Adjutant	Quartermaster	Surgeon	Assist.-Surgeons	Total Officers	Sergeants	Corporals	Drummers	Effective	Wanting to Complete	Remarks
1811—25th Dec.	1	1	1	10	13	4	1	1	1	1	1	35	43	40	22	734	75	Establishment reduced to 809 until the year 1852
1812—25th Dec.	1	1	2	10	14	8	1	1	1	1	2	42	44	39	22	705	104	
1813—25th Dec.	1	1	2	9	14	8	1	1	1	1	2	41	44	40	23	614	195	
1814—24th June	1	1	2	10	13	7	1	1	1	1	2	40	44	40	23	878		
1815—25th Dec.								1	1	1			27	27	10	27		69 Supernumeraries
1816—25th Dec.								1	1	1			26	27	12	26		Permanent Staff only. There are no Returns giving the number of Officers or Men enrolled.
1817—25th Dec.								1	1	1			27	27	11	27		
1818—25th Dec.								1	1	1			27	27	12	27		
1819—25th Dec.	1	1	2	10	10	5	1	1	1	1	2	35	21	20	7	572	237	
1820—16th June	1	1	2	10	10	3	1	1	1	1	2	32	20	20	7	710	99	
1821—15th June	1	1	1	9	11	6	1	1	1	1	2	35	20	17	12	830		21 Supernumeraries
1822—21st Dec.	1	1	2	9	11	5	1	1	1	1	2	35	20	17	6	830		"
1823—18th Nov.	1	1	2	8	11	5	1	1	1	1	2	34	20	18	5	791	18	"
1824—18th Nov.	1	1	1	7	10	3	1	1	1	1	2	30	20	20	8	658	151	
1825—17th June								1	1	1			20	16	7	13		Permanent Staff only. There are no Returns giving number of Officers or Men enrolled. Permanent Staff reduced in 1829.
1826—25th Dec.								1	1	1			20	14	7	14		
1827—25th Dec.								1	1	1			20	15	7	15		
1828—25th Dec.								1	1	1			20			7		
1829—25th Dec.								1	1	1			20			7		
1830—25th Dec.	1	1	2	7	7	3	1	1	1	1	1	26	20		5	195	614	
1831—9th March								1	1	1			17					
1832—1st Dec.								1	1	1			19					Permanent Staff only, from 1832 to 1852. There are no Returns giving the number of Officers or Men enrolled. The Permanent Staff was again reduced in 1835.
1833— ,,								1	1	1			19					
1834— ,,								1	1	1			12					
1835— ,,								1	1	1			12					
1836— ,,								1	1	1			12					
1837— ,,								1	1	1			12					
1838— ,,								1	1	1			11					
1839— ,,								1	1	1			10					
1840— ,,								1	1	1			9					
1841— ,,								1	1	1			10					
1842— ,,								1	1	1			10					
1843— ,,								1	1	1			10					

APPENDIX H.] THIRD WEST YORK LIGHT INFANTRY. 289

1844—														Permanent Staff only, from 1832 to 1852. There are no Returns giving the number of Officers or men enrolled. The Permanent Staff was again reduced in 1835
1845—														
1846—														
1847—														
1848—														
1849—														
1850—														
1851—														
1852— 1st June		1							10		9			No Returns. Establishment increased from 809 to the present Establishment of 1,036
1853—18th June	1	1		1	1		9	11	10	35	33	7	815	188	146 disembodied
1854— 1st Dec.	1	1		1	1		9	10	10	37	38	17	592	444	170 " " See pages 170-171
1855— 1st Dec.	1	1		1	1		9	10	10	37	38	12	725	125	7 " "
1856—30th June	1	1		1	1		9	10	10	38	40	9	615	251	
1857— 1st Oct.	1	1		1	1		8	10	9	33	38	21	1,023	8	
1858— 1st Dec.	1	1		1	1		9	10	9	35	40	17	809	220	
1859— 1st Dec.	1	1		1	1		9	10	9	37	48	17	766	270	No Returns. Not Trained
1860— 2nd May	1	1		1	1		9	10	9	36	50	16	789	247	
1861—															
1862—26th May	1	1		1	1		7	8	10	33	32	14	1,025	11	220 Supernumeraries. Ordered not to recruit above 700
1863—11th May	1	1		1	1		5	9	10	32	42	13	863	231	
1864— 3rd May	1	1		1	1		1	7	9	25	33	11	928	108	
1865—25th May	1	1		1	1			5	9	23	38	10	816		
1866—10th May	1	1	2	1	1			5	10	24	36	9	645	55	Ordered not to recruit above 1,000
1867—18th June	1	1	2	1	1			4	10	36	36	10	666	34	
1868—10th June	1	1	2	1	1			4	10	22	30	10	683	353	
1869—19th May	1	1	2	1	1			4	10	20	37	10	706	330	
1870—25th May	1	1	2	1	1			4	8	22	37	10	860	176	
1871—31st May	1	1	2	1	1			4	10	22	34	10	897	139	
1872—12th June	1	1	2	1	1			4	10	23	32	10	954	72	
1873—25th June	1	1	2	1	1			4	9	23	35	9	835	201	
1874— 2nd July	1	1	2	1	1		4	4	10	26	46	9	830	206	
1875—24th June	1	1	2	1	1		7	4	9	26	47	8	709	327	

(Hon. Colonel)

These numbers have been compiled from the Pay Lists in the Public Record Office from 1798 to 1831, and the remainder from the Returns at Head-quarters, and show the Strength of all ranks in the month of December, except in those years when the Regiment was Disembodied, or assembled for Training, when the numbers are given on the day the Regiment was Disembodied or Dismissed.

There were ten Companies previous to 1803, but, as the three senior Field Officers each had a Company, there were only seven Captains. From 1815 to 1852 only the number of the Permanent Staff on full pay are given, except in those years when the Regiment was assembled for Training.

The Paymaster, Quartermaster and Surgeon were retained on full pay on the Permanent Staff until 1829.

There are no Returns whatever giving the number of Officers or Men enrolled during the years the Regiment was not assembled for Training.

U

APPENDIX I.

PERIOD OF PRELIMINARY DRILL AND ANNUAL TRAINING

(IN THOSE YEARS WHEN THE REGIMENT WAS NOT EMBODIED)

FROM 1758 TO 1875.

Year	Preliminary Drill for Recruits				Regimental Training					Inspecting Officer
	No. of Days	From	To		No. of Days	From	To	Total No. of Days	Place	
1758	...	...	...		...	...	...	...	...	⎫
1764	...	...	...		...	...	...	...	...	⎬ No Records.
1797*	...	...	...		20	20th May	16th June	28	Doncaster	⎭
1820†	...	...	...		28	26th May	15th June	21	Pontefract	
1821	...	...	...		21	21st May	17th June	28	Doncaster	
1825‡	...	...	...		28	10th Feb.	9th March	28	Pontefract	
1831‡	...	...	...		28	25th April	21st June	28	Doncaster	
1853‡	...	...	...		35	18th April	25th May	38	Doncaster	Lieut.-Colonel J. Stoyte.
1854‡	14	24th April	7th May		21	8th May	25th May	35	Doncaster	Colonel M. J. Slade.
1862	14	8th April	21st April		21	22nd April	12th May	35	Doncaster	Colonel Goodwyn, C.B., 41st Foot.
1863	14	4th April	17th April		21	18th April	8th May	35	Doncaster	Lieut.-Gen. Sir G. A. Wetherall, K.C.B.
1864	7	24th April	30th April		27	1st May	27th May	34	Doncaster	Colonel Campbell, I.F.O., C.B.
1865	7	9th April	15th April		27	16th April	12th May	34	Doncaster	Col. G. W. P. Bingham, A.A.G., C.B.
1866	14	13th May	26th May		27	27th May	22nd June	41	Doncaster	Colonel Budd, 14th Foot.
1867	14	4th May	17th May		27	18th May	13th June	41	Doncaster	Colonel H. Bingham, C.B. Inspecting Field Officer.
1868	14	12th April	25th April		27	26th April	22nd May	41	Doncaster	Colonel A. Wombwell, Assistant Inspector

* The Regiment was embodied from 5th March, 1798, to 24th June, 1814 (except from 22nd April, 1802 to March, 1803).
† The Regiment was not assembled for Training in the following years (inclusive)—from 1815 to 1819 ; from 1822 to 1824 ; from 1826 to 1830 ; and from 1832 to 1852.
‡ The Regiment was Embodied from 26th May, 1854 to 2nd May, 1860 (except from July, 1856 to September, 1857). In 1861 the Training was dispensed with, the Regiment having been so recently Disembodied.
§ The Recruits did not attend the Regimental Training, being dismissed on the 20th of April.

APPENDIX J.

HALF-YEARLY AND ANNUAL INSPECTIONS.

DATE.	PLACE.	BY WHOM.	EFFECTIVE PRIVATES	REMARKS.
1759–1760	...	...	...	No Record
1761.—20th August	York	H.R.H. the Duke of York	...	No Record
1762-64	...	...	...	Amalgamated with 1st and 2nd West York.
1765–1796	...	...	...	No Record
1797	...	...	...	
1798.—23rd April	Doncaster	Major-General Lord Mulgrave	703	
„ 31st October	„	Major-General C. Horneck	...	
1799	...	...	...	No Record
1800.—7th June	York	Major-General Staveley	585	
„ 18th Sept.	Sunderland	Major-General Thomas Murray	...	
„ November	Stirling	Major-General Sir J. St. Clair Erskine, Bart.	...	
1801.—May	„	Major-General Sir J. St. Clair Erskine, Bart.	...	
„ September	Edinburgh	Lieut.-General Vyse	...	
1802	...	...	...	Disembodied 22nd April
1803.—August	Elmstead Heath	H.R.H. the Duke of York	1,127	Rank and File
„ 10th October	„	Major-General Lord Southampton	1,122	„
1804.—22nd May	„	Major-General Lord Southampton	1,168	„
„ 18th December	Feversham	Brigadier-General Coote Manningham	...	No Record
1805	...	...	...	
1806.—18th October	Sunderland	Major-General Cockburn	797	
1807.—30th April	„	Major-General Cockburn	786	
1808.—2nd May	Liverpool	Major-General Fisher	929	
„ 15th Sept.	„	Major-General Champagne	912	
1809.—10th May	Norman Cross	Major-General Williams	715	
„ 9th October	Ipswich	Brigadier-General Sir M. Burgoyne	751	
1810.—30th April	Harwich	Major-General Robinson	764	
„ 20th November	Colchester	Major-General J. C. Sherbrooke	886	

Year	Location	Commander	Number	Notes
1812.—1st May	Cork	Major-General S. Graham	739	
" 3rd October			689	
1813.—17th May	Cove	Major-General S. Graham	697	
" 19th October	"	Major-General Crowjoy	646	
1814.—May	Cork	Major-General S Graham	643 (?)	Disembodied 24th June
1815-19				No Training
1820			570	Rank and File
1821			732	
1822-24				" No Training
1825			657	Rank and File
1826-30				No Training
1831			192	Rank and File
1832-1852				No Training
1853.—18th June	Doncaster		848	
1854.—12th May	"	Lieut.-Colonel John Stoyte	877	Embodied 26th May
" 23rd October	Dublin	Colonel M. J. Slade, Inspecting Field Officer	563	
1855.—19th May	Waterford	Major-General William O. Cochrane	698	
" 1st November	The Curragh	Major-General John Eden	673	
1856.—21st May	Belfast	Colonel W. F. Bedford, Commanding 2nd Brigade		Disembodied 30th June
		Major-General J. B. Gough, C.B.		Embodied 1st October
1857			721	
1858.—18th May	Aldershot	Major-General Lawrence, C.B.	806	
" 11th December	Carlisle	Colonel Wilbraham, A.A.G.	753	
1859.—21st May	"	Colonel Wilbraham, A.A.G.	777	
" 25th October	Newcastle	Lieut.-General Sir J. L. Pennefather, K.C.B.		
1860			1,025	Disembodied 2nd May
1861			805	No Training
1862.—26th May	Doncaster	Colonel Goodwyn, C.B., 41st Foot	928	
1863.—11th May	"	Lieut.-General Sir G. A. Wetherall, K.C.B.	816	
1864.—3rd May	"	Colonel Campbell. I.F.O., C.B.	645	
1865.—25th May	"	Colonel G. W. P. Bingham, A.A.G., C.B.	666	
1866.—10th May	"	Colonel Budd, 1st Battalion 14th Foot	653	
1867.—18th June	"		706	
1868.—10th June	"	Colonel B. Bingham, C.B., Inspecting Field Officer	860	
1869.—19th May	"		897	
1870.—25th May	"	Colonel A. Wombwell, Assistant Inspector of Reserve Forces	964	
1871.—31st May	"		835	
1872.—12th June	"	Colonel Nason, Assistant-Adjutant-General	830	
1873.—25th June	"		709	
1874.—2nd July	"	Colonel Lightfoot, C.B., Commanding 7th and 8th Brigade Depôts.		
1875.—24th June	"			

NOTE.—There are no Returns in the Public Record Office, War Office, or Horse Guards, for the years which are not included, or are incomplete in this List.

APPENDIX K.

MISCELLANEOUS RETURNS.

NATIONALITY.
OFFICERS.—1806-13.

TABLE No. 1.

	1806.	1807.	1808.	1809.	1810.	1811.	1812.	1813.
English	32	30	37	33	31	34	27	37
Scotch	...	...	...	...	...	...	...	...
Irish	...	5	5	9	9	7	5	5
Foreigners	...	...	2	...	...	...	...	...
Total	32	35	44	42	40	41	32	42

PRIVATES.—1806-13.
TABLE No. 2.

	1806.	1807.	1808.	1809.	1810.	1811.	1812.	1813.
English	794	783	924	711	761	706	736	694
Scotch	1	1	2	1	...	1	...	...
Irish	2	2	3	3	3	3	3	3
Foreigners	...	...	...	...	...	...	...	...
Total	797	786	929	715	764	710	739	697

APPENDIX K.] THIRD WEST YORK LIGHT INFANTRY. 295

PRIVATES.—1854-1875.*

		1854	1855	1856	1857	1858	1859	1860	1861	1862	1863	1864	1865	1866	1867	1868	1869	1870	1871	1872	1873	1874	1875
English	Yorkshire	615	706	483	796	597	546	543	636	430	500	462	312	307	309	343	389	363	410	270	511	412
	Other Counties			128	157	147	138	146	144	140	190	102	104	128	150	150	170	200	216	211	195	151
Scotch		8	8	6	10	9	8	10	6	5	3	3	3	3	4	3	3	4	4	4	1	3
Irish		67	105	102	164	168	178	126	239	230	232	249	226	227	220	200	298	330	340	350	123	143
Total		690	819	719	1127	921	870	897	1025	805	925	816	645	666	683	796	866	897	964	835	830	709

* From 1854 to 1860 these numbers include Sergeants and Corporals, after that year Privates (Effective) only.

DESCRIPTION.†

TABLE No. 3.

	1808.	1809.	1810.	1811.	1812.	1813.	1814.	1820.	1855.	1856.	1857.	1858.	1859.	1860.
Principals	19	8	13	14	4	4	3	44	46	39	46	55	...	...
Substitutes	931	696	782	736	717	618	618	506	773	680	1081	866	47	48
Volunteers	11	62	128	24	23	22	22						823	849
Total	961	766	923	774	744	644	643	550	819	719	1127	921	870	897

† These numbers, which include Sergeants and Corporals, are made up on the 1st of December in each year from 1808 to 1813; in April, 1814 (previous to being disembodied), and in May, 1820, when assembled for Training, and consequently do not agree with the totals in the other Tables. The striking difference in the proportion of Substitutes and Volunteers is caused by the Militia having been raised exclusively by Voluntary Enlistment since 1852, instead of by Ballot.

SIZE.*

TABLE No. 4.

Height.	1803.	1804.	1805.	1806.	1807.	1808.	1809.	1810.	1811.	1812.	1813.
ft. in.											
6 0 and upwards	31	11		33	19	14	8	9	6	12	11
5 11	47	60		53	22	22	18	19	14	10	14
5 10	90	46		92	52	63	47	40	31	41	35
5 9	140	50	No Returns.	114	86	74	64	60	71	65	62
5 8	223	206		144	104	132	115	128	104	98	98
5 7	386	509		179	142	162	114	126	111	126	102
5 6	91	140		116	175	199	142	136	145	149	154
5 5	119	100		62	119	161	129	147	114	138	129
Under 5ft. 5in.	...	...		4	64	97	75	96	111	89	56
Boys	...	...		...	3	5	3	5	3	10	36
Total	1127*	1122*		797	786	929	715	764	710	739	697

TABLE No. 5.

AGES.—1803 TO 1813.

Years and Upwards.	1803.	1804.	1805.	1806.	1807.	1808.	1809.	1810.	1811.	1812.	1813.
Under 18	...	...		4	3	17	12	30	25	32	36
18	...	247		12	12	59	31	55	36	47	46
20	867	649		233	226	251	207	210	162	160	143
25			No Returns.	322	316	331	245	233	227	199	180
30	218	212		137	133	161	125	124	162	180	150
35				45	52	59	48	52	58	77	83
40	42	14		32	35	42	35	44	30	43	39
45				12	9	9	12	14	10	15	18
50	...	...		...	...	...	...	...	...	...	2
Total	1127*	1122*		797	786	929	715	764	710	739	697

AGES.†—1854–1860.

Years and Upwards.	1854.	1855.	1856.	1857.	1858.	1859.	1860.
Under 18	3	2	8	20	6	26	32
18 to 25	624	700	598	730	581	531	522
25 to 30	85	62	69	305	265	250	265
30 to 40	28	31	33	53	50	45	60
40 to 50	...	24	21	18	19	17	17
Upwards 50	...	...	...	1	...	1	1
Total	690	819	719	1127	921	870	897

* The numbers for the years 1803 and 1804, in Tables No. 4 and 5, are for Rank and File, the remainder Effective Privates only.
† From 1854 to 1860 these numbers include also Sergeants and Corporals.

LENGTH OF PAST SERVICE.

TABLE No. 6.

Years and Upwards.	1806.	1807.	1808.	1809.	1810.	1811.	1812.	1813.
25	...	...	...	2	3	2	1	2
21	...	9	12	10	10	4	10	10
18	...	6	4	4	4	6	9	8
14	...	24	10	14	16	25	56	60
12	...	21	18	31	42	83	21	21
10	...	52	54	48	18	40	13	144
8	60	95	43	32	23	121	217	79
7	...	24	28	24	259	138	18	11
6	...	31	24	220	37	12	3	17
5	...	42	195	46	5	1	3	129
4	...	368	142	10	4	8	178	29
3	737	92	13	2	5	158	14	26
2	...	12	1	4	222	35	39	62
1	...	2	3	266	3	40	63	39
Under 1 year	...	8	382	2	113	87	94	60
Total ...	797	786	929	715	764	710	739	697

TERM OF UNEXPIRED SERVICE.

TABLE No. 7.

Years.	1806.	1807.	1808.	1809.	1810.	1811.	1812.	1813.
Unlimited Service*	717	707	894	706	756	697	726	693
6								
5			10				3	
4				9		5		4
3					8		2	
2		14	10					
1	80	65	15			8	8	
Less than 1 year								
Total	797	786	929	715	764	710	739	697

NOTE.—The Statistics in these seven Tables are as complete as possible, there being no Inspection Returns (from which these have been compiled) for those years which are omitted, or incomplete. No details are given in the Returns previous to the year 1803, and in most of the later ones—after 1814, and again subsequently to 1860,—the details are so condensed or altered as to render them almost valueless for comparison. With the few exceptions noted in each Table, the numbers represent the Effective Privates present at the First Half-Yearly Inspection in each year (see Note to Table No. 3), and the total in each Table will be found to agree with the numbers given in Appendix J.

* The men were raised by Ballot to serve for five years, "*or for such further time as the Militia shall remain Embodied.*"

APPENDIX K.] THIRD WEST YORK LIGHT INFANTRY. 299

PRINCIPAL CHANGES IN THE ESTABLISHMENT OF THE REGIMENT
(Showing the various periods at which the Numbers of each Rank have been Increased or Reduced)
FROM 1758 TO 1875.
TABLE No. 8.

Year and Date.	Colonel.	Lieutenant-Colonels.	Majors.	Captains.	Lieutenants.	Ensigns and Sub-Lieutenants.	Paymaster.	Regimental Staff Officers — Adjutants.	Quartermaster.	Surgeon.	Assist.-Surgeons.	Total Officers.	Sergeants.	Corporals.	Drummers.	Privates.	Remarks.
1758-1764	1	1	1	7	10	10		1	1	1	1	33	20	20	20	400	
1797-1798	1	1	2	7	12	10		1	1	1	1	45	53	50	22	1,150	
1799—3rd Dec.	1	1	1	7	12	8		1	1	1	1	35	30	30	21	607	
1801—5th Aug.	1	1	2	10	14	5		1	1	1	1	34	66	32	27	809	
1803—27th Jan.	1	1	2	10	14	8		1	1	1	1	39	26	26	12		
—11th June	1	1	2	10	14	10		2	1	1	2	46	60	60	27	1,224	{ 1 Major, 1 Adjutant, 23 Sergeants, 12 Corporals, 5 Drummers, Supernumeraries. Increased from 10 to 12 Companies
1805—12th July	1	1	2	10	14	10		1	1	1	2	43	60	60	27	809	
1807—9th Dec.	1	1	2	10	12	10		1	1	1	2	46	56	55	27	1,135	
1808—21st Mar.	1	1	2	10	14	10		1	1	1	2	47	56	56	22		
1811—24th Sept.	1	1	2	10	14	8	1	1	1	1	1	40	40	40	22	809	Second Lieutenant-Colonel added
1814—24th Sept.	1	1	1	10	12	8	1	1	1	1	1	38	27	27	17		Reduced from 12 to 10 Companies
1819—24th April																		
1835—9th Sept.	1	1	1	10	10	10	1	1	1	1	1	37	12	30	7		
1853—10th Mar.	1	1	1	10	10	10	1	1	1	1	1	37	34	34	21	1,036	[on being embodied Non-Commissioned Officers increased
1854—26th May	1	1	2	10	12	10	1	1	1	1	1	41	54	40	21		
1858—17th Dec.																		
1864—23rd Aug.	1	1	2	10	12	10	1	1	1	1	2	43	41	34	10	760	
1867—16th Oct.																1,036	
1869—17th Mar.	1	1	1	10	10	10	1	1	1	1	2					1,090	
1870—25th April	1	1	1	10	10	10		1	1	1	2					1,036	
1874—11th May	1	1	2	10	10	10		1	1	1	2	47	40	40	10		

Since 1853 Paymasters have been only allowed when Embodied. The Sergeants and Drummers include the Permanent Staff (since 1853 27 of the former, and all the latter).

NOTE.—This table is not quite complete, or perfectly accurate, especially so far as it relates to the Non-commissioned Officers.

VOLUNTEERS INTO THE REGULAR ARMY DURING THE PENINSULA WAR.

TABLE No. 9.

Regiment.	1805.	1806.	1807.	1808.	1809.	1810.	1811.	1812.	1813.	1814.	Total, 1805-1814.
Royal Artillery	22										22
Royal Waggon Train									12		12
1st Foot (Grenadier) Guards					8		9	58	9	3	87
3rd Foot (Scots Fusiliers) Guards					5		3		3		8
1st Foot (The Royal Scots)				1	3		53				57
2nd (The Queen's Royal)											3
4th (The King's Own Royal)			18	27	35		38	2	1		76
7th (The Royal Fusiliers)	5		1	11							50
8th (The King's)				1							12
14th (Buckinghamshire)											1
15th (Yorkshire East Riding)							2				2
16th (Bedfordshire)	2										2
19th (First Yorkshire N.R., Princess of Wales's)							2				2
20th (East Devonshire)					1						1
24th (Second Warwickshire)				11							11
25th (The King's Own Borderers)				1				1			1
28th (North Gloucestershire)					4						4
29th (Worcestershire)				4	3						5
31st (Huntingdonshire)					2						3
32nd (Cornwall Light Infantry)				12	29		51	13	8		101
33rd (The Duke of Wellington's)	132		1	48	25			1	1		172
34th (Cumberland)	58		36		1						143
36th (Herefordshire)				1							1
38th (First Staffordshire)	1								1		2
39th (Dorsetshire)				25	31						31
40th (Second Somersetshire)	1				1		1		4		27
43rd (Monmouth Light Infantry)											1
45th (Nottingham Sherwood Foresters)											
46th (South Devonshire)					1			1			4
48th (Northamptonshire)	1				1						2
50th (The Queen's Own)					7						5
51st (The King's Own Light Infantry), Second West Riding Yorkshire			34	39	3				3	1	81
52nd (Oxfordshire Light Infantry)				5							8

THIRD WEST YORK LIGHT INFANTRY.

53rd (Shropshire)	...	...	...	8	...	...	29
55th (Westmoreland)	...	...	21	...	2	...	2
56th (West Essex)	12	...	...	...	...	...	12
59th (Second Nottinghamshire)	...	...	...	...	...	...	16
61st (South Gloucestershire)	...	1	14	2	...	...	4
65th (Second Yorkshire North Riding)	...	...	4	...	...	...	2
69th (South Lincolnshire)	...	...	2	...	...	...	4
73rd (Perthshire)	...	...	2	...	4	...	4
76th	...	...	...	1	...	...	10
77th (East Middlesex)	...	...	32	19	9	...	51
82nd (The Prince of Wales's Volunteers)	...	...	4	...	...	...	4
83rd (County of Dublin)	...	...	22	7	4	2	52
84th (York and Lancaster)	...	7	7	12	2	34	63
86th (Royal County Down)	...	...	...	...	17	14	19
88th (The Connaught Rangers)	...	...	8	1	3	...	36
95th ("Rifle Brigade" since 1816)	10	...	...	...	17	...	
Total	244	108	302	201	206	89	92	1,231

In 1798 the Bounty offered to Volunteers was seven guineas, to serve during the war and for six months after Peace had been concluded.

1799.—In July, the Bounty was increased to ten guineas.

1807.—In this year the conditions of service were changed, and the Bounty was fixed at fourteen guineas for unlimited service, and ten guineas for seven years.

1811.—In July the Bounty was reduced to ten guineas for unlimited service, and six guineas for seven years.

1812.—In May the Bounty was increased to fourteen guineas for unlimited service, or ten guineas for seven years, which was reduced in December to ten and six guineas respectively.

1813.—In July the Bounty was fixed at eleven guineas for unlimited service, and seven guineas for seven years; afterwards increased to sixteen and twelve guineas respectively.

In November eight guineas Bounty was offered to those who volunteered to serve abroad as Militia.

1814.—In April the Bounty was again reduced to twelve guineas for unlimited service, and eight guineas for seven years.

NUMBER OF VOLUNTEERS INTO THE ARMY AND MARINES DURING THE CRIMEAN WAR AND INDIAN MUTINY.

TABLE No. 10.

Year	When Embodied.			When Disembodied.	Grand Total.
	Army.	Marines.	Total.	Army.	
1854	324	25	350	53	403
1855	198	......	198	......	198
1856	263	1	264	......	264
1857	1	......	1	5	6
1858	231	9	240	......	240
1859	22	69	91	......	91
1860	......	......	......	30	30
1861 to 31st March	......	......	......	5	5
Total ...	1,039	105	1,144	93	1,237*

In 1852, 165 Volunteered, and in 1863-4, 317. The Regiment was not embodied in 1854 until the 14th of May, and remained embodied until June, 1856. In 1857 the Regiment was embodied; and again disembodied in May, 1860.

In November, 1854, the quota of Volunteers was fixed at 25 per cent. of the strength of the Regiment (762), or 190 men; an Ensign's Commission being given with every 75 men.

In 1856 the quota was fixed at 25 per cent. of the establishment, or 259.

In 1858 the quota was fixed first at 17 per cent. of the effectives on the 1st of January, or 135; on the 19th of August an Ensign's Commission was offered for every 75 men, which was increased to 100 on the 30th of August.

* The numbers given in every case far exceeded the quota, which, although compiled from Parliamentary Returns, are not complete; a Return dated 15th of March, 1856, gives the number of Volunteers from the Regiment from 1852 to 1855 as 2,302; of which number 256 had Volunteered since June, 1855.

APPENDIX K.] THIRD WEST YORK LIGHT INFANTRY. 303

BOUNTY PAID TO VOLUNTEERS DURING THE CRIMEAN WAR AND INDIAN MUTINY.

TABLE No. 11.

Year.	Army.		Marines.
	Cavalry.	Infantry.	
1854.—To 30th October*	£6 19 0	£5 6 0	£6
,, From 31st October	£7 15 6	£6 0 0	£7 (from November)
1855.—23rd January	£10 0 0	£8 0 0	£9
1856.—18th January to 28th April	£5 and a Free Kit	...	£6 and Free Kit, to May
,, From 29th April	£2 and ditto	...	£2 and ditto, from 6th May
1858.—4th February	£3 and ditto	...	£3 ,, ,,
1859.—	Ditto ditto	...	£5 ,, ,,

* All Volunteers between the 20th of November, 1854, and the end of the Crimean War, received an extra Pound.

NUMBER OF MEN ENROLLED, RE-ENROLLED, ABSENTEES, AND VOLUNTEERS INTO THE MILITIA RESERVE, IN EACH YEAR, FROM 1852 TO 1875.

TABLE No. 12.

Year.	Enrolled.*	Re-Enrolled.†	Absentees.‡	Militia Reserve.§	Remarks.
1852*	1036	...	...	...	Not Assembled for Training in 1852
1853	129	...	276	...	
1854	404	...	410	...	
1855	655	...	Embodied	...	
1856	379	...	"	...	
1857	340	21	"	...	
1858	333	9	"	...	
1859	137	30	"	...	
1860	284	26	...	...	Disembodied 3rd of May, 1860. Enrolment commenced
1861	...	84	...	...	Not Assembled for Training in 1861 [10th of May
1862	156	77	234	...	
1863	91	71	51	...	
1864	263	121	87	...	} Not allowed to recruit over 700 from 1864 to 1866
1865	57	88	71	...	
1866	2	78	50	...	
1867	144	92	40	...	
1868	205	121	60	21	
1869	181	50	53	33	} Not to recruit over 1000 in 1869-70
1870	297	96	117	196	232 Militia Reserve present at Training, 1870; 345 in 1871
1871	301	92	167	62	280 " " " " "
1872	204	58	51	...	259 " " " " "
1873	237	38	127	3	" " " " "
1874	202	39	138	25	246 " " " " "
1875*	365	58	93	47	

* Enrolment commenced the 25th of September, the engagement being for five years, which was increased to six years the 8th of December, 1873 (see pp. 155, 159). The number for 1875 is only up to 30th November inclusive.

† The first men were re-enrolled on the 3rd of October, 1857.

‡ This column shows the number of men who failed to attend the Training.

§ The Militia Reserve was not established until August, 1867 (see pp. 193, 194). Quota required 259.

This Table gives the number actually enrolled or re-enrolled in each year, and not the number of each description serving, which, of course, is much larger.

APPENDIX L.

SUMMARY OF STATUTES

FIXING THE NUMBER OF

VOLUNTEERS
REQUIRED FOR THE REGULAR ARMY.

35 Geo. III., Cap. 83, 2nd June, 1795.

Ten per cent of the establishment of privates to be allowed to volunteer into the Royal Navy, or Royal Artillery, at the usual bounty. To be replaced by recruits raised by beat of drum at a bounty of ten guineas.

38 Geo. III., Cap. 17, 12th January, 1798.

The Supplementary Militia, not exceeding 10,000 men, or one-fifth of the number to be raised in any County, to be allowed to enlist, their places not being filled by ballot. To serve during the war, and until six months after peace was concluded, and not liable to serve out of Europe.

39 Geo. III., Cap. 106, 12th July, 1799.

The King to appoint regiments of the Regular Army to receive volunteers. No regiment so appointed to be liable to serve out of Europe for five years, or during the war and six months after. The numbers of Volunteers not to exceed one-fourth of the quota, and to receive a bounty of ten guineas. (*See* Appendix M.)

39 and 40 Geo. III., Cap. 1, 8th October, 1799.

To enable the King to accept additional Volunteers at a bounty of ten guineas, to serve during the war and until six months after peace

x

had been concluded, and not liable to serve out of Europe. Men allowed to enlist as companies of not less than eighty, with one captain, one lieutenant, and one ensign; commissions as such being given to the Officers with temporary rank, and to be entitled to half-pay. The number volunteering not to exceed three-fifths of the quota, the difference, if any, to be dismissed to their homes.

42 Geo. III., Cap. 90, 26th June, 1802.

Expressly forbade the enlistment of Militiamen into the Regular Army, declaring the enlistment null and void, and imposed a fine of £20 upon the Officer or person so enlisting men from the Militia. (*See* Appendix M.)

45 Geo. III., Cap. 31, 10th April, 1805.

The number of **Volunteers not to** exceed the number of men above the original quota; one sergeant and one corporal to be allowed with every twenty men, the bounty being ten guineas. If four-fifths of the number required from any Regiment volunteer at once, **no more to be taken.** (Quota for Great Britain, 15,695, including 707 **Corporals.**)

47 Geo. III., Cap. 57, 13th August, 1807.

The **number** of **men to volunteer must leave** three-fifths of the establishment serving; if five-sixths volunteer no more to be allowed. (19,152 **volunteered** under this Act, see Parl. **Papers,** 1809 (49), **Vol. X., p. 257.)**

49 Geo. III., Cap. 4, 13th March, 1809.

Where the **number of the men** exceeds three-fifths of the present **establishment** (or less than two-fifths of the establishment in August, 1807), two-fifths **allowed to** enlist. (15,531 **volunteered** under this Act, see Parl. Papers, 1810 (129), Vol. XIII., p. **351.**)

51 Geo. III., Cap. 20, 11th April, 1811.

The **Militia, not exceeding 5,714 for** England and 1,142 for **Scotland** (total 6,856), **to be** enlisted *annually*, but not exceeding one-**seventh** of the **quota of any County.** The deficiency so caused to be supplied by **voluntary enlistment until** 1st July, 1813, and an equal number of supernumeraries as those allowed to volunteer to be raised annually, viz., 6,856. (*See* Appendix M.)

53 Geo. III., Cap. 81, 2nd July, 1813.

The proportion of Volunteers to be one-seventh of the establishment, and not in proportion to the number actually serving. (*See* Appendix M.)

54 Geo. III., Cap. 1, 24th November, 1813.   54 Geo. III., Cap. 20, 10th December, 1813.

Militia, not exceeding 30,000 men, called upon to volunteer to serve abroad in Europe, but in no case was any regiment to be reduced below three-fourths of the men actually serving. The bounty being eight guineas. This was not to affect volunteering under other Acts. Three Field Officers to be accepted with 900 men, two with 600, and one with 300 men (or three-fourths of the number actually serving), and the usual proportion of captains, subalterns, &c. Or men might enlist together as a company of not less than 100, the captain, lieutenant, and ensign receiving commissions as such in the Regular Army. (Similar to 39 and 40 Geo. III. c. 1, 1799.)

56 Geo. III., Cap. 64.

The supply of Volunteers to the Regular Army from the Militia was discontinued, and the statutes under which they had been obtained repealed, viz., 43 Geo. III., c. 100 ; 47 Geo. III., c. 71 ; 49 Geo. III., c. 53 ; 50 Geo. III., c. 24 ; and 51 Geo. III., c. 20.

APPENDIX M.

SUMMARY OF STATUTES

FIXING THE QUOTA OF MILITIA

IN ENGLAND AND WALES,

AND

SHOWING THE YEARS IN WHICH IT HAS BEEN INCREASED OR REDUCED.

---

30 GEO. II., CAP. 25, 28TH JUNE, 1757.

THE present Militia Force was first raised in England under this Act, the quota was fixed at 32,000 :—Yorkshire, 2,360 ; West Riding, 1,240 ; North Riding, 720 ; East Riding, 400 ; the Regiment, 400.

19 GEO. III., CAP. 76, 1779.

Militia *increased* by the addition of Volunteer Companies, which received same pay, and were subject to the same regulation, as the rest of the Force, and were to be reduced when the Militia was disembodied, the Act only remaining in force until the 1st December, 1782.

26 GEO. III., CAP 107, 1786.

Quota same as above.

34 GEO. III., CAP. 16, 28TH MARCH, 1794.

The Lords-Lieutenant were authorised to *augment* the Militia by accepting offers to raise Volunteer Companies or additional men for Regiments, to receive same pay, bounty, &c., as the other Militiamen ; the men being enlisted to serve until the Militia was disembodied, unless their services were dispensed with earlier. (Similar to 19 Geo. III., c. 76.)

37 GEO. III., CAP. 3, 11TH NOV., 1796 ; CAP. 22, 30TH DEC., 1796.

The Militia was *increased* by the Supplementary Militia, which was raised under these Acts, the quota being 63,878. Yorkshire, 6,915 ; West Riding, 4,694 ; North Riding, 1,360 ; East Riding, 861 ; the Regiment, 1,192. (In addition to numbers raised under 30 Geo. II., c. 25.)

38 GEO. III., CAP. 18, 20TH FEB., 1798 ; CAP. 19, DATED 23RD FEB.

One half of the Supplementary Militia to be embodied, the half to be embodied to be **balloted for**. Men to assemble not later than the 26th February, time extended to 10th March by 38 Geo. III., c. 19.

39 GEO. III., CAP. 106, 12TH JULY, 1799.

Quota *reduced* to 76,566 (partly by Volunteering). Any exceeding new establishment (raised under 37 Geo. III., caps. 3 and 22) who do not volunteer to be dismissed to their homes. Yorkshire, 7,318 ; West Riding, 4,555 ; North Riding, 1,707 ; East Riding, 1,056 ; the Regiment, 911. (*See* Appendix L.)

42 GEO. III., CAP. 12, 11TH DEC., 1801.

Establishment of Militia when disembodied (until 25th of March, 1803) to be *reduced* to 30,776. Yorkshire, 2,928 ; West Riding, 1,822 ; North Riding, 683 ; East Riding, 423 ; the Regiment, 607.

42 GEO. III., CAP. 90, 26TH JUNE, 1802.

This Act consolidated and amended the Militia Acts, and the quota then fixed is generally spoken of as " the Original Quota," and remained in force until 1852. The temporary increase which occurred on several occasions between the years 1802 and 1814 was calculated in proportion to the numbers fixed for the different counties by this Act, which *increased* the quota to 40,963. One half this number might be raised in addition, as " Supplementary Men," in case of war, rebellion, &c. Yorkshire, 3,904 ; West Riding, 2,429 ; North Riding 911 ; East Riding, 564 ; the Regiment, 809. (*See* Appendix L.)

44 GEO. III., CAP. 56, 29TH JUNE, 1804.—("ADDITIONAL FORCES ACT.")

This is not a Militia Act, but the 10th clause ordered the Militia to be *reduced* to the original quota fixed by 42 Geo. III., cap. 90. The number of men to be raised under this Act as the " Army Reserve " was: Yorkshire, 5,204 ; West Riding, 3,238 ; North Riding, 1,214 ; East Riding, 752. From the date of this Act to 1st October, 1805, a number, not exceeding 9,000, were to be raised annually to supply the place of those who volunteered into the Army from this Force, which was not liable for service out of the United Kingdom.

46 Geo. III., Cap. 91, 16th July, 1806.

As the number of men still exceed the original quota, the ballot to be suspended for two years except for supplying vacancies.

47 Geo. III., Cap. 71, 14th August, 1807.

The Militia *increased* by three-fourths of the original quota fixed by the 42 Geo. III. c. 90, or 30,720 men. Any County not raising the number required rendered liable to a fine of £60 for each man deficient. Yorkshire, 2,928; West Riding, 1,822; North Riding, 682; East Riding, 424; the Regiment, 607.

49 Geo. III., Cap. 53, 27th May, 1809.

The Militia *increased* by one half of the original quota, and from this date to 1st June, 1810, men to be raised by beat of drum at a bounty of twelve guineas; after that date, any deficiency to be made up by ballot. This increase amounted to 20,481. Yorkshire, 1,952; West Riding, 1,214; North Riding, 455; East Riding, 282; the Regiment, 405.

51 Geo. III. Cap. 20, 11th April, 1811.

The Militia to be gradually *reduced* to the original quota (partly by volunteering). Supernumeraries, not exceeding 6,856, to be raised annually by voluntary enlistment, to replace an equal number allowed to volunteer into the Army. Bounty, ten guineas. (*See* Appendix L.)

53 Geo. III., Cap. 81, 2nd July, 1813.

The Militia to be *increased* by beat of drum, by supernumeraries not exceeding one half of the original quota, or same number as raised under 49 Geo. III. c. 53, (one-seventh of the establishment to enlist,) one additional sergeant, one corporal, and one drummer being allowed for every fifty men so raised. (*See* Appendix L.)

15 & 16 Vic., Cap. 50, 30th June, 1852.

The Militia was first raised entirely by voluntary enlistment under this Act, and has continued to be so ever since. Quota for England and Wales, 80,000 in peace; 40,000 extra in time of war. Distribution of (peace) quota, as fixed by Orders in Council, 30th June and 16th October, 1852:—Yorkshire, 8,199; West Riding, 6,246; North Riding, 976; East Riding, 977; the Regiment, 1,036.

APPENDIX N.

DISTRIBUTION OF THE QUOTA

IN

THE SIX WAPENTAKES OF THE WEST RIDING IN WHICH THE REGIMENT WAS RAISED,

FROM 1797 TO 1852,

SHOWING

THE ORIGINAL QUOTA OF 809 MEN, OR THE REGULAR ESTABLISHMENT OF THE REGIMENT FROM 1802 TO 1852.

(*Raised under the 42 Geo. III., c. 90.*)

WAPENTAKES AND SUB-DIVISIONS.

	QUOTA.
AGBRIGG	60
BARKSTON ASH	83
OSGOLDCROSS	114
SKYRACK AND BOROUGH OF LEEDS	72
STAINCROSS	94
STRAFFORTH AND TICKHILL, UPPER DIVISION	290
,, ,, LOWER ,,	96
Total	809

TOWNSHIPS AND PARISHES.

	QUOTA.
AGBRIGG	60
Alverthorpe-with-Thornes	12
Crigglestone	4
Crofton	1
Wakefield	40
Warmfield-with-Heath	3
Total (Capt. Donelan's Company)	60
BARKSTON ASH	83
Barkstone Ash, and Saxton-cum-Scarthingwell	1
Barlow, and Drax	1

	QUOTA.
Biggin, *see* Fenton, and Ulleskelf.	
Birkin	1
Bootherton	5
Bootherton, and Lotherton-cum-Aberford	1
Bramham-cum-Oglethorpe, Newton, and Foulstone	1
Bramham-cum-Oglethorpe	3
Brayton	1
Burn	1
Burton Salmon, and Temple Hirst	1
Byram-cum-Poole, and Hirst Courtney	1

	QUOTA.
Camblesforth	1
Carlton	3
Cawood	3
Cawood, Carlton, and Newland	1
Chapel Haddlesey	1
Church Fenton, *see* Kirk Fenton.	
Clifford-cum-Boston	2
Drax, *see* Barlow	1
Fairburn	1
Fenton, and Biggin, *see* Ulleskelf	
Foulstone, *see* Bramham and Newton.	
Gateforth	1
Grimston, *see* Kirkby-cum-Milford.	
Hambleton	2
Hazlewood, *see* Sutton.	
Hillam, *see* Milford (South).	
Hirst Courtney, *see* Byram-cum-Poole.	
Hambleton, and Monk Fryston	1
Huddleston, Lumby, and Sutton	1
Hutton, *see* Ryther-cum-Ossendike.	
Kirkby-cum-Milford, Towton, and Grimston	1
Kirk Fenton (or Church Fenton)	2
Ledsham	1
Ledstone, *see* Ryther.	
Hoddlesey West	1
Ledstone, *see* Ryther-cum-Ossendike	1
Long Drax	1
Lotherton-cum-Aberford, *see also* Bootherton	1
Micklefield, and Newthorpe	1
Milford South	2
Milford South, and Hillam	1
Monk Fryston, *see also* Hambleton	1
Newland, *see* Cawood, and Carlton	1
Newthorpe, *see* Micklefield.	
Newton, and Foulstone, *see also* Bramham-cum-Oglethorpe	1
Ryther-cum-Ossendike	2
Ryther-cum-Ossendike, Hutton, and Ledstone	1
Saxton-cum-Scarthingwell, *see also* Barkston Ash	2
Selby	10
Sherburn	5
Stutton, with Hazlewood, *see* Huddleston	1
Tadcaster	6

	QUOTA.
Temple Hirst, *see* Burton Salmon.	
Thorpe Willoughby, *see* Wistow.	
Towton, *see* Kirkby-cum-Milford.	
Ulleskelf	1
Ulleskelf, Fenton, and Biggin	1
Wistow	2
Wistow, and Thorpe Willoughby	1
Total (Capt. Courtney's Company)	**83**
OSGOLDCROSS	114
Ackworth	6
Adlingfleet	1
Armin	2
Askern, *see* Sutton.	
Badsworth	1
Balne	2
Beaghill, *see* Cowick	2
Bramwith, *see* Fenwick Ferry.	
Burgh Wallis	1
Burgh Wallis, and Skellow	1
Campsall	1
Campsall, and North Elmsall	1
Carleton, *see* Tanshelf.	
Castleford	5
Cowick	3
Cowick, and Beaghill	1
Cridling Stubbs, *see* Womersley.	
Darrington, *see* Sutton	2
Eastoft, *see* Haldenby.	
Eggborough	1
Eggborough, Kirk Smeaton, and Little Smeaton	1
Elmsall North, *see* Campsall	1
Elmsall South, *see* Kirkby South	2
Featherstone	1
Fenwick Ferry	1
Fenwick, and Bramwith	1
Ferry Fryston	5
Fockerby, *see* Haldenby.	
Goole	2
Gowdall	1
Haldenby, Eastoft, and Fockerby	1
Hardwick West, *see* Purston Jaglin.	
Hardwick East, *see* Upton.	
Hook	1

APPENDIX N.]   THIRD WEST YORK LIGHT INFANTRY.   313

	QUOTA.		QUOTA.
Heck, and Walden Stubbs	1	Ansthorpe (?)	1
Hensall	1	Bardsey-cum-Rigton	2
Hook, see Snaith	1	Barwick-in-Elmet	6
Houghton	1	Beeston	6
Kellington	1	Collingham	1
Kellington, Swinfleet, and Whitgift	1	Garforth	3
Kirk Smeaton, see Eggborough	1	Headingley-cum Burley	6
Kirby, South, and South Elmsall	1	Hunslet	20
Kirby, South	2	Kippax	3
Knottingley	7	Keswick, East	2
Moss	1	Parlington	1
Norton	2	Preston, see Swillington.	
Ousefleet	1	Roundhay	1
Owston, see Sutton	1	Seacroft	2
Pollington	2	Shadwell	1
Pontefract	16	Swillington with Preston	4
Pontefract Park, see Purston Jaglin.		Templenewsam	4
Purston Jaglin, and West Hardwick	2	Thorner	4
Purston Jaglin (or Jackling), West Hardwick, and Pontefract Park	1	Total (Capt. Luard's Company)	72
Rawcliffe	4		
Reedness	2	STAINCROSS	94
Skelbrooke, and Stapleton	1		
Skellow, see Burgh Wallis.		Ardsley	2
Smeaton, Little, see Eggborough.		Barugh	2
Snaith	3	Barnsley	16
Snaith, and Hook	1	Bretton	2
Stapleton, see Skelbrooke.		Bretton Monk	2
Sutton, and Askern	1	Brierley, and Carlton	3
Sutton, Darrington, and Owston	1	Carlton, see Brierley.	
Swinfleet, see Kellington	3	Cawthorne, and Gunthwaite	5
Tanshelf	1	Chevet, see Notton.	
Tanshelf, and Carleton	1	Clayton, and Cudworth	5
Thorp Audlin	1	Cudworth, see Clayton.	
Upton, and East Hardwick	1	Cumberworth, and Darton	7
Walden Stubbs, see Heck.		Darton, see Cumberworth.	
Whitgift, see Kellington	1	Denby	3
Whitley	1	Dodworth	3
Womersley	1	Gunthwaite, see Cawthorne.	
Womersley, and Cridling Stubbs	1	Havercroft-with-Cold, and Wintersett	1
		Hemsworth	4
Total (Capt. MacAdam's Company)	114	Hiendley, South	1
		Hunshelf	2
SKYRACK, AND BOROUGH OF LEEDS	72	Hoyland, High	1
		Hoyland, Swaine	2
Aberford	2	Ingbirchworth	1
Allerton Bywater	2	Kexbrough, and Silkstone	4
Alwoodley	1	Langsett	1

314 FIRST REGIMENT OF MILITIA; OR, [APPENDIX N.

	QUOTA.
Monk Bretton, *see* Bretton, Monk.	
Notton, and Chevet	2
Oxspring	1
Penistone	1
Roystone	2
Ryhill, and Shafton	2
Shafton, *see* Ryhill.	
Silkstone, *see* Kexborough.	
Stainbrough	1
Tankersley, and Thurgoland	4
Thurgoland, *see* Tankersley.	
Thurlstone	5
Wintersett, *see* Havercroft-with-Cold.	
Woolley	2
Worsbrough, and Wortley	7
Wortley, *see* Worsbrough.	
Total (Capt. Wrather's Company)	94

UPPER STRAFFORTH AND TICKHILL, 290

Adwick-cum-Wheatcroft, *see* Ecclesfield.	
Anston-cum-Membris	2
Attercliffe-cum-Darnall	12
Aston-cum-Aughton	2
Bradfield	12
Braithwell	2
Bramley	1
Brampton Bierlow	3
Brampton-en-le-Morthen	1
Brightside Bierlow	26
Brinsworth, and Denaby	1
Catliffe, and Orgreave	1
Conisbrough	3
Dalton	1
Denaby, *see* Brinsworth.	
Dinnington, and Edlington	1
Ecclesall-Bierlow	18
Ecclesfield, and Adwick-cum-Wheatcroft	18
Edlington, *see* Dinnington.	
Firbeck	1
Greasbrough, and Letwell	4
Gelding Wells, *see* Wales.	
Hallam, Upper	4
Hallam, Nether	8
Handsworth	6

	QUOTA.
Harthill	1
Helaby, *see* Stainton.	
Hooton Roberts, *see* Hooton Levett.	
Hooton Levett, and Hooton Roberts	1
Hoyland	3
Kimberworth	12
(Total, Capt. Copley's Company, 144)	
Laughton-en-le-Morthen	2
Letwell, *see* Greasbrough.	
Maltby	2
Orgreave, *see* Catcliffe.	
Rawmarsh	3
Ravenfield, *see* Thorpe Salvin.	
Rotherham	12
Sheffield	106
Stainton-cum-Helaby	1
Swinton	3
Todwick, *see* Treeton.	
Thorpe, Salvin, and Ravenfield	1
Thrybergh, and Ulley	1
Tinsley	1
Treeton and Todwick	1
Ulley, *see* Thryberg.	
Wales and Woodsets, with Gilding-wells	1
Wath-upon-Dearne	3
Wentworth	3
Whiston	2
Wickersley	2
Wombwell	2
Woodsett, *see* Wales.	
(Total, Capt. Labourne's Company, 146). Total	290

LOWER STRAFFORTH and TICKHILL 96

Adwick-Le-Street and Armthorpe	1
Adwick-upon-Dearne and Bilham	1
Arksey, *see* Bentley.	
Armthorpe, *see* Ardwick-le-Street	1
Austerfield and Stainforth	1
Balby, *see* Hexthorpe.	
Barmbrough	1
Barmbrough, Brodsworth, with Frickley and Stotfold	2
Barnby-upon-Don	2
Bawtry	3

APPENDIX N.]   THIRD WEST YORK LIGHT INFANTRY.   315

	QUOTA.		QUOTA.
Bawtry and Loversall	1	Marr	1
Bentley-with-Arksey	5	Melton (High) and Thorpe-in-Balne	1
Billingley	1	Mexborough, *see* Hooton Pagnell	1
Bilham, *see* Ardwick-upon-Dearne.		Rossington	1
Bolton-upon-Dearne	2	Rossington, Stancil-with-Wellingley,	
Brodsworth, *see* also Barmbrough	1	Longthwaite-with-Tilts, Scaws-	
Cadeby and Sykehouse	1	by, and Wadworth	2
Cantley	2	Scawsby, Sandall, *see* Wheatley.	
Cantley and Darfield	1	Sprotbrough	2
Clayton-with-Frickley	1	Stainforth, *see* Austerfield	2
Darfield, *see* Cantley	1	Sykehouse, *see* also Cadeby	2
Doncaster	26	Stotfold, *see* Barmbrough.	
Fishlake	2	Stancit-with-Wellingley, *see* Rossington.	
Frickley, *see* Barmbrough and Clayton.		Thorne	7
Hampole and Hatfield	1	Thurnscoe	1
Hatfield, *see* also Hampole	5	Tickhill	6
Hexthorpe-with-Balby	1	Thorpe-in-Balne, *see* Melton (High)	
Hickleton and Little Houghton	1	Wadworth, *see* Rossington	1
Hooton Pagnell and Mexborough	1	Warmsworth	1
Houghton (Great)	1	Wheatley-with-Sandall	1
Houghton (Little), *see* Hickleton.		Wellingley, *see* Rossington.	
Kirk Sandall	1		
Loversall, *see* Bawtry.		Total (1st vacant Company)	96

APPENDIX O.

DISTRIBUTION OF THE QUOTA
IN
THE SIX WAPENTAKES OF THE WEST RIDING IN WHICH THE REGIMENT WAS RAISED,

FROM 1797 TO 1852,

SHOWING

THE QUOTA OF 1,214 MEN RAISED IN THE YEARS 1803,[*] 1809,[†] 1813,[‡] OR AN INCREASE OF 405 SUPPLEMENTARY MEN, BEING ONE-HALF OF THE ORIGINAL QUOTA OF 809 FIXED IN 1802 BY THE 42 GEO. III., C. 90.

(607 *Supplementary Men*, or *Three-Fourths of the Original Quota were raised in* 1807 *by the* 47 *Geo. III., c.* 71.)

WAPENTAKES AND SUB-DIVISIONS.

	QUOTA.
AGBRIGG	93
BARKSTON ASH	110
OSGOLDCROSS	171
SKYRACK AND BOROUGH OF LEEDS	109
STAINCROSS	141
STRAFFORTH AND TICKHILL, UPPER DIVISION ...	436
,, ,, LOWER ,, ...	154
Total ...	1,214

TOWNSHIPS AND PARISHES.

AGBRIGG	QUOTA. 93	BARKSTON ASH ...	QUOTA. 110
Alverthorpe-with-Thornes ...	20	Barkstone Ash, and Saxton-cum-Scarthingwell	1
Crigglestone	6		
Crofton	3	*See also* Bootherton.	
Heath, *see* Warmfield.		Barlow, and Drax	1
Wakefield	60	Barlow, and Brayton	1
Warmfield-with-Heath ...	4	Biggin, *see* Fenton, and Ulleskelf.	
		Birkin, and Camblesforth	1
Total	93	Birkin	1

[*] Under 42 Geo. III., c. 90.   [†] Under 49 Geo. III., c. 53.
[‡] Under 53 Geo. III., c. 81.

APPENDIX O.] THIRD WEST YORK LIGHT INFANTRY. 317

	QUOTA.
Bootherton	6
Bootherton, and Barkstone	1
Bootherton, and Sutton	1
Bootherton, and Lotherton-cum-Aberford	1
Bramham-cum-Oglethorpe	5
Bramham-cum-Oglethorpe, Newton, and Foulston	1
Brayton, *see* Barlow	1
Burn	1
Burn, Ledstone, Newton, and **Foulston**	2
Burton Salmon, **and Temple Hirst**, *see* Cawood	1
Byram-cum-Poole, and Hurst Courtney	1
Byram-cum-Poole, and Stutton	1
Camblesforth, *see* Birkin	1
Carlton, *see also* Cawood	4
Carlton and Gateforth	1
Cawood	4
Cawood and Burton Salmon	1
Cawood, Carlton, and Nowland	1
Chapel Haddlesey	1
Chapel Haddlesey, and Fairburn	1
Church Fenton, *see* **Kirk Fenton.**	
Clifford	3
Clifford, Drax, and Saxton-cum-Scarthingwell	1
Drax, *see* Barlow, Clifford, and Long Drax	1
Fairburn, *see* Chapel Haddlesey	1
Fenton, and Biggin, *see* Ulleskelf	1
Fenton, Biggin, and Hirst Courtney	1
Foulston, *see* Bramham, and Newton.	
Gateforth, *see* Carlton	1
Grimston, *see* Lotherton, and Kirkby.	
Haddlesey, West, *see* Sherburn	1
Hambleton	3
Hambleton, **Huddleston-cum-Lumby, and Micklefield**	1
Hambleton, and **Monk Frystone**	1
Hazlewood, *see* Sutton.	
Hirst Courtney, *see* Byram-cum-Poole and Fenton.	
Huddleston-cum-Lumby, **and Sutton,** *see* Hambleton	1
Ledstone, *see also* Ryther-cum-Ossendike	1

	QUOTA.
Ledsham, *see* Sherburn	1
Long Drax	1
Long Drax, Wistow, and Kirkby-cum-Milford	1
Lotherton-cum-Aberford, *see also* Bootherton	1
Lotherton, Thorpe Willoughby, and Grimston	1
Kirkby-cum-Milford, **Towton, and** Grimston, *see* Long **Drax**	1
Kirk Fenton (or Church **Fenton**)	2
Kirk Fenton, and Newthorpe	1
Micklefield, and Newthorpe, *see* Hambleton	1
Milford, South, *see* Newland.	
Milford, South, and Hillam	2
Milford, South	3
Monk Frystone, *see* Temple Hirst and Monk Frystone	1
Newland, *see* Cawood	1
Newland, and South Milford	1
Newton, and Foulston, *see* Bramham, and Burn	1
Newthorpe, *see* Kirk Fenton, and Micklefield.	
Ryther-cum-Ossendike	3
Ryther-cum-Ossendike, Sutton, and Ledstone	1
Saxton-cum-Scarthingwell, *see* Barkstone, and Clifford.	
Saxton-cum-Scarthingwell	3
Sherburn	7
Sherburn, West Haddlesey, and Ledsham	1
Stutton, and Hazlewood, *see* Byram-cum-Poole	1
Sutton, *see* Bootherton, Huddleston, **Lumby, and Ryther.**	
Tadcaster	8
Tadcaster, and Hillam	1
Temple Hirst, and Monk Frystone, *see* Burton Salmon	1
Thorpe Willoughby, *see* Lotherton, and Wistow.	
Towton, *see* Kirby and Ulleskelf.	
Ulleskelf	1
Ulleskelf, and Towton	1
Ulleskelf, Fenton, and Biggin	1

	QUOTA
Wistow, *see* Landrax	3
Wistow, and Thorpe Willoughby	1
Total	110
OSGOLDCROSS	171
Ackworth	9
Adlingfleet	1
Adlington, **Haldenby**, and **Eastoft**	1
Armin	3
Armin, and Hook	1
Askern, *see* Bramwith, and Sutton.	
Badsworth	1
Balne	3
Burgh Wallis	1
Burgh **Wallis**, and **Moss**	1
Burgh Wallis, and Skellow	1
Badsworth	1
Badsworth, Upton, and South Elmsall	1
Beaghall, *see* Cowick	3
Bramwith, Sutton, Askern, and Darrington, *see* Fenwick	1
Campsall	2
Campsall, and North Elmsall	1
Castleford	7
Castleford, and Featherstone	1
Carleton, *see* Tanshelf.	
Cowick, and Beaghall	2
Cowick	4
Cridling Stubbs, *see* Womersley.	
Darrington, *see* Bramwith, and Sutton	3
Eastoft, *see* Adlingfleet, and Haldenby.	
Eggborough	1
Eggborough, Kirk Smeaton, and Little Smeaton	2
Elmsall, North, *see* Campsall	1
Elmsall, South, *see* Badsworth	3
Featherstone, *see* Castleford	1
Fenwick	1
Fenwick, and Bramwith	1
Fenwick, and Pontefract Park	1
Ferry Frystone	7
Fockerby, *see* Haldenby, and Kellington.	
Goole	3
Gowdall	1
Gowdall, and Hensall	1
Haldenby, Eastoft, and **Fockerby**, *see also* Adlingfleet	1
Hardwick, West, *see* Purston Jaglin.	
Hardwick, East, *see* Thorpe Audlin, and Upton	1
Heck	1
Heck, and Walden Stubbs	1
Hensall, *see* Gowdall	1
Hook, *see* **Armin**, and **Snaith**	1
Houghton, *see* Knottingley	3
Kellington	1
Kellington, Fockerby, and Ousefleet	1
Kellington, Swinfleet, and Whitgift	1
Kirby, South, and North Elmsall	1
Kirby, South, and South Elmsall	1
Kirk Smeaton, *see* Eggborough	1
Kirk Smeaton, **and** Skellow	1
Knottingley	10
Knottingley, and Houghton	1
Moss, *see* Burgh Wallis	1
Norton	3
Owston, *see* Sutton	1
Owston, and Skelbrooke	1
Ousefleet, *see* Kellington, and Whitgift	1
Pontefract, *see* Fenwick, and Purston Jaglin	23
Pontefract, and Purston Jaglin	1
Purston Jaglin, and West Hardwick, *see also* Pontefract	3
Purston Jaglin, and Pontefract Park	1
Purston Jaglin, West Hardwick, and Pontefract Park	1
Pollington	3
Rawcliffe	6
Reedness	3
Skellow, *see* Burgh **Wallis**, and Swinfleet.	
Skelbrooke, and Stapleton, *see* Owston	1
Skellow, *see* Kirk Smeaton.	
Sutton, and Askern, *see* Bramwith	1
Sutton, Darrington, and Owston	1
Swinfleet, and Reedness	1
Swinfleet, *see* Kellington	3

APPENDIX O.]   THIRD WEST YORK LIGHT INFANTRY.   319

	QUOTA.		QUOTA.
Snaith	4	Templenewsam	7
Snaith, and Whitley	1	Thorner	6
Snaith, and Hook	1		
Smeaton, Little, see Eggborough.			109
Stapleton, see Skelbrooke, and Thorpe Audlin.			
Tanshelf	1	STAINCROSS	141
Tanshelf, and Carleton	2		
Thorpe Audlin	1	Ardsley	3
Thorpe Audlin, East Hardwick, and Stapleton	1	Barnsley	24
		Barugh	3
Upton, and East Hardwick, see Badsworth	1	Bretton, Monk	3
		Bretton, West	3
Walden Stubbs, see Hock.		Brierley, and Carlton	4
Witgift, and Ousefleet, see Kellington	2	Carlton, see Brierley.	
		Cawthorne, and Gunthwaite	7
Witgift	1	Chevet, see Notton.	
Womersley, and Cridling Stubbs	1	Clayton, and Cudworth	7
Whitley, see Snaith	1	Cudworth, see Clayton.	
Womersley	1	Cumberworth, and Darton	10
		Darton, see Cumberworth.	
Total	171	Denby	5
		Dodworth	5
		Gunthwaite, see Cawthorne.	
		Havercroft-with-Cold, and Wintersett	1
SKYRACK	109	Hiendley, South, see Longsett	1
		Hemsworth	6
Aberford	3	Hoyland, High	1
Alwoodley	1	Hoyland, Swaine	4
Allerton Bywater	2	Hunshelf	2
Bardsey-cum-Rigton	3	Ingbirchworth	1
Barwick	6	Kexbrough, and Silkstone	7
Barwick-in-Elmet	3	Langsett	1
Beeston	10	Langsett, and South Hiendley	1
Collingham	2	Notton, and Chevet	3
Garforth	5	Osspring	2
Heddingley	6	Penistone	2
Heddingley-cum-Burley	3	Royston	3
Hunslett	31	Ryhill, and Shafton	3
Keswick, East	2	Shafton, see Ryhill.	
Kippax	5	Silkstone, see Kexbrough.	
Parlington	2	Stainbrough	1
Preston, see Swillington.		Tankersley	3
Roundhay	1	Thurgoland	3
Seacroft	3	Thurlstone	8
Shadwell	2	Wintersett, see Havercroft-with-Cold.	
Swillington, and Preston	6		

	QUOTA		QUOTA
Woolley	3	Thorpe Salvin	1
Worsbrough, and Wortley	11	Thrybergh	2
		Tinsley	1
Total	141	Todwick	1
		Treeton	2
STRAFFORTH AND TICKHILL		Ulley	1
(UPPER DIVISION)	436	Wales	2
		Wath-upon-Dearne	6
Adwick-cum-Wheatcroft	1	Wentworth	5
Anston-cum-Membris	3	Whiston	5
Aston-cum-Aughton	2	Wickersley	3
Attercliffe-cum-Darnall	11	Wombwell	3
Bradfield	15	Woodsets and Gilding Wells	1
Braithwell, and Micklebrig	4		
Bramley	1	Total	436
Brampton Bierlow	5		
Brampton-en-le-Morthen	2	STRAFFORTH AND TICKHILL	
Brightside Bierlow	19	(LOWER DIVISION)	154
Brinsworth	2		
Catcliffe	1	Arksey, *see* Bentley.	
Coulsbrough	5	Armthorpe	2
Dinington	2	Austerfield	2
Ecclesall Bierlow	23	Adwick-le-Street	2
Ecclesfield	19	Adwick-upon-Dearne	1
Edlington	1	Barnby-upon-Don	3
Firbeck	2	Bawtry	6
Gilding Wells, *see* Woodsett.		Billingley	2
Greasbrough	5	Bilham	—
Hallam (Upper)	3	Brodsworth and Pigburn	1
Hallam (Nether)	8	Bramwith, *see* Stainforth.	
Handsworth and Woodhouse	7	Bolton-upon-Dearne	4
Hartbill-cum-Woodall	2	Bentley and Arksey	6
Hellaby, *see* Stainton-cum-Hellaby.		Barmbrough	3
Hooton Levett	—	Clayton-with-Frickley	1
Hooton Roberts	1	Cantley	5
Hoyland	6	Cadeby (in Sprotbrough Parish).	
Kimberworth	14	Cusworth, *see* Sprotbrough.	
Laughton-en-le-Morthen	3	Darfield	2
Letwell	1	Doncaster Town and Soke	51
Maltby	4	Fishlake	3
Micklebrig, *see* Braithwell.		Frickley, *see* Clayton.	
Orgreave	1	Hooton Pagnell	2
Ravenfield	2	Houghton (Great)	2
Rotherham	18	Houghton (Little)	1
Rawmarch	8	Hickleton	2
Sheffield	107	Hampole and Stubbs	1
Swinton	4	Hatfield	8
Stainton-cum-Hellaby	1	Kirk Sandall	2

[APPENDIX O.] THIRD WEST YORK LIGHT INFANTRY.

	QUOTA		QUOTA
Longthwaite-with-Tilts	—	Stotfold	—
Marr	1	Thorpe-in-Balne	1
Melton (High)	2	Tilts, see Longthwaite.	
Mexborough	1	Thorne	10
Pigburn, see Brodsworth.		Thurnscoe	2
Sprotbrough and Cusworth	2	Tickhill	11
Stainforth and Bramwith	2	Wadworth	3
Stancil-with-Wellingley	1	Warmsworth	3
Stubbs, see Hampole.			
Sykehouse	3	Total	154
Scausby	—		

ACTIVE ARMY.

IV. ARMY CORPS.
Head-Quarters, Dublin.

1st DIVISION (Dublin).

1st Brigade (Dublin).	2nd Brigade (Belfast).
3 Regiments of the Line.	126th (Edinburgh), or Queen's Regiment of Light Infantry Militia.
	74th, or 1st Royal Lanark.
	78th, or 2nd Royal Lanark.

DIVISIONAL TROOPS.*
Cavalry, Artillery, and Engineers.
Infantry—76th, or The Highland Light Infantry Militia.

2nd DIVISION (Curragh).

1st Brigade.	2nd Brigade.
3 Regiments of the Line.	1st, or 3rd West York Light Infantry.
	5th, or 1st West York Rifles.
	21st, or 2nd West York Light Infantry

DIVISIONAL TROOPS.*
Cavalry, Artillery, and Engineers.
Infantry—133rd, or 4th West York Militia.

3rd DIVISION (Cork).

1st Brigade.	2nd Brigade.
16th, or 1st Somerset Light Infantry.	36th, or 1st Warwick.
47th, or 2nd Somerset.	44th, or Royal Glamorgan Light Infantry.
67th, Worcester.	53rd, or 2nd Warwick.

DIVISIONAL TROOPS.*
Cavalry, Artillery, and Engineers.
Infantry—1 Regiment of the Line.

CAVALRY BRIGADE (Curragh).
3 Regiments; 1 Battery R.H.A.

CORPS ARTILLERY (Dublin).
3 Batteries R.H.A.; 2 Batteries R.A.; Corps Ammunition Reserve.

CORPS ENGINEERS (Dublin),
1 Troop (Pontoons); ½ Troop (Telegraph); 1 Company and Field Park.

Note.—By the Mobilisation of the Forces, as established 8th December, 1875, the Regiment forms part of the Fourth Army Corps quartered in Ireland. The Line Brigades will be composed of whatever Regiments happen to be quartered in the District. The Militia Brigades are permanent.

---

* The Divisional Troops, in addition to the Infantry Regiments named, each consist of—1 Cavalry Regiment; 1 Company R.E.; 3 Batteries R.A.; and the Infantry Ammunition Reserve.

RECORDS

OF THE

FIRST WEST YORK
SUPPLEMENTARY REGIMENT

OR,

THIRD WEST YORK MILITIA.

RAISED—FEBRUARY, 1797;

DISBANDED—DECEMBER, 1799.

THE FIRST WEST YORK SUPPLEMENTARY REGIMENT;

OR,

THIRD WEST YORK MILITIA.

From the Formation of the Regiment in February, 1797

until Disbanded in December, 1799.

This Regiment, which was commanded by Lord Harewood, was embodied on the 20th of February, 1798. The Headquarters were established at Leeds, where they occupied a house as store-rooms, &c., during the disembodied period from the 30th of June, 1797, to the 20th of February, 1798, for the rent of which they paid £30; and a field for exercise, at the same place, from the 5th of March to the 20th of May, 1798, for which they paid five guineas; another at Whitby cost fourteen guineas.*

An Order, dated War Office, the 28th of April, directed the Regiment to march on the second day (Sunday excepted) prior to that which might be appointed for assembling the second half of the Supplementary Militia at that place to the following quarters:—three companies to Tadcaster, Sherburn, Bramham, and Aberford; four companies to Knaresborough, Ripley, and Harrowgate; two companies to Bradford; and one company to Harewood and Otley; but to leave such detachment at Leeds as should be directed by the Adjutant-General.† Orders of the

---

* Pay Lists.

† Militia Marching Book, Vol. XCVII., pp. 57, 59, 61.

same date were sent to the 2nd West York, at Ashford, to send ten men to the Regiment at Knaresborough. On the 9th of May the Regiment assembled at Leeds, 411 strong. On the 12th of May, the Regiment went from Leeds to the following places—two companies from Leeds to Knaresborough; two to Bradford; two to Harrowgate; two to Tadcaster; one to Otley; and one to Aberford; returning again on the 21st, with the exception of the Tadcaster and Aberford companies, which went on to Hull.

By an Order, dated War Office, the 11th of May, the Supplementary Militiamen belonging to the 1st West York Militia at Horsham were ordered to march to join their Regiment on the 19th, to replace an equal number who had been sent to train the Regiment.*

An Order, dated the 12th of May, was addressed to the "Officer Commanding the Detachment of Supplementary Militia of the West Riding of York, at Wakefield," to send the Supplementary men apportioned to the Regiment to Leeds so as to join on Monday, the 21st of May. Another Order of the same date, to the Officer Commanding the 3rd West Riding Yorkshire Militia at Knaresborough, directed him to return to Leeds on the 21st inst., to join the Supplementary men there.† In May a second major and second adjutant were appointed in consequence of the augmented establishment.‡

Between the 25th and 30th of May, four companies went from Leeds to Whitby, four companies from Leeds to Scarborough, and a detachment was sent to Hull to augment the flank companies.

In August, a Warrant was issued to supply the Regiment with Colours. The Regimental Colour was apple-green, with the words "III. Regiment West York Militia" on a shield in the centre, surrounded by a wreath.

On the 28th of September, the two flank companies at Hilston Camp returned to Hull; and between the 1st and

---

* Militia Marching Book, Vol. XCVII., pp. 90, 91.
† Idem, p. 93.
‡ Militia, No. 31 (Home Office).

5th of October the four companies at Scarborough, and the four companies at Whitby, returned to Leeds. On the 24th of December, there were 54 sergeants, 50 corporals, 26 drummers, and 988 privates.

1799.—On the 29th of April, four companies went from Leeds to Scarborough, and the following day the remaining four companies at Leeds proceeded to Whitby; the two flank companies at Hull went into camp at Roos on the 12th of June, and on the 4th of July to Scarborough. On the 9th of July, one company was sent from the latter place to Whitby. The five companies at Scarborough and the five companies at Whitby returned to Leeds on the 2nd of October; and four companies were sent to Wakefield on the 10th of October, returning to Leeds on the 12th of December.

On the 18th of February, 1799, there were 1,036 privates, or only fourteen short of the establishment of 1,050. In this year the Regiment supplied a number of men to the Regular Army; 166 went into the following Regiments: Royal Artillery, ten (a Warrant, dated the 17th of February, 1798, authorised the Royal Artillery to enlist 400 men from the Supplementary Militia); 1st Foot Guards, twenty-one; 9th Foot, thirty-three; 15th Foot, eight; 16th Foot, three; 31st Foot, sixteen; 35th Foot, seventy-five.*

The Regiment was disbanded on the 24th of December, 1799, after a short existence of rather less than three years. Six months' allowance was granted to the officers, several of whom subsequently joined the 3rd Regular Regiment, the men receiving fourteen days' pay, and "half mounting," either in kind or value.†

---

* Pay List. † See page 75.

SUCCESSION OF OFFICERS

OF THE

First West York Supplementary Regiment;

OR,

THIRD WEST YORK MILITIA.

FROM 1797 TO 1799.

COLONEL.	DATE OF APPOINTMENT.	REMARKS.
Edwin, Lord Harewood	25th Feb., 1797	
LIEUTENANT-COLONEL.		
William Sotheron ...	25th Feb., 1797	Lt.-Col. Pontefract Volunteers
MAJORS.		
John Tottenham ...	25th Feb., 1797	
Hon. Henry Lascelles	24th June, 1798	From Captain
CAPTAINS.		
Henry Wickham ...	25th Feb., 1797	
Hon. Henry Lascelles	26th Feb., 1797	Prom. to Major, 24th June, 1798
Samuel Buck	27th Feb., 1797	
Charles Hoare	28th Feb., 1797	
Thomas Slingsby	1st March, 1797	
John Cockshott ...	2nd March, 1797	Died 24th April, 1798
William Cookson	3rd March, 1797	
Thomas Duncombe	24th April, 1798	From Lieutenant
Richard Broom	2nd July, 1798	From Captain-Lieut. to Captain 2nd W. Y., June, 1801
George Waugh	1st April, 1799	From Captain-Lieut. to Captain 3rd W.Y.L.I., 25th June, 1800
Richard Yorke	2nd April, 1799	From Lieutenant
Daniel Smalpage	3rd April, 1799	From Lieutenant
David Swale	22nd Aug., 1799	
CAPTAIN-LIEUTENANTS.		
Henry Greville ...	25th Feb., 1797	
Thomas Duncombe ...	17th April, 1798	Vice Greville, promoted to Captain, 24th April, 1798

THE FIRST WEST YORK SUPPLEMENTARY MILITIA. 329

CAPT.-LIEUTS.—Cont.	DATE OF APPOINTMENT.	REMARKS.
George Waugh	3rd July, 1798	Prom. to Capt., 1st April, 1799
Richard Broom	26th April, 1798	From Lieut., promoted to Captain 2nd July, 1798
David Swale	4th April, 1799	Quartermaster, promoted to Captain 22nd August, 1799
George Vincent ...	22nd Aug., 1799	From Lieutenant

LIEUTENANTS.

Thomas Duncombe	25th Feb., 1797	Promoted to Captain-Lieut. 17th April, 1798
Richard Broom ...	26th Feb., 1797	Promoted to Captain-Lieut. 25th April, 1798
William Barnett	27th Feb., 1797	
Brook Richmond	28th Feb., 1797	
Wm. Thompson Dunderdale	2nd March, 1797	
Josiah Tetley.	3rd March, 1797	
Richard Yorke	4th March, 1797	Prom. to Capt., 2nd April, 1799
David Swale	5th March, 1797	Quartermaster, 19th Mar., 1798
Daniel Smalpage	6th March, 1797	Prom. to Capt., 3rd April, 1799
George Vincent	7th March, 1797	Adjutant, 2nd March, 1797; Capt.-Lieut.,22nd Aug., 1799
William Molineaux	8th March, 1797	
St. Andrew Ward	9th March, 1797	
John Child	10th March, 1797	
Gervais Charles Seaton ...	11th March, 1797	
James Rawstone ...	12th March, 1797	
John Bayley	13th March, 1797	
Bryan Hesledon ...	11th April, 1797	From Ensign to Captain 1st W. Y., 26th Feb., 1800
Robert Priestley	16th April, 1797	Surgeon, 20th Feb., 1798
Thomas Skin... ...	12th June, 1798	Adjutant, 22nd June, 1798
Samuel Copperthwaite	13th June, 1798	From Ensign, to Lieutenant 1st W. Y., April, 1800
Richard Richardson ...	14th June, 1798	From Ensign
John Wareham	15th June, 1798	From Ensign
Thomas Johnson	16th June, 1798	From Ensign
William Gott	17th June, 1798	
William Overend	1st Feb., 1799	From Ensign
John Moxon ...	2nd Feb., 1799	From Ensign
James Rimington	3rd Feb., 1799	From Ensign
John Wrigglesworth	4th Feb., 1799	From Ensign
George Platt	5th Feb., 1799	From Ensign, to Lieut. 1st W.Y., April, 1800
Henry Zouch	6th Feb., 1799	From Ensign
Edwin Halwell Haywood ...	1st May, 1799	
Thomas Wilson	22nd Aug., 1799	From Ensign, to Lieut. 3rd W.Y. L. I., 24th Feb., 1800
Thomas Brooke ...	23rd Aug., 1799	From Ensign, to Lieut. 2nd West York, Aug., 1800

ENSIGNS.	DATE OF APPOINTMENT.	REMARKS.
Bryan Hesledon	26th Feb., 1797	Prom to Lieut. 11th Apr., 1797
Thomas Foster	27th Feb., 1797	—
Thomas William Tottie	7th Mar., 1797	
Samuel Copperthwaite	25th Mar., 1798	Prom. to Lieut. 13th June, 1798
Richard Richardson	26th Mar., 1798	Prom. to Lieut. 14th June, 1798
Thomas Johnson	27th Mar., 1798	Prom. to Lieut. 16th June, 1798
John Wareham	28th Mar., 1798	Prom. to Lieut. 15th June, 1798
William Overend	12th June, 1798	Prom. to Lieut. 1st Feb., 1799
John Moxon	13th June, 1798	Prom. to Lieut. 2nd Feb., 1799
James Rimington	14th June, 1798	Prom. to Lieut. 3rd Feb., 1799
John Wrigglesworth	15th June, 1798	Prom. to Lieut. 4th Feb., 1799
George Platt	16th June, 1798	Prom. to Lieut. 5th Feb., 1799
Henry Zouch	26th Oct., 1798	From Ens. Westmoreld. Militia, prom. to Lieut. 6th Feb., 1799
Thomas Wilson	27th Oct., 1798	Prom. to Lieut. 22nd Aug., 1799
Thomas Brooke	7th Dec., 1798	Prom. to Lieut. 23rd Aug., 1799
William Blanchard	1st April, 1799	To Ensign 1st W. York Militia, April, 1800
James Ray, Jun.	1st May, 1799	
James Bruton	2nd May, 1799	
Henry Booth	22nd Aug., 1799	To Ensign 2nd W. York Militia, August, 1800

ADJUTANTS.		
George Vincent	2nd Mar., 1797	Lieut. 7th March, 1797; Capt.-Lieut. 22nd Aug., 1799
George Waugh		
Thomas Skin	22nd June, 1798	**Lieut. 12th June, 1798**

PAYMASTER.		
Gervais Charles Seaton	... ...	Lieut. 11th March, 1797

QUARTERMASTER.		
David Swale	19th Mar., 1798	Lieut. 5th Mar., 1797; prom. to Capt.-Lieut. 4th April, 1799

SURGEON.		
Robert Priestley	**20th Feb., 1798**	Lieut. 16th Feb., 1797

ASSISTANT-SURGEON (SURGEON'S MATE).		
John Moxon		

AGENT.		
Mr. Stables	1798-1799	Pay Office, Whitehall

ALPHABETICAL LIST OF OFFICERS

OF THE

First West York Supplementary Regiment;

OR,

THIRD WEST YORK MILITIA.

BARNETT, WILLIAM.—Lieutenant 27th February, 1797, *en second* *
(Jamaica).

BAYLEY, JOHN.—Lieutenant 13th March, 1797.

BLANCHARD, WILLIAM.—Ensign 1st April, 1799; Ensign 1st West
    York Militia April, 1800 (commission dated 5th April,
    1799).

BOOTH, HENRY.—Ensign 22nd August, 1799; Ensign 2nd West
    York Militia August, 1800 (commission dated 22nd August,
    1799); Lieutenant 8th June, 1803.

BROOKE, THOMAS.—Ensign 7th December, 1798; Lieutenant 23rd
    August, 1799; Lieutenant 2nd West York Militia August,
    1800 (commission dated 23rd August, 1799).

BROOM, RICHARD.—Lieutenant 26th February, 1797; Captain-Lieu-
    tenant 26th April, 1798; Captain 2nd July, 1798; Captain
    2nd West York Militia June, 1801 (commission dated 2nd
    July, 1798).

BRUTON, JAMES.—Ensign 2nd May, 1799.

BUCK, SAMUEL.—Captain 27th February, 1797.

CHILD, JOHN.—Lieutenant 10th March, 1797.

COCKSHOTT, JOHN.—Captain 2nd March, 1797.

COOKSON, WILLIAM.—Captain 3rd March, 1797.

---

* A **Seconded Officer** holds a Commission which is in abeyance, until he returns
to actual service.—Clode's Military Forces of the Crown, Vol. II., Appendix EE.,
p. 469.

COPPERTHWAITE, SAMUEL.—Ensign 25th March, 1798; Lieutenant 13th June, 1798; Lieutenant 1st West York Militia April, 1800 (commission dated 13th June, 1798); Captain 16th May, 1803.

DUNCOMBE, THOMAS.—Lieutenant 25th February, 1797; Captain-Lieutenant 17th April, 1798; Captain 24th April, 1798.

DUNDERDALE, WILLIAM THOMPSON.—Lieutenant 2nd March, 1797, *en second* (in America).

FOSTER, THOMAS.—Ensign 27th February, 1798.

GOTT, WILLIAM.—Lieutenant 17th June, 1798.

GREVILLE, HENRY.—Captain-Lieutenant 25th February, 1797.

HAREWOOD, LORD EDWIN.—Colonel 25th February, 1797.

HAYWOOD, EDWIN HALWELL.—Lieutenant 1st May, 1799.

HESLEDON, BRYAN.—Ensign 26th February, 1798; Lieutenant 11th April, 1797; Captain 1st West York Militia 26th February, 1800; Major 21st January, 1808.

HOARE, CHARLES.—Captain 28th February, 1797.

JOHNSON, THOMAS.—Ensign 27th March, 1798; Lieutenant 16th June, 1798.

LASCELLES, HON. HENRY.—Captain 26th February, 1797; Major 24th June, 1798.

MOLINEAUX, WILLIAM.—Lieutenant 8th March, 1797.

MOXON, JOHN.—Ensign 13th June, 1798; Lieutenant 2nd February, 1799.

OVEREND, WILLIAM.—Ensign 12th June, 1798; Lieutenant 1st February, 1799.

PLATT, GEORGE.—Ensign 16th June, 1798; Lieutenant 5th February, 1799; Lieutenant 1st West York Militia April, 1800 (commission dated 3rd February, 1798).

PRIESTLEY, ROBERT.—Lieutenant 16th April, 1797; Surgeon 20th February, 1798.

RAWSTONE, JAMES.—Lieutenant 12th March, 1797; Resigned 29th May, 1798.

RAY, JAMES, Jun.—Ensign 1st May, 1799.

RICHARDSON, RICHARD.—Ensign 26th March, 1798; Lieutenant 14th June, 1798.

RICHMOND, BROOK.—Lieutenant 28th February, 1797.

RIMINGTON, JAMES. — Ensign 14th June, 1798; Lieutenant 3rd February, 1799.

SEATON, GERVAIS CHARLES.—Lieutenant 11th March, 1797.

SKIN, THOMAS.—Lieutenant 12th June, 1798; Adjutant 22nd June, 1798.

SLINGSBY, THOMAS.—Captain 1st March, 1797.

SMALPAGE, DANIEL.—Lieutenant 6th March, 1797; Captain 3rd April, 1799.

SOTHERON, WILLIAM.—Cornet Royal Horse Guards (Blues) 6th June, 1770; Lieutenant 3rd November, 1773; Captain 62nd Foot 29th February, 1776; Major 31st October, 1789; Retired H.-P. 11th August, 1790; Lieut.-Colonel 1st West York Supplementary Regiment 25th February, 1797; M.P. for Pontefract from 1784 to 1796; Lieut.-Colonel Pontefract Volunteers 9th August, 1803.

SWALE, DAVID.—Lieutenant 5th March, 1797; Quartermaster 19th March, 1798; Captain-Lieutenant 4th April, 1799; Captain 22nd August, 1799.

TETLEY, JOSIAH.—Lieutenant 3rd March, 1797.

TOTTENHAM, JOHN.—Major 25th February, 1797.

TOTTIE, THOMAS WILLIAM.—Ensign 2nd March, 1798; Resigned May, 1798.

VINCENT, GEORGE.—Ensign 9th Foot 5th June, 1771; Lieutenant 31st May, 1773; Captain-Lieutenant 28th September, 1781; Retired 19th October, 1787; Adjutant 1st West York Supplementary Militia 2nd March, 1797; Lieutenant 7th March, 1797; Captain-Lieutenant 22nd August, 1799; Died at Thorp Arch 7th September, 1834; Served in America under General Burgoyne.

WARD, ST. ANDREW.—Lieutenant 9th March, 1797.

WAREHAM, JOHN.—Ensign 25th March, 1798; Lieutenant 13th June, 1798.

WAUGH, GEORGE.—Captain-Lieutenant 3rd July, 1798; Captain 1st April, 1799; Captain 3rd West York Light Infantry 25th June, 1800; Displaced 7th July, 1804.

WICKHAM, HENRY.—Captain 25th February, 1797.

WILSON, THOMAS.—Ensign 27th October, 1798; Lieutenant 22nd August, 1799; Lieutenant 3rd West York Light Infantry 24th February, 1800; Ensign 34th Foot 2nd May, 1805; Lieutenant 56th Foot 4th February, 1807; Retired H.P. 25th April, 1817; Died at Wrexham 27th October, 1827.

WRIGGLESWORTH, John.—Ensign 15th June, 1798; Lieutenant 4th February, 1799.

YORKE, RICHARD.—Lieutenant 4th March, 1797; Captain 2nd April, 1799.

ZOUCH, HENRY.—Ensign Westmoreland Militia 20th December, 1797; Ensign 1st West York Supplementary Regiment 26th October, 1798; Lieutenant 6th February, 1799.

This List contains the names of 51 Officers. Of this number, 2 had previously served in the Regular Army; 1 was appointed from another Militia Regiment; 4 were appointed to the 1st West York, 3 to the 2nd West York, and 2 to the 3rd West York Regiments of Militia.

ERRATA.

1853.—Page 158, lines 13, 14, *for* Colonel M. J. Slade, *read* Lieutenant-Colonel J. Stoyte.

1854.—Page 162, fourth line from bottom, *for* 259, *read* 762.

Page 234, Howard, Hon. F. C., *add* Hythe Musketry Certificate, dated 5th October, 1872.

Page 250, Willcocks, J. G. S., *for* Adjutant, *read* Captain and Adjutant.

Page 257, Table No. 6, *add* Captain George Waugh, 1st West York Supplementary Regiment.

www.ingramcontent.com/pod-product-compliance
Lightning Source LLC
Chambersburg PA
CBHW020314240426
43673CB00039B/798